T0214135

Communications
in Computer and Information Science   1409

More information about this series at http://www.springer.com/series/7899

Patricia Pesado · Jorge Eterovic (Eds.)

Computer Science – CACIC 2020

26th Argentine Congress, CACIC 2020
San Justo, Buenos Aires, Argentina, October 5–9, 2020
Revised Selected Papers

 Springer

Editors
Patricia Pesado 🆔
National University of La Plata
La Plata, Argentina

Jorge Eterovic 🆔
National University of La Matanza
San Justo, Argentina

ISSN 1865-0929   ISSN 1865-0937 (electronic)
Communications in Computer and Information Science
ISBN 978-3-030-75835-6   ISBN 978-3-030-75836-3 (eBook)
https://doi.org/10.1007/978-3-030-75836-3

This Springer imprint is published by the registered company Springer Nature Switzerland AG
The registered company address is: Gewerbestrasse 11, 6330 Cham, Switzerland

Preface

Welcome to the selected papers of the 26th Argentine Congress of Computer Science (CACIC 2020), held in San Justo, Buenos Aires, Argentina, during October 5–9, 2020. CACIC 2020 was organized by the National University of La Matanza (Buenos Aires) on behalf of the Network of National Universities with Computer Science Degrees (RedUNCI).

CACIC is an annual congress dedicated to the promotion and advancement of all aspects of computer science. Its aim is to provide a forum within which the development of computer science as an academic discipline with industrial applications is promoted, trying to extend the frontier of both the state of the art and the state of the practice. The main audience for and participants of CACIC are seen as researchers in academic departments, laboratories, and industrial software organizations.

CACIC 2020 covered the following topics: intelligent agents and systems; distributed and parallel processing; computer technology applied to education; graphic computation, visualization and image processing; databases and data mining; software engineering; hardware architectures, networks and operating systems; innovation in software systems; signal processing and real-time systems; innovation in computer science education; computer security; digital governance and smart cities.

This year, the congress received 118 submissions. Each submission was reviewed by at least 2, and on average 3.2, Program Committee members and/or external reviewers. In total, 79 full papers, involving 267 different authors from 38 universities, were accepted. According to the recommendations of the reviewers, 24 of the papers were selected for this book.

During CACIC 2020, special activities were also carried out, including three plenary lectures, two discussion panels, a special track of Digital Governance and Smart Cities, and an International School with four courses.

Special thanks to the members of the different committees for their support and collaboration. Also, we would like to thank the local Organizing Committee, reviewers, lecturers, speakers, authors, and all conference attendees. Finally, we want to thank Springer for their support of this publication.

April 2021

Patricia Pesado
Jorge Eterovic

Organization

The 26th Argentine Congress of Computer Science (CACIC 2020) was organized by the School of Computer Science of the National University of La Matanza (UNLaM) on behalf of the Network of National Universities with Computer Science Degrees (RedUNCI).

Editors

Patricia Pesado[1]   National University of La Plata, Argentina
Jorge Eterovic   National University of La Matanza, Argentina

Editorial Assistant

Pablo Thomas   National University of La Plata, Argentina

Program Committee

Jorge Eterovic   National University of La Matanza, Argentina
Maria Jose Abásolo   National University of La Plata, Argentina
Claudio Aciti   National University of Central Buenos Aires, Argentina
Hugo Alfonso   National University of La Pampa, Argentina
Jorge Ardenghi   National University of the South, Argentina
Marcelo Arroyo   National University of Río Cuarto, Argentina
Hernan Astudillo   Technical University Federico Santa María, Chile
Sandra Baldasarri   University of Zaragoza, Spain
Javier Balladini   National University of Comahue, Argentina
Luis Soares Barbosa   University of Minho, Portugal
Rodolfo Bertone   National University of La Plata, Argentina
Oscar Bria   National University of La Plata, Argentina
Nieves R. Brisaboa   University of La Coruña, Spain
Carlos Buckle   National University of Patagonia San Juan Bosco, Argentina
Alberto Cañas   University of West Florida, USA
Ana Casali   National University of Rosario, Argentina
Silvia Castro   National University of the South, Argentina
Alejandra Cechich   National University of Comahue, Argentina
Edgar Chávez   Michoacana University of San Nicolás de Hidalgo, Mexico
Carlos Coello Coello   CINVESTAV, Mexico

---

[1] RedUNCI Chair

Uriel Cuckierman	National Technological University, Argentina
Armando E. De Giusti	National University of La Plata, Argentina
Laura De Giusti	National University of La Plata, Argentina
Marcelo De Vincenzi	Inter-American Open University, Argentina
Claudia Deco	National University of Rosario, Argentina
Beatriz Depetris	National University of Tierra del Fuego, Argentina
Javier Díaz	National University of La Plata, Argentina
Juergen Dix	TU Clausthal, Germany
Ramón Doallo	University of La Coruña, Spain
Domingo Docampo	University of Vigo, Spain
Jozo Dujmovic	San Francisco State University, USA
Marcelo Estayno	National University of Lomas de Zamora, Argentina
Elsa Estevez	National University of the South, Argentina
Marcelo A. Falappa	National University of the South, Argentina
Pablo Rubén Fillotrani	National University of the South, Argentina
Jorge Finocchieto	CAECE University, Argentina
Daniel Fridlender	National University of Cordoba, Argentina
Fernando Emmanuel Frati	National University of Chilecito, Argentina
Carlos Garcia Garino	National University of Cuyo, Argentina
Luis Javier García Villalba	Complutense University of Madrid, Spain
Marcela Genero	University of Castilla-La Mancha, Spain
Sergio Alejandro Gómez	National University of South, Argentina
Eduard Groller	Vienna University of Technology, Austria
Roberto Guerrero	National University of San Luis, Argentina
Jorge Ierache	National University of Buenos Aires, Argentina
Tomasz Janowski	Danube University Krems, Austria
Horacio Kuna	National University of Misiones, Argentina
Laura Lanzarini	National University of La Plata, Argentina
Guillermo Leguizamón	National University of San Luis, Argentina
Fernando Lopez Gil	University of Zaragoza, Spain
Ronald Prescott Loui	Washington University in St. Louis, USA
Emilio Luque Fadón	Autonomous University of Barcelona, Spain
Maria Cristina Madoz	National University of La Plata, Argentina
Maria Alejandra Malberti	National University of San Juan, Argentina
Maria Malbrán	National University of Buenos Aires, Argentina
Cristina Manresa Yee	University of Baleares Islands, Spain
Javier Marco	University of Zaragoza, Spain
Mauricio Marin	National University of Santiago de Chile, Chile
Ramon Mas Sanso	University of Baleares Islands, Spain
Orlando Micolini	National University of Cordoba, Argentina
Alicia Mon	ITBA, Argentina
Regina Motz	University of the Republic, Uruguay
Marcelo Naiouf	National University of La Plata, Argentina
Antonio Navarro Martin	Complutense University of Madrid, Spain
Jose Angel Olivas Varela	University of Castilla-La Mancha, Spain
Ariel Pasini	National University of La Plata, Argentina

Alvaro Pardo	University of the Republic, Uruguay
Patricia Pesado	National University of La Plata, Argentina
Mario Piattini Velthuis	University of Castilla-La Mancha, Spain
María Fabiana Piccoli	National University of San Luis, Argentina
Marcela Printista	National University of San Luis, Argentina
Enrico Puppo	University of Genoa, Italy
Hugo Ramón	National University of Northwestern Buenos Aires, Argentina
Dolores Isabel Rexachs del Rosario	Autonomous University of Barcelona, Spain
Nora Reyes	National University of San Luis, Argentina
Rosabel Roig Vila	University of Alicante, Spain
Gustavo Rossi	National University of La Plata, Argentina
Paolo Rosso	Technical University of Valencia, Spain
Sonia V. Rueda	National University of the South, Argentina
Francisco Ruiz González	University of Castilla-La Mancha, Spain
Claudia Russo	National University of Northwestern Buenos Aires, Argentina
Carolina Salto	National University of La Pampa, Argentina
Cecilia Sanz	National University of La Plata, Argentina
Guillermo Ricardo Simari	National University of the South, Argentina
Osvaldo Spositto	National University of La Matanza, Argentina
Ralf Steinmetz	TU Darmstadt, Germany
Remo Suppi	Autonomous University of Barcelona, Spain
Liane Tarouco	Federal University of Rio Grande do Sul, Brazil
Francisco Tirado	Complutense University of Madrid, Spain
Luis Velho	Federal University of Rio Grande do Sul, Brazil
Eduardo Vendrell	Technical University of Valencia, Spain
Marcelo Vénere	National University of Central Buenos Aires, Argentina
Horacio Villagarcía Wanza	National University of La Plata, Argentina
Dante Zanarini	National University of Rosario, Argentina

Sponsors

RedUNCI
Network of Universities
with Degrees in Computer Science

National University of La Matanza

Contents

Software Engineering

Databases and Data Mining

Hardware Architectures, Networks, and Operating Systems

Innovation in Software Systems

Signal Processing and Real-Time Systems

Innovation in Computer Science Education

Computer Security

Digital Governance and Smart Cities

Intelligent Agents and Systems

Modeling Human Decision Making with an Abstract Dynamic Argumentation Framework

Maximiliano Sapino[1,2,3], Edgardo Ferretti[1,2(✉)] ⓘ,
Luciana Mariñelarena Dondena[1], and Marcelo Errecalde[1,2] ⓘ

[1] Universidad Nacional de San Luis (UNSL), San Luis, Argentina
{mesapino,ferretti,lucianamd,merreca}@unsl.edu.ar
[2] Laboratorio de Investigación y Desarrollo en Inteligencia Computacional, UNSL,
San Luis, Argentina
[3] National Council of Scientific and Technical Research (CONICET),
San Luis, Argentina

Abstract. Human-beings everyday decisions are often based on arguments and counter-arguments, and *Argumentation* has shown –within the research field of Artificial Intelligence– to be an appropriate way to advocate for a choice, given its explanatory power. For human beings it worth having a decision making approach in which one can better understand the underpinnings of the evaluation. In this work we show the adequacy of an abstract dynamic argumentation framework to model the Dictator Game by emulating the answers contained in a survey we conducted. The Dictator Game is a well-known problem belonging to the field of experimental economic studies related to human decision making.

Keywords: Human decision making · Abstract dynamic argumentation · Experimental economic studies · Dictator game

1 Introduction

As stated in [23], in Artificial Intelligence (AI) all the developed systems that concern thinking and acting can be broadly classified depending on whether they follow a human-centered approach or a rationalist approach. The former approach measures the systems success in terms of the fidelity to *human* performance, while the latter involves measuring the systems performance against the *ideal* one, so-called *rationality*.

Unless a system be a purely reactive one, *decision making* (DM) is an underlying task related to both thinking and acting, and it can be tackled in as many ways as different research areas deal with the problems belonging to its field of study—using their particular tools and methodologies. For example, as discussed in [16], from a *psychological* perspective it is necessary to examine individual decisions in the context of the set of needs and preferences that people have.

© Springer Nature Switzerland AG 2021
P. Pesado and J. Eterovic (Eds.): CACIC 2020, CCIS 1409, pp. 3–18, 2021.
https://doi.org/10.1007/978-3-030-75836-3_1

This is due to the fact that people evaluate their chances based on subjective expected values. From a *cognitive* perspective DM is considered the result of a mental process in continuous interaction with the environment, in order to select a course of action among the possible ones. The *normative* analysis emphasizes the definition of rationality and the logic of DM, since many axioms and principles have been proposed to govern the preferences of a rational decision maker. Alternatively, the *descriptive* analysis of decisions concern people's beliefs and preferences as they are, and not as they should be. Even at another level, DM can be conceived as a problem solving activity whose completion is given by obtaining a satisfactory solution. Therefore, in general, it could be said that decision making is a reasoning process (rational) or emotional (perhaps irrational), and which may be based on explicit or implicit assumptions.

In Computer Science, DM problems have been mainly tackled from the research field of AI—and *Argumentation* [20] has contributed with its unique strengths. Argumentative reasoning for decision making is an active research trend [2,4,6,7,9–13,17,19,21,24–26]. The state of the art is vast, and the different proposals published roughly differ in two aspects: (a) the underlying argumentation framework used, viz. structured [6,9–12,17,24–26] or abstract (e.g., [2,4,13,19]), and (b) whether decision behavior is formalized with respect to a classical decision approach [2,10–13,17] or not [4,6,9,24,26]. This latter aspect is comprehended in the distinction made at the beginning of this section whether a rationalist approach is followed or not.

In this context, the work reported in [4] is a notable paper, where different studies from experimental economic are modeled using an argumentative framework to reproduce the qualitative decisions that humans exhibited in the studies conducted. In particular two well-known games were studied, the Dictator game [14] and the Ultimatum game [18] and results were compared with those reported by humans with different cultural background. Argument schemes were used as the underlying argumentation approach and they were instantiated with Action-based Alternating Transition Systems (AATS) [27] to obtain the set of conflicting arguments. Once this set has been produced, in order to evaluate the arguments acceptability, they are organized in a Value-based Argumentation Framework (VAF) [3]. A VAF is an extension of the standard Argumentation Framework (AF) [8]. VAFs extend AFs in that each argument in the graph is associated with the value promoted by that argument. Whereas in an AF attacks always succeed, in a VAF they succeed only if the value associated with the attacker is ranked by the audience evaluating the VAF equal to, or higher than, the argument it attacks. Unsuccessful attacks are removed, and then the resulting framework is evaluated as a standard AF. The VAF thus accounts for elements of subjectivity in that the arguments that are acceptable are dependant upon the audience's ranking of the values involved in the scenario.

Another interesting proposal reported in [24], also tackles the Dictator game by means of *Defeasible Logic Programming* (DeLP) [15], a formalism that combines results of Logic Programming and Defeasible Argumentation. The argumentative model presented in [24] is simpler than the one proposed in [4], since all the modeling is carried out within DeLP formalism instead of performing the two-stage process described above.

In the paper at hand, we extend the work presented in [24] by using an abstract dynamic argumentation framework instead of a structured one like DeLP. By performing this abstraction we make us independent of the explicit features that this structured formalism has, thus being able on getting more focused on the high-level details involved in modeling human decision making; like the composition of the working set of arguments where different kind of arguments exist—the ones that compare actions among each other based on the preference criteria, and those aiming at choosing a particular action based on the supporting arguments of the afore-mentioned pairwise comparison of actions. This possibility allowed us to obtain a simpler epistemic component for example, than the one defined in [13]—where the proposed Abstract Argumentation Decision Framework (AADF) generalizes the classical maximum-expected utility model using a Dynamic Argumentation Framework [22].

As mentioned above, non-rational decision making is not the primary focus of [13] but interesting comments are posed on this matter. Moreover, modeling the Dictator game with this abstract dynamic argumentation framework also paves the way to tackle non-rational decision making with other structured argumentation formalism like Possibilistic Defeasible Logic Programming [1]—by instantiating our proposed abstract framework following the methodology described in [12], and thus making richer the application field of the original AADF posed in [13].

The rest of the paper is organized as follows. Section 2 introduces the theoretical concepts relative to the AADF used to model the Dictador game while the formulation of this game based on the AADF is presented in Sect. 3. Finally, Sect. 4 discuss the model proposed considering other related works and draws the conclusions.

2   A Dynamic Argumentation Framework for Decision Making: A Brief Overview

Dynamic Argumentation Frameworks (or DAF for short) were introduced in [22] and provide a formalization for abstract argumentation systems where the current set of *evidence* dynamically activates arguments that belong to a *working set* of arguments. The main objective of DAFs is to extend Argumentation Frameworks [8] to provide the ability of handling dynamics; for achieving that, at a given moment, the set of available *evidence* determines which arguments are *active* and can be used to make inferences to obtain justified conclusions.

In [13], a DAF is used for representing preference relations and the conflicts among the available alternatives. Four other components complete the formalism: a set X of mutually exclusive *alternatives* which are available to the agent; a set of *distinguished literals* representing different binary preference relations for comparing the alternatives; a *strict total order* over the set of distinguished literals to represent the priority among the preference criteria provided to the agent; and a set of *decision rules* that implement the agent's decision making policy. This decision device will not be used in this work since we pursue to model human decision making rather than rational decision making. A key concept that brings together the former three of the afore-mentioned components is that of epistemic component, stated in Definition 1; but before, other notions on which this definition is built upon, are introduced.

The working set of arguments W contains every argument that is available for use by the reasoning process, and in this particular case it contains arguments for reasoning about when an alternative is better than other, as well as which alternative to choose. Note that in a DAF, an argument $\mathcal{A}$ is a reasoning step for a claim α from a set of premises $\{\beta_1, \ldots, \beta_n\}$ denoted as the pair $\langle \{\beta_1, \ldots, \beta_n\}, \alpha \rangle$. An argument will be *active* if its premises are satisfied based on the current evidence. Given an evidence set E, an argument's premise is satisfied whether it belongs to E, or it is the conclusion of an active argument according to E. In this DAF the set $\bowtie$ will contain the conflicts among arguments in W. Given an argument $\mathcal{A} \in W$, $cl(\mathcal{A})$ denotes the claim of $\mathcal{A}$ and $\overline{cl(\mathcal{A})}$ represents the complement of $cl(\mathcal{A})$ with respect to negation ($\sim$). Finally, the preference function $\mathfrak{pref}$ will consider all the agents' criteria represented by (distinguished) literals in $\mathcal{C}$, and, if it is possible, it will return the argument that is based on a better distinguished literal with respect to the order $>_\mathcal{C}$.

Since the epistemic component is defined in an abstract form, the function $\mathfrak{pref}$ is defined in terms of *argumental structures* –or *a-structures* for short– (denoted with Σ) which are built with one or more arguments from W. When the set of arguments in an a-structure is a singleton, that is, $args(\Sigma) = \{\mathcal{A}\}$,[1] the a-structure is called *primitive*. In order to compare two a-structures, distinguished literals will be used.

Definition 1 (Epistemic component). *Let X be the set of all the possible candidate alternatives, $\mathcal{C}$ be a set of distinguished literals in $\mathcal{L}$ and $>_\mathcal{C}$ be a strict total order over $\mathcal{C}$. An epistemic component $\mathcal{K}_\mathcal{A}$, is a DAF $\langle E, W, \bowtie, \mathfrak{pref} \rangle$ where:*

- *The evidence E is a consistent set of sentences of the form $c(x, y)$, such that $x, y \in X$ and $c \in \mathcal{C}$.*
- *The working set W will be such that if $c \in \mathcal{C}$, $\{x, y\} \subseteq X$ ($x \neq y$), better $\notin \mathcal{C}$ and choose $\notin \mathcal{C}$ then:*

$$\langle \{c(x, y)\}, better(x, y) \rangle \in W$$
$$\langle \{better(x, y)\}, choose(x) \rangle \in W$$
$$\langle \{better(x, y)\}, \sim choose(y) \rangle \in W$$

- $\bowtie = \{(\mathcal{A}, \mathcal{B}) | \{\mathcal{A}, \mathcal{B}\} \subseteq W, cl(\mathcal{A}) = \overline{cl(\mathcal{B})}\}$.
- *Let Σ_1 and Σ_2 be two argumental structures in W, then*

$$\mathfrak{pref}(\Sigma_1, \Sigma_2) = \begin{cases} \Sigma_1 \text{ if } \forall c \in dlits(\Sigma_2), \exists c' \in dlits(\Sigma_1) \text{ st. } (c', c) \in >_\mathcal{C}, \\ \Sigma_2 \text{ if } \forall c \in dlits(\Sigma_1), \exists c' \in dlits(\Sigma_2) \text{ st. } (c', c) \in >_\mathcal{C} \\ \epsilon \quad otherwise \end{cases}$$

---

[1] $args(\Sigma)$ denotes the set of arguments belonging to a-structure Σ.

where dlits(Σ) $\subseteq$ $\mathcal{C}$ is the set of distinguished literals that are contained in arguments of an argumental structure Σ.

In the AADF, the exchange of arguments resembles a dialogical discussion where different alternatives are compared. As such, it makes sense that the introduction of a new argument by one of the participants should be consistent with the previously posed arguments. Indeed, it is also desirable to require that none of the parties be allowed to introduce an argument already posed by them. The set of all the arguments posed by the proponent is referred as *pro*, while the set of all the arguments posed by the opponent is referred as *con*. Definition 2 formalizes the intuitions referred above on what is called an *acceptable argumentation line*. Indeed, several argumentation lines starting with the same a-structure resemble the intuition of a discussion around a topic. This notion known as *dialectical tree* is also formalized next, in Definition 3.

Definition 2 (Acceptable Argumentation Line). *Given an argumentation line λ in the context of a DAF, $\mathbf{F} = \langle E, W, \bowtie, \mathfrak{pref} \rangle$, λ is acceptable in $\mathbf{F}$ iff it holds that:*

- *There is no repetition of structures in λ (non-circularity), and*
- *Sets* pro *and* con *are consistent with respect to the conflict relation among argumental structures (concordance).*

It is worth mentioning that an acceptable argumentation line is *exhaustive* if it is not possible to insert more argumental structures in the sequence.

Definition 3 (Dialectical Tree). *Given a DAF $\mathbf{F}$ and a set S of exhaustive argumentation lines in $\mathbf{F}$ rooted in Σ_1, such that S is maximal wrt. set inclusion, a dialectical tree for an argumental structure Σ_1 is a tree $\mathcal{T}_\mathbf{F}(\Sigma_1)$ verifying:*

- *Σ_1 is the root;*
- *A structure $\Sigma_{i \neq 1}$ in a line $\lambda_i \in S$ is an inner node, iff has as children all the Σ_j in lines $\lambda_j \in S$ such that $\Sigma_j \Rightarrow \Sigma_i$ and $\lambda^\uparrow[\Sigma_i] = \lambda^\uparrow(\Sigma_j)$;[2]*
- *The leaves of the tree correspond to the leaves of the lines in S.*

Dialectical trees are defined over the working set of arguments, and hence they can contain active and inactive a-structures. A dialectical tree that contains only active structures is called *active dialectical tree*, and it is denoted $\mathbb{T}_\mathbf{F}(\Sigma)$. Once a dialectical tree has been built for an a-structure, a marking criterion determines which structures in the tree are defeated and which ones remain undefeated. This criterion is specified by a marking function. Definition 4 introduces the marking function used in the AADF.

---

[2] The defeat relation between argumental structures is denoted as "$\Rightarrow$". Moreover, given an argumentation line $\lambda = [\Sigma_1, \ldots, \Sigma_n]$, the *top segment* of Σ_i ($1 < i \leq n$) in λ is $[\Sigma_1, \ldots, \Sigma_i]$ and it is denoted as $\lambda^\uparrow(\Sigma_i)$. The *proper top segment* of Σ_i in λ is $[\Sigma_1, \ldots, \Sigma_{i-1}]$ and is denoted $\lambda^\uparrow[\Sigma_i]$.

Definition 4 (Skeptical Marking Function). *Given an argumental struc-ture Σ_i in a line λ_i in a dialectical tree $\mathcal{T}_F(\Sigma)$, the skeptical marking function m_e is defined as follows: $\mathrm{m}_e(\Sigma_i, \lambda_i, \mathcal{T}_F(\Sigma)) = D$ iff $\exists \Sigma_j$ s.t. $\mathrm{m}_e(\Sigma_j, \lambda_j, \mathcal{T}_F(\Sigma)) = U$, where Σ_j is a child of Σ_i in $\mathcal{T}_F(\Sigma)$.*

Once the marking function has been defined, the warranty status of the root of a dialectical tree can be determined, as defined next.

Definition 5 (Warrant). *Given a DAF $\mathbf{F}$ and a marking function m, an a-structure Σ from $\mathbf{F}$ is warranted in $\mathbf{F}$, iff $\mathrm{m}(\Sigma, \lambda, \mathbb{T}_F(\Sigma)) = U$, where λ is any argumentation line from $\mathbb{T}_F(\Sigma)$. The conclusion $cl(\Sigma)$ is justified by $\mathbf{F}$.*

To conclude, it is worth mentioning that the notion of warrant is defined on active dialectical trees, since all the reasoning only can be carried out over the set of active arguments. Considering that this section aims at introducing the minimal theoretical concepts underpinning the AADF used to model the Dictator Game, for more details the interested reader is referred to [13,22].

3   Modeling the Dictator Game

We begin by considering the problem formulation as posed in [4] and [24]. We will consider the same limited number of options that comprise the set of alter-natives X and we assume 1000 units of money to be divided. Thus, the five actions belonging to set $X = \{a_1, a_2, a_3, a_4, a_5\}$ correspond to different divi-sions of the money, namely: $a_1 = give(70\%)$, $a_2 = give(100\%)$, $a_3 = give(50\%)$, $a_4 = give(0\%)$ and $a_5 = give(30\%)$. The dictator starts having the whole money and the "motivations" to share it that we have considered are mentioned below:

Money: Most obvious is money's value. This is what the economic man is sup-posed to maximize. Given that we need to recognize that the other player having money may be considered positively by the dictator, we need to dis-tinguish money for the dictator himself from money for the other.

Giving: It can be held that giving a gift is a source of pleasure, and this is what motivates the dictator to share.

Image: Another consideration is the desire not to appear mean before the exper-imenter that motivates sharing. It could even be that one does not want to appear mean to oneself.

Equality: Equality, as defined by an equal distribution, characterizes a sense of fairness.

In our model, these motivations are used as the criteria to compare the alternatives among each other and they will be represented by the set of distin-guished literals $\mathcal{C} = \{ms, mo, giv, im, eq\}$. Some of these motivations establish well-defined preference orderings among the alternatives; for example, the money the dictator has for himself (ms), clearly produces the following ordering among the alternatives: $a_4 \prec a_5 \prec a_3 \prec a_1 \prec a_2$—where $a_i \prec a_j$ denotes that action a_i is preferred to a_j. Conversely, "the money for the other" motivation (mo) generates a mirror-like ordering of the alternatives: $a_2 \prec a_1 \prec a_3 \prec a_5 \prec a_4$.

The remaining motivations are more subjective and different orderings can be obtained depending on the individuals' personality and cultural background. In this context, one possible ordering of all the alternatives according to these motivations is the one presented below, as facts belonging to evidence set E. These facts were stated considering the rules of the game and our understanding of some of the elements of subjectivity—like for instance, if giving more than half of the money is a source of pleasure for the dictator. In our view it is not, and that is why facts like $giv(a_2, a_1)$, $giv(a_2, a_3)$, $giv(a_2, a_4)$, $giv(a_2, a_5)$, $giv(a_1, a_3)$, $giv(a_1, a_4)$, $giv(a_1, a_5)$ and $giv(a_5, a_4)$ are not present in E.

$$E = \left\{ \begin{array}{lllll}
ms(a_4, a_1), & mo(a_2, a_1), & giv(a_3, a_4), & im(a_1, a_4), & eq(a_3, a_1), \\
ms(a_4, a_2), & mo(a_2, a_3), & giv(a_3, a_5), & im(a_2, a_4), & eq(a_3, a_2), \\
ms(a_4, a_3), & mo(a_2, a_4), & giv(a_3, a_2), & im(a_3, a_4), & eq(a_3, a_4), \\
ms(a_4, a_5), & mo(a_2, a_5), & giv(a_3, a_1), & im(a_5, a_4), & eq(a_3, a_5), \\
ms(a_5, a_3), & mo(a_1, a_3), & giv(a_5, a_4), & im(a_2, a_1), & eq(a_5, a_4), \\
ms(a_5, a_2), & mo(a_1, a_4), & giv(a_5, a_2), & im(a_2, a_3), & eq(a_5, a_2), \\
ms(a_5, a_1), & mo(a_1, a_5), & giv(a_5, a_1), & im(a_2, a_5), & eq(a_1, a_2) \\
ms(a_3, a_1), & mo(a_3, a_4), & giv(a_4, a_1), & im(a_1, a_3), & \\
ms(a_3, a_2), & mo(a_3, a_5), & giv(a_4, a_2), & im(a_1, a_5), & \\
ms(a_1, a_2), & mo(a_5, a_4), & giv(a_1, a_2), & im(a_3, a_5), &
\end{array} \right\}$$

Our survey is composed by 276 samples, *i.e.*, 276 different people that played the Dictador game. They are mainly students of the National University of San Luis but also 2.9% of the people are employed in the private industry and 3.3% work in the public sector. Considering their origin, 84% were born in the capital of San Luis and the remaining 16% were born in 19 different cities from San Luis province and other provinces from Argentina. All the people live in San Luis at present. Ages ranged from 17 to 54 years old, with an approximate mean of 22 years old. Regarding educational level, 96% of the participants have completed secondary education and only 4% have completed a tertiary level. When gender is considered, 73% of the samples correspond to female individuals and 27% to male individuals. Finally, it is worth mentioning that 93% of the people do not have children, while the remaining 7% do.

The answers obtained from the survey reported that 66.67% of people chose $a_3 = give(50\%)$, 10.87% chose $a_2 = give(100\%)$, 9.78% chose $a_4 = give(0\%)$, 9.42% chose $a_5 = give(30\%)$ and 3.26% chose $a_1 = give(70\%)$. It is beyond the scope of our present study to analyze the possible reasons of these behaviors, and this ordering of the alternatives resulted in the following order $>_C = \{(giv, mo), (giv, ms), (giv, im), (giv, eq), (mo, ms), (mo, im), (mo, eq), (ms, im), (ms, eq), (im, eq)\}$ of the distinguished literals.

As mentioned above, the evidence set E contains factual information where actions are compared in a pairwise manner considering the motivations to share the money that the dictator has. In this way, taking into account the factual information present in E about the distinguished literal giv where alternative a_3 is deemed better than the other ones, provided us a firm reason to set this distinguished literal as the most preferred one in the order $>_C$.

Then *mo* is the second most preferred in $>_C$ given its direct relation with the fact that a_2 was the second action chosen in the survey. Following a similar pattern of reasoning *ms* was considered third in the preference ordering given its relation with a_4. Finally, *im* and *eq* take fourth and fifth places in $>_C$, respectively—*im* is more preferred than *eq*, given that all the actions can be compared against each other with this criterion and with *eq* cannot.

Due to space constraints, Figs. 1 and 2 condense a lot information that will be detailed next. First, we can see that they show 94 active a-structures. Second, we have abbreviated literals *better* and *choose* as *bt* and *ch* respectively, to improve reading. Besides, to avoid a visual overload in these figures we have omitted the names of all the arguments, except two, in order to introduce how to denote them from the numbers of the a-structures they belong to. In this respect, we can see in the top-left corner of Fig. 1 that a-structure Σ_1 is highlighted and its two composing arguments are denoted with letters a and b as subscripts. Hence, $args(\Sigma_i) = \{\mathcal{A}_{ia}, \mathcal{A}_{ib}\} \, \forall i = 1 \ldots 94$. It is clear that this notation style introduces some redundancy given that the same argument will be referred with different names depending on the a-structure it belongs to.

Next, we present the exhausted list of denoting equalities among arguments from Figs. 1 and 2 whose subscript is a: $\mathcal{A}_{1a} = \mathcal{A}_{5a}$, $\mathcal{A}_{2a} = \mathcal{A}_{9a}$, $\mathcal{A}_{3a} = \mathcal{A}_{12a}$, $\mathcal{A}_{4a} = \mathcal{A}_{16a}$, $\mathcal{A}_{6a} = \mathcal{A}_{10a}$, $\mathcal{A}_{7a} = \mathcal{A}_{13a}$, $\mathcal{A}_{8a} = \mathcal{A}_{17a}$, $\mathcal{A}_{11a} = \mathcal{A}_{18a}$,$\mathcal{A}_{14a} = \mathcal{A}_{89a}$, $\mathcal{A}_{15a} = \mathcal{A}_{91a}$, $\mathcal{A}_{19a} = \mathcal{A}_{29a}$, $\mathcal{A}_{20a} = \mathcal{A}_{31a}$, $\mathcal{A}_{21a} = \mathcal{A}_{36a}$, $\mathcal{A}_{22a} = \mathcal{A}_{23a}$, $\mathcal{A}_{24a} = \mathcal{A}_{30a}$, $\mathcal{A}_{25a} = \mathcal{A}_{32a}$, $\mathcal{A}_{26a} = \mathcal{A}_{37a}$, $\mathcal{A}_{27a} = \mathcal{A}_{33a}$, $\mathcal{A}_{28a} = \mathcal{A}_{38a}$, $\mathcal{A}_{34a} = \mathcal{A}_{35a}$, $\mathcal{A}_{39a} = \mathcal{A}_{43a}$, $\mathcal{A}_{40a} = \mathcal{A}_{88a}$, $\mathcal{A}_{41a} = \mathcal{A}_{49a}$, $\mathcal{A}_{42a} = \mathcal{A}_{53a}$, $\mathcal{A}_{44a} = \mathcal{A}_{50a}$, $\mathcal{A}_{45a} = \mathcal{A}_{87a}$, $\mathcal{A}_{46a} = \mathcal{A}_{54a}$, $\mathcal{A}_{47a} = \mathcal{A}_{51a}$, $\mathcal{A}_{48a} = \mathcal{A}_{55a}$, $\mathcal{A}_{52a} = \mathcal{A}_{56a}$, $\mathcal{A}_{57a} = \mathcal{A}_{61a}$, $\mathcal{A}_{58a} = \mathcal{A}_{90a}$, $\mathcal{A}_{59a} = \mathcal{A}_{62a}$, $\mathcal{A}_{60a} = \mathcal{A}_{68a}$, $\mathcal{A}_{63a} = \mathcal{A}_{65a}$, $\mathcal{A}_{64a} = \mathcal{A}_{67a}$, $\mathcal{A}_{66a} = \mathcal{A}_{69a}$, $\mathcal{A}_{70a} = \mathcal{A}_{77a}$, $\mathcal{A}_{71a} = \mathcal{A}_{93a}$, $\mathcal{A}_{72a} = \mathcal{A}_{84a}$, $\mathcal{A}_{73a} = \mathcal{A}_{92a}$, $\mathcal{A}_{74a} = \mathcal{A}_{78a}$, $\mathcal{A}_{75a} = \mathcal{A}_{94a}$, $\mathcal{A}_{76a} = \mathcal{A}_{85a}$, $\mathcal{A}_{79a} = \mathcal{A}_{81a}$, $\mathcal{A}_{80a} = \mathcal{A}_{83a}$, $\mathcal{A}_{82a} = \mathcal{A}_{86a}$.

Likewise, we introduce the exhausted list of denoting equalities among arguments from Figs. 1 and 2 whose subscript is b: $\mathcal{A}_{1b} = \mathcal{A}_{39b}$, $\mathcal{A}_{2b} = \mathcal{A}_{40b}$, $\mathcal{A}_{3b} = \mathcal{A}_{41b}$, $\mathcal{A}_{4b} = \mathcal{A}_{42b}$, $\mathcal{A}_{5b} = \mathcal{A}_{43b}$, $\mathcal{A}_{6b} = \mathcal{A}_{87b}$, $\mathcal{A}_{7b} = \mathcal{A}_{44b}$, $\mathcal{A}_{8b} = \mathcal{A}_{46b}$, $\mathcal{A}_{9b} = \mathcal{A}_{88b}$, $\mathcal{A}_{10b} = \mathcal{A}_{45b}$, $\mathcal{A}_{11b} = \mathcal{A}_{48b} = \mathcal{A}_{64b} = \mathcal{A}_{80b}$, $\mathcal{A}_{12b} = \mathcal{A}_{49b}$, $\mathcal{A}_{13b} = \mathcal{A}_{50b}$, $\mathcal{A}_{14b} = \mathcal{A}_{51b} = \mathcal{A}_{65b} = \mathcal{A}_{81b}$, $\mathcal{A}_{15b} = \mathcal{A}_{52b} = \mathcal{A}_{66b} = \mathcal{A}_{82b}$, $\mathcal{A}_{16b} = \mathcal{A}_{53b}$, $\mathcal{A}_{17b} = \mathcal{A}_{54b}$, $\mathcal{A}_{18b} = \mathcal{A}_{55b} = \mathcal{A}_{67b} = \mathcal{A}_{83b}$, $\mathcal{A}_{19b} = \mathcal{A}_{57b} = \mathcal{A}_{70b}$, $\mathcal{A}_{20b} = \mathcal{A}_{71b}$, $\mathcal{A}_{21b} = \mathcal{A}_{72b}$, $\mathcal{A}_{22b} = \mathcal{A}_{58b} = \mathcal{A}_{73b}$, $\mathcal{A}_{23b} = \mathcal{A}_{90b} = \mathcal{A}_{92b}$, $\mathcal{A}_{24b} = \mathcal{A}_{59b} = \mathcal{A}_{74b}$, $\mathcal{A}_{25b} = \mathcal{A}_{75b}$, $\mathcal{A}_{26b} = \mathcal{A}_{60b} = \mathcal{A}_{76b}$, $\mathcal{A}_{29b} = \mathcal{A}_{61b} = \mathcal{A}_{77b}$, $\mathcal{A}_{30b} = \mathcal{A}_{62b} = \mathcal{A}_{78b}$, $\mathcal{A}_{31b} = \mathcal{A}_{93b}$, $\mathcal{A}_{32b} = \mathcal{A}_{94b}$, $\mathcal{A}_{36b} = \mathcal{A}_{84b}$, $\mathcal{A}_{37b} = \mathcal{A}_{68b} = \mathcal{A}_{85b}$, $\mathcal{A}_{56b} = \mathcal{A}_{69b} = \mathcal{A}_{86b} = \mathcal{A}_{91b}$, $\mathcal{A}_{47b} = \mathcal{A}_{63b} = \mathcal{A}_{79b} = \mathcal{A}_{89b}$.

As we can see in evidence set E, we have 47 facts which compare the possible actions among each other considering the preference criteria provided to the dictator. From Definition 1 we can observe that there are two kind of arguments in the working set W, those with a premise of the kind $c(x, y)$ and claim $better(x, y)$ and those having $better(x, y)$ as a premise and $choose(x)$ or $\sim choose(y)$ as possible claims based on x and y comparison. The former kind corresponds to the arguments denoted with subscript a in Figs. 1 and 2 while the latter kind corresponds to the arguments denoted with subscript b. Since these 47 arguments

–having as premises the facts in the evidence– will support arguments' premises whose claim allow to decide whether to choose x or similarly not to choose y, we will have the 94 active a-structures presented in Figs. 1 and 2, respectively. Figures 1 and 2 also introduce all the active arguments from the working set W that will interact among each other to decide which action is warranted. Let analyze each action one by one.

Tables 1, 3, 5, 7 and 9 present the active a-structures supporting whether to choose or not action $a_{i=1\ldots5}$, together with their corresponding sets of distinguished literals $dlits(\Sigma_i)$ (cf. Definition 1). Besides, Tables 2, 4, 6, 8 and 10 introduce in a tabular way, the existing preferences according to function $\mathfrak{pref}$ among conflicting a-structures. For instance, first row of Table 2 compares Σ_1 which supports $\sim choose(a_1)$ against the a-structures supporting $choose(a_1)$. The output of function $\mathfrak{pref}$ is ϵ when Σ_1 is compared against Σ_2, Σ_3 and

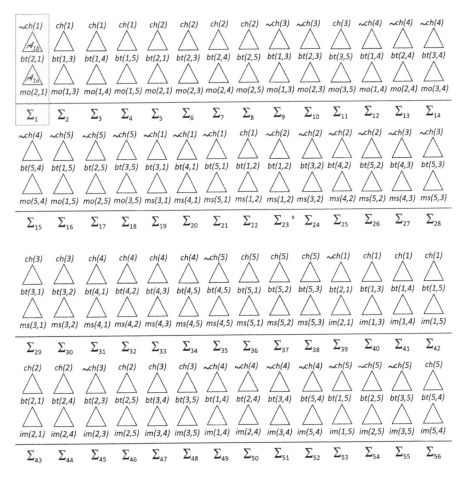

Fig. 1. Active a-structures and active arguments from the working set W

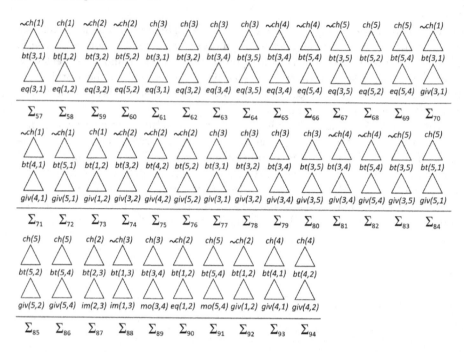

Fig. 2. Active a-structures and active arguments from the working set W

Σ_4 since all the a-structures are based on distinguished literal mo and none is preferred. When Σ_1 is compared against Σ_{73} this latter a-structure is preferred given that it is based on the distinguished literal giv and $(giv, mo) \in >_C$. Conversely, Σ_1 is preferred when compared against the remaining a-structures because $\{(mo, ms), (mo, im), (mo, eq)\} \subset >_C$.

Table 1. Argumental structures supporting whether to choose or not action a_1

$choose(a_1)$								
Σ_2	Σ_3	Σ_4	Σ_{22}	Σ_{40}	Σ_{41}	Σ_{42}	Σ_{58}	Σ_{73}
$\{mo\}$	$\{mo\}$	$\{mo\}$	$\{ms\}$	$\{im\}$	$\{im\}$	$\{im\}$	$\{eq\}$	$\{giv\}$
$\sim choose(a_1)$								
Σ_1	Σ_{19}	Σ_{20}	Σ_{21}	Σ_{39}	Σ_{57}	Σ_{70}	Σ_{71}	Σ_{72}
$\{mo\}$	$\{ms\}$	$\{ms\}$	$\{ms\}$	$\{im\}$	$\{eq\}$	$\{giv\}$	$\{giv\}$	$\{giv\}$

The same analysis can be made for Tables 2, 4, 6, 8 and 10. Considering the way the epistemic component has been defined, the a-structures based on the most preferred distinguished literal will allow to build an active dialectical tree with an acceptable argumentation line of one a-structure only that will be in consequence the root and the only node of this tree. The skeptical marking function from Definition 4 will mark with U the root of this particular tree, and by Definition 5 the conclusion $cl(\Sigma)$ will be justified. This warrant of a claim can be appreciated in a tabular fashion when a whole column or row contains the same a-structure. Only Tables 4 and 6 present this situation. In Table 4, the last four columns shows that a-structures Σ_{75}, Σ_{76}, Σ_{90} and Σ_{92} are preferred against the other a-structures supporting $choose(a_2)$. This means that $\sim choose(a_2)$ is warranted and $choose(a_2)$ is not. In Table 6, we can observe that a-structures Σ_{77}, Σ_{78}, Σ_{79} and Σ_{80} are preferred against the other a-structures supporting $\sim choose(a_3)$. Hence, $choose(a_3)$ is warranted and $\sim choose(a_3)$ is not.

A blocking situation arises in Table 2, where the output of function $\mathfrak{pref}$ is ϵ when Σ_{70}, Σ_{71} and Σ_{72} are compared against Σ_{73} since all the a-structures are based on distinguished literal giv and none is preferred; but they are preferred to all the other a-structures because giv is the most preferred distinguished literal.

Table 2. Output values of function $\mathfrak{pref}(\cdot,\cdot)$ for a-structures supporting whether to choose or not action a_1

$\mathfrak{pref}(\cdot,\cdot)$	Σ_2	Σ_3	Σ_4	Σ_{22}	Σ_{40}	Σ_{41}	Σ_{42}	Σ_{58}	Σ_{73}
Σ_1	ϵ	ϵ	ϵ	Σ_1	Σ_1	Σ_1	Σ_1	Σ_1	Σ_{73}
Σ_{19}	Σ_2	Σ_3	Σ_4	ϵ	Σ_{19}	Σ_{19}	Σ_{19}	Σ_{19}	Σ_{73}
Σ_{20}	Σ_2	Σ_3	Σ_4	ϵ	Σ_{20}	Σ_{20}	Σ_{20}	Σ_{20}	Σ_{73}
Σ_{21}	Σ_2	Σ_3	Σ_4	ϵ	Σ_{21}	Σ_{21}	Σ_{21}	Σ_{21}	Σ_{73}
Σ_{39}	Σ_2	Σ_3	Σ_4	Σ_{22}	ϵ	ϵ	ϵ	Σ_{39}	Σ_{73}
Σ_{57}	Σ_2	Σ_3	Σ_4	Σ_{22}	Σ_{40}	Σ_{41}	Σ_{42}	ϵ	Σ_{73}
Σ_{70}	Σ_{70}	Σ_{70}	Σ_{70}	Σ_{70}	Σ_{70}	Σ_{70}	Σ_{70}	Σ_{70}	ϵ
Σ_{71}	Σ_{71}	Σ_{71}	Σ_{71}	Σ_{71}	Σ_{71}	Σ_{71}	Σ_{71}	Σ_{71}	ϵ
Σ_{72}	Σ_{72}	Σ_{72}	Σ_{72}	Σ_{72}	Σ_{72}	Σ_{72}	Σ_{72}	Σ_{72}	ϵ

Table 3. Argumental structures supporting whether to choose or not action a_2

$choose(a_2)$									
Σ_5	Σ_6	Σ_7	Σ_8	Σ_{43}	Σ_{44}	Σ_{46}	Σ_{87}		
$\{mo\}$	$\{mo\}$	$\{mo\}$	$\{mo\}$	$\{im\}$	$\{im\}$	$\{im\}$	$\{im\}$		
$\sim choose(a_2)$									
Σ_{23}	Σ_{24}	Σ_{25}	Σ_{26}	Σ_{59}	Σ_{60}	Σ_{75}	Σ_{76}	Σ_{90}	Σ_{92}
$\{ms\}$	$\{ms\}$	$\{ms\}$	$\{ms\}$	$\{eq\}$	$\{eq\}$	$\{giv\}$	$\{giv\}$	$\{giv\}$	$\{giv\}$

Table 4. Output values of function $\mathfrak{pref}(\cdot,\cdot)$ for a-structures supporting whether to choose or not action a_2

$\mathfrak{pref}(\cdot,\cdot)$	Σ_{23}	Σ_{24}	Σ_{25}	Σ_{26}	Σ_{59}	Σ_{60}	Σ_{75}	Σ_{76}	Σ_{90}	Σ_{92}
Σ_5	Σ_5	Σ_5	Σ_5	Σ_5	Σ_5	Σ_5	Σ_{75}	Σ_{76}	Σ_{90}	Σ_{92}
Σ_6	Σ_6	Σ_6	Σ_6	Σ_6	Σ_6	Σ_6	Σ_{75}	Σ_{76}	Σ_{90}	Σ_{92}
Σ_7	Σ_7	Σ_7	Σ_7	Σ_7	Σ_7	Σ_7	Σ_{75}	Σ_{76}	Σ_{90}	Σ_{92}
Σ_8	Σ_8	Σ_8	Σ_8	Σ_8	Σ_8	Σ_8	Σ_{75}	Σ_{76}	Σ_{90}	Σ_{92}
Σ_{43}	Σ_{23}	Σ_{24}	Σ_{25}	Σ_{26}	Σ_{43}	Σ_{43}	Σ_{75}	Σ_{76}	Σ_{90}	Σ_{92}
Σ_{44}	Σ_{23}	Σ_{24}	Σ_{25}	Σ_{26}	Σ_{44}	Σ_{44}	Σ_{75}	Σ_{76}	Σ_{90}	Σ_{92}
Σ_{46}	Σ_{23}	Σ_{24}	Σ_{25}	Σ_{26}	Σ_{46}	Σ_{46}	Σ_{75}	Σ_{76}	Σ_{90}	Σ_{92}
Σ_{87}	Σ_{23}	Σ_{24}	Σ_{25}	Σ_{26}	Σ_{87}	Σ_{87}	Σ_{75}	Σ_{76}	Σ_{90}	Σ_{92}

Table 5. Argumental structures supporting whether to choose or not action a_3

$choose(a_3)$

Σ_{11}	Σ_{29}	Σ_{30}	Σ_{47}	Σ_{48}	Σ_{61}	Σ_{62}	Σ_{63}	Σ_{64}	Σ_{77}	Σ_{78}	Σ_{79}	Σ_{80}	Σ_{89}
$\{mo\}$	$\{ms\}$	$\{ms\}$	$\{im\}$	$\{im\}$	$\{eq\}$	$\{eq\}$	$\{eq\}$	$\{eq\}$	$\{giv\}$	$\{giv\}$	$\{giv\}$	$\{giv\}$	$\{mo\}$

$\sim choose(a_3)$

Σ_9	Σ_{10}	Σ_{45}	Σ_{88}										
$\{mo\}$	$\{mo\}$	$\{im\}$	$\{im\}$										

Table 6. Output values of function $\mathfrak{pref}(\cdot,\cdot)$ for a-structures supporting whether to choose or not action a_3

$\mathfrak{pref}(\cdot,\cdot)$	Σ_{11}	Σ_{29}	Σ_{30}	Σ_{47}	Σ_{48}	Σ_{61}	Σ_{62}	Σ_{63}	Σ_{64}	Σ_{77}	Σ_{78}	Σ_{79}	Σ_{80}	Σ_{89}
Σ_9	ϵ	Σ_9	Σ_9	Σ_9	Σ_9	Σ_9	Σ_9	Σ_9	Σ_9	Σ_{77}	Σ_{78}	Σ_{79}	Σ_{80}	ϵ
Σ_{10}	ϵ	Σ_{10}	Σ_{10}	Σ_{10}	Σ_{10}	Σ_{10}	Σ_{10}	Σ_{10}	Σ_{10}	Σ_{77}	Σ_{78}	Σ_{79}	Σ_{80}	ϵ
Σ_{45}	Σ_{11}	Σ_{29}	Σ_{30}	ϵ	ϵ	Σ_{45}	Σ_{45}	Σ_{45}	Σ_{45}	Σ_{77}	Σ_{78}	Σ_{79}	Σ_{80}	Σ_{89}
Σ_{88}	Σ_{11}	Σ_{29}	Σ_{30}	ϵ	ϵ	Σ_{88}	Σ_{88}	Σ_{88}	Σ_{88}	Σ_{77}	Σ_{78}	Σ_{79}	Σ_{80}	Σ_{89}

Table 7. Argumental structures supporting whether to choose or not action a_4

$choose(a_4)$

Σ_{31}	Σ_{32}	Σ_{33}	Σ_{34}	Σ_{93}	Σ_{94}						
$\{ms\}$	$\{ms\}$	$\{ms\}$	$\{ms\}$	$\{giv\}$	$\{giv\}$						

$\sim choose(a_4)$

Σ_{12}	Σ_{13}	Σ_{14}	Σ_{15}	Σ_{49}	Σ_{50}	Σ_{51}	Σ_{52}	Σ_{65}	Σ_{66}	Σ_{81}	Σ_{82}
$\{mo\}$	$\{mo\}$	$\{mo\}$	$\{mo\}$	$\{im\}$	$\{im\}$	$\{im\}$	$\{im\}$	$\{eq\}$	$\{eq\}$	$\{giv\}$	$\{giv\}$

Table 8. Output values of function $\mathfrak{pref}(\cdot,\cdot)$ for a-structures supporting whether to choose or not action a_4

$\mathfrak{pref}(\cdot,\cdot)$	Σ_{12}	Σ_{13}	Σ_{14}	Σ_{15}	Σ_{49}	Σ_{50}	Σ_{51}	Σ_{52}	Σ_{65}	Σ_{66}	Σ_{81}	Σ_{82}
Σ_{31}	Σ_{12}	Σ_{13}	Σ_{14}	Σ_{15}	Σ_{31}	Σ_{31}	Σ_{31}	Σ_{31}	Σ_{31}	Σ_{31}	Σ_{81}	Σ_{82}
Σ_{32}	Σ_{12}	Σ_{13}	Σ_{14}	Σ_{15}	Σ_{32}	Σ_{32}	Σ_{32}	Σ_{32}	Σ_{32}	Σ_{32}	Σ_{81}	Σ_{82}
Σ_{33}	Σ_{12}	Σ_{13}	Σ_{14}	Σ_{15}	Σ_{33}	Σ_{33}	Σ_{33}	Σ_{33}	Σ_{33}	Σ_{33}	Σ_{81}	Σ_{82}
Σ_{34}	Σ_{12}	Σ_{13}	Σ_{14}	Σ_{15}	Σ_{34}	Σ_{34}	Σ_{34}	Σ_{34}	Σ_{34}	Σ_{34}	Σ_{81}	Σ_{82}
Σ_{93}	Σ_{93}	Σ_{93}	Σ_{93}	Σ_{93}	Σ_{93}	Σ_{93}	Σ_{93}	Σ_{93}	Σ_{93}	Σ_{93}	ϵ	ϵ
Σ_{94}	Σ_{94}	Σ_{94}	Σ_{94}	Σ_{94}	Σ_{94}	Σ_{94}	Σ_{94}	Σ_{94}	Σ_{94}	Σ_{94}	ϵ	ϵ

Table 9. Argumental structures supporting whether to choose or not alternative a_5

$choose(a_5)$									
Σ_{36}	Σ_{37}	Σ_{38}	Σ_{56}	Σ_{68}	Σ_{69}	Σ_{84}	Σ_{85}	Σ_{86}	Σ_{91}
$\{ms\}$	$\{ms\}$	$\{ms\}$	$\{im\}$	$\{eq\}$	$\{eq\}$	$\{giv\}$	$\{giv\}$	$\{giv\}$	$\{mo\}$

$\sim choose(a_5)$								
Σ_{16}	Σ_{17}	Σ_{18}	Σ_{35}	Σ_{53}	Σ_{54}	Σ_{55}	Σ_{67}	Σ_{83}
$\{mo\}$	$\{mo\}$	$\{mo\}$	$\{ms\}$	$\{im\}$	$\{im\}$	$\{im\}$	$\{eq\}$	$\{giv\}$

Table 10. Output values of function $\mathfrak{pref}(\cdot,\cdot)$ for a-structures supporting whether to choose or not action a_5

$\mathfrak{pref}(\cdot,\cdot)$	Σ_{36}	Σ_{37}	Σ_{38}	Σ_{56}	Σ_{68}	Σ_{69}	Σ_{84}	Σ_{85}	Σ_{86}	Σ_{91}
Σ_{16}	Σ_{16}	Σ_{16}	Σ_{16}	Σ_{16}	Σ_{16}	Σ_{16}	Σ_{84}	Σ_{85}	Σ_{86}	ϵ
Σ_{17}	Σ_{17}	Σ_{17}	Σ_{17}	Σ_{17}	Σ_{17}	Σ_{17}	Σ_{84}	Σ_{85}	Σ_{86}	ϵ
Σ_{18}	Σ_{18}	Σ_{18}	Σ_{18}	Σ_{18}	Σ_{18}	Σ_{18}	Σ_{84}	Σ_{85}	Σ_{86}	ϵ
Σ_{35}	ϵ	ϵ	ϵ	Σ_{35}	Σ_{35}	Σ_{35}	Σ_{84}	Σ_{85}	Σ_{86}	Σ_{91}
Σ_{53}	Σ_{36}	Σ_{37}	Σ_{38}	ϵ	Σ_{53}	Σ_{53}	Σ_{84}	Σ_{85}	Σ_{86}	Σ_{91}
Σ_{54}	Σ_{36}	Σ_{37}	Σ_{38}	ϵ	Σ_{54}	Σ_{54}	Σ_{84}	Σ_{85}	Σ_{86}	Σ_{91}
Σ_{55}	Σ_{36}	Σ_{37}	Σ_{38}	ϵ	Σ_{55}	Σ_{55}	Σ_{84}	Σ_{85}	Σ_{86}	Σ_{91}
Σ_{67}	Σ_{36}	Σ_{37}	Σ_{38}	Σ_{56}	ϵ	ϵ	Σ_{84}	Σ_{85}	Σ_{86}	Σ_{91}
Σ_{83}	Σ_{83}	Σ_{83}	Σ_{83}	Σ_{83}	Σ_{83}	Σ_{83}	ϵ	ϵ	ϵ	Σ_{83}

An analogous situation occurs in Table 8 among a-structures Σ_{81} and Σ_{82} when compared against Σ_{93} and Σ_{94}; and it Table 10 among a-structures Σ_{84}, Σ_{85} and Σ_{86} when compared against Σ_{83}. These blocking situations yields that claims $choose(a_i)$ and $\sim choose(a_i)$ are undecided for $i = 1, 4, 5$.

4 Conclusions

In this paper we have given an account of argumentation-based decision making in a simple scenario from experimental economics, like the Dictator game. In particular we use an Abstract Dynamic Argumentation Framework, so-called AADF, to model human choice behavior from a survey we conducted. Our model obtained that $choose(a_3)$ was warranted—coinciding with the most preferred action in the survey; and no other literal of the kind $choose(x)$ was warranted.

This AADF is a simpler version of the original one proposed in [13] since the conflict relation among arguments concerns only the arguments supporting claims of the kind $choose(x)$ or $\sim choose(x)$ and not pairwise comparison of the kind $better(x, y)$ and $\sim better(x, y)$. Indeed, these former arguments are new with respect to the original ones present in the epistemic component of the AADF proposed in [13]. This is due to the fact that the agent's decision behavior now is included in the epistemic component instead of using the decision device called *decision rules*; a device widely used in previous works [10,11,13] where rational decision making was pursued rather than human decision making.

Besides, as mentioned in the introductory section, this present work extends [24]; an approach to model the Dictator game using a structured argumentative formalism like DeLP. Performing this abstraction helped us to get more focused on the high-level details involved in modeling human decision making; like the composition of the working set of arguments. In this respect, as previously said, not only the kind of arguments in the working set changed but also the number of arguments is less than those that would be generated by the DeLP approach.

In this study, we have worked with the so-called *active instance* of a DAF (cf. Sect. 3.1 in [22]) and hence, all the work done on acceptability of arguments and argumentation semantics can be applied to it. Therefore, the decision making problem tackled in this work could be solved with a library such as ConArgLib [5]—which supports the solution of problems in Abstract Argumentation. In this way, our proposed decision framework can also be applied to solve problems in practice and not to model them just in theory.

Finally, as also stated in the introductory section, modeling the Dictator game with this abstract dynamic argumentation framework also paves the way to tackle non-rational decision making with other structured argumentation formalism, thus making richer the application field of abstract argumentation for decision making.

Acknowledgments. This work was partially supported by CONICET and Universidad Nacional de San Luis (PROICO 03-0620).

References

1. Alsinet, T., Chesñevar, C.I., Godo, L., Simari, G.: A logic programming framework for possibilistic argumentation: formalization and logical properties. Fuzzy Sets Syst. **159**(10), 1208–1228 (2008)

2. Amgoud, L., Prade, H.: Using arguments for making and explaining decisions. Artif. Intell. **173**(3–4), 413–436 (2009)

3. Bench-Capon, T.: Persuasion in practical argument using value-based argumentation frameworks. J. Log. Comput. **13**(3), 429–448 (2003)

4. Bench-Capon, T., Atkinson, K., McBurney, P.: Using argumentation to model agent decision making in economic experiments. Auton. Agent. Multi-Agent Syst. **25**(1), 183–208 (2011)

5. Bistarelli, S., Rossi, F., Santini, F.: ConArgLib: an argumentation library with support to search strategies and parallel search. J. Exp. Theor. Artif. Intell. 1–28 (2020)

6. Buron Brarda, M., Tamargo, L.H., García, A.J.: An approach to enhance argument-based multi-criteria decision systems with conditional preferences and explainable answers. Expert Syst. Appl. **126**, 171–186 (2019)

7. Carstens, L., Fan, X., Gao, Y., Toni, F.: An overview of argumentation frameworks for decision support. In: Croitoru, M., Marquis, P., Rudolph, S., Stapleton, G. (eds.) GKR 2015. LNCS (LNAI), vol. 9501, pp. 32–49. Springer, Cham (2015). https://doi.org/10.1007/978-3-319-28702-7_3

8. Dung, P.M.: On the acceptability of arguments and its fundamental role in non-monotonic reasoning, logic programming and n-person games. Artif. Intell. **77**(2), 321–358 (1995)

9. Fan, X., Toni, F.: Decision making with assumption-based argumentation. In: Black, E., Modgil, S., Oren, N. (eds.) TAFA 2013. LNCS (LNAI), vol. 8306, pp. 127–142. Springer, Heidelberg (2014). https://doi.org/10.1007/978-3-642-54373-9_9

10. Ferretti, E., Errecalde, M., García, A., Simari, G.: Decision rules and arguments in defeasible decision making. In: 2nd International Conference on Computational Models of Arguments (COMMA), pp. 171–182. IOS Press (2008)

11. Ferretti, E., Errecalde, M., García, A., Simari, G.: A possibilistic defeasible logic programming approach to argumentation-based decision-making. J. Exp. Theor. Artif. Intell. **26**(4), 519–550 (2014)

12. Ferretti, E., Errecalde, M.: Argumentation-Based Proofs of Endearment: Essays in Honor of Guillermo R. Simari on the Occasion of His 70th Birthday, chap. A P-DeLP Instantiation of a Dynamic Argumentation Framework for Decision Making. College Publications, England (2018)

13. Ferretti, E., Tamargo, L.H., García, A.J., Errecalde, M.L., Simari, G.R.: An approach to decision making based on dynamic argumentation systems. Artif. Intell. **242**, 107–131 (2017)

14. Forsythe, R., Horowitz, J.L., Savin, N.E., Sefton, M.: Fairness in simple bargaining experiments. Games Econom. Behav. **6**(3), 347–369 (1994)

15. García, A., Simari, G.: Defeasible logic programming: an argumentative approach. Theory Pract. Logic Program. **4**(1–2), 95–138 (2004)

16. Kahneman, D., Tversky, A. (eds.): Choice, Values, and Frames, 1st edn. Cambridge University Press, Cambridge (2000)

17. Matt, P.-A., Toni, F., Vaccari, J.R.: Dominant decisions by argumentation agents. In: McBurney, P., Rahwan, I., Parsons, S., Maudet, N. (eds.) ArgMAS 2009. LNCS (LNAI), vol. 6057, pp. 42–59. Springer, Heidelberg (2010). https://doi.org/10.1007/978-3-642-12805-9_3

18. Nowak, M.A., Page, K.M., Sigmund, K.: Fairness versus reason in the ultimatum game. Science **289**, 1773–1775 (2000)

19. de Oliveira Gabriel, V., Panisson, A.R., Bordini, R.H., Adamatti, D.F., Billa, C.Z.: Reasoning in BDI agents using Toulmin's argumentation model. Theoret. Comput. Sci. **805**, 76–91 (2020)
20. Rahwan, I., Simari, G.R. (eds.): Argumentation in Artificial Intelligence. Springer, Heidelberg (2009)
21. Rieke, R.D., Sillars, M.O., Peterson, T.R.: Argumentation and Critical Decision Making, 8th edn. Pearson, London (2012)
22. Rotstein, N., Moguillansky, M., García, A., Simari, G.: A dynamic argumentation framework. In: Computational Models of Argument: Proceedings of COMMA 2010, pp. 427–438 (2010)
23. Russell, S., Norvig, P.: Artificial Intelligence: A Modern Approach, 3 edn. Prentice Hall (2010). Chapter 1
24. Sapino, M., Ferretti, E., Mariñelarena-Dondena, L., Errecalde, M.: Modeling human decision making with defeasible logic programming. In: Pesado, P.M., Eterovic, J. (eds.) Actas del XXVI Congreso Argentino de Ciencias de la Computación (CACIC). Universidad Nacional de La Matanza (2020). ISBN 978-987-4417-90-9
25. Sosa Toranzo, C., Ferretti, E., Errecalde, M.: Intention reconsideration like dichotomous choice: an argumentation-based approach. In: XLIII Latin American Computer Conference (CLEI), Córdoba, Argentina. IEEE, September 2017
26. Teze, J.C., Gottifredi, S., García, A.J., Simari, G.R.: An approach to generalizing the handling of preferences in argumentation-based decision-making systems. Knowl.-Based Syst. **189**, 105–112 (2020)
27. Wooldridge, M., van der Hoek, W.: On obligations and normative ability: towards a logical analysis of the social contract. J. Appl. Log. **3**, 396–420 (2005)

Hybrid Simulated Annealing to Optimize the Water Distribution Network Design: A Real Case

Carlos Bermudez[1], Hugo Alfonso[1], Gabriela Minetti[1]([✉]),
and Carolina Salto[1,2]

[1] Facultad de Ingeniería, Universidad Nacional de La Pampa, Santa Rosa, Argentina
{bermudezc,alfonsoh,minettig,saltoc}@ing.unlpam.edu.ar
[2] CONICET, Buenos Aires, Argentina

Abstract. A water distribution network consists of many nodes interconnected to provide water to consumers. The importance and huge capital cost of the system lead to their design optimization. The present work proposes an intelligent optimization solver based on a Hybrid Simulated Annealing (HSA) to solve this problem. One of the main HSA control parameters is the Markov Chain Length (MCL), which is the number of moves to reach the equilibrium state at each temperature value. Our main objective is to analyze the HSA behavior by considering static and dynamic methods to compute the MCL. We test the HSA approaches using networks reported in the state-of-the-art and a real and new median size network that arises from a regional requirement. The experimentation suggests the use of a dynamic method, which exhibits the balance between solution quality and computational effort.

Keywords: Water Distribution Network Design · Optimization · Simulated Annealing · Markov Chain Length

1 Introduction

Water is one of the most important natural resources, becoming an essential commodity for human life. Public water services provide more than 90% of the water supply in the world today, and therefore a safe drinking water distribution system is a critical component for any city. Consequently, the design and optimization of a water distribution network gain prime importance to minimize the cost and simultaneously maximize the network reliability and benefits. The network should supply water at all the intended places with sufficient pressure head, fulfilling the fire hydrant demands and having minimum leakages to ensure the non-degradation of water quality. The distribution system has many components to be considered, such as pipes of various sizes for carrying water, valves for controlling the flow, service connections to the individual homes, and distribution reservoirs for storing the water to be fed into the distribution pipes. This problem is known as Water Distribution Network Design (WDND) and requires

© Springer Nature Switzerland AG 2021
P. Pesado and J. Eterovic (Eds.): CACIC 2020, CCIS 1409, pp. 19–34, 2021.
https://doi.org/10.1007/978-3-030-75836-3_2

handling a large number of variables and constraints, and in consequence, it is classified as NP-hard [1]. The water distribution network optimization aims to find the optimal pipe diameters in the network for a given layout and demand, satisfying the conservation of mass and energy in addition the constraints.

The design process also involves the growth of city sizes. General Pico (La Pampa, Argentina) has a new neighborhood of around five km^2, which needs an infrastructure to provide this essential public service to their citizens. Consequently, a design of an independent water distribution network is necessary for this neighborhood. CORPICO[1] is the organization in charge of distributing this essential element in this city. This cooperative specifically requires an optimization system to determine the best engineering solution in meeting established design criteria while at the same time minimizing capital costs.

The design problem is not simple at all and requires considerable effort. Efficiency and reduction of costs have been important reasons for managers to progressively migrate from manual design based on experience to the development of suitable intelligent optimization tools. Some works expressed the WDND problem as a multi-objective optimization problem and applied a multi-objective evolutionary algorithm [2]. A genetic algorithm was developed to solve six small networks [3], which considered the velocity constraint on the water flowing through the pipes. In [4] also regarded this constraint, but the authors used mathematical programming on bigger, closer-to-reality networks. Other metaheuristics were used to tackle more complex WDND formulations [5–7]. In this line, an Iterative Local Search [8] (ILS) considered that every demand node has 24 hrs water demand pattern and included a new constraint related to the limit of the maximal velocity of water through the pipes. The objective of our research is to develop an intelligent solver based on state-of-the-art optimization techniques, which intends to support the decision making during the design, plan, and management of complex water systems. The focus is on the optimization of the design of water distribution network with time-varying demand patterns (extension known as multi-period setting) and the maximum water velocity constraint as formulated in [8]. This problem formulation is more realistic and complex than the problems solved in [2,3].

This study is a continuation and refinement of a previous work [9], which presents a Hybrid Simulated Annealing (HSA) [10,11] to optimize the pipe diameters involved in the WDND by using a local search technique based on GRASP. In [9], we analyzed the HSA behavior by studying the Markov Chain Length (MCL), an HSA control parameter. The computation of its appropriate length is a difficult task to apply in practice. Consequently, we consider three different strategies to set the MCL to understand their effectiveness regarding solution quality and runtime. In order to mitigate the lack of information about the behavior of each variant of the HSA solver, in the present we define the following research questions:

---

[1] CORPICO is the Regional Cooperative for Electricity, Works and other Services in the city of General Pico, province of La Pampa, Argentina.

- *RQ1*: How does the MCL affect the performance of the HSA solver to tackle the WDND problem?
- *RQ2*: Is the HSA capable of solving a real case?
- *RQ3*: Does HSA improve the techniques reported in the state-of-the-art to solve this problem?

To address these *RQ*s, we analyze how the MCL variants can affect the performance of the HSA solver. For that, we use the publicly available HydroGen network instances [12] to test the performance of our HSA solver. Moreover, we describe and give the features of a real medium size distribution network, which is also used to test the capabilities of the HSA solver developed. In the present work, we give more details about the WDND problem and its restrictions, the HSA description is improved with more features, and the experimentation is enlarged by including statistical studies that allow determining which variant is the most appropriate to solve the WDND problem. Later on, we analyze and compare these HSA solvers considering relevant aspects such as solution quality and runtime to solve different WDND problem sizes, from artificial to real networks. Furthermore, a new section is introduced where we compare the results obtained by our proposals with the literature ones.

The remainder of this article is structured as follows. Section 2 introduces the problem definition. Section 3 explains our algorithmic proposal, HSA, to solve the WDND optimization problem and the HSA's configurations. Section 4 describes the experimental analysis and the methodology used. Then, Sects. 5 and 6 present the result analysis of the variants and the comparison with an ILS [8] from the literature, respectively. Finally, Sect. 9 summarizes our conclusions and sketches out our future work.

2   Multi-period Water Distribution Network Design

The mathematical formulation of the WDND is often treated as the least-cost optimization problem. The decision variables are the diameters for each pipe in the network. The problem can be characterized as simple-objective, multi-period, and gravity-fed. Two restrictions are considered: the limit of water speed in each pipe and the demand pattern that varies in time. The network can be modeled by a connected graph, which is described by a set of nodes $N = \{n_1, n_2, ...\}$, a set of pipes $P = \{p_1, p_2, ...\}$, a set of loops $L = \{l_1, l_2, ...\}$, and a set of commercially available pipe types $T = \{t_1, t_2, ...\}$. The objective of the WDND problem is to minimize the Total Investment Cost (TIC) in a water distribution network design. The TIC value is obtained by the formula shown in Eq. 1.

$$\min TIC = \sum_{p \in P} \sum_{t \in T} L_p IC_t x_{p,t} \tag{1}$$

where IC_t is the cost of a pipe p of type t, L_p is the length of the pipe, and $x_{p,t}$ is the binary decision variable that determines whether the pipe p is of type t or not. The objective function is constrained by: physical laws of mass and energy conservation, minimum pressure demand in the nodes, and the maximum speed in the pipes, for each time $\tau \in T$.

2.1   Objective Function Constraints

Generally, the WDND optimization constraints include mass and energy conservation in each primary loop, flow continuity at each node, and the minimum allowable head requirement at each node. In other words, to minimize the TIC value, a WDND solution requires to satisfy the physical laws described in the following paragraphs.

Mass Conservation Law. It must be satisfied for each node N in each period of time τ. This law establishes that the volume of water flowing towards a node in an unit of time must be equal to the flow that leaves it (see Eq. 2).

$$\sum_{n_1 \in N/n} Q_{(n_1,n),\tau} - \sum_{n_2 \in N/n} Q_{(n,n_2),\tau} = WD_{n,\tau} - WS_{n,\tau} \quad \forall n \in N \quad \forall \tau \in T \quad (2)$$

where $Q_{(n_1,n),\tau}$ is the flow from node n_1 to node n at time τ, $WS_{n,\tau}$ is the external water supplied and $WD_{n,\tau}$ is the external water demanded.

Energy Conservation Law. It states that the sum of pressure drops in a closed circuit in an instant of time τ is zero. These drops can be approximated using the Hazen-Williams equations with the parameters used in EPANET 2.0 [13] (the hydraulic solver used in this paper), as indicated in Eq. 3.

$$\sum_{p \in l} \left[\frac{10.6668 y_{p,\tau} Q_{p,\tau}^{1.852} L_p}{\sum_{t \in T} (x_{p,t} C_t^{1.852} D_t^{4.871}} \right] = 0 \quad \forall l \in L \quad \forall \tau \in T \quad (3)$$

where $y_{p,\tau}$ is the sign of $Q_{p,\tau}$ that indicates changes in the water flow direction relative to the defined flow directions, $Q_{p,\tau}$ is the amount of water flowing through pipe p in time τ, L_p is the pipe length, C_t is the Hazen-Williams roughness coefficient of pipe type t, and D_t is the diameter of pipe type t.

Minimum Pressure Head Requirements. For each node n in each period of time τ, it must be satisfied (see Eq. 4),

$$H_{n,\tau}^{min} \leq H_{n,\tau} \quad \forall n \in N \quad \forall \tau \in T \quad (4)$$

being H^{min} the minimum node pressure and $H_{n,\tau}$ the node's current pressure.

Maximum Water Velocity. The water velocity $v_{p,\tau}$ can not exceed the maximum stipulated speed $v_{p,\tau}^{max}$. Equation 5 shows this relationship.

$$v_{p,\tau} \leq v_{p,\tau}^{max} \quad \forall p \in P \quad \forall \tau \in T \quad (5)$$

3   A Real WDND Problem

The principal motivation of this research is to get involved in solving community problems, in particular the water distribution network design. To provide some context, the water access problem in the province of La Pampa is a priority treatment for being a scarce natural resource. CORPICO, the supplier of

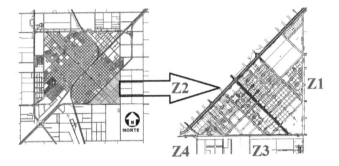

Fig. 1. Map of the water distribution networks in General Pico.

this essential service in General Pico, has to design an independent drinking water distribution network for a new neighborhood of five km², minimizing the network cost through the proper selection of the pipe dimensions according to consumption and the physical laws of this type of problem. The water distribution network should cover an area called "Barrio Quintas Sur" identified as Zone 2 or Z2 (shaded region of Fig. 1). Initially, the network has an extension of $1.65 \, km^2$ foreseeing for the next ten years an adjacent extension of $3.4 \, km^2$, identified as the zones Z1, Z3, and Z4. The network designed for Z2 is independent but requires taking into consideration the demand of the other zones to become an extra supply network or to receive water from them (bypass).

4   HSA Solver for the Multi-period WDND Problem

Simulated Annealing (SA) [14] belongs to the class of local search algorithms that allow upward movements to avoid getting stuck prematurely at a local optimum. More specifically, SA is a simple and efficient trajectory-based metaheuristic. SA is based on the principles of statistical thermodynamics, which models the physical process of heating material. The SA algorithm simulates the energy changes in a system subjected to a cooling process until it converges to an equilibrium state (steady frozen state). The physical material states correspond to problem solutions, the energy of a state to cost of a solution, and the temperature to a control parameter.

The SA algorithm slowly reduces the temperature to decrease defects, thus minimizing the system energy. Similarly, at each virtual annealing temperature, the SA algorithm generates a new potential solution (or neighbor of the current state) to the problem considered by altering the current state, according to a predefined criterion. The acceptance of the new state is based on the Boltzman criterion satisfaction. This procedure is iterated until convergence. In other words, SA evolves by a sequence of transitions between states. These transitions are generated by transition probabilities. Therefore, SA can be modeled mathematically by Markov chains, where a sequence of chains is generated by a transition probability calculated involving the current temperature.

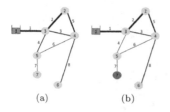

Pipe ID	Length (m)
1	31
2	20
3	35
4	37
5	24
6	50
7	12
8	65

(c)

Diam. (mm)	Roughness unitless	Cost
60	130	22
80	130	35
100	130	38
150	130	50
200	130	61

(d)

(a)   (b)

Fig. 2. Different solutions or network designs. (a) Solution 1; (b) Solution 2; (c) Pipe lengths; (d) Available pipe types with their corresponding costs.

Table 1. Different solutions or network designs in vector representation.

Solution	Pipe ID	1	2	3	4	5	6	7	8	Feasibility
	Length (m)	31	20	35	37	24	50	12	65	TIC
1	diam. (mm)	150	150	80	80	100	60	60	80	feasible
	cost	1550	1000	1225	1295	912	1100	264	2275	9621
2	diam. (mm)	150	150	80	60	100	60	60	80	infeasible
	cost	1550	1000	1225	814	912	1100	264	2275	9140

The proposed HSA is a hybridization of the SA algorithm to solve the Multi-Period WDND optimization problem. In this work, we extend the study of the HSA as WDND solver, initiated in [9]. The performance of the HSA is related to the fine-tuning of their main control parameters, which include the definition of the Markov Chain Length (MCL) [15]. Particularly, we focus on the way to calculate the Markov chain length. The next sections describe the solution representation, the HSA algorithm, and the MCL variants.

4.1 Solution Representation for the WDND Problem

The first design issue to solve is how to represent a solution for the WDND problem. The decision variables are the diameters for each pipe in the network (see Sect. 2). Therefore, a solution is a network, as shown in Fig. 2 (a) and (b), which is represented by a vector. Each vector element is the diameter selected for the pipe it represents. Table 1 shows the vectors that correspond to the candidate solutions in Fig. 2(a) and (b). The TIC for each solution is calculated by the Eq. 1, using the input data from tables (c) and (d) of Fig. 2. The first solution is hydraulically feasible (satisfying all constraints mentioned in Sect. 2) and the second one is infeasible (violating the minimum pressure constraint in node 7). HSA uses the EPANET 2.0 toolkit [13] to solve the hydraulic equations since this hydraulic solver is applied in most existing works.

4.2 HSA Solver Description

The pseudo-code of the HSA solver proposed to optimize the WDND problem is shown in Algorithm 1. HSA begins with the initialization of the temperature

Algorithm 1. HSA to solve the WDND Optimization Problem

1: $k = 0$;
2: initTemp(T)
3: initialize(S_0);
4: TIC_0 = evaluate(S_0);
5: **repeat**
6:    **repeat**
7:       $k = k + 1$;
8:       S_1 = MP-GRASP_LS(S_0);
9:       TIC_1=evaluate(S_1);
10:      **if** $TIC_1 < TIC_0$ **then**
11:         $S_0 = S_1$; $TIC_0 = TIC_1$
12:      **end if**
13:      S_2 = perturbation_operator(S_0);
14:      TIC_2 = evaluate(S_2);
15:      **if** $(TIC_2 < TIC_0)$ **or** $(exp^{((TIC_2-TIC_0)/T)} > random(0,1))$ **then**
16:         $S_0 = S_2$; $TIC_0 = TIC_2$
17:      **end if**
18:   **until** $(k \bmod MCL == 0)$
19:   update(T);
20: **until** *stop criterion is met*
21: **return** S_0;

Algorithm 2. Pseudocode of algorithm for setting initial temperature T_0

1: **function** initTemp (T_s)
2: $T_0 = T_s$;
3: initialize(S_1);
4: E_1=evaluate(S_1);
5: **while** acceptability rate is not reached **do**
6:    update T_0 ;
7:    $S_2 = S_1$;
8:    E_2=evaluate(S_2);
9:    **for** i=0 to test **do**
10:      S_2 = MP-GRASP_LS(S_1);
11:      E_2=evaluate(S_2);
12:   **end for**
13: **end while**
14: **return** T_0

(line 2). The choice of the right initial temperature plays a crucial role in the HSA performance to find good solutions. Algorithm 2 presents the procedure to compute the initial temperature, having as input a seed temperature T_s. The output, T_0, is determined such that, when applying the Boltzmann criterion, worse solutions are accepted with a high probability value. This algorithm starts from T_s that is increased until the aforementioned acceptance is reached. After that, HSA generates a feasible initial solution S_0 applying both HighCost and LowCost mechanisms proposed in [8] (line 3), which is then evaluated (line 4).

Once the initialization process ends, an iterative process starts (lines 5 to 20). The first step in the iteration involves a hybridization to intensify the exploration into the current search space. In this way, a feasible solution, S_1, is obtained by applying the MP-GRASP local search [8] to S_0 (line 8), and then a greedy selection mechanism is performed (lines 10–12). Therefore, S_0 can be replaced by S_1 if it is better than S_0. In the next step, a perturbation operator is used to obtain a feasible neighbor, S_2, from S_0 (line 13), to explore other areas of the search space. This perturbation randomly changes some pipe diameters. If

S_2 is worse than S_0, S_2 can be accepted under the Boltzmann probability (line 15, second condition). In this way, the search space exploration is strengthened when the temperature (T) is high. In contrast, at low temperatures the algorithm only exploits a promising region of the solution space, intensifying the search. To update T, a random cooling schedule [11] is used (line 19), which combines three traditional cooling schemes (the proportional [14], exponential [14], and logarithmic [16] schemes) in only one schedule process. The cooling schedule is applied after a certain number of iterations (k) given by the Markov Chain Length (MCL) (line 18). Finally, SA ends the search when the total evaluation number is reached or $T = 0$.

4.3 Markov Chain Length

One of the main search components of the HSA solver that deserves study is the MCL, which is the number of required transitions k (moves) to reach the equilibrium state at each T. This number can be either static or adaptive. In the first case, the number of movements is set before the search starts. The static approach, named as MCLs, assumes that each temperature T is held constant for a sufficient and fixed number of iterations. In this work, each T is held constant for $k = 30$ iterations, a widely used number in the scientific community.

For the adaptive cases, the Markov Chain Length depends on the characteristics of the search. For instance, Cardoso et al. [17] consider that the equilibrium state is not necessarily attained at each level of the temperature. Consequently, the cooling schedule is applied as soon as an improved candidate (neighbor) solution is generated. In this way, the computational effort can be drastically reduced without compromising the solution quality. This approach is referred as MCLa1. Another adaptive approach is proposed by Ali et al. [18], named as MCLa2, which uses both the worst and the best solutions found in the Markov chain (inner loop) to compute the next MCL. This strategy allows to increase the number of function evaluations at a given temperature if the difference between the worst and the best solutions increases, but if an improved solution is found the MCL remains unchanged.

5 Experimental Design

In this section, we explain the experimental design followed in this work so that our conclusions could be both objective and valid. To evaluate the HSA solver with the three MCL configurations, 50 HydroGen instances of WDND optimization problem [12] are solved. After that, we optimize a real case the GP-Z2-2020 instance that we generated using the data given by CORPICO.

In our experiments, we use the best HSA's variant found in [10] to solve the multi-period WDND problem, named $HSA_{Rand100}$, which uses the random cooling scheme and 100 as seed temperature. This variant, renamed HSA in what follows, is executed under the three approaches to compute the MCL, as a consequence, three new HSA's configurations arise. The stop condition is to reach 1,500,000 evaluations (Epanet calls) of the objective function to make a fair comparison with the literature algorithms. We performed 30 independent runs for each instance and HSA's configuration because of the stochastic nature of the HSA solver, in order to gather meaningful experimental data and apply statistical confidence metrics to validate our results and conclusions. Before performing the statistical tests, we first checked whether the data followed a normal distribution by applying the Shapiro-Wilks test. Where the data was distributed normally, we later applied an ANOVA test. Otherwise, we used the Kruskal Wallis (KW) test. This statistical study allows us to assess whether or not there were meaningful differences between the compared algorithms with $\alpha = 0.05$. The way to determine these algorithm pairwise differences is by carrying out a post hoc test, as is the case of the Mann-Whitney-Wilcoxon test if the KW test is used.

5.1 HydroGen Networks

The HydroGen networks [12] arise from 10 different distribution networks, named as HG-MP-i with $i \in \{1, 10\}$, which use set of 16 different pipe types. The demand nodes are divided into five categories (domestic, industrial, energy, public services, and commercial demand nodes), each one with a corresponding base load and demand pattern[2]. In this way, each HG-MP-i network consists of five different instances, totaling 50 instances. The combinations of 16 pipe types and the number of pipes of each instance determines the network complexity. In this way, four different categories are obtained, to know HG-MP1-3, HG-MP4-6, HG-MP7-9, and HG-MP10, regarding the number of pipes of each instance.

5.2 GP-Z2-2020: A Real Network

The GP-Z2-2020 network, which arises from CORPICO's requirements, is composed of 222 domestic demand nodes and only one water reservoir. Moreover, this zone is connected with three other ones through some peripherical nodes which have different demand patterns, as explained in Sect. 3. Table 2 summarizes available pipe diameters in the local market, their corresponding roughness, and their unit costs (expressed in US dollars). The area is residential with demand according to the current distribution of the customers in 584 plots but considering a development pattern over a timespan of 30 years. The daily pattern demand corresponds to the summer period (based on the model demand of historical records) having a maximum resolution of one hour. The total number of possible combinations of design for a set of 8 commercial pipe types and 282 pipes is 8^{282} that makes the instance in a difficult case to solve; this shows the importance of optimization.

---

[2] The base loads can be found in the EPANET input files of the instances.

Table 2. Pipe types and their corresponding costs for the GP-Z2-2020 network.

Number	Diam. (mm)	Roughness	Cost	Number	Diam. (mm)	Roughness	Cost
1	63	110	2.85	5	315	110	69.10
2	90	110	5.90	6	400	110	110.89
3	110	110	8.79	7	450	110	140.15
4	125	110	11.00	8	630	110	273.28

Table 3. Averages of the best TIC values found by each HSA's configurations.

Network	MCLs	MCLa1	MCLa2	KW
HG-MP-1	**335723**	336984	337809	0,87
HG-MP-2	298430	298652	**297823**	0,85
HG-MP-3	**384210**	384665	384687	0,92
HG-MP-4	683780	**682361**	685424	0,80
HG-MP-5	719569	717268	**711906**	0,40
HG-MP-6	739923	**735738**	738108	0,93
HG-MP-7	807367	**792435**	801907	0,27
HG-MP-8	843657	841653	**841240**	0,13
HG-MP-9	823783	817325	**816485**	0,00
HG-MP-10	787399	**771461**	784385	0,08

Table 4. Wilcoxon p-values from the comparison of TIC values obtained for the HG-MP-9 network.

HSA Conf.	MCLs	MCLa1
MCLa1	4.20e−06	–
MCLa2	5.63e−06	1.47e−07

6   Analysis of the HydroGen Instance Results

In the following paragraphs, we summarize and analyze the results of using the three new HSA's configurations to solve the 50 Hydrogen instances grouped by their corresponding distribution network. To answer how the MCL affect the HSA performance, as formulated in *RQ1*, and also discover the configuration with the best performance, the following methodology is carried out. First, we analyze the behavior of these configurations by considering the results shown in Table 3, taking the different MCL approaches into account. The columns 2–4 show the average of the best TIC values found by the three HSA's configurations. The last column presents the p-value obtained by the KW test. The boxplots shown in Fig. 3 represent graphically the distribution of results obtained in each case, coloring in gray the case where significant differences are found. Finally, we analyze the computational effort for each HSA proposed, considering the time to find the best solution (see Fig. 4) and the total runtime (see Fig. 5) of the search measured in seconds.

Firstly, the analysis focus on the quality point of view. The three approaches behave statistically similar for 90% of the instances with KW p-values are bigger than $\alpha = 0.05$). The HSA with the adaptive options (MCLa1 and MCLa2) find the best TIC values in 80% of the cases. However, for the HG-MP-9 network, the HSA's behaviors are significantly different, we apply the post hoc Wilcoxon

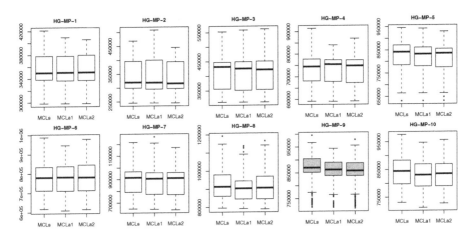

Fig. 3. Boxplots of the TIC values for Hydrogen network found by each HSA.

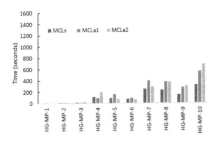

Fig. 4. Runtimes consumed by each HSA's configuration to find the best solution.

Fig. 5. Total runtimes consumed by each HSA's configuration.

test to verify that MCLa2 is the configuration for HSA that allows finding the lowest TICs values, as shown the p-values $< \alpha$ in Table 4.

Finally, the analysis covers the computational effort. For all configurations, the HSA's runtimes grow as the instance complexity increases. HSA with MCLa2 is the slowest configuration, whereas HSA with MCLs reduces significantly the total runtime (approximately 30–50%). The KW p-values $< \alpha$ corroborate these differences and the Wilcoxon p-values, in Table 5, indicate which algorithms differ from each other. The latter can be seen graphically in Fig. 6 for each network, whose boxplots are colored in gray. However, when the time values to reach the best solution are analyzed, these differences are noticeably narrowed, minimizing the gap between the three HSA's configurations.

Summarizing, these results clearly state that the MCLa1 configuration exhibits a good trade-off between the solution quality and the required runtime. This adaptive approach interrupts the Markov chain when the candidate solution is better than the current one, reducing the computational effort in comparison with MCLa2. In this way, we explain how the MCL affects the performance of HSA solver configuration, answering the *RQ1*.

Table 5. Wilcoxon p-values from the comparison of the total runtime of each HSA's configuration for Hydrogen networks.

Network	HSA Conf.	MCLs	MCLa1
HG-MP-1	MCLa1	1.47e−26	–
	MCLa2	8.42e−25	1.47e−26
HG-MP-2	MCLa1	4.59e−26	–
	MCLa2	1.47e−26	1.47e−26
HG-MP-3	MCLa1	2.36e−24	–
	MCLa2	3.14e−24	5.02e−18
HG-MP-4	MCLa1	2.63e−23	–
	MCLa2	5.75e−23	1.52e−15
HG-MP-5	MCLa1	2.33e−26	–
	MCLa2	2.33e−26	1.56e−06
HG-MP-6	MCLa1	7.77e−29	–
	MCLa2	7.77e−29	1.31e−08
HG-MP-7	MCLa1	4.23e−29	–
	MCLa2	4.23e−29	1.18e−08
HG-MP-8	MCLa1	4.23e−29	–
	MCLa2	4.23e−29	1.54e−08
HG-MP-9	MCLa1	4.23e−29	–
	MCLa2	4.23e−29	4.21e−09
HG-MP-10	MCLa1	9.24e−29	–
	MCLa2	9.24e−29	1.10e−09

7   Analysis of the GP-Z2-2020 Network Results

To answer the *RQ2* about the HSA ability to solve a real instance, we analyze the results of the HSA when solving the real GP-Z2-2020 network. Table 6 presents the results of the three HSA's configurations for different metrics: average TIC values (row 1) and the average total runtime (row 2), expressed in seconds. The minimal values found by each metric are boldfaced. Finally, the KW p-values are shown in the last column.

HSA using MCLa2 finds minimal TIC values. This is an expected result since similar observations were made in the previous analysis taking into account networks of comparable complexity. This outcome is statistically supported by the results obtained via the KW and Wilcoxon tests and the boxplots shown in Table 6 and Fig. 7.a), respectively. An analogous situation is observed regarding the runtimes, as is shown in Table 6 and Fig. 7.b), respectively. The red boxplots in both figures indicate that the compared algorithms are statistically different.

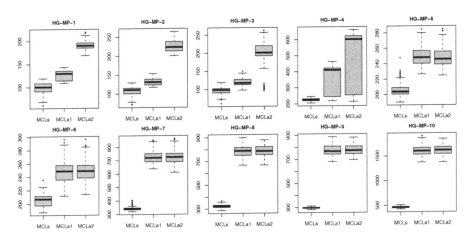

Fig. 6. Boxplots of the total runtimes (in seconds) found by each HSA to solve Hydrogen networks.

Table 6. Average results of the GP-Z2-2020 Network.

Metrics	MCLs	MCLa1	MCLa2	KW
TIC values	420949.53	408075.93	**401570.20**	0.04
Total runtime	**186.46**	627.97	615.52	1.08e−13

Table 7. Wilcoxon p-values from comparison of the results found by each HSA to solve the GP-Z2-2020 network.

TIC values			Total runtimes		
HSA Conf.	MCLs	MCLa1	HSA Conf.	MCLs	MCLa1
MCLa1	0.07	–	MCLa1	1.61e−06	–
MCLa2	0.12	0.03	MCLa2	1.61e−06	0.03

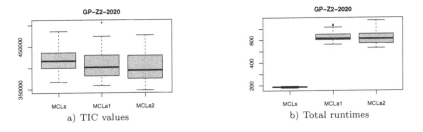

a) TIC values b) Total runtimes

Fig. 7. Boxplots of the results found by the each HSA to solve the GP-Z2-2020 network.

Table 8. The best known TIC values found by our proposals and ILS.

Network	MCLs	MLCa1	MLCa2	ILS
HG-MP-1	**298000**	**298000**	**298000**	**298000**
HG-MP-2	245330	245330	245330	**245000**
HG-MP-3	310899	310706	**310493**	318000
HG-MP-4	592048	**590837**	592036	598000
HG-MP-5	**631000**	**631000**	**631000**	**631000**
HG-MP-6	617821	**609752**	614917	618000
HG-MP-7	648372	644568	**639932**	653000
HG-MP-8	795996	792436	**790037**	807000
HG-MP-9	716944	715863	**712450**	725000
HG-MP-10	730916	**712847**	727818	724000
GP-Z2-2020	366684.00	358717.00	**347596.00**	355756.00

8   Comparison of the HSA Solver with the State-of-the-Art

The performance of the HSA's configurations proposed in this work is compared with the ILS metaheuristic, introduced in [8] for solving the WDND problem, to answer the *RQ3*. This metaheuristic is chosen from literature for this comparison since its authors also used the HydroGen instances to test it. In this way, our results can be compared with ones of the state-of-the-art, allowing us to know the level of quality reached by our proposal (Table 7).

The methodology used to analyze the results is described in the following. First, to ensure a fair comparison, the compared algorithms use the same stop criterion that is set in 1,500,000 Epanet calls. Secondly, we also use the ILS algorithm to solve the real GP-Z2-2020 instance. Finally, we study the HSA behavior comparing the best TIC values found by the HSA's configuration and ILS [8] for the Hydrogen Networks, grouped by their corresponding distribution network, as presented in Table 8 (the minimal values are boldfaced). Note that, we only present the HSA's total runtimes for the Hydrogen networks tested in this work, because no data about this metric are reported in [8].

Analyzing the best-known TIC values found by these four algorithms, we conclude that our proposals obtain the best results in eight of the eleven networks, including the real case GP-Z2-2020. In so far as for another two cases the outcomes are equal, and in only one network the ILS presents a minimum TIC value. In this way, we can say that the answer to the *RQ3* is affirmative. In other words, HSA improves the techniques reported in the state-of-the-art to solve the WDND problem.

9   Conclusions

Our goal in this work was to develop an intelligent HSA solver, by focusing on the optimization of the design of water distribution network with multi-period setting and the maximum water velocity constraint. Consequently, we statistically analyzed the control parameter MCL influence on the HSA solver performance, by considering a static (MCLs) and two adaptive (MCLa1 and MCLa2) MCL configurations. For this analysis, the solver was evaluated by optimizing 50 Hydrogen networks and a new WDND real case.

The experimentation results allow us to answer the research questions formulated in our study. For the first one, *RQ1*, we can respond that the adaptive configurations find better solutions than the static one by adapting the MCL to the search context. These adaptations require an extra computational effort to calculate the MCL during the search. The HSA with MCLa1 presents a good trade-off between solution quality and computational effort since this adaptive method interrupts the Markov chain if a better solution than the current one is found. The *RQ2* is affirmatively answered because the real case is efficiently solved by the HSA solver. When our proposals are contrasted against ILS [8], the HSA's configurations outperform or equal ILS in every WDND network, answering the third research question, *RQ3*, satisfactorily.

In future works, we will deal with high-dimensional WDND networks considering big-data frameworks, which will be used to implement our HSA solver.

Acknowledgments. The authors acknowledge the support of Universidad Nacional de La Pampa (Project FI-CD-151/15 and POIRe-03-2019) and the Incentive Program from MINCyT. The last author is also funded by CONICET.

References

1. Yates, D., Templeman, A., Boffey, T.: The computational complexity of the problem of determining least capital cost designs for water supply networks. Eng. Optim. **7**(2), 143–155 (1984)
2. Farmani, R., Walters, G.A., Savic, D.A.: Trade-off between total cost and reliability for anytown water distribution network. J. Water Resour. Plan. Manag. **131**(3), 161–171 (2005)
3. Gupta, I., Gupta, A., Khanna, P.: Genetic algorithm for optimization of water distribution systems. Environ. Model. Softw. **14**(5), 437–446 (1999)
4. Bragalli, C., D'Ambrosio, C., Lee, J., Lodi, A., Toth, P.: On the optimal design of water distribution networks: a practical MINLP approach. Optim. Eng. **13**(2), 219–246 (2012)
5. Uma, R.: Optimal design of water distribution network using differential evolution. Int. J. Sci. Res. (IJSR) **5**(11), 1515–1520 (2016)
6. Mansouri, R., Mohamadizadeh, M.: Optimal design of water distribution system using central force optimization and differential evolution, vol. 7, no. 3. http://ijoce.iust.ac.ir/article-1-310-en.html
7. Sedki, A., Ouazar, D.: Hybrid particle swarm optimization and differential evolution for optimal design of water distribution systems. Adv. Eng. Inform. **26**, 582–591 (2012)

8. De Corte, A., Sörensen, K.: An iterated local search algorithm for water distribution network design optimization. Network **67**(3), 187–198 (2016)
9. Alfonso, H., Bermudez, C., Minetti, G., Salto, C.: A real case of multi-period water distribution network design solved by a hybrid SA. In: XXVI Congreso Argentino de Ciencias de la Computación (CACIC), pp. 21–23 (2020). http://sedici.unlp.edu.ar/handle/10915/113258
10. Bermudez, C., Salto, C., Minetti, G.: Designing a multi-period water distribution network with a hybrid simulated annealing. In: XLVIII JAIIO: XX Simposio Argentino de Inteligencia Artificial (ASAI 2019), pp. 39–52 (2019)
11. Bermudez, C., Minetti, G., Salto, C.: SA to optimize the multi-period water distribution network design. In: XXIX Congreso Argentino de Ciencias de la Computación (CACIC 2018), pp. 12–21 (2018)
12. De Corte, A., Sörensen, K.: Hydrogen. http://antor.uantwerpen.be/hydrogen. Accessed 27 June 2018
13. Rossman, L.: The EPANET Programmer's Toolkit for Analysis of Water Distribution Systems (1999)
14. Kirkpatrick, S., Gelatt, C.D., Vecchi, M.P.: Optimization by simulated annealing. Science **220**, 671–680 (1983)
15. Talbi, E.-G.: Metaheuristics: From Design to Implementation. Wiley, Hoboken (2009)
16. Hajek, B.: Cooling schedules for optimal annealing. Math. Oper. Res. **13**(2), 311–329 (1988)
17. Cardoso, M., Salcedo, R., de Azevedo, S.: Nonequilibrium simulated annealing: a faster approach to combinatorial minimization. Ind. Eng. Chem. Res. **33**, 1908–1918 (1994)
18. Ali, M., Törn, A., Viitanen, S.: A direct search variant of the simulated annealing algorithm for optimization involving continuous variables. Comput. Oper. Res. **29**(1), 87–102 (2002)

Distributed and Parallel Processing

Comparison of HPC Architectures for Computing All-Pairs Shortest Paths. Intel Xeon Phi KNL vs NVIDIA Pascal

Manuel Costanzo[1] , Enzo Rucci[1]([✉]) , Ulises Costi[2], Franco Chichizola[1] , and Marcelo Naiouf[1]

[1] III-LIDI, Facultad de Informática, UNLP – CIC, 1900 La Plata, Bs As, Argentina
{mcostanzo,erucci,francoch,mnaiouf}@lidi.info.unlp.edu.ar
[2] Facultad de Informática, UNLP, 1900 La Plata, Bs As, Argentina

Abstract. Today, one of the main challenges for high-performance computing systems is to improve their performance by keeping energy consumption at acceptable levels. In this context, a consolidated strategy consists of using accelerators such as GPUs or many-core Intel Xeon Phi processors. In this work, devices of the NVIDIA Pascal and Intel Xeon Phi Knights Landing architectures are described and compared. Selecting the Floyd-Warshall algorithm as a representative case of graph and memory-bound applications, optimized implementations were developed to analyze and compare performance and energy efficiency on both devices. As it was expected, Xeon Phi showed superior when considering double-precision data. However, contrary to what was considered in our preliminary analysis, it was found that the performance and energy efficiency of both devices were comparable using single-precision datatype.

Keywords: Shortest paths · Floyd-Warshall · Xeon Phi · Knights landing · NVIDIA Pascal · Titan X

1 Introduction

In the last decade, the quest to improve the energy efficiency of high-performance computing (HPC) systems has fueled the trend toward heterogeneous computing and massively parallel architectures [7]. Heterogeneous systems combine CPUs with accelerators (such as NVIDIA and AMD GPUs or Intel's Xeon Phi many-core co-processors), delegating code sections with high computational demand to them. According to the Green500[1] ranking, the November 2010 edition featured 17 systems that integrated accelerators. However, 10 years later, this number has increased to 145, evidencing the great popularity of this strategy.

Today, GPUs can be considered the dominant accelerator class due to their high computing power and energy efficiency, in addition to their low cost. In the opposite sense, one of their weaknesses is the need to learn a specific language

---

[1] https://www.top500.org/green500/.

© Springer Nature Switzerland AG 2021
P. Pesado and J. Eterovic (Eds.): CACIC 2020, CCIS 1409, pp. 37–49, 2021.
https://doi.org/10.1007/978-3-030-75836-3_3

in order to make the most of them, such as CUDA and OpenCL. Among the manufacturing companies, NVIDIA stands out as the largest provider for the high-performance segment.

On the other hand, Intel introduced the second generation of its Xeon Phi processors in 2016, codenamed Knights Landing (KNL). Unlike its predecessor, Knights Corner (KNC), KNL can operate as a standalone processor. Among its main features, the large number of cores with hyper-threading support, the incorporation of AVX-512's 512-bit vector instructions, and the integration of a high-bandwidth memory (HBM), among others [14], can be mentioned. Generations aside, the outstanding feature in this family is that it offers support for x86 architectures, which allows programmers to use traditional models in HPC, such as OpenMP and MPI.

Because each accelerator has its advantages and disadvantages for certain classes of problems [3, 17, 22], selecting the best option for a given application is key when searching for maximum performance. To provide some guidelines for such selection, this article presents a comparative analysis between two different HPC architectures (Intel Xeon Phi KNL vs. NVIDIA Pascal). As a case study, the Floyd-Warshall (FW) algorithm was selected for computing the all-pairs shortest paths in a graph, as a representative case of graph applications that are memory-bound [16]. We hope that development teams will find this analysis useful when choosing the most suitable architecture for their applications.

The remaining sections of this article are organized as follows: in Sect. 2, the general background and other works that are related to this research are presented. Next, in Sect. 3, the implementations used are described, and in Sect. 4, the experimental work carried out is detailed and the results obtained are analyzed. Finally, in Sect. 5, our conclusions and possible lines of future work are presented.

2   Background and Related Works

First, the Intel Xeon Phi KNL and NVIDIA Pascal architectures are briefly described and compared. Then, the FW algorithm for all-pair shortest paths computation in a graph is described. Finally, some works related to this article are detailed.

2.1   Intel Xeon Phi KNL Vs NVIDIA Pascal

Intel Xeon Phi KNL. Unlike a GPU or a co-processor such as KNC, KNL is a standalone processor, capable of booting operating systems and directly accessing DDR memory. The scalable unit of replication of the KNL architecture is the *tile*. Each tile houses 2 cores, a L2 cache shared between both cores, and a portion of the distributed directory. The cores of a tile implement *simultaneous multi-threading* (4 hw threads per core) and out-of-order execution in its pipeline, in addition to having 2 vector units that support AVX-512's new 512-bit instructions [14].

A KNL chip has between 32 and 36 active tiles (between 64 and 72 cores), depending on each specific model. The tiles are interconnected by a 2D mesh, with cache coherence based on distributed directory and MESIF protocol. This mesh can be configured in five different execution modes (cluster modes). Based on the execution mode selected, the distributed directory will be split among the tiles in the chip, which will have an impact on latency and bandwidth in memory access.

KNL comes with a 16 GB HBM called MCDRAM, which is built into the same processor package. This memory can be configured in three different modes. In *flat* mode, the address space is mapped between the two memories (MCDRAM and DDR), so it is the programmer who has the responsibility of defining how to use them. On the other hand, *cache* mode leaves the system in charge of managing the MCDRAM as a DDR cache. Finally, the *hybrid* mode assigns part of the MCDRAM as flat, and part as cache [1].

NVIDIA Pascal. Pascal is the penultimate micro-architecture introduced by NVIDIA for the high-performance segment, successor to Maxwell. In this segment, a GPU of this family can have up to 3840 CUDA cores distributed among (at most) 60 Streaming Multiprocessors (SM). Compared to its predecessor, Pascal doubles the number of registers per core and increases the available size of shared memory.

This micro-architecture features several significant improvements over Maxwell. Among them, we can highlight the inclusion of an HBM of up to 16GiB in some of its chips, which allows them to reach a bandwidth of up to 720 GB/s. It also replaces the traditional PCIe bus used for CPU-GPU communication by a high-speed bus (NVLink), which significantly improves communication speed. Finally, the provision of a *unified memory*, consisting of a virtual address space between the CPU and GPU memories, aimed at simplifying programming [13].

As regards peak performance, some Pascal chips can achieve double-precision (DP) throughput rates that are half of the single-precision (SP) ones. On the other hand, they can double SP performance if they apply half-precision computing [5].

Brief Comparison. Table 1 presents a comparison of these architectures and, in particular, considers the models used in the experimental work. From the point of view of the theoretical peak performance in SP, the Titan X is far superior to the KNL 7230 (10.97 TFLOPS vs. 6 TFLOPS). However, due to the weak support of the former for DP, it is the KNL in this case that has a remarkable superiority (3 TFLOPS vs. 0.342 TFLOPS).

As regards main memory, the KNL has an HBM that puts it almost on par with Titan X in terms of bandwidth, since KNL has DDR4 technology while Titan X has GDDR5X. However, since it is a co-processor, the Titan X has a much smaller memory size than the KNL, which is a *host* unto itself.

Finally, when considering the (theoretical) energy efficiency, even though the Titan X has a higher thermal design power (TDP), its TFLOPS/W ratio in SP

Table 1. Intel Xeon Phi KNL 7230 vs NVIDIA Titan X

Device	Intel Xeon Phi KNL	NVIDIA Titan X
Chip	7230	GP102
Clock Frequency	1.3–1.5 GHz	1.42–1.53 GHz
Cores	64 (256 hw threads)	28 SMs (3584 CUDA cores)
Cache	1 MB L2	3 MB L2
SIMD	512-bit	–
HBM	16 GB MCDRAM (450 GB/s)	–
RAM Memory	192 GB DDR4 (115.2 GB/s)	12 GB GDDR5X (480.4 GB/s)
Bus	–	PCI-Express 3.0 x 16
Peak Theoretical performance SP (DP)	6 (3) TFLOPS	10.97 (0.342) TFLOPS
TDP	215W	250W
TFLOPS/W (SP/DP)	0.028/0.014	0.051/0.001
Launch Date	June 2016	August 2016

almost doubles that of KNL due to its higher theoretical performance peak. On the contrary, the poor performance of the Titan X for DP results in KNL being vastly superior in this case. Despite the fact that some years have passed since their launch, both architectures remain relevant, as shown by the latest edition of the Top500[2] ranking, where 17 systems are equipped with Xeon Phi KNL and an additional, 30 with GPUs from the Pascal family.

2.2 All-Pair Shortest Paths Computation in a Graph

FW Algorithm. The pseudocode of FW is shown in Algorithm 2.2. Given a graph G of N vertexes, FW receives as input a dense $N \times N$ matrix D that contains the distances between all pairs of vertexes from G, where $D_{i,j}$ represents the distance from node i to node j[3]. FW computes N iterations, evaluating in the k-th iteration all possible paths between vertexes i and j that have k as the intermediate vertex. As a result, it produces an updated matrix D, where $D_{i,j}$ now contains the shortest distance between nodes i and j up to that step. Also, FW builds an additional matrix P that records the paths associated with the shortest distances.

Blocked FW Algorithm. At first glance, the nested triple loop structure of this algorithm is similar to that of dense matrix multiplication (MM). However, since read and write operations are performed on the same matrix, the three loops cannot be freely exchanged, as is the case with MM. Despite this, the FW algorithm can be computed by blocks under certain conditions [21].

---

[2] Top500 www.top500.org.

[3] If there is no path between nodes i and j, their distance is considered to be infinite (usually represented as the largest positive value).

Algorithm 1. Pseudocode of the FW algorithm

for $k \leftarrow 0$ to $N - 1$ do
  for $i \leftarrow 0$ to $N - 1$ do
    for $j \leftarrow 0$ to $N - 1$ do
      if $D_{i,j} \geq D_{i,k} + D_{k,j}$ then
        $D_{i,j} \leftarrow D_{i,k} + D_{k,j}$
        $P_{i,j} \leftarrow k$
      end if
    end for
  end for
end for

The blocked FW algorithm (BFW) divides matrix D into blocks of size $TB \times TB$, totaling $(N/TB)^2$ blocks. Computation is organized in $R = N/TB$ rounds, where each round consists of 4 phases ordered according to the data dependencies between the blocks:

1. Phase 1: Update the $D^{k,k}$ block because it only depends on itself.
2. Phase 2: Update the blocks in row k of blocks $(D^{k,*})$ because each of these depends on itself and on $D^{k,k}$.
3. Phase 3: Update the blocks in column k of blocks $(D^{*,k})$ because each of these depends on itself and on $D^{k,k}$.
4. Phase 4: Update the remaining $D^{i,j}$ blocks of the matrix because each of these depends on blocks $D^{i,k}$ and $D^{k,j}$ on its row and column of blocks, respectively.

Figure 1 shows each of the computation phases and the dependencies between blocks. The yellow squares represent blocks that are being computed, gray squares are those that have already been processed, and green squares are the ones that have not been computed yet. Last, arrows show the dependencies between blocks for each phase.

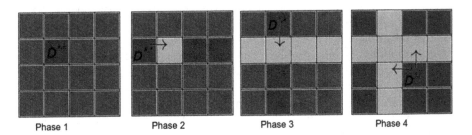

Phase 1   Phase 2   Phase 3   Phase 4

Fig. 1. BFW computation phases and block dependencies

2.3   Related Works

The comparison of HPC architectures is a topic widely studied by the scientific community. In particular, there are several articles involving comparative studies between Xeon Phi KNL and NVIDIA Pascal in the field of large-scale economic modeling [19] linear algebra [4], computational fluid dynamics [15], and automatic deep learning [6], among others. However, as far as we know, this is the first to consider graph algorithms, in particular the FW algorithm for all-pair shortest paths.

The contributions of this work can be seen as an extension of a previous work of the authors [2], where the comparison of HPC architectures just considered performance and theoretical energy efficiency. By incorporating actual power consumption and programming cost to the comparison, this work is able to offer a more comprehensive analysis of the pro and cons of each architecture for graph applications.

3   FW Optimization

This section describes the Xeon Phi implementation followed by the GPU one.

3.1   Implementation on Xeon Phi KNL 7230

The implementation used considers the following optimizations:

- *Data locality.* By computing with BFW, it is not only possible to exploit data locality, but it is also possible to increase the parallelism available in the application.
- *Parallelism at thread level.* Using OpenMP, a multi-threaded version is obtained. Both Phase 2 and Phase 3 blocks are distributed among the different threads by means of the `for` directive with `dynamic` scheduling. In the case of Phase 1, since it consists of a single block, the iterations within it are distributed among the threads.
- *Parallelism at data level.* Using the OpenMP `simd` directive, the operations of the innermost loop are vectorized when computing each block, which allows taking advantage of the AVX-512 instructions.
- *Loop unrolling.* By fully unrolling the innermost loop and loop i only once.
- *Branch prediction.* By including the built-in `__builtin_expect` compiler macro, `if` statement branches can be better predicted.
- *MCDRAM.* Since this is a bandwidth-limited application, using this special memory is greatly beneficial. Executions are done using the `numactl` command.

It should be noted that this implementation can be considered as an optimized version of [16], since it also includes intra-block parallelization for Phase 1 and the improvement in branch predictions.

3.2   Implementation on NVIDIA Titan X

The implementation used considers the optimizations known for GPU-based FW solutions at the moment [10,11]. Among those, the following can be mentioned:

- *Concurrency.* Three kernels have been developed that are invoked once for each BFW computation round. On round k, the first kernel computes block $D^{k,k}$ (Phase 1) and is instantiated with a single grid made up of a single block. Next, the second kernel is invoked, which computes both Phase 2 and Phase 3 blocks ($D^{k,*}$, $D^{*,k}$), and is instantiated with a single grid of $2 \times (R-1)$ blocks. Finally, the third kernel, which computes the remaining blocks corresponding to Phase 4 ($D^{i,j}$), is invoked. This kernel is instantiated with a single grid of $(R-1)^2$ blocks. In all cases, blocks are made up of $TB \times TB$ threads.
- *Exploitation of memory hierarchy.* For BFW computation, the use of shared memory is not only convenient but also necessary, especially in Phases 1–3 since the threads read and write to the same blocks of the matrix due to their dependencies. In the case of Phase 4, it is possible to take advantage of the private memory for the write block ($D^{i,j}$), which improves access times even more. Finally, the main memory accesses were organized so that they are coalescent.
- *Resource occupation.* In order to optimize this aspect, different thread block sizes were tried (using $TB = \{8, 16, 32\}$) to find the one that leads to the maximum possible number of active *warps*.
- *Loop unrolling.* By fully unrolling the loop that computes each thread.

4   Experimental Results

In this section, the experimental setup and methodology are described. Next, the results found are presented and analyzed. Last, the limitations of this research are mentioned.

4.1   Experimental Setup and Methodology

The tests were carried out on two different platforms[4]. On the one hand, an Intel Xeon Phi KNL 7230 server configured in *all-to-all* cluster mode and with *flat* memory (ICC v19.0.0.117). On the other, an Intel Core i7-7700 3.6 GHz and 16 GB RAM, which integrates an NVIDIA Titan X GPU (CUDA v9.0).

For both platforms, the variation in the size of the distances matrix ($N = \{4096, 8192, 16384, 32768, 65536\}$) and data type (*float*, *double*) were considered. In the case of KNL, different values for both the number of OpenMP threads $T = \{64, 128, 192, 256\}$ and $TB = \{16, 32, 64, 128\}$ were tried to identify the optimal values of $T_{float} = 128$, $T_{double} = 64$ and $TB = 64$. As regards the GPU, the best performances were obtained when using $TB_{float} = 32$ and $TB_{double} = 16$.

---

[4] The characteristics of each platform were described at the end of Sect. 2.1.

Finally, to minimize variability, each specific test was repeated 15 times and the average values were calculated.

Since this paper considers power consumption as well as performance, the measurement environment used on each platform is described as follows:

- *Intel Xeon Phi KNL*. Intel has developed the Intel PCM[5] (Performance Counter Monitor) to take power measurements on both Intel Xeon and Xeon Phi processors. With Intel PCM interface, any programmer can perform an analysis of CPU resource consumption by means of hardware counters.
- *NVIDIA Titan X*. In modern NVIDIA GPUs, the NVIDIA System Management Interface utility (*nvidia-smi*[6]) can be used to query power consumption at runtime. This tool is based on the NVIDIA Management Library (NVML) and is intended to help in the management and monitorization of NVIDIA GPU devices.

4.2   Performance Results

The GFLOPS metric is used for performance evaluation:

$$GFLOPS = \frac{2 \times N^3}{t \times 10^9} \tag{1}$$

where N is the size of the distances matrix, t is execution time (in seconds), and factor 2 represents the number of floating-point operations required by each iteration of the innermost loop.

Figure 2 shows the performance obtained by each implementation with different values for both matrix and data type used. In SP (*float*), it can be seen that the GPU achieves a better performance with smaller matrix sizes, being approximately 19% higher when $N = 4096$. In these cases, GPU is better suited than KNL, which requires higher workloads to reach its maximum use. This is reflected in the graph, since, as the size of the distances matrix increases, KNL achieves the best performance, reaching an additional 7% difference. It should be noted that with $N = 65536$, KNL experiences a performance loss of approximately 30%, due to the fact that, with this value, the available size of the MCDRAM is exceeded and partial use of DDR4 is required, which has a much lower bandwidth. Even so, it is more convenient than using GPU, which cannot compute cases with $N > 32768$ because the available main memory space is exceeded[7].

As regards DP (*double*), the results obtained are as expected due to the weak support of Titan X for this class of operations. While GPU obtains an

---

[5] Intel Performance Counter Monitor: http://www.intel.com/software/pcm.

[6] NVIDIA System Management Interface: https://developer.nvidia.com/nvidia-system-management-interface.

[7] Naturally, it is also possible to develop an implementation that processes the matrix in parts and does not have this memory limitation. However, the need to run I/O operations for each round would significantly degrade performance.

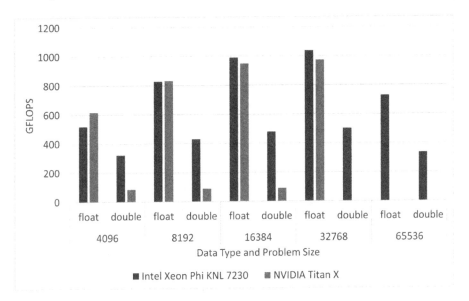

Fig. 2. Performance obtained with different data types and distances matrix sizes with Intel Xeon Phi KNL 7230 and NVIDIA Titan X

almost constant performance of $\sim$90 GFLOPS, KNL improves its performance as N increases and eventually surpasses the size of the MCDRAM. In particular, KNL gets about half the FLOPS of SP but improves to 4.3$\times$ those of Titan X. Lastly, the memory limit issue in GPU is also worse due to the fact that the *double* type requires more space (cases with $N > 16384$ could not be processed).

4.3   Power and Energy Efficiency Results

As mentioned in Sect. 1, application performance is not the only point of interest to be considered, energy efficiency also matters. Table 2 lists energy efficiency ratios taking into account the GFLOPS peaks reached and the TDP of the platforms used. As it can be seen, KNL is superior in both cases. In particular, KNL gets a GFLOPS/Watt ratio that is 1.2$\times$ better than that of Titan X in SP. However, this factor increases up to 5.5$\times$ in DP, due to the weak support of this GPU for these operations. It should be noted that for this analysis, *host* consumption by GPU was not taken into account, so the differences could be even greater.

TDP can be useful for qualitative comparison purposes and sometimes is the only valid metric when power measuring is not possible. However, actual power readings can differ from TDP due to a variety of reasons (power saving techniques available in modern processors/accelerators, specific workload in the target application, among others) [9]. For this reason, this work also includes an empirical power-performance analysis between platforms.

Table 2. Theoretical comparison of performance and power efficiency by platform

Precision	Platform	GFLOPS (peak)	TDP (Watt)	GFLOPS/Watt
SP	*Xeon Phi KNL 7230*	1037	215	4.82
	NVIDIA Titan X	972	250	3.89
DP	*Xeon Phi KNL 7230*	501	215	2.33
	NVIDIA Titan X	90	250	0.36

Table 3. Comparison of performance and power efficiency by platform

Precision	Platform	GFLOPS (peak)	Power (Watt)	GFLOPS/Watt
SP	*Xeon Phi KNL 7230*	1037	229.7	4.51
	NVIDIA Titan X	972	209.5	4.64
DP	*Xeon Phi KNL 7230*	501	261	1.92
	NVIDIA Titan X	90	144.8	0.62

Table 3 shows a summary of the best performance and the corresponding average power consumption on the different architectures under study.

These power measurements reinforce the idea that actual power readings can differ from the TDP of each platform. In the KNL architecture, a higher power consumption is observed in both SP and DP scenarios; however, the difference is larger in the DP case. Hence, DP not only affects execution time but also increases power consumption, as it was also observed in other recent studies [8, 18].

In opposite sense to the KNL case, average power consumption is lower than the corresponding TDP in Titan X. Considering this issue, Titan X becomes slightly better than KNL when SP is used. Nevertheless, it must be remarked that host power consumption in not included in the GPU estimation; so, KNL still remains as probably the best option from this perspective. Despite the fact that energy efficiency gets almost doubled in DP, this improvement is virtually useless due to the poor performance of the Titan X.

4.4   Programming Cost

As well as general-purpose architectures, KNL supports widely extended parallel programming models in HPC (such as OpenMP or MPI). On the other hand, CUDA is the *de facto* standard for GPU programming nowadays. This fact puts KNL in a favourable position with respect to GPUs, since code development and portability get simplified.

Beyond specific language learning, GPUs may require additional programming efforts. Even though it experienced a significant performance loss when matrix size exceeded that of the MCDRAM, KNL was able to process all graphs. On the other hand, Titan X was not able to process those that exceeded the size of its RAM memory. While it is possible to develop an implementation that does, it would also have an associated performance loss and would require additional programming effort (not required in the case of KNL).

4.5 Limitations

Two possible limitations of this research can be mentioned:

- In 2019, Intel cancelled the KNL line [20]. Even though, several features of there processors (like AVX-512 floating point unit, the mesh interconnect on the die, and the integration of high bandwidth stacked memory into the processor) have gone mainstream in the current Xeons [12]. Thus, part of the results found in this research can be extrapolated to Xeon processors.
- This analysis focuses on two specific architecture models and that, as such, some of the results found could change if different models were used. For example, the NVIDIA GP100 (Pascal) GPU has a slightly lower peak SP performance than the Titan X (10.1 TFLOPS). However, its support for DP is vastly higher, being half SP (5 TFLOPS). In this sense, it is considered that the comparison is equally valuable to show trends and the distinctive characteristics of each architecture, even when there are different models that may present variations in their specifications.

5 Conclusions and Future Work

This work focuses on the comparison of Intel Xeon Phi KNL and NVIDIA Pascal architectures. Taking the FW algorithm for computing all-pairs shortest paths in a graph as a case study, optimized implementations were used to compare the achievable performance on each platform and thus be able to extract some general guidelines. Among those, the following can be mentioned:

- Despite the fact that the preliminary analysis indicated that Titan X was far superior to KNL, the performances (SP) obtained for FW were comparable. While the GPU performed better for small graphs, as the size of the distances matrix increased, it was the KNL that performed better. This fact leads to KNL's need for large workloads in order to make the most of it.
- As regards energy efficiency, contrary to what was found in the preliminary analysis, no significant difference was observed in SP. This result contributes to the fact that device sustainable performance and energy efficiency vary depending on each particular problem and its corresponding software implementation.
- Beyond specific language learning, GPUs may require additional programming efforts due to their co-processor nature (they are not hosts per se) and limited memory sizes.

Future works include:

- Extending the GPU implementation to support graphs larger than the main memory size.
- Including other models of the studied architectures (especially Pascal GPUs).

The development of these activities would give greater robustness and representativeness to the study carried out.

Acknowledgments. The authors are grateful for the support of NVIDIA through the donation of the Titan X GPU used in this research.

References

1. Codreanu, V., Rodríguez, J., Saastad, O.W.: Best practice guide - knights landing (2017). https://bit.ly/2CEolbR
2. Costanzo, M., Rucci, E., Costi, U., Chichizola, F., Naiouf, M.: Comparación de Arquitecturas HPC para Computar Caminos Mínimos en Grafos. Intel Xeon Phi KNL vs NVIDIA Pascal. In: Actas del XXVI Congreso Argentino de Ciencias de la Computación (CACIC 2020), pp. 82–92 (2020)
3. Deng, L., Bai, H., Zhao, D., Wang, F.: Kepler GPU vs. Xeon phi: performance case study with a high-order CFD application. In: 2015 IEEE International Conference on Computer and Communications (ICCC), pp. 87–94 (2015)
4. Deveci, M., Trott, C., Rajamanickam, S.: Multithreaded sparse matrix-matrix multiplication for many-core and GPU architectures. Parallel Comput. **78**, 33–46 (2018). https://doi.org/10.1016/j.parco.2018.06.009. http://www.sciencedirect.com/science/article/pii/S0167819118301923
5. Foley, D., Danskin, J.: Ultra-performance pascal GPU and NVLINK interconnect. IEEE Micro **37**(2), 7–17 (2017)
6. Gawande, N.A., Daily, J.A., Siegel, C., Tallent, N.R., Vishnu, A.: Scaling deep learning workloads: Nvidia DGX-1/pascal and intel knights landing. Futur. Gener. Comput. Syst. **108**, 1162–1172 (2020)
7. Giefers, H., Staar, P., Bekas, C., Hagleitner, C.: Analyzing the energy-efficiency of sparse matrix multiplication on heterogeneous systems: a comparative study of GPU, Xeon Phi and FPGA. In: 2016 IEEE International Symposium on Performance Analysis of Systems and Software (ISPASS), pp. 46–56 (2016)
8. Hashemi, S., Anthony, N., Tann, H., Bahar, R.I., Reda, S.: Understanding the impact of precision quantization on the accuracy and energy of neural networks. In: Design, Automation Test in Europe Conference Exhibition (DATE), pp. 1474–1479 (2017). https://doi.org/10.23919/DATE.2017.7927224
9. Igual, F.D., García, C., Botella, G., Piñuel, L., Prieto-Matías, M., Tirado, F.: Non-negative matrix factorization on low-power architectures and accelerators. Comput. Electr. Eng. **46**(C), 139–156 (2015). https://doi.org/10.1016/j.compeleceng.2015.03.035
10. Katz, G.J., Kider, Jr, J.T.: All-pairs shortest-paths for large graphs on the GPU. In: Proceedings of the 23rd ACM SIGGRAPH/EUROGRAPHICS Symposium on Graphics Hardware, GH 2008, pp. 47–55. Eurographics Association, Aire-la-Ville (2008)

11. Lund, B.D., Smith, J.W.: A multi-stage CUDA kernel for Floyd-Warshall. CoRR abs/1001.4108 (2010). http://arxiv.org/abs/1001.4108
12. Morgan, T.P.: The end of Xeon Phi - It's Xeon and Maybe GPUs from here (2018). https://www.green500.org/
13. NVIDIA: NVIDIA Tesla P100. https://bit.ly/2Ozrrk1
14. Reinders, J., Jeffers, J., Sodani, A.: Intel Xeon Phi Processor High Performance Programming Knights, Landing edn. Morgan Kaufmann Publishers Inc., Boston (2016)
15. Robertsén, F., Mattila, K., Westerholm, J.: High-performance SIMD implementation of the lattice-Boltzmann method on the Xeon Phi processor. Concurr. Comput. Pract. Exp. **31**(13), e5072 (2019). https://doi.org/10.1002/cpe.5072
16. Rucci, E., De Giusti, A., Naiouf, M.: Blocked all-pairs shortest paths algorithm on Intel Xeon Phi KNL processor: a case study. In: De Giusti, A.E. (ed.) CACIC 2017. CCIS, vol. 790, pp. 47–57. Springer, Cham (2018). https://doi.org/10.1007/978-3-319-75214-3_5
17. Rucci, E., Garcia, C., Botella, G., De Giusti, A., Naiouf, M., Prieto-Matias, M.: SWIFOLD: Smith-Waterman implementation on FPGA with OpenCL for long DNA sequences. BMC Syst. Biol. **12**(5), 96 (2018). https://doi.org/10.1186/s12918-018-0614-6
18. Sakamoto, R., Kondo, M., Fujita, K., Ichimura, T., Nakajima, K.: The effectiveness of low-precision floating arithmetic on numerical codes: a case study on power consumption. In: Proceedings of the International Conference on High Performance Computing in Asia-Pacific Region, HPCAsia2020, pp. 199–206. Association for Computing Machinery, New York (2020). https://doi.org/10.1145/3368474.3368492
19. Scheidegger, S., Mikushin, D., Kubler, F., Schenk, O.: Rethinking large-scale economic modeling for efficiency: optimizations for GPU and Xeon Phi clusters. In: 2018 IEEE International Parallel and Distributed Processing Symposium (IPDPS), pp. 610–619 (2018)
20. Trader, T.: Requiem for a Phi: knights landing discontinued (2018). https://www.hpcwire.com/2018/07/25/end-of-the-road-for-knights-landing-phi
21. Venkataraman, G., Sahni, S., Mukhopadhyaya, S.: A blocked all-pairs shortest-paths algorithm. SWAT 2000. LNCS, vol. 1851, pp. 419–432. Springer, Heidelberg (2000). https://doi.org/10.1007/3-540-44985-X_36
22. Véstias, M., Neto, H.: Trends of CPU, GPU and FPGA for high-performance computing. In: 2014 24th International Conference on Field Programmable Logic and Applications (FPL), pp. 1–6 (2014). https://doi.org/10.1109/FPL.2014.6927483

Computer Technology Applied to Education

Virtual Reality Serious Game to Bring the History of Key Figures of Computer Science Closer to Young People

Mariano Ariel Mazza[1] (ID), Cecilia Sanz[2,3](✉) (ID), and Verónica Artola[2] (ID)

[1] Facultad de Informática Universidad Nacional de La Plata, La Plata, Argentina
[2] Instituto de Investigación en Informática LIDI, CIC, Facultad de Informática, UNLP, La Plata, Argentina
{csanz,vartola}@lidi.info.unlp.edu.ar
[3] Investigador Asociado a La Comisión de Investigaciones Científicas de La Prov. De Buenos Aires, Buenos Aires, Argentina

Abstract. This paper presents a virtual reality serious game for mobile devices, called Innovática, whose educational goal is to introduce some central figures in the history of Computer Science. Innovática has been designed and developed from the consideration of a set of heuristics created for the development of serious games that served as guides from the moment of defining the concept of this game. The design considerations and guidelines addressed in the game creation process are presented here, as well as the application of Innovática with different users (N = 22), mainly teachers and students. With respect to the results, the participants have shown great interest in the virtual reality game, highlighting their preference for the history of some figures with stories they did not know, and with a high appreciation of the scenarios of each character. The game fulfilled its objective in this sense, since it managed to bring the contributions of innovators in Computer Science closer and make them known.

Keywords: Virtual reality · Serious games · Heuristics for game design · Innovators in Computer Science

1 Introduction

Serious games are those that have a characterizing objective that goes beyond entertainment. In general, they have an educational objective [1, 2]. At present, there is a remarkable interest in research linked to the use of this type of games in educational contexts [3, 4]. These studies analyze the effects of serious games on student motivation, learning, academic performance, and attitudes, among others.

At the same time, virtual reality constitutes an interaction paradigm that offers user immersion in a virtual environment. Immersion can be partial or complete, according to the type of virtual reality being implemented. This is linked to the senses that are involved and stimulated during the use of the virtual reality system, and the physical input/output devices used. "Depending on the degree of identification and involvement

P. Pesado and J. Eterovic (Eds.): CACIC 2020, CCIS 1409, pp. 53–66, 2021.
https://doi.org/10.1007/978-3-030-75836-3_4

of the user in the system, it can go from a weak interactivity or simulation - such as, for example, that of the fictional image as an intentional construction of structures that have a limited real experience, to that of games, in which the user maintains awareness of its non-truth - to a strong simulation or fiction, a fact that can be experienced in isolation or be shared by other observers who are in the same fictional space" [5].

Research on the possibilities of virtual reality for education is a current topic [6], in addition to its combination with serious games, giving rise to works that focus on the design, development and evaluation of serious educational games based on virtual reality [7, 8].

This paper deals with this topic in which the possibilities of serious games based on virtual reality are studied, it is an extension of the one presented in [9], where the background analysis is deepened. This work explains in more detail the components and aspects considered for the design of the serious game Innovática, the interaction models selected for virtual reality, and the results regarding the usability and experience of a group of 22 users (mainly teachers and students) with this game are presented. In other words, the results have also been extended with respect to [9].

From here on, this paper is organized as follows: in Sect. 2, some definitions and components considered in the literature for the design of serious games based on virtual reality are presented, in Sect. 3 some background of this type of games for educational contexts is described, and in Sect. 4 the game Innovática, created by the authors, is introduced. Then, Sect. 5 presents the experience carried out to study the usability and game experience with Innovática, to finally analyze the results and conclusions of the work.

2   Virtual Reality and Serious Games

Virtual reality technologies are being used in schools and universities around the world [10, 25]. They are increasingly inserted in the educational system due to the benefits they provide, for example, they allow students not only to learn about certain topics but also to experience them, based on situations that may only exist in the imagination of the individual. This is why this potential can be exploited and interest in important topics can be awakened, based on the richness of the multisensory virtual experience, which can also make learning meaningful [25].

Virtual reality is a particularly suitable technology for educational contexts, due to its ability to capture the attention of students through immersion in virtual worlds related to different branches of knowledge, which can help in the learning of the contents of any subject [11]. At the same time, this type of tools can also be used to promote the development of skills with digital technologies, which is required as a necessary competence in this century [10, 22, 23].

Beyond the possibilities of virtual reality, when designing a system with this interaction paradigm, certain important variables must be taken into account in order to achieve the expected objectives. Aspects such as immersion, the sense of presence, the quality of the images in the scenes, interactivity, the types of senses involved, and the forms of interaction proposed influence the user's experience and the achievement of the objectives proposed with the system [12, 13].

In relation to the design of serious games, various components must also be taken into account. These are constrained by rules established by the gameplay [14] that put a limit to the player's actions, while guiding him in a direction, seeking to lead him to fulfill an objective; in a context in which the player himself wishes to achieve it [5]. These objectives are carried out in a scenario in which the actions take place. In these scenarios the player can find different characters that can fulfill the function of being allies and help them in their journey, or play the role of enemy and thus seek to be a challenge that the player must overcome. Once the objectives have been achieved, the player usually moves on to the next level, in general of a higher difficulty. This causes the progress of a story that guides the game experience, story with which the mechanics are adapted to an environment of certain verisimilitude [15]. This story is related to the facts that thread and give meaning to the events that unfold, those through which the player passes. The story has a narrative that determines how the events are presented throughout the video game [14].

When designing a virtual reality serious game, the objectives of the game, which go beyond entertainment, must be defined initially. Both the story and the mechanics must be oriented to achieve a balance between entertainment and educational achievement. In addition, since it is a game with virtual reality, important aspects must be considered at the time of design, such as: the student's immersion, the sense of presence in the simulated environment, the consideration of how much realism is to be achieved, what emotions to mobilize, what interactivities will be part of the experience, feedbacks of interest for learning, game times, among other aspects of interest. This is why work is being done in the development of methodologies for this type of specific systems that have the characteristic of being virtual reality serious games [15].

In this context, one of the key concepts in the design is playability. This is a term used in game design and analysis that describes the quality of the game in terms of its operating rules and its design as a game. It refers to all the experiences of a player during interaction with game systems. It can also be defined as what makes a game easy and fun to use, with emphasis on the interactive style and quality of gameplay, affected by usability, narrative and story, interactive intensity, degree of realism, etc. [15, 16, 22]. Several authors have presented heuristics related to gameplay design and also for its evaluation. Some have relied on the processing model described by [17], which establishes a separation between affective and cognitive mechanisms by which humans interact with their media, and which is also taken as a basis for emotional design. This model considers three levels of processing: visceral (low), behavioral (intermediate) and reflexive (high). The visceral is part of human nature, of the player in this case, and is generated automatically from the stimulation of the senses; the behavioral is part of human behavior in general and can be fostered from the actions and consequences of these during the game process; while the cognitive is a higher layer, which influences the behavioral level in the medium and long term. In the case of games, it is possible to work from the thoughts and memories that the player has, to activate other thinking skills. Thus, when designing the game, according to its objectives, one can seek to stimulate the three levels of processing in order to achieve them and balance educational and entertainment objectives. These design aspects become relevant when designing a virtual reality serious game. In this work, the dimensions and heuristics presented in [13] have been also taken into account. The dimensions are: intrinsic, mechanical, interactive, artistic, personal and social playability. Section 4 will explain how they were used for the design of Innovática.

3   Background of Virtual Reality Serious Games

This section presents some background information on serious games based on virtual reality. This study has made it possible to review aspects of design and integration of virtual reality in educational scenarios.

The case of Labster was studied, which is a VR laboratory that seeks to encourage students in the educational process through an innovative approach to science teaching. Its creators were based on the idea of using simulators, and this resulted in the development of virtual laboratories. In these laboratories, students can perform experiments with results similar to what would happen in a real laboratory. In [18], the use of Labster in two case studies at a university is described. The first case study integrates 197 students who completed the simulation with Labster as a formative exercise to introduce the use of hazardous equipment in a laboratory practicum. The results show that the students achieved the educational objectives proposed and showed a high level of satisfaction during the experience. This case was analyzed since it deals with simulated laboratories to enrich educational practices. It is a case of partial virtual reality since only sight and hearing are stimulated and a PC is used for navigation of the simulated environment.

Nefertari is a game developed by the company Experius VR for the PC, designed to be used with a virtual reality helmet. The game aims to allow students in the same classroom to visit the tomb of Queen Nefertari, appreciate the illustrations, the hieroglyphics on the walls and learn about Egyptian mythology through narratives, interactive surfaces and exploration. The player must enter the experience through the use of high-end virtual reality headsets, such as the HTC Vive or the Oculus. These headsets track the player's position, head movements, rotation, and body tilt in detail. They also have two controllers, one for each hand, which allow you to track the position of your arms, so that you can interact with each of the different surfaces in the game. This is a case of full virtual reality in which it is possible to interact with the whole body. The game allows experiencing full immersion in the tomb of Nefertari. The place is recreated just as it can be seen in reality, even the imperfections on the surface caused by the passage of time are maintained. The elements in the environment such as the illustrations on the walls are selectable. When selected, a voice narrator provides information about them. The place is illuminated by digital lights that do not illuminate the whole place, so the player carries a flashlight that can be moved by the controls, which is used to investigate the place. It was used at the University of Melbourne as an experience for multiple simultaneous users in the same virtual environment, all represented by their avatars [19]. In this experience, realism and the immersion feature and sense of presence are highlighted to aid learning.

In [20] a virtual reality serious game in which a story is told is presented. The paper highlights the importance of story structure in the educational context, citing research indicating its impact on content retention and retrieval. The authors' study focuses on analyzing how story structure and designed interactivities impact student learning. The game "The Chantry", available for the PlayStation VR platform, is used. The app tells the story of Dr. Edward Jenner and his invention of the smallpox virus vaccine (https://jennermuseum.com/). They work with elementary school students, and two modes of walkthrough are discussed, one guided and structured and one free-exploration mode. In the conclusions it is discussed that, while in the guided environment the students show greater retention of the knowledge worked on through the questions asked, in the second mode they show more sense of presence, more involvement with the experience.

Another case is "Immersive training of first responder squad leaders in untethered virtual reality" [21], an immersive training platform for firefighters. This experience allows professional firefighters to train to be prepared for different emergencies, but avoiding the limitations of time, cost and safety that traditional training in a physical environment brings. This proposal is a case of complete and immersive virtual reality; composed of a virtual reality helmet, a controller for easy interaction with the virtual environment, and an omnidirectional treadmill that allows the person to walk freely to recreate the stress and physical fatigue of the event. Tests conducted on 41 participants showed a wide acceptance of this technology, with the majority of these participants reporting a high degree of presence and the perception of great potential in the prototype presented.

This background is of interest as it recaptures central aspects of the design of serious VR games and their educational possibilities. While the first case presents a partial VR game design based on a 3D web-based environment, it enables the achievement of risky practices in science laboratories. In addition, it has a high level of interactivity throughout the experience, with feedback on the different possibilities of action that the student has. In the second example, the high quality of the environment generated with virtual reality is highlighted, which has given rise to an immersion almost as if one were in the physical location of Nefertari's tomb. In the third case analyzed, attention is paid to the story component, and its mode of interaction with it: free or guided, and how they impact on attitude and learning. In the fourth, the benefits that these technologies bring to a high-risk work environment can be seen.

4   Description of Innovática

Innovática (Computer Innovators) is a mobile-based, virtual reality serious game. Its educational goal is focused on showing young people important figures in the history of Computer Science. Specifically, it is aimed at students in their final years of secondary school and first years of university, so as to connect them more affectively with these figures who have been Computer Science innovators. At the same time, the goal of the game is to repair a time-space anomaly, which has affected the history of Computer Science. Students become a lead character in this story, and they are tasked with repairing historical facts related to the characters by traveling through portals and accessing the specific contexts.

The following central aspects were considered for the design of Innovática: story creation, mechanics to achieve game objectives, the trajectory in a semi-structured way, with certain aspects that are guided while others are free (so as to achieve greater involvement information retention), inclusion of feedback and information for learning, and a prize at the end of the full trajectory (as a motivational aspect for the end of the game).

In addition, the three processing levels in the model presented in [17] are taken into account, as described later. Character backgrounds, although fictional, were planned to be close to the real situation.

Regarding its implementation, the application was developed in Unity 2019.3.0f6. It has been compiled for Android devices, and it requires an accelerometer and gyroscope in the cell phone where it is run to detect player head movements. The application is available on Google Play.

Design aspects taken into account are described in more detail below.

4.1 Heuristics and Design Aspects Considered

The gameplay heuristics presented in [14] were used for the design. As regards dimensions, the intrinsic, mechanical, interactive, artistic and personal dimensions proposed by this author were used. For each one, the following attributes are analyzed: satisfaction, learning, effectiveness, immersion, motivation, emotion, and the social aspect (bonding

Table 1. Example of the table used, in this case for intrinsic gameplay and its attributes. For each attribute, the corresponding plan for achieving it is described, along with its corresponding design aspects.

Attribute	Design aspects based on the attribute
Satisfaction	Students are involved as the lead character of the story. They have an active role in solving the space-time anomaly and saving Computer Science history. Real facts are combined with fiction
Learning	The story guides students to save a part of the history of prominent figures in Computer Science, such as Babbage, Ada Lovelace and John Von Neumann. When students travel through portals, they experience anecdotes and situations that were part of the lives of these figures, they get familiar with their stories, workplaces or homes. By solving the anomaly, students return to the present time knowing information about some innovative ideas and contributions these characters made to the history of Computer Science
Effectiveness	The entire journey takes 15 min at most to help students keep their focus. The learning experience and entertainment are combined through the resolution of simple challenges, with stories that bring the characters closer together in a more affective way. The story is partially guided, with the possibility of choosing which rooms to visit
Immersion	Virtual reality glasses are used with mobile devices, meaning that students are visually and audibly immersed in the story. The journey is done through head movements and no other device is required. Audio and image quality contributes to the immersion, as well as the first-person approach students take as the lead character who is responsible for repairing history
Motivation	To motivate students, a high level of interactivity was planned, adding actions such as crossing portals, character-specific environments, character anecdotes, exploring the objects surrounding these characters, prizes awarded for repairing some invention of the character in question, and closing the story with affective feedback. Motivation was also reinforced through the story itself and attention to the three levels used for processing the model [17]: visceral (arousing emotions through stories), behavioral (inviting players to solve small challenges through interaction), and reflective (offering to engage with stories about each character's contributions)
Emotion	Surprise at the beginning of the story when the space-time anomaly occurs. Joy when each challenge is solved. At the visceral level, students are expected to initially experience surprise when they start the museum tour and suddenly the anomaly takes place and the paintings fall. By solving the challenges, it is expected, through a semi-guided or semi-structured exploration, to lead the student to witness some experience or anecdote of one of the characters. After repairing each challenge, students are expected to achieve a more reflective level, based on a specific story about the contributions of that character to the history of Computer Science

with others). This was done using a table. Table 1 shows only one of the dimensions as way of example. The decisions related to emotions and stimuli pertaining to the three levels presented by [17] are also highlighted.

4.2 The Story

The story of Innovática starts at a museum, where participating students meet a robot that, through its movements and audio stories, guides them through the given path. The robot initially offers three rooms for students to choose which one they want to visit. Each room introduces the story of some outstanding figures linked to Computer Science. Students are free to choose any room, although room numbering (1, 2 and 3) would take them through the events in chronological order, according to the historical moment of the characters (see Fig. 1).

When entering a room, the pictures on the walls suddenly fall (see Fig. 2, left and right), which is intended as an element of surprise that would catch the players off-guard. The robot announces that a space-time anomaly has occurred, and that this should not be happening. Players are invited to take a leading role: they will have to travel through portals to repair the history of Computer Science. Through each portal, a completely different scenario is accessed, showing the background for one of the characters (depending on the room and the portal used). In the first room, they meet Charles Babbage (see Fig. 3, Babbage's workplace) and Ada Lovelace (see Fig. 4 a room in Ada's house); in the second room, they meet Alan Turing, John Von Neumann and Grace Hopper; finally, in the third room, part history must be recovered through figures such as Linus Tovalds, Vinton Cerf and Jack Kilby.

At the end of the tour, if the students managed to repair all character stories, they receive an award and congratulatory feedback, appealing to a type of affective feedback.

Fig. 1. Central game room.

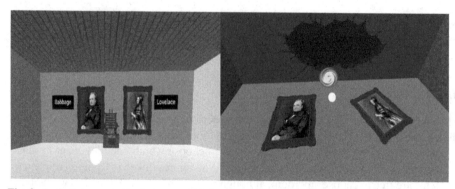

Fig. 2. Left: Entrance to the first room with the pictures of Babbage and Lovelace. Right: moment when the anomaly occurs, the pictures fall off the walls and the portal opens

Fig. 3. Charles Babbage's workplace with objects to explore.

Fig. 4. Living room in Ada Lovelace's house.

4.3 Mechanics and Their Relationship to Learning Objectives

The game proposes interacting with a guide robot, as seen in Figs. 1 and 3. Robot audios serve as guidance and present part of the story and the knowledge the students are encouraged to learn. Audio stories are short for effectiveness and to favor attention. Also, characters are initially approached in a more experiential way, appealing to a more visceral level of processing, with some story that helps students connect with that character in an affective way. For example, in the case of Grace Hopper, the origin of the term "bug" is retrieved as a reference to an error in the system caused by an insect. Students must catch the insect that causes the malfunction in the machine that Hopper was using, which originated the expression "bug". When traveling through the portal, the experience is exploratory and experiential, with affective components that help students feel a connection with the characters and remember part of their stories (thus appealing to the visceral and behavioral levels of the model of [17]).

On each journey, the experience involves exploring objects with the cross-hair to solve a challenge. When focused on, objects provide feedback in the form of a brief audio message from the robot that tells what the object is, and how it is linked to the character in question. Once the challenge has been solved, the students go through the same portal to return to the museum room, where now there appears an invention/contribution of the character to the history of Computer Science that works as a reward for having repaired history. By interacting with this object, a more formal account is displayed about what this innovator has contributed to Computer Science (reflective level).

Thus, both the mechanics used to solve the challenges and thus "fix history" are opportunities for learning through the use of different levels of processing.

5 Experience with Innovática for Its Evaluation and Results

Innovática was planned to be used during 2020 with first-year students of the Computer Science courses of studies at UNLP. Due to the pandemic, a distance experience has been carried out with several users ($N = 22$), mostly students and teachers from various backgrounds, in order to evaluate game usability and aspects related to experience and learning.

5.1 Methodology Used for the Evaluation

To carry out the experience, students (especially from the first year) and teachers from the School of Computer Science were invited to participate. Other users close to the creators of the game were also invited because of their interest in this type of games. Our goal was to include educators so that we could know their point of view regarding the application, since later they can be the driving force that integrates Innovática into the educational context. For this, an email was sent with an overview of the game, detailing its objective, the context in which it was developed, instructions for its use, and the link to download the.apk. Also, after using Innovática they were asked to respond to a survey submitted through Google Forms, whose link was also included in the email.

The survey used included four items about participant data such as age, gender, their role (student or educator), and the context in which they study or work. Then, there were three items devoted to asking how satisfied they were with the experience, and two final items where they were asked to pick their favorite character and sum up the lessons learned from the stories. All ten items are then considered together to assess game usability as measured by the SUS (System Usability Scale) instrument [24]. The SUS questionnaire provides a reliable and fast method for measuring usability. It consists of a 10-point questionnaire with a scale of 5 possibilities that range from "strongly disagree" to "strongly agree" (using values 1–5 to analyze the results). To calculate the result of this instrument, the following method is used: first, the average of all responses for each point is calculated. Then, the total value of each item is calculated, assigning a value of the mean minus 1 for odd items, and 5 minus the mean for even items. The total sum of all the items is multiplied by 2.5, which yields a final result between 0 and 100. This result should not be confused with a percentage [24]. The average score of the questionnaire is 68. This means that a SUS score greater than 68 is above average, and a score lower that 68 is below average.

A total of 22 participants responded to this invitation, 59% male and 41% female. Eighteen participants were aged between 21 and 35 y/o, and only 4 participants were over the age of 35 y/o. The disciplines to which they belong are: 7 Computer Science/Engineering, 3 Multimedia Design, 1 Medicine student, 1 Film student, 1 Chemistry student, 1 Social Communication student, and 1 Economics student. Overall, 14 participants were students, 3 were unemployed, and the rest were educators.

5.2 Results

As regards the question of what they liked the least about the game, aimed at identifying weak points in user experience, some participants made reference to navigation when working without visors and using only the cell phone in their hands. This is because, as the experience was carried out remotely, some participants did not have a visor and used only their cell phones.

Regarding what they liked the most about the game, participants made reference to the anecdotes and contexts (scenarios) of the characters with comments such as: "*Being able to know fun facts about the innovators. It was not like reading a Wikipedia article, I also learned curious and fun facts*"; "*The environments are very well achieved, they look striking and interesting, you can notice the different personalities of the historical figures and the time in which they lived. The game invites you to see the whole place, the guide is very helpful and does not clash with the experience*". The mechanics chosen for entertaining and learning were also referenced as a positive aspect: "*I like the idea itself of doing something fun with time-travels and saving the world as a way to teach you about any particular subject.*"

When asked about the character of choice, the most chosen stories were those of Alan Turing and Ada Lovelace, followed by Grace Hopper (see Fig. 5).

In the question about what they remembered from the characters' stories, things that had caught their attention, such as the history of the term "bug" (5 people referred to this), the personalities of Babbage and Von Neumann, the story of Kilby's storm, and the setting of Ada's house were mentioned the most. This shows that they managed to pay attention to the stories and get involved with some of the characters.

Finally, as regards SUS, the values described in the following paragraphs were obtained.

On the question about how complex the game seemed, 20 out of the 22 participants rated 1, meaning that they strongly disagreed that the game was complex. This result was achieved by targeting interaction mechanics and a simple thematic approach. The person can get into the game without a big learning curve. These simple interaction mechanics prove their effectiveness, this is observed from the 14 users who rated 5 when asked if the functions of the game were well integrated. There were 7 participants that rated 4 in this category, an equally very favorable opinion.

The previous item is closely related to the question as to whether the game was easy to use. In this case, 21 of the responses were distributed between a rating of 4 and 5 (agree and strongly agree).

When asked if most people would learn to use this game quickly, 11 users fully agreed with the statement, and another 8 users rated 4, that is, they agreed with it. One aspect that has been observed in this regard is that players need a few moments until they get used to lowering their gaze to move forwards along the path. This method was implemented to avoid the use of additional peripherals, leading to a broader chance of arrival by requiring nothing more than the visor.

As regards the need for assistance from a person with technical knowledge to be able to use the game, 11 participants strongly disagreed with the statement, and 7 participants rated with a 2, that is, they were in disagreement. The game is distributed in the form of an APK, that is, a downloadable installer, for Android. This is a common and recognized way to install applications today, and the average user finds no major problem in doing so. This is why, when asked if they needed to learn a lot before being able to use this game, 18 of the participants fully disagreed with the statement.

When considering if there are inconsistencies in the game, 16 rated the statement with a value of 1, meaning that they fully disagreed with it. The remaining 6 participants rated this statement with a 2. The game remains constant in relation to its rhythm and the interaction it proposes with the environment, and there is coherence in the design of the mechanics and the story.

When asked about how comfortable and safe they felt while playing the game, 17 participants rated the statement with a 5, 4 did so with a 4, and only 1 rated with a 3. These numbers indicate that the game was well received by the users who tried it.

Finally, when these items corresponding to the SUS were processed following the methodology described in Sect. 5, a mean of 85.7 was obtained, which is well above the average, and is considered a very positive result regarding usability.

Which historical character shown in the game was the most interesting?

22 answers

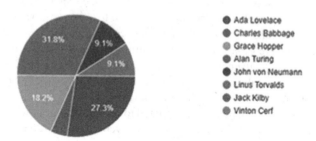

Fig. 5. Poll asking which was the most liked character in the story.

6   Conclusions and Future Work

This work contributes to research on the design of serious games based on virtual reality and its educational possibilities. Design-related aspects are discussed, where a variety of components related to games and virtual reality are considered. Previous background has allowed obtaining key elements that were considered for the design and creation of Innovática, such as different processing levels and gameplay heuristics. This game has made it possible to bring educators and students participating in the Innovática experience closer to prominent figures in the history of Computer Science. The design aspects taken into account have been positively perceived by the participants, with a very good value yielded by the SUS instrument in terms of application usability. Even though we have worked with a reduced sample, the door is open to deepen this study with new audiences. At the same time, questions such as the strategies used for the tour (is it better to follow a sequential order to visit the rooms (1, 2, 3) or any order of preference is fine) or the impact the stories have on the students, among others, will be further researched.

Acknowledgments. This work was carried out as part of a graduate dissertation of the School of Computer Science, National University of La Plata, Argentina. We also thank LIDI III Project 11/F023: Software Engineering Methodologies, Techniques and Tools in Hybrid Scenarios. Process Improvement, which provides the context to research these issues, and Project RTI2018–096986-B-C31: "PERGAMEX: PERVASIVE GAMING EXPERIENCES FOR ALL," which works on similar topics.

References

1. Archuby, F., Sanz, C., Pesado, P.: Experience analysis for the use of desafiate serious game for the self-assessment of students. In: Pesado, Patricia, Arroyo, Marcelo (eds.) CACIC 2019. CCIS, vol. 1184, pp. 110–123. Springer, Cham (2020). https://doi.org/10.1007/978-3-030-48325-8_8
2. Dörner, R., Göbel, S., Effelsberg, W., Wiemeyer, J. (eds.): Serious Games. Springer, Cham (2016). https://doi.org/10.1007/978-3-319-40612-1

3. Kiili, K.: Ketamo, H: Evaluating cognitive and affective outcomes of a digital game-based math test. IEEE Trans. Learn. Technol. **11**(2), 255–263 (2018)
4. Chittaro, L., Buttussi, F.: Assessing knowledge retention of an immersive serious game vs. a traditional education method in aviation safety. IEEE Trans. Visual Comput. Graphics **21**(4), 529–538 (2015)
5. Giannetti, C.: Estética de la simulación como endoestética. En: Estética, ciencia y tecnología, creaciones electrónicas y numéricas. Iliana Hernández García (comp.), pág. 92 (2005)
6. Kavanagh, S., Luxton-Reilly, A., Wuensche, B.: A systematic review of virtual reality in education - The Open University. Themes Sci. Technol. Educ. **2**, 85–119 (2017)
7. Chirinos, Y., Sanz, C., Rucci, A., Comparato, G., Gonzalez, G., Dapoto, S.: HUVI: una aplicación de realidad virtual para acercar el patrimonio argentino. Congreso de Tecnología en Educación y Educación en Tecnología (2020)
8. Schott, C., Marshall, S.: Virtual reality and situated experiential education: a conceptualization and exploratory trial. J. Comput. Assist. Learn. (2018)
9. Mazza, M., Sanz, C., Artola, V.: Juego serio de realidad virtual para acercar la historia de figuras claves de la historia de la Informática. In: Congreso Argentino en Ciencias de la Computación. CACIC 2020, pp. 133 – 143. ISBN 978–987–4417–90–9
10. Faaborg, A.: [TEDx Talks]. Designing for virtual reality and the impact on education (2015). https://www.youtube.com/watch?v=DQMA5NNhN58
11. Merchant, Z., Goetz, E., Cifuentes, L., Keeney-Kennicutt, W., Davis, T.: Effectiveness of virtual reality-based instruction on students' learning outcomes in K-12 and higher education: a meta-analysis. Comput. Educ. **70**, 29–40 (2014). ISSN 0360–1315. https://doi.org/10.1016/j.compedu.2013.07.033
12. Tsaramirsis, G., Buhari, S., AL-Shammari, K.O., Ghazi, S., Nazmudeen, M.S., Tsaramirsis, K.: Towards simulation of the classroom learning experience: Virtual Reality approach. In: Mn, H. (ed.) The 10th Indiacom - 2016 3rd International Conference on Computing for Sustainable Global Development, pp. 1343–1346. New Delhi, India: IEEE (2016)
13. Ritz, L.T.: Teaching with CAVE virtual reality systems: instructional design strategies that promote adequate cognitive load for learners (2015)
14. González Sánchez, J.L., Gutierrez Vela, F.: Jugabilidad: caracterización de la experiencia del jugador en videojuegos. Tesis doctoral de la Universidad de Granada (2010)
15. Chirinos, Y., Sanz, C., Dapoto, S.: Tesis de Maestría: La Realidad Virtual como Mediadora de Aprendizajes. Desarrollo de una aplicación móvil de Realidad Virtual orientada a Niños (2020)
16. Usability First. Website. https://uxplanet.org/usability-first-why-usability-design-matters-to-ui-ux-designers-9dfb5580116a
17. Normal, D.: El Diseño Emocional: Por Que Nos Gustan (O No) los Objetos Cotidianos. Ed. Paidós (2004)
18. Smith, C.L., Coleman, S.K.: Using Labster to improve Bioscience student learning and engagement in practical classes. Heads of Biological Sciences, Royal Society of Biology. Spring 2017 meeting. University of Leicester (2017)
19. Hilliker, H.: A Guided Tour of Queen Nefertari's Tomb With a Docent in High Fidelity VR. https://www.youtube.com/watch?v=yX_rDXOL2oA
20. Ferguson, C., van den Broek, E., van Oostendorp, H.: On the role of interaction mode and story structure in virtual reality serious games. Comput. Educ. 143, 103671 (2020). ISSN 0360–1315. https://doi.org/10.1016/j.compedu.2019.103671
21. Mossel, A., Schoenuaer, C., Froeschl, M., Peer, A., Goellner, J., Kaufmann, H.: Immersive training of first responder squad leaders in untethered virtual reality (2020)
22. Giannakos, M.: Enjoy and learn with educational games: examining factors affecting learning performance (2013)

23. Kenwright, B.: Virtual Reality: Ethical Challenges and Dangers (2018)
24. Brooke, J.: SUS: a retrospective. J. Usability Stud. **8**, 29–40 (2013). https://uxpajournal.org/sus-a-retrospective
25. González Izard, S., Vivo Vicent, C., Juanes Méndez, J.A., Palau, R.: virtual reality in higher education: an experience with medical students: research into how virtual reality can be used as a powerful training tool for medicine students. In: Eighth International Conference on Technological Ecosystems for Enhancing Multiculturality. (TEEM 2020), pp. 414–421. Association for Computing Machinery, New York (2020). https://doi.org/10.1145/3434780.3436539

Serious Mobile Games Development. Possibilities and Challenges for Teachers

Edith Lovos[1,3](✉) ⓘ, Iván Basciano[1,3] ⓘ, Evangelina Gil[1,3] ⓘ, and Cecilia Sanz[2,3] ⓘ

[1] Universidad Nacional de Río Negro, Sede Atlántica, Viedma, Río Negro, Argentina
`elovos@unrn.edu.ar`
[2] III-LIDI, Facultad de Informática, Universidad Nacional de la Plata, La Plata, Argentina
`csanz@lidi.info.unlp.edu.ar`
[3] Investigador Asociado de la Comisión de Investigaciones Científicas de la Pcia. de Bs. As,,
Buenos Aires, Argentina

Abstract. The possibilities that digital games allow in a didactic proposal are not new, however, and in relation to the specific experiences of integration of digital games in teaching and learning scenarios, a limitation is observed given by the adaptability of them to specific contexts. Thus, it is important to advance in the search for tools that are preferably free and open access that allow teachers to create their own games or edit others created by third parties, based on profiles with different degrees of programming knowledge. This work presents the results obtained from the search, selection and analysis of tools, including web platforms, software applications, and/or frameworks, which allow the creation of serious games, particularly those considered mobile, and which include interactions using augmented reality through QR codes and/or user location, by users with different technical profiles.

Keywords: Serious games · Authoring tools · Frameworks · Augmented reality · M-learning

1 Introduction

Michel & Chen [1] define serious game (SG) as a way of combining video games and education, where the main objective is education (in any of its forms), and whose main components are: objectives, rules, challenges and interaction. SGs enable another mechanism to carry out teaching and learning, at the same time that it extends the training objectives and generates not only conditions for the player (student) to learn but also to apply and demonstrate what has been learned [1]. On the other hand, a mobile serious game (MSG) is a SG that can be executed on a mobile device such as cell phones or tablets or laptops, providing the player with the possibility of playing at any time and place, that is, making possible the generation of less rigid, personalized and ubiquitous learning environments [2, 3]. In addition, the common elements of these types of devices such as: cameras, gyroscopes, etc., give rise to the use of emerging technologies such as augmented reality (AR), which allows enriching a physical context

P. Pesado and J. Eterovic (Eds.): CACIC 2020, CCIS 1409, pp. 67–79, 2021.
https://doi.org/10.1007/978-3-030-75836-3_5

with virtual information. AR is characterized by: (a) a combination of virtual and real objects in a real environment, (b) users interacting in real time, and (c) an alignment between real and virtual objects [4]. There are different levels of AR, depending on the element that is used as the trigger for it. Thus, level 0 uses QR codes that only make it possible to link other content without any type of interaction or monitoring, level 1 uses markers (quadrangular black and white images with schematic drawings) that allow recognition of 2D patterns and 3D objects. Level 2 includes the recognition of images or objects and/or the positioning of the user giving rise to other types of interactions and the superposition of virtual elements in the captured physical world, and in the last level special devices such as AR lenses are used or others, which allows a more complete integration between the physical and virtual worlds and thus the experiences that can be generated are more immersive and personalized [5]. Regarding to its potential in the educational context, AR allows incorporating multimedia into the teaching-learning process, increasing the richness of the physical context and thus, innovating in teaching practice from the design of educational activities that contribute to the understanding of abstract concepts, of spatiality, student motivation and discovery-based learning, among others [3, 5–7]. Hence, the combination of AR and mobile devices together with the characteristics of the games allow an instructional design that can help to achieve both affective and cognitive learning outcomes [8, 9].

This article is an extension of a previous work [31] in which different tools that can assist teachers with different levels of programming skills to produce their own serious games were analyzed. This new version extends the analysis with new tools that are considered, and it offers a richer discussion.

1.1 Serious Games Development

SGs development requires matching instructional design (ID) with game design (game characteristics, mechanics, and playability), thus advancing in the development of a SG requires knowledge of game design, learning theories and mastery of the content to be addressed with it. By the ID, it is possible to define the contents, the skills to be developed, the strategies that will be used to offer the contents and the evaluation mechanisms, all based on the needs of the students, their characteristics and the learning context of application [10]. However, although teachers have expertise in ID, in many cases they do not have the technical knowledge, particularly in programming, to allow them to advance in the development of a SG tailored to the context of their teaching practice. At this point, in the literature [11–15, 17] on the subject some possibilities appear through the so-called authoring tools (AT) and also frameworks that can assist in the design and development process of SGs with little or no programming knowledge.

The term authoring tool (AT) is associated with the idea of software that enables the creation and editing of learning content in multimedia format, so that it can be used in teaching and learning proposals in different media, giving rise to processes of e-learning and m-learning. In this sense, an AT is a software that facilitates the production of applications, which can be used by profiles that do not necessarily have technical knowledge. So, the software will be equipped with a set of functionalities and characteristics (friendly interfaces, templates or models, tutoring systems, interoperability with other resources, among others) that allow progress in this sense [16, 17].

From the point of view of software engineering [18], a framework represents a skeletal abstraction of solutions to a series of similar problems. In a framework, the steps or stages to follow to implement the solution are described without going into details about the activities that will be carried out in each of the steps. In the specific case of video game development, frameworks allow, with minimal or in some cases without programming knowledge, to accelerate the development process by offering predefined solutions with extension and/or customization possibilities. There are frameworks such as the case of Construct2, which use the drag-and-drop system allowing to create the game logic through pre-built scripts that are associated with the elements of the game that is being built visually. Beyond ease of use, a desirable feature of a framework for SG development is, as Paiva [21] points out, the possibility of changing the (learning) content by re-using the structure of the game, without having to start from scratch.

This work presents a list of ATs and frameworks collected through a bibliographic review process, as well as the criteria established for their evaluation. Then the results achieved with the evaluation of those selected are described and, finally, a discussion and the conclusions reached are presented along with future work. It is important to highlight that this work was carried out in the context of a research project (PI-UNRN-40C-750), accredited and funded by the National University of Río Negro (UNRN). The project seeks to generate knowledge about the design, development and application of mobile educational games with augmented reality, in teaching and learning context of medium and higher level of the UNRN.

2 Authoring Tools and Frameworks Selection

In the research project mentioned in the previous section, a bibliography review was carried out with the intention of recovering authoring tools and frameworks that can be used for the development of MSGs, in particular those that allow including interactions using AR (where the trigger elements are QR codes and/or the geographic location of the player). The review was limited to the period 2015–2019 and was focused to answer the following questions:

- What technological infrastructure is necessary for its use?
- Do you require programming knowledge? What level?
- What types of games can be built with these tools?
- What level of AR can be implemented?

From this review process, the tools presented in Table 1 were collected, and they have been categorized according to their type (AT or Framework), access form, platform to which the developed game can be exported, type of element used to activate AR, type of activities that can be included in the game using AR (ARAT), the language in which the tool is available, and finally the country of origin.

The selection presents on Table 1 was filtered, taking into account the following criteria: free access, possibility of exporting the game to be developed to mobile devices with Android operating system, possibility of including activities with augmented reality using QR codes and/or user location. Finally, it was important to take into account the

Table 1. ATs and frameworks collected.

	Access	Platform	AR trigger	ARAT	Language	Country
ARIS [19]	Free (open source)	Mobile (iOS)	QR GPS	Interactive tours. Puzzles	English	United States
ARLEARN [20]	Free (open source)	Mobile (Android)	GPS	Interactive tours. Puzzles	English	The Netherlands
I_learnTest [21]	Free. User register required	Web	No available	Quizzes Association	English	Portugal
FJSU [22]	Free	Mobile (Android, iOS)	No available in the actual version	Adaptive games, shooters, RPG Puzzles	Portuguese	Brazil
MAGIS [23]	Free	Mobile (Android, iOS)	Fiducially markers, GPS	Adventure Interactive tours Puzzles	English	Philippines
MOLE [11]	Prototype	Mobile (Android, iOS)	QR	Interactive tours Puzzles	Spanish	Argentine
SG Generator from a base project in HTML5 [30]	Prototype	Multi-device	Fiducially markers, images	Rules Games, Memory Games	Spanish	Mexico
TaleBlazer [29]	Free. User register required	Mobile (Android, iOS)	GPS	Interactive tours	English	United States
U-Adventure [24]	Free	Mobile (Android, iOS), Console	GPS QR	Adventures Interactive tours Puzzles	Spanish	Spain
VEDILS [13]	Free. User register required	Mobile (Android)	Images, Fiducially markers, text	Interactive tours Puzzles	English/Spanish	Spain

context of application (UNRN), the possibility of using the tool in Spanish language and/or in a visually way. This reduced the possibilities to the following ATs: MOLE [11], SG Generator [30], U-Adventure [23], TaleBlazer [29], VEDILS [13]. However the first two were discarded because at the time of the evaluation, the tools were still in the version of prototype. On the other hand, in the case of [30] although the tool is presented as a possibility to produce multi-device SG that include AR interactions, it requires technical profiles with knowledge in HTML 5 to specify the SG structure. In the case of frameworks, iLearnTest [21] and FSJU [22] have been discarded for not presenting support for the development of games that include interactions with AR.

2.1 Evaluation Criteria

For the evaluation of ATs, the criteria established in other investigations [15, 25, 26] have been followed as well as others established by the authors of this work have also been incorporated. The contributions of [15], allow to evaluate the characteristics of the authoring tools for the development of educational materials that include augmented reality. In other work [25], it is proposed to carry out the evaluation of authoring tools, from the perspective called Critical Success Factor (CSF), analysing factors such as: infrastructure (technological requirements), user (levels, skills and knowledge) and community (of practice), and other aspects such as learning strategies and styles, teaching methods, social presence (interaction, engagement and realism), the degree of commitment generated by the developed product and the fun provided both from the point of view of the person who is carrying out the design and the end user (in this context teachers and students). Based on this, Table 2 presents the evaluation criteria used to analyse the authoring tools and frameworks selected for this study.

2.2 Analysis and Discussion of the Selected ATs and Frameworks

The results of the analysis are described below.

U-Adventure. It is a SGs editor that is distributed and it works as an extension of the Unity game engine, and according to its creators, the e-UCM Research Group of the Complutense University of Madrid, allows the production of games to user profiles that do not necessarily have programming knowledge. The tool is built on the basis of a previous version called e-Adventure [27]. So U-Adventure seeks to solve problems of its obsolescence previous version, as well as to open the possibility to the generation of multiplatform games [14]. Among the potentialities of U-Adventure, the potential to include in the game interactions using AR both outdoor, through user location and indoor using QR codes as triggers stands out (this last option was part of the e-adventure version). Likewise, it is possible to define on which game events it collects information during its execution, and then carry out an analysis of this as part of the learning evaluation process. Regarding the generation of games for mobile devices, although programming knowledge is not required, the process of exporting projects to the Android operating system is not transparent for the user, since it requires the installation and configuration of Android Studio. At this point, it is observed that although the tool has the desirable features for an AT, it is necessary to have different user profiles during the MSG production process. Table 3 presents the results of the analysis of the tool based on the established criteria.

Table 2. Evaluation criteria

Edition Tool	Name	
Analysis Criteria (ACX)		Detail
ACx0	License	Cost of access and use of the tool
ACx1	Technical Requirements	Technical requirements (hardware, software, connectivity) required by the tool
ACx2	Shared and collaborative Edition	It is possible to edit the game in a shared/collaborative way
ACx3	User Profile	Digital skills required to use the tool
ACx4	Templates	Templates or models provided by the tool for the generation of games based on them
ACx5	Games Types	Games types that could be generated by the tool
ACx6	AR level supported	QR, fiducially markers, user location, images
ACx7	Augmented information supported	Supported augmented information types (images, videos, audio, 3D objects, etc.)
ACx8	Accessibility	The tool enables the development of games that can be considered accessible
ACx9	Content distribution	Forms provided by the tool for the distribution of the developed game
ACx10	Analytics	The tool allows to collect and record information about player interactions during the execution game

TaleBlazer. It is an online and free platform accessible through any browser by https://taleblazer.org/. It allows the development of educational games that include AR interactions using the user's location both outdoors and indoors. The platform was developed by MIT under the Scheller Teacher Education Program and has a game editor that uses a block-based visual scripting language, similar to the Scratch language. The TaleBlazer editor allows the user to create a game from scratch or remix a game already created by the author himself or others.

A game developed with TaleBlazer involves the following elements: agents (characters or objects that the player can interact with during the game execution), regions (real-world locations where the game can be played), scenarios (allows generate different versions of the game based on the starting point selected by the player at the start) and roles (refers to the character a player plays during the game execution). To design the

Table 3. U-Adventure analysis based on Table 2 criteria

Edition Tool	U-Adventure
Analysis Criteria (ACx)	Details
ACx0	Download, installation and free use from https://github.com/e-ucm/uAdventure. No user registration required
ACx1	Requires the Unity game development engine (version 2017.3) installed
ACx2	No shared edition allowed
ACx3	Although it does not require programming knowledge to use the tool, it is necessary to have technical knowledge on how to link the U-Adventure with the Unity engine and it is also necessary to know how to install and configure Android Studio to export projects in Android format
ACx4	A user manual and an installation guide are available through the site https://github.com/e-ucm/uAdventure, which is currently in English
ACx5	Templates not available
ACx6	Classical adventures
ACx7	QR, user location
ACx8	Images (jpg y png), videos(mp4), audio (mp3), web page links
ACx9	The tool allows to include text and audio for greater accessibility in the development of projects
ACx10	Analytics are integrated into the tool through the Experience API (xAPI), allowing its use both online and offline [28]. It has a specific editor to select the events to be recorded

game's elements, the editor consists of 6 tabs: map, agents, player, world, configuration and beacons, through which the game is configured and built. It is important to note that the current version is available only in English language.

Once a game is created, it is stored in the cloud, and a code is generated that makes it accessible to download and play from the TaleBlazer mobile application. This application is available for mobile devices with operating system like Android 4.0 or higher, and Ios 6.0 or higher. The platform has an emulator option, however in the current version it is not enabled, so the developer can only test a game through the mobile application.

An interesting aspect of the platform is the possibility of generating information about the game regarding its recipients (age range), the type of difficulty involved and the physical space that it intends to travel. This information is presented when downloading the game from the mobile application.

Through the mobile application it is possible to view other games developed with TaleBlazer that are in locations close to the user, making it a very interesting possibility to share the productions of a work team. Regarding the possibility of collecting and retrieving information about the player's interactions during the game, the functionality is only available for special users (officially featured organizations). Table 4 presents the results of the analysis of TaleBlazer based on the established criteria.

Table 4. TaleBlazer analysis based on Table 2 information

Edition Tool	TaleBlazer
Analysis Criteria (ACx)	Details
ACx0	Open-source, free, cloud-based platform. It can be accessible at https://taleblazer.org/
ACx1	Internet connection. User register
ACx2	Shared edition not allowed
ACx3	Block programming knowledge required
ACx4	Allow create a game from scratch or remix games already created by the author himself or others. It also has detailed documentation about the creation of different types of games
ACx5	Location based narratives
ACx6	Location outdoor e indoor
ACx7	Image (jpg, png, jpeg, gif), audio (mp3, wma, m4a, wav, 3gp) and links (web pages or e-mail addresses)
ACx8	It does not present specific functionality
ACx9	Through code generation. It is transparent by the game developer
ACx10	Only available for special users (officially featured organizations)

VEDILS. It was developed at the University of Cádiz (Spain), and its authors [13] define it as a visual environment that allows the design of interactive learning scenarios, in which it is possible to include technologies such as AR among others. VEDILS is based on MIT's App2Inventor development environment and enables the production of augmented content for mobile devices (cell phones and tablets), through a cloud platform, after registration and authorization for use. The tool, which is currently in version 1.6, is made up of two parts: one where you work on the design of the application to be developed, and another called blocks where it is possible to define the logic of the application using a visual language. At this point, the user of the tool must have knowledge of programming using blocks, as indicated in other investigations [11]. VEDILS has a component called ActivityTracker that makes it possible to collect information on the interactions that occur as part of the game execution, although it must be taken into account that they are registered and processed using the Google Fusion Tables and MongoDB services. Although using this functionality may not be easy for a novel user, VEDILS offers videos and tutorials that can accompany the component configuration process, as well as how to carry out the information analysis process. Regarding the export of the project, it is transparent for the user and can choose between exporting the project as APK (download it on the computer) and then distribute it in the way that is convenient, or generate a QR code to access it, in this case the code will last 2 h. On the other hand, it is advisable to download the generated projects since they can be removed from the platform for maintenance reasons. Table 5 presents the results of the analysis of the tool based on the established criteria.

Table 5. VEDILS analysis based on Table 2 criteria

Edition Tool	VEDILS
Analysis Criteria (ACx)	Details
ACx0	Free cloud-based platform
ACx1	Internet connection. User registration required
ACx2	Not available
ACx3	Not programming knowledge required for interface design, but it is necessary have block programming knowledge for define the logic interaction between game elements [11]
ACx4	Has many tutorials and step-by-step explanations of applications developed with the tool
ACx5	It is possible import others games (.aia) for use in a new one
ACx6	Puzzle
ACx7	QR, location, text and image recognition
ACx8	Images (.png and.jpg), videos(mp4), audio (mp3), 3D models (obj, 3ds, mds)
ACx9	Allow include text and audio for a greater accessibility in the game
ACx10	Allow collect and register information on player interactions during the game execution. To do so, use a non-proprietary service (Google Fusion Tables). Use this functionality maybe not be easy for a novel user

MAGIS. It is a framework designed and created by a group of researchers from the Ateneo de Manila University in Philippines. The framework is an extension of the Unity engine and, seeks to simplify the design of narrative-based games that use the player's location, such as historical or museum tours. [23] Game development using MAGIS implies the creation of scenes where for each one of the objects included in it, a script is generated in the form of a script based on the framework's own commands (and not in the C# language) and with the format TSV (Tab Separated Values) and the extension.txt. On this point, as the authors themselves point out, creating this type of files manually can be complex and prone to errors, and to avoid this they have developed a free access AT, which tries to automate the task, however it presents an interface that it's not visually friendly, which can be daunting specially for an inexperienced user. Likewise, the generation of fiducial markers that can be used to activate AR must be generated with other applications such as Vuforia. Regarding the possibility of recording and processing the information that occurs as part of the player's interactions, its authors indicate that it has an analysis subsystem that can be activated in two ways: through the events that take place during the game (i.e., scanning a scoreboard) or through the scripts that define the game logic using the specific @analytics commands. The game stores the collected data in cache and then sends it to the analysis server, where it is recorded for later viewing and analysis. At this point, the MAGIS user guide does not provide specific information. Table 6 presents the results of the analysis of MAGIS based on the established criteria.

Table 6. MAGIS analysis based on Table 2 criteria

Edition Tool	MAGIS
Analysis Criteria (CAX)	Details
ACx0	Free under GNU license
ACx1	Unity 5 (2016)
ACx2	Not available
ACx3	Knowledge programming required
ACx4	Has a framework user's guide and an scripting guide on creating game engine scripts using the AT
ACx5	Location based adventures
ACx6	Markers, Location
ACx7	Images (.png), audio (.ogg), 3D models (FBX)
ACx8	Audio could be used as a resource to provide accessibility
ACx9	Using the functionalities provided by Unity personal version it can be distributed as APK
ACx10	It has an analysis subsystem, but its use is not specified in the user manual

3 Conclusion and Perspectives

The possibilities offered by the MSGs into learning activities are varied and allow to attend to different aspects: cognitive, emotional and motivational among others, and in the particular case of those games that include interactions using AR, these possibilities allow to take advantage of the physical environment in which they are carried out, giving rise to contextualized learning and discovery. However, existing games are not always adapted to the needs of the application context, so there is a need for tools that enable teachers with different levels of technical knowledge to advance in the development and subsequent re-use of SGs. In the case of the tools that were analyzed in the previous section, TaleBlazer and VEDILS are presented as an alternative that allow to edit from the cloud, from scratch or based on other games, and where the distribution of the game developed is carried out in a transparent way for the user, however it will be necessary to have knowledge of programming using blocks. About TaleBlazer, although it presents a more limited set of supported augmented information, it has tutorials that not only facilitate and guide the use of the platform, but also allow to understand the process of design a serious game. Here, an obstacle to overcome, may be in some cases the AT language.

In the case of U-Adventure and MAGIS, both are presented as alternatives for user profiles with technical knowledge (configuration in the case of the first and programming in the case of the second) that allow them to advance with the use of a generation game engine like Unity. In the case of MAGIS, the language used to script the game scenes can be confusing for a novel user.

Regarding the possibility of having specific functionalities to carry out learning analytics about the interactions that take place during the game execution, any of the AT and frameworks analysed, requires an extra effort by the user, although in the case of U-Adventure having a specific editor integrated into the tool, may be of support for the process.

In conclusion, so that teachers can advance in the production of MSGs that include interactions using AR, it will be necessary not only to have knowledge of instructional design but also technical knowledge that allows to maximize the use of tools (whether ATs or frameworks) and put them at the service of the pedagogical proposal.

Although the tools analyzed in this work, improve the possibilities of intervention for development of MSGs by non-technical users, we agree with recent research [29] that points out the need to advance in the development of tools that improve usability. At this point it is fundamental the access and use of the tools by profiles with different degrees of programming knowledge, do not became in a technical problem.

It is proposed as future work, to approach the design and production of a MSG with one of these tools, analyzing the roles and interventions of a team in which teachers with different technical profiles have an active participation in this process.

References

1. Michael, D.R., Chen, S.L.: Serious Games: Games That Educate, Train, and Inform. Muska & Lipman/Premier-Trade, New York (2005)
2. Demir, K., Akpinar, E.: The effect of mobile learning applications on students' academic achievement and attitudes toward mobile learning. Malays. Online J. Educ. Technol. 6(2), 48–59 (2018)
3. De la Torre Cantero, J., Martin-Dorta, N., Pérez, J.L.S., Carrera, C.C., González, M.C.: Entorno de aprendizaje ubicuo con realidad aumentada y tabletas para estimular la comprensión del espacio tridimensional. Revista de Educación a Distancia (37) (2015)
4. Azuma, R., Baillot, Y., Behringer, R., Feiner, S., Julier, S., MacIntyre, B.: Recent advances in augmented reality. Naval Research Lab Washington Dc (2001)
5. Melo, I.M.: Realidad aumentada y aplicaciones. TIA 6(1), 28–35 (2018)
6. Fonseca Escudero, D., Redondo Domínguez, E., Valls, F.: Motivación y mejora académica utilizando realidad aumentada para el estudio de modelos tridimensionales arquitectónicos. Teoría de la Educación. Educación y Cultura en la Sociedad de la Información 17(1) (2016)

7. Salazar Mesía, N., Gorga, G., Sanz, C.V.: EPRA: Herramienta para la enseñanza de conceptos básicos de programación utilizando realidad aumentada. In: X Congreso sobre Tecnología en Educación & Educación en Tecnología (TE & ET) (Corrientes, 2015) (2015)

8. Schmitz, B., Klemke, R., Specht, M.: Effects of mobile gaming patterns on learning outcomes: a literature review (2013)

9. Chang, C.Y., Hwang, G.J.: Trends in digital game-based learning in the mobile era: a systematic review of journal publications from 2007 to 2016. Int. J. Mob. Learn. Organ. **13**(1), 68–90 (2019)

10. Fernández-Robles, J.L., Hernández-Gallardo, S.C.: Diseño instruccional de un juego serio que facilite a niños de tercer grado de primaria el ejercicio de operaciones matemáticas básicas

11. Dal Bianco, P.A., Mozzon Corporaal, F., Lliteras, A.B., Grigera, J., Gordillo, S.E.: MoLE: a web authoring tool for building mobile learning experiences. In: XXV Congreso Argentino de Ciencias de la Computación. CACIC 2019. Universidad Nacional de Río Cuarto (2019)

12. Firssova, O., Vogel, C., Brouns, F., Diegel, N., Forsman, P., Stracke, C.M.: Designing for virtual mobility: potentials and caveats. In: Fessl, A., Zdolšek Draksler, T. (eds.) EC-TEL Practitioner Proceedings 2019: 14th European Conference on Technology Enhanced Learning, Delft, Netherlands, 16–19 September 2019. CEUR Workshop Proceedings, vol. 2437. Springer (2019). https://ceur-ws.org/Vol-2437/paper4.pdf

13. Mota, J.M., Ruiz-Rube, I.: VEDILS: a toolkit for developing Android mobile apps supporting mobile analytics. In: Seventh European Business Intelligence & Big Data Summer School (eBISS 2017) (2017)

14. Perez-Colado, I.J., Perez-Colado, V.M., Martínez-Ortiz, I., Freire-Moran, M., Fernández-Manjón, B.: UAdventure: the eAdventure reboot: combining the experience of commercial gaming tools and tailored educational tools. In: 2017 IEEE Global Engineering Education Conference (EDUCON), pp. 1755–1762. IEEE, April 2017

15. Moralejo, L.: Análisis comparativo de herramientas de autor para la creación de actividades de realidad aumentada. Doctoral dissertation, Facultad de Informática (2014)

16. Cubillo, J.: ARLE: una herramienta de autor para entornos de aprendizaje de realidad aumentada. Doctoral dissertation, UNED. Universidad Nacional de Educación a Distancia (España) (2014)

17. Karoui, A., Marfisi-Schottman, I., George, Sébastien.: Mobile learning game authoring tools: assessment, synthesis and proposals. In: Bottino, R., Jeuring, J., Veltkamp, R.C. (eds.) GALA 2016. LNCS, vol. 10056, pp. 281–291. Springer, Cham (2016). https://doi.org/10.1007/978-3-319-50182-6_25

18. Mnkandla, E.: About software engineering frameworks and methodologies. In: AFRICON 2009, pp. 1–5. IEEE (2009)

19. https://arisgames.org/editor/

20. https://portal.ou.nl/web/topic-mobile-learning/home/-/wiki/Main/ARLearn

21. Paiva, A.C., Flores, N.H., Barbosa, A.G., Ribeiro, T.P.: iLearnTest–framework for educational games. Procedia-Soc. Behav. Sci. **228**, 443–448 (2016)

22. Silveira Júnior, G.D.: FJSU: Um Framework para o desenvolvimento de jogos sérios ubíquos (2019)

23. Vidal, E.C.E., Jr., Ty, J.F., Caluya, N.R., Rodrigo, M.M.T.: MAGIS: mobile augmented-reality games for instructional support. Interact. Learn. Environ. **27**(7), 895–907 (2019)

24. Pérez-Colado, V.M., Pérez-Colado, I.J., Freire-Morán, M., Martínez-Ortiz, I., Fernández-Manjón, B.: uAdventure: simplifying narrative serious games development. In: 2019 IEEE 19th International Conference on Advanced Learning Technologies (ICALT), vol. 2161, pp. 119–123. IEEE (2019)

25. Teoh, K.K., Sliuzas, R.: Multimedia development of online literacy objects: an evaluation of authoring tools for novice authors. In: Hamerton, H., Fraser, C. (eds.) Te tipuranga – Growing

Capability: Proceedings of the 2015 National Tertiary Learning and Teaching Conference, pp. 70–76. Bay of Plenty Polytechnic, Tauranga (2016)

26. Christopoulou, E., Xinogalos, S.: Overview and comparative analysis of game engines for desktop and mobile devices (2017)
27. https://e-adventure.e-ucm.es/
28. Perez-Colado, I., Perez-Colado, V., Freire-Moran, M., Martinez-Ortiz, I., Fernandez-Manjon, B.: Integrating Learning Analytics into a Game Authoring Tool. In: Xie, H., Popescu, E., Hancke, G., Fernández Manjón, B. (eds.) ICWL 2017. LNCS, vol. 10473, pp. 51–61. Springer, Cham (2017). https://doi.org/10.1007/978-3-319-66733-1_6
29. Ahmad, A., Law, E.L., Moseley, A.: Integrating instructional design principles in serious games authoring tools: insights from systematic literature review. In: Proceedings of the 11th Nordic Conference on Human-Computer Interaction: Shaping Experiences, Shaping Society, pp. 1–12 (2020)
30. Aguilar, G., Gregorio, J.: Desarrollo de un generador de juegos serios educativos multi-dispositivo con implementación de realidad aumentada. Doctoral dissertation (2019)
31. Lovos, E., Basciano, I., Gil, E., Sanz, C.V.: La Producción de Juegos Serios Móviles. Posibilidades y Desafíos para el Docente de Nivel Superior. In: Congreso Argentino de Ciencias de la Computación (CACIC 2020), La Matanza, 8 al 12 de Octubre de 2020 (2020)

MEHI - Interactive Hypermedial Educational Material for a General Chemistry Course. Result of Virtual Educational Experience

Ricardo García[1](✉) ⓘ, Gladys Gorga[2] ⓘ, and Rodolfo Bertone[2] ⓘ

[1] Universidad Nacional del Noroeste de La Pcia de Bs. As, Junín, Argentina
[2] III-Lidi Facultad de Informática UNLP, La Plata, Argentina
`{ggorga,pbertone}@lidi.info.unlp.edu.ar`

Abstract. The incorporation and integration of multimedia material in educational settings opens the possibility of change and renewal in classroom dynamics, the didactic processes involved, the facilities, the activity of the teacher and the role of the student. The use of these resources affects cognitive processes, increasing the capacity to encode, store and process information. In this context, the design and development of digital educational materials to integrate them into different contexts and paradigms is of utmost importance. Consequently, the design, production and evaluation in a pilot test of an interactive hypermedia educational material (IHEM) aimed at learning General Chemistry content was launched in 2019.

The pandemic unleashed in early 2020, led to the need to virtualize the General and Inorganic Chemistry Course at UNNOBA. Since the MEHI tool had been tested in a pilot test cohort in 2019, it was decided to launch it in the 2020 cohort, using it for teaching Unit 10 of the subject General and Inorganic Chemistry, in which the contents of Electrochemistry that addresses the hypermedial MEHI material are developed.

The work begins with a brief introduction that reviews the state of the arts and then presents the methodology and description of the sample used in the new educational experience and the data collection instruments for its evaluation. Finally, the results obtained and analysis data and the conclusions are developed.

Keywords: Hypermedia educational material · General Chemistry · Data collection instruments · Virtual educational experience

1 Introduction

Applying new technologies in the classroom can develop innovative teaching strategies, optimizing the learning process, and redefining the activity of the teacher and the role of the student [1].

The adequate complementation between the technological, disciplinary and didactic-pedagogical knowledge of the designs, the trends and experiences that allow validating their effectiveness, are considerations to take into account when designing these multimedia materials [2].

P. Pesado and J. Eterovic (Eds.): CACIC 2020, CCIS 1409, pp. 80–88, 2021.
https://doi.org/10.1007/978-3-030-75836-3_6

The growing trend towards the use of digital educational materials oriented to the teaching and learning of Sciences in general and Chemistry in particular is evident, with the purpose of assisting the teacher in the development of certain contents [3, 4].

Research in the field of science didactics shows the usefulness of these resources to face the difficulties of learning abstract content that is difficult to acquire, or for the development of virtual and remote laboratories as scenarios of great interest in the educational field. It is thus achieved overcoming physical limitations and equipment, allowing to improve the forms of spontaneous reasoning, acting as an epistemological and methodological obstacle or thought. In this way, functional fixation is avoided, which leads to avoid learning that does not favor analysis, reflection and creative thinking to solve a situation, fact or problem, and functional reduction that does not allow the correlation of different variables or causes of a phenomenon [5, 6].

The application in the educational field of multimedia resources provides a great deal of interesting data. This includes not only text, but also other media such as static images (photographs, graphics or illustrations), moving images (videos or animations) and audio (music or sounds), giving greater flexibility to the expression of the content developed in the form of multimedia [7]. On the other hand, hypertext provides a structure that allows data to be presented and explored in different sequences. Thus, the integration of hypertext and multimedia allows accessibility to multimedia content, according to the needs or interests of the user. The use of a more natural and friendly multidimensional medium, not limited to linear presentations, allows the student to choose the hyperlinks they want at all times. This freedom of choice stimulates curiosity and the possibility of managing their own learning process, become a tool that facilitates autonomous learning [8, 9].

This article be an extension of a previous work [10], which considered a non-pandemic, educational context. In this extended version, a richer discussion is offered by analyzing the new educational context in which the IHEM was used during the first four-month period of the 2020 and the evaluation tools provided for the study of this educational experience.

In this context, research was carried out in two stages. The first one provides literature review of backgrounds and experiences using hypermedia materials for teaching and learning chemistry and authoring tools for designing digital materials. The second stage focused on the design and implementation of a digital educational material for the learning of General Chemistry contents, the material produced was evaluated in a pilot test carried out in the General and Inorganic Chemistry Subject of UNNOBA in the 2019 cohort [10].

The pandemic unleashed at the beginning of 2020, led to the need to virtualize the General and Inorganic Chemical Subject at UNNOBA. Given that the MEHI tool was available and that it had been evaluated in a pilot test in the 2019 cohort, it was decided to include it in the 2020 cohort, using it to teach Unit 10 of the General and Inorganic Chemistry subject, which is the unit where the contents of Electrochemistry are developed, which addresses the Interactive Hypermedia Educational Material (IHEM) produced, available to download at: https://ricardogarciaquimica.github.io/electroquimica/.

The new educational context in which the IHEM was used during the first four-month period of the 2020 cohort and the evaluation tools provided for the study of this educational experience are described below.

2 Methodology

The use of a tool in one educational experience is proposed, in which students of the subject General and Inorganic Chemistry of UNNOBA use the hypermedia materials IHEM in one virtual mode, through the platform of Digital Education University, using Google MEET for synchronous activities.

The General and Inorganic Chemistry course is introduced on the platform with an initial cover page and a design in tabs, one for each thematic unit.

In each unit the student can find reading material, solved activities, proposed activities, explanatory videos and, as assessment tools, a quiz with multiple-choice questions and an activity returned to the tutor.

In the case of unit 10, the MEHI is included theoretical as the main tool of the -practical activity.

3 Sample Selection

255 students (Cohort 2020) of the Bachelor's degrees in Genetics and Industrial, Mechanical and Food Engineering participated in this experience.

4 Design of the Electrochemistry Unit 10 on the Platform

The unit includes:

- **Theory:** in Power point presentation with audio, with the topics

a) Commercial batteries
b) Corrosion

- **Theoretical-practical activity**

a) IHEM
b) Ion-electron and battery method (power point presentation used in the synchronous class)
c) Electrolytic cell (power point presentation used in the synchronous class)
d) Stack: problems solved and proposed
e) Electrolytic cell: solved and proposed problems

- **Evaluations**

a) Unit 10 quiz
b) Unit 10 Activities to be checked by tutor

5 Course Methodology

The development of the unit takes two weeks. The student has all the tools available from the beginning of the study unit. In the first week the study materials stack and ion electron method are reviewed, and as a theoretical and practical activity the IHEM tool develops the aspects related to the battery issue. During this week, two to one-hour synchronous activities are carried out to reinforce theoretical and practical content.

In the second week, the electrolytic cell and corrosion study materials are introduced, and as a theoretical-practical activity to use the chapter on Electrolytic Cell from the MEHI. During this week, two synchronous activities are carried out again, with similar aims to those of the previous week.

6 Data Collection Instruments

a) **Quiz.** The quiz consists of 5 questions with four options each. Students completed the quiz in 30 min. The system marks the quiz by question and the total score is calculated with feedback on incorrect choices.

b) **Test checked by tutor.** Students are provided with this activity from the beginning; they can download it and solve it as their learning develops. Once resolved, it is sent to the tutors for correction.

The proposed activity is the following:

1- Balance the following redox reaction by the Ion electron method $MnO_2 + KCl + H_2SO_4 \rightarrow KClO_3 + MnSO_4 + H_2O$
2- Balance the following redox reaction by the Ion electron method $MnO_2 + KClO_3 + KOH \rightarrow K_2MnO_4 + KCl + H_2O$
3- For the cell made up of Cd^{+2} (1 M)/Cd (s) and Ag^+ (0.1M)/Ag (s) Indicate: a) Hemi anodic and cathodic reaction b) Oxidizing and reducing agent. c) Stack notation or diagram d) Stack EMF
4- Calculate a pile has as half cells: Cu^{+2}/Cu and Ag^+/Ag. Write the global stack equation and calculate the equilibrium constant
5- An electric current flows for a certain time through two electrolytic cells connected in series. In cell A, 0.0240 g of Cu from a solution of. Cell B contains $AgNO_3$. ¿How many moles of Ag will be deposited on the cathode of cell B?

c) **Partial test and make-up partial tests.** The students must do two partial exams. In the second integrative exam, 4 units are included, among them unit 10 with the analyzed topics. This exam contains three questions related to that unit, which is assigned 10 points in Total. The exam is passed with 5 points. The students who do not pass the course, can do a make-up test similar to the first one. Table 1 shows the assessment tools used.

Table 1. Data collection instruments

Instrument	Evaluators	Application time
a) Questionnaire	Automatic by system	During the experience
b) Activity with answer	Tutors	During the experience
c) Partial exam	Tutors	After the experience
d) Rec. partial EXAM	Tutors	After the experience

7   Analysis of Results

a) **Quiz.** Of the 255 participant students, 210 questionnaires were received; but only 197 were included in the study, corresponding to the students who had also sent the activities checked by the tutor.

The quizzes were scored on a scale from 0 to 10, with automatic correction. The exam consists of 5 questions with a value of two points each. Each question has four options with one or more correct answers. For each incorrect answer the system deducted 25% of the score.

The data received is classified into a frequency table in four intervals: 0 to 4.00 points interpreted as Insufficient, 4.10 to 5.00 points interpreted as Acceptable, from 5.10 to 7.00 points Good and 7.10 to 10.00 points Very good. The absolute frequencies in the intervals were calculated, using an Excel spreadsheet and then the relative percentage frequency. The data obtained can be seen in Table 2.

Table 2. Relative frequencies by interval for the quiz

Unit 10 quiz				
Interpretation	Note range		Frequency	% relative frequency
	Lower limit	Upper limit		
Insufficient	0	4.00	60	30
Acceptable	4.10	5.00	18	9
Good	5.10	7.00	73	37
Very good	7.10	10.00	46	24
Total students			**197**	

b) **Tutor- assessed task.** 197 tasks were received. The activity had 5 questions, which, again, were assigned two points per question, if it was all correct. Partially correct questions were assigned a score from 0 to 2 according to the degree of resolution.

Obtained from the scores, is the calculation performed the absolute frequency and relative percentage in the same ranges as defined in the case of the questionnaire and the same meaning. The results data can be seen in Table 3.

Table 3. Relative frequencies by Tutor-assessed task

Tutor-assessed task unit 10				
Interpretation	Note range		Frequency	% relative frequency
	Lower limit	Upper limit		
Insufficient	0	4.00	55	28
Acceptable	4.10	5.00	31	16
OK	5.10	7.00	50	25
Very good	7,10	10.00	61	31
Total students			**197**	

b) **Partial and make-up tests.** Students sit for a second partial test, which included 4 thematic units including Electrochemistry (Unit 10). In this evaluation, consisting of a quiz of 10 questions, 3 correspond to that unit. Only the results corresponding to unit 10 were considered for this presentation.

Two of the questions were assigned a score of 3, while the others were assigned 4 points. In all cases, this score corresponds to a question correctly answered, subsequently subtracting said value, according to the degree of resolution carried out. With data from this evaluation, they were calculated f absolute and relative percentage frequency in same note intervals defined in the case of the quiz and the same meaning. The data obtained can be seen in Table 4.

Table 4. Relative frequencies per interval for the partial test

Partial test: unit 10 questions				
Interpretation	Note range		Frequency	% relative frequency
	Lower limit	Upper limit		
Insufficient	0	4.00	70	35
Acceptable	4.10	5.00	36	18
OK	5.10	7.00	38	19
Very good	7.10	10.00	50	28
Total students			**194**	

The students who did not get 5 points in the partial evaluation had to sit for, as previously mentioned, a recovery. The results and the data obtained can be seen in Table 5.

Table 5. Relative frequencies by Interval for make –up test.

Make –up test notes unit 10 questions				
Interpretation	Note range		Frequency	% relative frequency
	Lower limit	Upper limit		
Insufficient	0	4.00	29	37
Acceptable	4.10	5.00	16	20
OK	5.10	7.00	14	18
Very good	7.10	10.00	19	25
Total students			**78**	

Table 6 shows the percentage relative frequencies per interval obtained with the four assessment tools applied to the classroom experience performed using the IHEM: QUIZ, Activities checked by tutor, Partial and Make -up Partial test.

Table 6. Relative frequencies by interval for the four evaluations

Unit 10 assessments				
	Quiz	Activity	Partial	Make up partial
Insufficient	30	28	35	37
Acceptable	9	16	18	20
OK	37	25	19	18
Very good	24	31	28	25
N students	**197**	**197**	**194**	**78**

The Fig. 1 shows the relative frequencies valuations considered in the analysis, linked to the four evaluation tools.

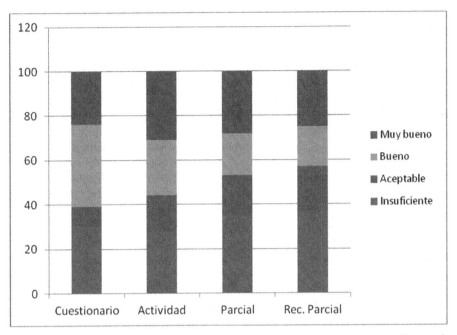

Fig. 1. Percentage relative frequencies for the four assessment tools corresponding to the assessments considered

8 Conclusions Obtained

The results obtained for the 2020 cohort are analyzed, which was developed in virtuality; and later, they are compared with those obtained in the previous pilot test.

In the first place, when analyzing the parameters obtained with the four assessment tools applied to the virtual experience using the IHEM: Quiz, Activities checked by tutor, Partial test and its make -up, it can be seen that the relative frequencies of the marks for each interval shows striking similarities. That is, the frequency for intervals of values Very Good, Good, Acceptable and Insufficient results are equivalent in the four tools used, which, as it can be concluded, similarly characterize the studied population.

During the pilot classroom experience, a proposal for flipped classroom with application of the MEHI was held in the 2019 cohort, in which six instruments of assessment were used: assessment of production phases, survey for teachers and students, activities to be checked by the tutor, Partial exam, Participant observation and Triangulation of data [10].

There were four activities checked by the tutor, carried out during the pilot experience, one for each chapter of the IHEM. The correct responses as a percentage of the maximum possible score for the four activities, ranged between 65% and 95%, with a number of evaluations analyzed that ranged from 20 to 27.

Comparatively, in the 2020 study, analyzing the results obtained with the quiz, the frequencies of the intervals Good (37%) and Very good (24%) add up to 61% with 197 quiz sent in a completely remote context. virtual experience.

In the case of the activities Tutor- assessed task in the 2020 experience, the frequencies for the Very Good and Good intervals add up to 56% with 197 activities analyzed. Showing that the results obtained in both experiences are similar.

In the partial examination then the pilot made of 2019 is working with three groups of 27 students each. One group took part in the experience, while the other two groups were controlled. The partial exam consisted of two exercises, A and B, about Electrochemistry. The data obtained expressed as a percentage of the maximum possible score for Exercise A was 41.1% while the controlled groups, the 15.5% and 15.9%. While for Exercise B, shows the group that used the IHEM obtained or 30% while the controls 21.1% and 16.3%.

In a study carried out during the virtual experience of 2020, in the first partial, adding the percentage frequencies of the intervals Good (19%) and Very good (28%) add up to 47% with 194 evaluations carried out. Comparing the results of both experiences midterms the data get gone, again, are similar.

Quantitative assessment tools applied in both experiences characterize the study sample similarly, although the population in the case of the virtual experience is 7 times larger.

While both experiences were carried out in different cohorts, and the didactic pedagogical proposals were different, the results of the experience in 2020 with a larger sample, it validates those obtained in the pilot. This larger sample (the entire 2020 cohort) was due to the prevailing virtual condition of the pandemic. The conditions likely to work for the first half of 2021 will allow for a new virtual experience with high samples.

References

1. Salinas, J.: Teaching innovation and use of ICT in university teaching. University and Knowledge Society Magazine (RUSC). UOC, vol. 1, no. 1 (2004)
2. Dell´Arciprete, R.: Proposal for Specialization in TIAE: survey of digital educational materials for the teaching and learning of Chemistry. Faculty of Informatics. UNLP (2013)
3. Mayer, R.E.: Introduction to multimedia learning. In: Mayer, R.E. (ed.) The Cambridge Handbook of Multimedia Learning, 2nd edn., pp. 1–25. Cambridge University Press, Cambridge (2014)
4. Litwin, E.: The office of teaching. Conditions and contexts, Paidós, Buenos Aires (2008)
5. Furió, C., Calatayud, M.L.: Difficulties with the geometry and polarity of molecules: beyond misconceptions. J. Chem. Educ. **73**, 37–41 (1996)
6. Furió, C., Furió, C.: Conceptual and epistemological difficulties in learning chemical processes. Chem. Educ. **11**(3), 300–308 (2000)
7. Jiménez, G., Llitjós, A.: Cooperation in telematic environments and the teaching of chemistry. Eureka Mag. Sci. Teach. Dissemination **3**(1), 115–133 (2006)
8. Deslie, N., Schwartzs, M.D.: Collaborative writing with hypertext. IEEE Trans. Prof. Commun. **32**(3), 183–188 (1989)
9. Whittington, C.D.: MOLE: computer-supported collaborative learning. Comput. Educ. **26**(1/3), 153–161 (1996)
10. García, R.G., Bertone, R.G.: IHEM - Interactive Hypermedial Educational Material for a General Chemistry course. Results of a classroom experience. CACIC 2020. Red UNCI. pp. 186–196 (2020). ISBN 978-987-4417-90-9

Graphic Computation, Images and Visualization

Stereoscopic Image-Based Rendering Technique for Low-Cost Virtual Reality

Matías N. Selzer[1,2]($^\boxtimes$), M. Luján Ganuza[1,2], Dana K. Urribarri[1,2], Martín L. Larrea[1,2], and Silvia M. Castro[1,2]

[1] VyGLab Research Laboratory, UNS-CICPBA, 8000 Bahía Blanca, Argentina
[2] Institute for Computer Science and Engineering, CONICET-UNS, Bahía Blanca, Argentina
{matias.selzer,mlg,dku,mll,smc}@cs.uns.edu.ar
http://vyglab.cs.uns.edu.ar

Abstract. Mobile phones offer an excellent low-cost alternative for Virtual Reality. However, the hardware constraints of these devices restrict the displayable visual complexity of graphics. Image-Based Rendering techniques arise as an alternative to solve this problem, but usually, generating the stereoscopic effect to improve depth perception presents a challenging problem. In this work, we present an Image-Based Rendering technique for low-cost virtual reality that incorporates stereoscopy to improve depth perception. We also conducted a user evaluation to analyze the stereoscopic effect of the technique, especially considering the effect on depth perception, presence, and navigation. The results prove the benefits of our technique for both virtual and real-world environments.

Keywords: Virtual Reality · Low-Cost VR · Navigation · Image-Based Rendering

1 Introduction

Virtual Reality (VR) is an already established technology that immerses users into computer-generated 3D environments. In the last years, many different VR systems have been developed and most of them are very expensive for the regular consumer. VR is advancing as a very versatile alternative for a variety of applications in multiple areas as diverse as entertainment, medical, education, tourism, and architecture, among many others. This strong interest in VR is reinforced by the rapid evolution of the technology and the possibility of applying it in everyday devices, demanding the creation of increasingly realistic applications. On the other hand, there are low-cost alternatives that use mobile phones. This low-cost VR brings a new world of possibilities to those users who cannot afford a high-end VR system [1,2].

Since mobile devices usually present hardware and graphical processing limitations, compared to modern gaming computers, the video games and experiences designed for this type of VR are graphically very simple.

© Springer Nature Switzerland AG 2021
P. Pesado and J. Eterovic (Eds.): CACIC 2020, CCIS 1409, pp. 91–101, 2021.
https://doi.org/10.1007/978-3-030-75836-3_7

In recent years there has been tremendous growth in the number and variety of GPU-intensive mobile applications, enabling users to interact and navigate virtual environments. Given their high demand on both application data and network and computing resources, a key element in designing cost-effective mobile applications is the careful consideration of these resources according to the application goals.

Traditional geometry rendering and image-based rendering (IBR) are two of the most popular render techniques for this purpose. Even though traditional geometry rendering can be used to overcome some of the performance limitations of mobile devices by integrating progressive meshes and using catching and restricting objects resolution techniques, rendering high visual-quality 3D scenes on limited mobile devices still obtains a very low level of performance [3–7]. IBR, on the other hand, is a technique that emerged in the late 1990s to overcome this kind of limitations, especially when representing photo-realistic 3D scenes in real-time [8–10]. This rendering process requires less computational resources than traditional geometry rendering.

Even though some of the most recent methods generate new views based on captured panoramas from both video and images, these methods only run on PC and free navigation is not available. Also, the synthesis of intermediate views is performed by computationally intensive warping and interpolation techniques [11,12]. The main issue with some of the approaches that include image interpolation and free navigation is that they only run on PC [13–17]. In 2019, Dai et al. [16] proposed a method based on panoramic images, supporting the free exploration of the scene with a 360° field of view, but they synthesized new views using an intensive warping algorithm, part of which was carried out offline. In [13] they present an IBR system to interactively viewpoint-navigate through space and time of general real-world, dynamic scenes (camera recording arrangements). It is a free-viewpoint navigation system but the virtual viewpoint is spatially restricted because they can viewpoint-navigate on the spanned by all camera recording positions, looking at the scene from different directions, but they cannot move into the scene or fly through it. For high-quality rendering results, they observed that the angle between adjacent cameras should not exceed 10 degrees, independent of scene content. For greater distances, missing scene information appears to become too large to still achieve convincing interpolation results. The same is true for too fast scene motion.

The literature presents different approaches for mobile devices that manage different image types and qualities [8,18]. Some approaches generate high-quality scenes in a server [19,20]. IBR is more suitable to represent high-quality 3D scenes in mobile devices since the rendering is based on images that do not depend on the scene complexity but the final image resolution.

Stereopsis enables a very strong depth cue that is very powerful in VR. Many studies have investigated the relative importance of stereopsis for different tasks. Some performed path tracing experiments where the participants had to find the endpoint of a line. The target line was presented among other distracting lines on a 3D display that allowed experiencing stereopsis [21,22].

The use of binocular stereopsis and 3D displays also improves spatial comprehension and the performance of spatial understanding tasks [23]. Another study that showed a benefit of stereopsis was reported by Hassaine et al. [24], in which stereopsis showed to be more valuable in visual tasks regarding reaching objects.

In another behavioral study, Boustila et al. [25] implemented a technique to evaluate the influence of stereopsis in the context of visiting houses using VR. They used a CAVE VR system and the participants traveled to virtual houses where they had to answer questions about the geometry of the rooms and the difficulty of the task. The results indicated that stereopsis was very valuable for judging the geometry of the rooms. The perceived task difficulty was also higher when stereopsis was removed.

In our previous work, we introduced a novel technique to display high visual-quality 3D scenes in low-cost VR devices [26]. That technique simulates a 3D environment by using a spherical-panorama 3D-texture matrix and dynamic image warping for a smooth transition between image points. Also, a performance evaluation was performed.

The mentioned technique immerses the user in a fully navigable virtual environment created by spherical panoramic images. The technique also calculates the image that corresponds to the current camera point of view. Even though the user is immersed in an image-based virtual environment, the stereoscopic effect is not provided since both eyes are presented with the same image.

In this paper, we extend the work presented at CACIC 2020 [26] to include the stereoscopic effect, thus improving depth perception. More specifically, the present work yields a fully 3D stereo VR navigation through the following contributions:

- A novel IBR technique for low-cost VR that simulates a stereo view in a 3D environment by using two spherical panorama 3D textures, one for each eye.
- A novel image warping technique that enables a smooth transition between image points for both eyes, thus simulating a stereoscopic effect.

2   Technique Overview

The original technique presented a novel Image-Based Rendering technique based on spherical panoramic images to simulate high-visual quality 3D environments for low-cost VR devices. Considering a user that is navigating through a virtual environment, one of the main goals of this technique is to efficiently present the corresponding view. In such visualization, the virtual environment is not rendered in 3D as usual, but instead, it is simulated by using stored images that correspond to the user's current point of view.

2.1   Image Repository

The Image Repository is a component that stores a set of 360° panoramic images that represent the original virtual environment that we want to simulate. In order to get these images, the environment has to be sampled by capturing 360° panoramic images from different and specific positions.

It is important to mention that one of the benefits of our technique is that all the images stored in the Image Repository do not necessarily have to be captured from a rendered 3D environment. They can also be taken from a real-life environment by taking the pictures separated by a Δ distance. In order to calculate and generate a better projection, the Warping Component requires the approximate dimensions of each room in the environment. This can also be provided by the Image Repository together with the images. If for any reason these measurements are not provided, our technique uses approximations. The Image Repository must be able to send images on demand. For example, an Apache HTTP Server[1] running in a local computer can be used.

2.2   Local Image Management - Texture Matrix

The Texture Matrix is a component that loads, stores, and manages the 360° panoramic images in the local memory of the device. Those images correspond to the current position of the cameras and their surroundings. This matrix is eventually capable of storing every sample of the scene.

In an ideal case, where memory size is not a problem, it would be possible to retrieve from the Image Repository and store in memory all the 360° panoramic images captured from the original scene, avoiding depending in the future on the download times of the server. Unfortunately, this is not possible, especially considering the low-memory of mobile devices. This restriction presents the challenge of efficiently loading and managing images.

The Texture Matrix works efficiently since a small number of images is loaded in memory at any time. These images correspond to the current camera position and its surroundings. Every time the camera moves, the Texture Matrix is updated. Furthermore, the images located at a certain distance from the current position of the camera are deleted, thus the matrix is cleaned.

2.3   Image Warping

When the camera moves, the Image Warping component calculates and generates a new image that corresponds to the specific camera's current position. This avoids the user from noticing jumps between samples. For this reason, a smooth function for transitions was implemented [26].

Let us assume that two contiguous spherical panoramic images $\mathcal{I}_A$ and $\mathcal{I}_B$ were taken at points A and B, then if the user stands at one of those points the system shows the corresponding image. However, while the user is moving from point A to B the system should show an intermediate image that smoothly switches from $\mathcal{I}_A$ to $\mathcal{I}_B$.

The only information we have about the panoramic images is the point in space where it was taken, and the room to which it belongs. However, we do not

---

[1] https://httpd.apache.org/.

have the real depth information of the objects in the image, hence to simplify and allow rooms of any shape, we consider that the spherical panoramic images correspond to an equirectangular projection of a circular room that fully contains the original one (see Fig. 1).

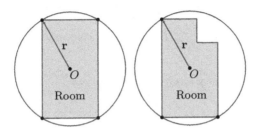

Fig. 1. Cross-section of the sphere with center O and radius r containing two different rooms.

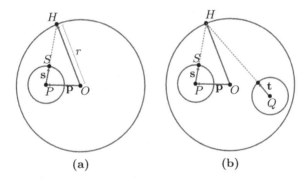

(a)   (b)

Fig. 2. Cross-section of a room centered at O and two unitary spheres centered at P and Q. (a) Point H over the room corresponding to the projection S. The unitary sphere is centered at P, where the equirectangular panoramic image $\mathcal{I}_P$ was taken. (b) Projection of point H over the unitary sphere centered at Q, where no image was taken.

Let O be the center of the circle of radius r that contains the room, Q be the point where the user stands and P be the point where the nearest panoramic image $\mathcal{I}_P$ was taken. The strategy is to warp $\mathcal{I}_P$ to match the panoramic image that should have been taken from the point of view of Q. If $(u, v) \in [0, 1]^2$ is a texture coordinate over the panoramic image $\mathcal{I}_P$, we invert the projection to obtain the point S over a unitary sphere centered at P that projects onto (u, v) (see Fig. 2a). Since the panoramic image is the result of a equirectangular projection, the vector $\mathbf{s}$ between P and S is:

$$\mathbf{s} = (x, y, z) = (\sin(\phi)\cos(\theta), \sin(\theta)\sin(\phi), \cos(\phi)), \qquad (1)$$

where

$$\theta = 2u\pi \tag{2}$$

and

$$phi = v\pi. \tag{3}$$

Now, let H be the point over the room of radius r that projects on S. Then,

$$H = k\mathbf{s} + \mathbf{p} \tag{4}$$

where

$$\mathbf{p} = Q - O, |k\mathbf{s} + \mathbf{p}| = r \tag{5}$$

and

$$k = \frac{-(\mathbf{p} \cdot \mathbf{s}) + \sqrt{(\mathbf{p} \cdot \mathbf{s})^2 - |\mathbf{s}|^2(|\mathbf{p}|^2 + r^2)}}{|\mathbf{s}|^2}. \tag{6}$$

To warp the image to match the point of view of Q, we find the projection $\mathbf{t}$ of H over the unitary sphere centered at Q (see Fig. 2b),

$$\mathbf{t} = \frac{H - Q}{|H - Q|}. \tag{7}$$

Finally, the 2D projection (u, v) of $\mathbf{t} = (x, y, z)$ over the equirectangular texture is

$$(u, v) = (\frac{\theta}{2\pi}, \frac{\phi}{\pi}) \tag{8}$$

where

$$\theta = \text{atan2}(y, x) \tag{9}$$

and

$$\phi = \text{atan2}(\sqrt{x^2 + y^2}, z). \tag{10}$$

The next section presents an example of this Image Warping technique in action.

3   Technique Methodology

In order to generate the stereoscopic effect, we need to dynamically obtain the images corresponding to both eyes. The interpupillary distance (IPD) is the distance measured in millimeters between the centers of the pupils of the eyes. This measurement is different from person to person and this technique allows users to input their IPD. Otherwise, a general IPD of 64 mm is used.

As mentioned before, we have extended the technique presented in [26] to incorporate stereopsis. In the first step of the technique process, the images that correspond to the user's eyes are calculated, based on the user's IPD. The technique main steps are described next, following the example presented in Fig. 3:

1. The user's position is represented by a point denominated *camera center*. Therefore, the left camera is represented by a position on the left of the camera center, with a distance of -IPD/2; and the right camera is represented by a position on the right of the camera center, with a distance of IPD/2. In this step, every time the user moves, the camera center informs its current position to the Texture Matrix component. In this example, the camera center is at the position $(1.0; 1.7; 3.28)$ and the technique must obtain the image corresponding to that position.

2. The Image Repository does not contain images for every decimal value. This depends on the capture technique used. For this reason, the Texture Matrix requests the nearest available image and the surrounding ones to the Image Repository. If any of the images are already in the Texture Matrix, that image is not requested.

3. The Image Repository sends the requested images to the Texture Matrix component. The necessary images are now loaded into the Texture Matrix in the local memory.

4. The Texture Matrix component sends the nearest image corresponding to the camera center's current position to the Image Warping component.

5. Based on the provided image, the Image Warping component calculates and generates images that correspond exactly to the camera center's current position and, by considering the IPD, it calculates and generates the image that corresponds to the left eye and the right eye.

6. Finally, the new left eye image is displayed to the left camera and the right eye image to the right camera, thus simulating the scene from the point of view of the camera's current position and generating also a stereoscopic effect based on the user IPD.

This process is continuously repeating as the user is moving, creating the sensation of a smooth transition through the virtual environment.

4 Case Study

This technique is especially useful for mobile devices with limited resources since performance evaluations have shown it performs better than traditional geometry rendering [26]. In this study we present a case study to evaluate the stereoscopic effect.

For this study, we used a 3D virtual scenario called "Doctor's Office" [27] that runs in Unity3d [28]. Regarding the hardware, we used the mobile phone *Le Eco Max 2* which has Android 6.0.1, a screen resolution of 2560×1440 pixels, Adreno (TM) 530 GPU, 2048 MB VRAM, Quad-core 2.1 GHz Snapdragon-820 GPU, and 5774 MB RAM.

A tool called Unity360ScreenshotCapture [29] was used to create the image dataset. This tool helps to create a 360° panoramic image based on the position of the virtual camera. By doing this, the whole dataset is created automatically by iterating along the desired volume.

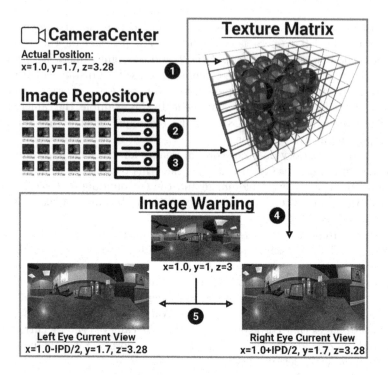

Fig. 3. Technique overview.

In order to create the dataset, we need to define the boundaries of the used virtual scenario, and the distance between samples we want to use. Since the average distance between both eyes is approximately 6 cm, a distance between samples below 4.24 cm will assure that both eyes see different images [15], thus improving the stereoscopic effect. For this reason, in this experiment we considered samples separated by 4 cm.

In this experiment, since the camera is not moving in the y axis, all images were taken on a fixed height of 1.68 m. We covered an area of 20 m × 27 m, and with a distance between samples of 4 cm, this conforms a total of 337500 samples. The images size was 1024px × 512px each. Hence, the total size of the dataset is around 18 GB. Finally, the name of each image file corresponded to the position where it was captured. For instance, the image "0.1 4.5 7.3.jpg" corresponds to the image captured on position $(0.1, 4.5, 7.3)$.

In order to test the stereoscopic effect, three participants navigated through the image-based virtual environment. We measured the IPD of each participant, which was configured in the system. After that, the participants put on the low-cost VR headset with the mobile phone and started the experience.

The participants had up to 10 min to navigate through the environment by using a wireless joystick. They could withdraw the experiment at any time in case they felt cybersickness symptoms. After that, they were interviewed about the whole experience, especially considering the stereoscopic effect.

The three participants reported having a very strong stereoscopic effect and sense of depth perception. They mentioned that the distance of the scene objects was noticeable, which provided a strong sense of presence. One of them complained about the environment being "too big", which may be caused by some error in the provided IPD. On the other hand, the three participants commented about the use of a joystick for navigation and suggested other alternatives, such as real walking or walking-in-place.

5   Conclusions and Future Work

In this paper, we extend a novel IBR technique designed to present high-quality virtual environments in low-cost VR devices. VR headsets benefit from the stereoscopic effect achieved by the device being near the user's face. Improving the technique with stereoscopic effect increases the users' depth perception and improves the sense of presence.

In this work, we used a very small distance between samples (4 cm) to assure a different image provided to each user's eye. However, our technique works for any distance between samples. As expected, bigger distances would cause strange deformations that may cause cybersickness symptoms. This effect is more noticeable for near objects in the environment. Future work should therefore perform a user evaluation regarding the limits on sample distance and cybersickness symptoms.

To properly use our technique, an image server is required. This brings many advantages. First, the size of the exported mobile application would be very small. Then, many mobile phones can be running at the same time and use the same image dataset without replicating the images. Also, if needed, the images can be altered, optimized, adjusted, etc., and the technique will still work. If we want to change the virtual environment, we can only change the images and the applications do not have to be compiled again. Finally, the server not necessarily has to be hosted locally. The images can be hosted online and the technique will still work for any mobile phone connected to the Internet.

In this work, we used sample images separated by 4 cm. However, some trade-offs should be considered when selecting the distance between samples. When covering the same area, the less the distance between samples, the more samples that will be required. The size of a sample depends on its size and quality. This directly impacts the total size of the dataset. Furthermore, the less the size of a sample, the faster that sample can be downloaded and displayed. If the images can be downloaded faster, the user would be able to move faster around the virtual environment.

We performed a case study designed to evaluate the effectiveness and usefulness of the included stereoscopic effect. The technique takes advantage of the efficiency of the Texture Matrix Component which already had the images surrounding the camera center position. Therefore, the communication overhead between the system and the server is not increased.

The inclusion of the stereoscopic effect was shown to increase the sense of depth perception and thus the sense of presence. The participants commented about the navigation technique and future work should therefore study different navigation techniques to allow more natural navigation through the virtual environment.

Since our technique does not depend on the complexity of the scene, it will also work with real-world images. To do this, the real-world environment has to be sampled by capturing 360° panoramic spherical pictures delimited by a defined distance. Future work should investigate the use of real-world images, especially considering the navigation techniques to provide a very natural experience.

References

1. Selzer, M.N., Gazcon, N.F., Larrea, M.L.: Effects of virtual presence and learning outcome using low-end virtual reality systems. Displays **59**, 9–15 (2019)
2. Selzer, M.N., Larrea, M.L., Castro, S.M.: Realidad virtual: maximizando presencia, inmersión y usabilidad. In: XXII Workshop de Investigadores en Ciencias de la Computación, WICC 2020, El Calafate, Santa Cruz (2020)
3. Engel, K., Sommer, O., Ertl, T.: A framework for interactive hardware accelerated remote 3d-visualization. In: de Leeuw, W.C., van Liere, R. (eds.) Data visualization 2000. Eurographics, pp. 167–177. Springer, Vienna (2000). https://doi.org/10.1007/978-3-7091-6783-0_17
4. Ma, J., Chen, Q., Chen, B., Wang, H.: Mobile 3D graphics compression for progressive transmission over wireless network. In: 11th IEEE Interenational Conference on CAD and Computer Graphics, pp. 357–362. IEEE (2009)
5. Isenburg, M., Lindstrom, P.: Streaming meshes. In: VIS 2005. IEEE Visualization, 2005, pp. 231–238. IEEE (2005)
6. Shen, Z., Liu, J., Zheng, Y., Cao, L.: A low-cost mobile VR walkthrough system for displaying multimedia works based on Unity3D. In: 14th International Conference on Computer Science & Education (ICCSE), pp. 415–419. IEEE (2019)
7. Fathy, G., Hassan, H., Sheta, W., Bahgat, R.: Efficient framework for mobile walkthrough application. Pervasive Mob. Comput. **18**, 40–54 (2015)
8. Chen, S.E.: Quicktime VR: an image-based approach to virtual environment navigation. In: Proceedings of the 22nd Annual Conference on Computer Graphics and Interactive Techniques, pp. 29–38 (1995)
9. Noimark, Y., Cohen-Or, D.: Streaming scenes to MPEG-4 video-enabled devices. IEEE Comput. Graph. Appl. **23**(1), 58–64 (2003)
10. Chim, J., Lau, R.W., Leong, H.V., Si, A.: Cyberwalk: a web-based distributed virtual walkthrough environment. IEEE T. Multimed. **5**(4), 503–515 (2003)
11. Kowdle, A., Sinha, S.N., Szeliski, R.: Multiple view object cosegmentation using appearance and stereo cues. In: Fitzgibbon, A., Lazebnik, S., Perona, P., Sato, Y., Schmid, C. (eds.) ECCV 2012. LNCS, vol. 7576, pp. 789–803. Springer, Heidelberg (2012). https://doi.org/10.1007/978-3-642-33715-4_57
12. Chaurasia, G., Duchene, S., Sorkine-Hornung, O., Drettakis, G.: Depth synthesis and local warps for plausible image-based navigation. ACM Trans. Graph. (TOG) **32**(3), 1–12 (2013)

13. Lipski, C., Linz, C., Berger, K., Sellent, A., Magnor, M.: Virtual video camera: image-based viewpoint navigation through space and time. In: Computer Graphics Forum, vol. 29, pp. 2555–2568. Wiley Library (2010)
14. Stich, T., Linz, C., Wallraven, C., Cunningham, D., Magnor, M.: Perception-motivated interpolation of image sequences. ACM Trans. Appl. Percept. (TAP) 8(2), 1–25 (2011)
15. Zhang, Y., Zhu, Z.: Walk-able and stereo virtual tour based on spherical panorama matrix. In: De Paolis, L.T., Bourdot, P., Mongelli, A. (eds.) AVR 2017. LNCS, vol. 10324, pp. 50–58. Springer, Cham (2017). https://doi.org/10.1007/978-3-319-60922-5_4
16. Dai, F., Zhu, C., Ma, Y., Cao, J., Zhao, Q., Zhang, Y.: Freely explore the scene with 360° field of view. In: IEEE Conference on Virtual Reality and 3D User Interfaces (VR), pp. 888–889. IEEE (2019)
17. Liu, C., Shibusawa, S., Yonekura, T.: A walkthrough system with improved map projection panoramas from omni directional images. In: 7th International Conference on Ubiquitous Intelligence & Computing and 7th International Conference on Autonomic & Trusted Computing, pp. 45–51. IEEE (2010)
18. Lei, Yu., Jiang, Z., Chen, D., Bao, H.: Image-based walkthrough over internet on mobile devices. In: Jin, H., Pan, Y., Xiao, N., Sun, J. (eds.) GCC 2004. LNCS, vol. 3252, pp. 728–735. Springer, Heidelberg (2004). https://doi.org/10.1007/978-3-540-30207-0_89
19. Doellner, J., Hagedorn, B., Klimke, J.: Server-based rendering of large 3D scenes for mobile devices using G-buffer cube maps. In: Proceedings of the 17th International Conference on 3D Web Technology, pp. 97–100 (2012)
20. Reinert, B., Kopf, J., Ritschel, T., Cuervo, E., Chu, D., Seidel, H.P.: Proxy-guided image-based rendering for mobile devices. In: Computer Graphics Forum, vol. 35, pp. 353–362. Wiley Library (2016)
21. Naepflin, U., Menozzi, M.: Can movement parallax compensate lacking stereopsis in spatial explorative search tasks? Displays 22(5), 157–164 (2001)
22. van Beurden, M.H., Kuijsters, A., IJsselsteijn, W.A.: Performance of a path tracing task using stereoscopic and motion based depth cues. In: 2010 Second International Workshop on Quality of Multimedia Experience (QoMEX), pp. 176–181. IEEE (2010)
23. McIntire, J.P., Liggett, K.K.: The (possible) utility of stereoscopic 3D displays for information visualization: the good, the bad, and the ugly. In: 2014 IEEE VIS International Workshop on 3dvis (3dvis), pp. 1–9. IEEE (2014)
24. Hassaine, D., Holliman, N.S., Liversedge, S.P.: Investigating the performance of path-searching tasks in depth on multiview displays. ACM Trans. Appl. Percept. (TAP) 8(1), 1–18 (2010)
25. Boustila, S., Bechmann, D., Capobianco, A.: Effects of adding visual cues on distance estimation, presence and simulator sickness during virtual visits using wall screen. In: Proceedings of the Computer Graphics International Conference, pp. 1–6 (2017)
26. Selzer, M.N., Ganuza, M.L., Urribarri, D.K., Larrea, M.L., Castro, S.M.: Simulation of high-visual quality scenes in low-cost virtual reality. In: XXVI Congreso Argentino de Ciencias de la Computación (CACIC) (Modalidad virtual, 5 al 9 de octubre de 2020) (2020)
27. Studio, B.P.: Doctorsoffice (2020). http://sojaexiles.com/. Accessed July 2020
28. Unity: Unity3d (2020). https://unity.com. Accessed July 2020
29. yasirkula: Unity3d (2020). https://github.com/yasirkula/. Accessed July 2020

Software Engineering

Systematic Literature Review on the Implementation of Software Architectures for Critical Systems

Joaquín Acevedo, Andrea Lezcano, Juan Pinto Oppido, and Emanuel Irrazábal[✉]

Grupo de Investigación en Innovación de Software y Sistemas Computacionales,
FaCENA – UNNE, Corrientes, Argentina
{jacevedo,alezcano,jpoppido,eirrazabal}@exa.unne.edu.ar

Abstract. Context: critical systems present specific functionalities and a set of regulatory best practices which seek to ensure minimum security levels at each life cycle stage. This defines restrictions on the software present in critical systems that require integration with hardware, the latter being a characteristic present in embedded systems. Therefore, it is possible to find techniques that can meet the required safety levels, but using different strategies and resources. Objective: execute and report a systematic secondary study on the software architectures applied in the domain of critical systems, the level of security achieved and the tools used to achieve it. Method: a systematic literature review was used to identify studies published from January 1999 to December 2019 on software architectures for critical systems. Results: the most widely used types of architecture were identified according to the intended security level. Likewise, study evidence was found in different application domains, with special emphasis on automotive and industrial regulations.

Keywords: ISO 61508 · Architecture · Software · Secondary study · Systematic literature review

1 Introduction

1.1 A Subsection Sample

It is becoming more and more common to work with dedicated purpose systems, especially in applications such as industrial processes, automotive, or avionics. In particular, certain applications are used in critical environments in such a way that failures could cause financial loss or even human life loss [1]. In response to this, there are regulatory frameworks that stipulate the need to demonstrate the safety of the built system. Regarding embedded software, the main standards in critical systems come from the IEC 61508 - part 3. In addition, the IEC 61508 standard details the concept of safety integrity level (SIL) which provides a scale against which to measure and quantify the safety level of a system, from SIL 1, the lowest possible level, up to SIL 4.

P. Pesado and J. Eterovic (Eds.): CACIC 2020, CCIS 1409, pp. 105–122, 2021.
https://doi.org/10.1007/978-3-030-75836-3_8

The appropriate treatment of the characteristics of the software in charge of controlling industrial processes was a recurrent matter since the modernization and diversification of industrial applications. The regulation of this aspect started with the standardization of functional safety measures in the field of critical systems with the publication of the IEC 61508 standard [1] in 1998. Thus, for example, the automotive industry and its ISO 26262 standard [2] establishes the automotive safety integrity levels (ASIL) or the avionics industry and its DO-178B standard [3] that establishes the development assurance levels (DAL).

In particular, section 7.4.3 of the IEC 61508-3 standard specifies best practices when building the software architecture in terms of activities, documentation, comprehensive specification of each module of the architecture and use of programming best practices. From the point of view of this standard, the software architecture consists of the definition of the subsystems or modules together with their interconnections and, especially, the way in which the SIL level is achieved. It also defines the general behavior of the software, its interfaces, and the decisions that will underpin the detailed component design techniques.

Therefore, the choices of the types of software architecture that comply with the aforementioned good practices can be complex. Currently there are different studies that present software architectures for critical systems, but standard architectures by level of comprehensive security and oriented to cover the largest number of problem domains do not emerge.

For all these reasons, in this article a Systematic Literature Review (SLR) has been carried out to identify common software architectures in software development for critical systems that have been shown to be validated for certain security levels. Likewise, application domains and related technologies have been analyzed.

The paper is organized as follows: Sect. 2 describes secondary studies related to the subject. In Sect. 3, the methodology used for the study corresponding to the planning phase of an SLR is detailed and the research questions are presented in Table 1. In Sect. 4 the activities corresponding to the SLR conduction stage are reported. Section 5 provides the results obtained; for its presentation, the results of 23 studies were synthesized and the research questions were answered. Finally, Sect. 6 includes the conclusion of the SLR.

2 Related Works

There are works related to the objective of this review and that provide a state of the art about different issues related to architectures for critical systems. In [4] the authors present a systematic mapping of the literature focused on model-based tests for software security. This study includes an analysis of different publications that present software development on a specific domain of software security. However, questions related to security levels are not included. In [5] the state of the art of combining model-driven engineering techniques and product line engineering for the development of software architectures for critical systems is presented. In this case, the questions are focused on identifying studies that deal with embedded systems from the dimension of model-driven engineering. This approach compromises the internal validity of the evidenced techniques and the requirements that ensure the criticality of the systems resulting from the techniques recorded in the secondary study are not discussed in depth.

Also, in [6] a characterization of different techniques used to represent software architectures for embedded systems is presented. The associated risks of complying with critical system architectures are discussed without including a direct analysis of the security level. For all these reasons, this review differs from the mentioned reviews as follows:

- Norms and standards related to critical systems are identified.
- Includes studies published from 1999 to 2019.
- The relationship between software architectures and the level of security they present is characterized when considering their application in a critical system.
- The technology used for the development of architectures is described.
- An analysis of each included study is provided in terms of rigor, validity and applicability.

The present study is an extension of the work [7], having been extended including in the report of the RSL more details about the search strategy, the data synthesis and the data discussion.

3 Methodology

This section describes the method used to carry out the secondary study. In this case, the approach identified by the guidelines for conducting Systematic Literature Reviews

Table 1. Research questions

Research question	Motivation
RQ 1. What software architectures exist for critical software?	Identify the different software architectures in the field of application of critical systems and the frequency of their use and reporting in academic studies
RQ 2. What regulations do they comply with?	Identify the regulations that were presented as requirements to be met by the architectures presented and the degree of compliance with them
RQ 3. What level of security do they verify?	Determine the evaluation carried out regarding compliance with the level of security that the software architecture presents
RQ 4.1 What technologies do they use?	Determine the technologies used for the development of software architectures and their ability to achieve compliance with the requirements included in the regulations
RQ 4.2 What platforms are used?	Identify the platforms on which software architectures are developed, if proprietary or open source, own or third-party tools are used
RQ 5. What are the application domains?	Determine the evaluation carried out regarding compliance with the level of security that the software architecture presents
RQ 6. What are the reported activities?	Determine the technologies used for the development of software architectures and their ability to achieve compliance with the requirements included in the regulations

in Software Engineering [8] has been followed. As described in the introduction to this work, the objective of this SLR is to identify the software architectures used for critical applications of embedded systems, the evidence of compliance with international regulations and the technologies used for it. The analysis is based on research questions found in Table 1.

3.1 Search Strategy

This section describes the search strategy, explaining the scope in terms of sources, the method used and the search string. The searches were performed manually and systematically. The automated search was carried out through the entry of search strings in the search engines of the digital sources. The manual search was effectuated through the exploration of the important sources. The specific implementation of the search string for each chosen database was similar in each case and is presented in Table 2.

Table 2. Syntax of the search string for each digital library.

Search engine	Search string
SCOPUS	TITLE-ABS-KEY ((embedded OR "safety*" OR "functional safety" OR critical OR "mission-critical" OR "fault tolerance" OR "fault tolerant" OR "fault-tolerance" OR "fault-tolerant" OR sil OR ssil OR rams) AND (architect* OR "architectural pattern" OR "architectural design" OR design) AND (software OR application OR "source code" OR firmware) AND (61508 OR 61508–3 OR 50128 OR misra OR "MISRA C" OR 62279 OR do-178* OR 26262))
IEEE	("All Metadata": embedded OR safety* OR "functional safety" OR critical OR "mission-critical" OR "fault tolerance" OR "fault tolerant" OR "fault-tolerance" OR "fault-tolerant" OR sil OR ssil OR rams) AND ("All Metadata":architect* OR "architectural pattern" OR "architectural design" OR design) AND ("All Metadata":software OR application OR "source code" OR firmware) AND (61508 OR 61508–3 OR 50128 OR misra OR "MISRA C" OR 62279 OR do-178* OR 26262)
ACM	((embedded OR safety* OR "functional safety" OR critical OR "mission-critical" OR "fault tolerance" OR "fault tolerant" OR "fault-tolerance" OR "fault-tolerant" OR sil OR ssil OR rams)AND (architect* OR "architectural pattern" OR "architectural design" OR design)AND (software OR application OR "source code" OR firmware) AND (61508 OR 61508–3 OR 50128 OR misra OR "MISRA C" OR 62279 OR do-178* OR 26262))
SPRINGER	((embedded OR safety* OR "functional safety" OR critical OR "mission-critical" OR "fault tolerance" OR "fault tolerant" OR "fault-tolerance" OR "fault-tolerant" OR sil OR ssil OR rams)AND (architect* OR "architectural pattern" OR "architectural design" OR design)AND (software OR application OR "source code" OR firmware) AND (61508 OR 61508–3 OR 50128 OR misra OR "MISRA C" OR 62279 OR do-178* OR 26262))

It was decided to search databases containing articles related to computer science and engineering. The databases generally used in other reviews of the same subject were used: Scopus, IEEE Xplore, ACM Digital Library and Springer Link. The article was made based on the review of publications in magazines, conferences and articles. Table 3 presents each term together with its keywords.

Table 3. Key terms and synonyms used to create the search string.

Terms	Keywords
Safety	"safety*" OR "functional safety" OR critical OR "mission-critical" OR "fault tolerance" OR "fault tolerant" OR "fault-tolerance" OR "fault-tolerant" OR sil OR ssil OR rams
Architecture	architect* OR "architectural pattern" OR "architectural design" OR design
Software	software OR application OR "source code" OR firmware
61508	61508 OR 61508–3 OR 50128 OR MISRA OR "MISRA C" OR 62279 OR do-178* OR 26262

3.2 Search Strategy

Articles referring to the development of software architectures for applications in critical systems, which present a level of security and published since 1999 in indexed journals and at conferences are included. Tool description or use articles, duplicates, and conference presentations are excluded. Regarding content, studies that describe, implement or evaluate requirements description languages are excluded.

Table 4. Study inclusion criteria.

Identifier	Description
CRI1	The article belongs to a prestigious database
CRI2	Full access to the article is provided
CRI3	The publication date of the article is after 1998
CRI4	The article deals with quality regulations and/or risk treatment
CRI5	The model (s) discussed in the article have a section on risk treatment with a standard metric (SIL, ASIL)
CRE1	The article is focused on testing software architectures
CRE2	The article treats only hardware architectures
CRE3	The article uses a software architecture as an example to demonstrate the reliability of a framework or framework without presenting specifications
CRE3	The article uses a software architecture as an example to demonstrate the reliability of a framework or framework without presenting specifications
CRI1	The article belongs to a prestigious database

To select the primary studies, the inclusion/exclusion criteria are applied by reading the abstracts of the articles found. The identifier with a CRI prefix indicates that it is an inclusion criterion and the CRE prefix, that it is one of exclusion (Table 4).

In case there are doubts about its relevance, the full article will be read. The review process will be accompanied by the criteria of the researchers to agree on the correct application of the inclusion/exclusion criteria.

3.3 Strategy for Data Extraction and Synthesis

The procedure used for data extraction consists of a first ordering of all the publications resulting from the query to the research database in a spreadsheet respecting the export identifiers of the source added to a control field to indicate the status of inclusion or exclusion of the article. Each database has its own fields to index publications, therefore, after reaching the set of all the studies to include in the study, all their identifiers were normalized.

To perform the synthesis of the data, each accepted publication was organized in a directory according to the access source. Labels were then created to identify each analysis dimension corresponding to the criteria on the research questions. The result of this procedure was to present the information of each publication that means concise descriptions related to the research questions.

The data obtained were qualitatively analyzed through the open coding of the texts [9]. The first and second authors carried out the process separately and identified disagreements, these were resolved by adding a third researcher who visited the information source again and considered the justifications given by the two original members. As the next step, closed coding [10] was used to identify and resignify the categories analyzed. Again, the first two study authors performed the initial coding and disagreements were resolved by presentation to a third investigator.

4   Conducting the Review

The SLR was carried out following all the steps of the protocol defined in the previous section and completed in one year, in this period the time required for each of the three phases is included, that is, planning, carrying out and reporting. Initially, 7550 publications were found. Each search phase is detailed in Table 5 and Table 6.

4.1 Selection of Primary Studies

At this stage of selection of the primary studies are the assurance criteria, application of the assurance criteria and extraction of data from the articles. A total of 7550 articles were found applying the search strategy defined in the protocol. The search was carried out using title, abstract and indexed keywords (see Table 5).

Filtering of the first 7550 results was carried out using the checklist established in the protocol, repeated reviews were carried out until a final number of 24 articles was reached with publication dates ranging from 2004 to 2017 (see Table 6).

In addition to the inclusion/exclusion criterion, the quality assurance of primary studies is also considered to provide a more detailed criterion and in order to assess the importance of individual studies when the results are being synthesized. This section discusses quality in terms of minimizing bias and maximizing internal and external

Table 5. Automated search details.

Database	Search results
IEEE Xplore	295
SCOPUS	696
ACM Digital Library	2000
Springer Link	4559
TOTAL	7550

Table 6. Details of each phase of selection of primary studies.

Phase	Description	Included	Excluded
Phase 1	Search results	7550	0
Phase 2	Selection by inclusion criteria	2899	4651
Phase 3	Selection by exclusion criteria	57	2842
Phase 4	Selection by title and abstract	26	31
Phase 5	Joint validation	24	2

validity as outlined in the Cochrane manual for systematic reviews of interventions [11] from the practices adopted by good practice for SLR [8]. For this stage, a series of questions were used to evaluate the way in which the primary studies present the information related to the objective, as well as the rigor of the topics developed[1].

Next, quantitative and qualitative data were extracted from each of the 23 articles to have valid and objective information. Each study was organized in an arrangement to focus the contents of each publication, for the purposes of the research. The importance of this activity lies in the appropriate presentation of the review report at the time of the discussion, presented in Sect. 5.

The results of the quality assurance of the selected studies were presented using the five-likert scale to visualize the dimensions of quality assurance analysis addressed, as well as the impact of the studies themselves[2]. As a result, it was established that the average rigor is 91% grouping based on the way in which the study answered questions PQA1 and PQA2. The validity of the set of studies is 84% based on the way in which each study answers questions PQA3, PQA4, PQA5, PQA6 and PQA7. Finally, the applicability of the set of studies is 72% based on the way in which each study answers the questions PQA8, PQA9, PQA10 and PQA11. The three quality measures adopted for the study, in terms of rigor, validity and applicability, are shown in Fig. 1.

---

[1] Attached: https://bit.ly/slrappendixacevedoetal, table A2.
[2] Attached: https://bit.ly/slrappendixacevedoetal, table A3.

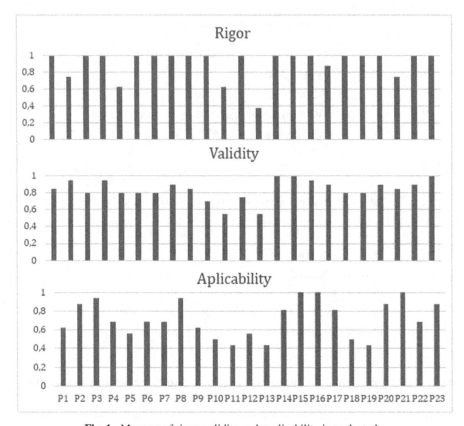

Fig. 1. Measure of rigor, validity and applicability in each study.

For the synthesis of the representative data of each publication, the methods established in Sect. 3 were used. Carrying out this activity made it possible to characterize and evaluate each publication jointly using the complete study and the extended information from the classification table and the ordering of the support tools. At the time of collecting the information related to each research question, specific data were recorded in each field of the extraction form.

5 Review Report

The results organized by research question are described below. In the discussion of the results, reference is made to the articles with the form Px, where "x" is the article number as described in Table A1 of the documentation attached to this work[3].

---

[3] Attached: https://bit.ly/slrappendixacevedoetal, list of articles in table A1.

5.1 RQ1. What Software Architectures Exist for Critical Systems?

Table 7 summarizes the software architectures found in the analysis of the articles and the total number found. 39% of the works under study apply an implementation of layered architectures. This design decision of the systems under study requires extensive testing and a clear separation of functions that can introduce more possibilities of failure; therefore, selecting a layered architecture ensures that each function has its failure probability limited. P3 shows a modular security case for a work network that requires compliance with the IEC 61508 standard and describes a protocol to transfer data safely, complying with SIL level 3.

30% of the publications use an architecture with a voting scheme of the M-out-of-N type and 70% of this subset specifically uses the 1oo2 scheme. This distribution among the studies is justified since certain domains require that the system remain functional under extreme conditions and meeting the required SIL level. In work P20 the authors present a solution that implements redundant hardware and given the case of implementation of the solution on a high-pressure high temperature environment, they do not recommend the use of their double pressure transmitter scheme because they could add a failure in the complete sensor.

About 26% of the works mention and apply a software scheme in conjunction with hardware redundancy as a risk mitigation measure. In P13 hardware redundancy is mentioned as a safe monitoring method under comparison tests using a voter.

Also, 13% of publications employ master-slave architecture as a proposed solution. Thus, in P9 a master microcontroller and different slave microcontrollers are recommended, with their respective treatment of possible faults.

Only 8% of the papers propose an architecture that includes software redundancy and they do not cover the entire certification procedure necessary for the implementation of a critical software-driven system.

Table 7. Types of software architecture used.

Identifier	Architecture	Article that implements the solution	Total
MooN	m-out-of-n	P5 P6 P8 P9 P13 P14 P15 P20	8
MS	Master-Slave	P9 P18 P19	3
RHW	Hardware redundancy	P7 P13 P14 P16 P20 P21	6
AC	Layered architecture	P3 P10 P11 P16 P17 P19 P20 P21 P22	9
RSW	Software redundancy	P1 P2	2
FSM	Finite state machine	P12	1
SCP	Safety channel pattern	P23	1

5.2 RQ2. What Regulations do they Comply With?

About 78% of the studies expressly address the IEC 61508 standard, while the remaining 22% indicate specific regulations of the domain and scope of application of software architecture in a critical system, referring to the characteristics and design restrictions demanded: automotive [P7] [P25] [P15] avionics [P22] and specific telecommunication regulations [P3].

A notable result is the growing development of automatic driving technologies addressed in the recommended practices for surface vehicles [12], increasing the rigor required for software components and programmable circuits, with limited response times. Mention is made, then, of the ISO/IEC/IEEE 42010 standard that regulates this new area without excluding the existing ISO 26262 standard.

Paper P19 does not make direct reference to the IEC 61158 standard because the scope of the study in question is the implementation of a secure communication protocol. Technically the IEC 61784 standard defines protocols based on the standard mentioned above and includes other extended definitions.

In P21 experimental results on the system audit under a fault injection test are presented to verify the implementation of the security concepts, it also indicates the possibility of carrying out automated tests for system validation in accordance with the ISO7637 standard [13]. Table 8 summarizes the regulations that are intended to be complied with and the articles that mention them.

Table 8. Regulations identified in each article.

Normative	Article
IEC 61508	P1 P2 P3 P4 P5 P6 P7 P9 P10 P11 P13 P14 P15 P16 P18 P19 P20 P21
DO 178	P12
EN 14908	P5
EN 50126	P13
EN 50128	P13
EN 50129	P13
ISO 26262	P8 P9 P11 P17 P21 P22 P23
IEC 61131	P7
EN 954-1	P6
IEC 61800	P6
IEC 60204	P6
IEC 61511	P16
API RP 14C	P16
IEC 61784	P19 P22
IEC 61158	P22
ISO/IEC/IEEE 42010	P23

5.3   RQ3. What Level of Security do they Verify?

The 60% of the works included in the study aim to reach SIL 3 or similar level in accordance with the specific regulations. The distribution of publications referring to software architectures for critical systems that address this level of comprehensive security allows viewing the presence of software solutions in this area that comply with the standards in force in each domain covered (see Table 9).

Around 39% of the papers reviewed aim to certify up to a SIL4 level or equivalent in ASIL and DAL. Finally, 30% of the publications aim to achieve a SIL2 level or lower, it is important to clarify that the required safety level varies according to the domain of the critical system and in the presence of publications that mention these levels of SIL1 and SIL2. It is possible to use elements of different SIL to achieve a higher SIL, in particular, IEC 61508 part 2 7.4.3.2 [1] clarifies that there must be sufficient independence between the elements present in the combination. Several studies suggest that the proposed systems can be presented in combination to achieve higher SIL levels. P1 includes the cyclically operating programmable electronic system as an alternative to verify SIL 4. n P2 the problem of SIL apportionment is discussed and it says that applying rules for apportionment must be studied in detail to avoid inconsistency. According to 61508 Annex B, for SIL3 and SIL4, dynamic analysis is required to validate the results that can be obtained by means of static analysis and failure analysis. In P21, a combination of quantitative analysis is used to achieve the proposed ASIL level and qualitative analysis to complement the proposed safety goals.

Table 9. SIL level identified in each article.

SSIL	Article
SIL1/ASIL A	P2 P15
SIL2	P2 P6 P10 P11 P16 P20
SIL3/ASIL B/DAL B	P1 P2 P3 P4 P5 P6 P7 P9 P12 P14 P16 P18 P19 P22
SIL4/ASIL D/DAL A	P1 P2 P4 P8 P12 P13 P17 P21 P23

5.4   RQ4.1 What Technology do They Use?

The technology section chosen as the implementation platform is the analysis dimension that presents the greatest diversity of results. All publications use their own high-level software scheme to reduce the complexity of the specific hardware schemes. 30% of the included studies use a framework as technology for software development. 48% of the included studies present software development using libraries. To a lesser extent, about 22% of the included studies only describe software development at the source code level.

In some cases, in the automotive domain the use of a CAN bus [P8] [P11] [P17] [P23] is described, which at the software technology level use libraries or a framework for greater integration of functions. The implementation of the bus is specific for each case treated. The variety of technologies available to support the development cycle of an architecture is due to restrictions on the hardware on which the implementation is made. In P10 it uses state simulation software tools. In P13 it uses the development tools of the chosen ARM7 board. Table 10 shows the articles by technology.

Table 10. Technologies used for software architectures.

Technology	Article	Total
Framework	P3 P10 P13 P14 P19 P21 P22	7
Libraries	P2 P4 P5 P6 P7 P8 P11 P15 P17 P20 P23	11
Source Code	P1 P9 P12 P16 P18	5

5.5   RQ4.2 What Platforms are Used?

The distribution of platforms evidenced to implement software architecture is displayed in Table 11. About 65% of the studies use their own solution, 21% of the studies describe the use of a commercially available microcontroller. A notable result is the one described in article [P18], which uses a platform that is certified by IEC61508 SIL 3 and ISO26262 ASIL D. To a lesser extent is the use of software architectures on programmable logic controllers (PLC), representing 13% of the total of studies included. In the cases that contemplate the use of programmable logic controllers, their implementation was accompanied by an operating environment using a real-time operating system to validate the expected behavior of the system under test. And finally, there is the choice of a real-time operating system (RTOS) as a platform, representing about 8% of the included studies. In P6 the use of a real-time operating system is mentioned for its implementation in control systems. Therefore, it can be ensured that there is no predominance of a platform for any type of implementation of a critical system, the use of microcontrollers is just one more part of the system and by itself does not influence Systematic Capability.

Table 11. Platforms used in each type of software architecture developed.

Platform	Article	Total
Specific solution	P1 P2 P3 P4 P5 P8 P10 P11 P14 P15 P16 P17 P19 P22 P23	15
MCU	P9 P12 P13 P18 P21	5
PLC	P6 P7 P20	3
RTOS	P6 P7	2

5.6 RQ5. What are the Application Domains?

To answer this section, the domain to which the critical system worked in the publication belongs is taken into consideration. 43% of the reviewed publications use software architecture for a critical system under the domain of security in industrial equipment.

Around 26% of the studies describe systems that are used under the domain of the automotive industry, including the activities of validation, analysis and development of software architecture. About 8% of the studies reviewed present a system that is used under the domain of trains [P23] [P9]. P20 deals with the implementation of critical systems in the security domain in offshore facilities. The application domains for critical systems that include software architecture (see Table 12). The growth of domains in which critical systems applications are presented prompts revisions to existing regulations and leads in many cases to the creation of new regulations. Specific restrictions can be presented to a domain, and when trying to treat these restrictions from a single general standard, it can lead to a loss of specificity in the correct analysis of the measures to take into account for the development.

Table 12. Domain of the critical system treated in each article.

Domain	Article	Total
Industrial equipment safety	P1 P2 P3 P4 P5 P6 P7 P14 P15 P16	10
Automotive	P8 P9 P10 P11 P17 P21 P23	7
Avionics	P12	1
Secure communication networks	P19 P22	2
Railway	P13 P18	2
Offshore facility security	P20	1

5.7 RQ6 What are the Reported Activities?

Activities that describe architecture design including security cases are required, and activities that ensure the application of the system using certified electronic components and the respective test roles following the security cases developed in a particular way. The activities covered in each publication differ because each level of security integrity has greater stringency in the requirements. 50% of this set of studies mentioned describe the system testing stage. One of the notable characteristics in this domain is the comprehensive evaluation of all the constraints of the environment in which the critical system is to be implemented, this fact requires correct documentation of the software and hardware to be used.

Finally, P23 and P9 include validation activities at the system test level, this is related to the SIL level that is intended to be achieved in these two articles. The identification by activity and article is found in Table 13. There is no homogeneous development when proposing the activities reported in each study. Standard [1] suggests a guided development cycle, however the implementation of said development cycle will vary due to human resources and the instances set for each stage. One of the variations present in the activities refers to the use of existing and certified hardware, a fact that by itself does not guarantee a SIL compliance application, however it allows consistent results in the validation stage.

Table 13. Activities reported in the development of software architectures for critical systems.

Activity	Article	Total
Analysis	All articles	23
Research	P4 P5 P7 P9 P10 P11 P17	7
Development	P1 P2 P3 P5 P6 P8 P9 P10 P12 P13 P14 P15 P16 P17 P18 P19 P20 P21 P23	19
Validation	P1 P2 P3 P4 P6 P7 P8 P9 P11 P12 P13 P14 P15 P16 P17 P18 P19 P20 P21 P22 P23	22
Implantation	P13 P16	2

5.8 Additional Results

As shown in Fig. 2, the distribution of publications that meet the proposed research criteria presents a fluctuation that reaches its maximum between the years 2009 to 2012.

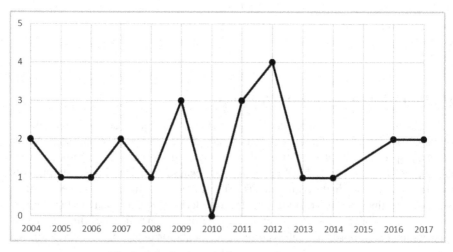

Fig. 2. Distribution of primary studies by domain.

Once the relevant data had been extracted from the set of studies selected to conduct the review, a scheme was reached that describes it based on the parameters that are directly related to the research questions, meaning information with granularity based on the oneness of each publication and the excluding and non- excluding characteristics indicated in the methodology. This change in the schemes presented respecting the criterion of uniqueness of the publications and presenting links has been formally studied in works such as Hashemi et al. [14]. Implemented on the set of studies, an important grouping of publications is observed that treat a layered architecture with SIL 2 and SIL 3. And another grouping presenting an architecture taking a base scheme of M-out-of-N grouped in the levels SIL 3 and SIL 4, this is presented in Fig. 3. Regarding the proportion in the way of presenting software developments related to the included architectures, keeping in mind the temporal dimension, there were no groupings greater than two publications and their distribution is displayed in Fig. 4.

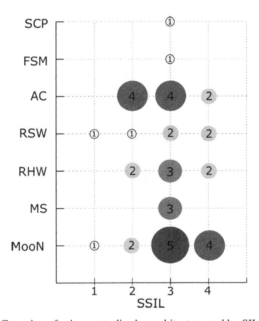

Fig. 3. Grouping of primary studies by architecture and by SIL treated.

5.9 Threats to Validity

The threats to validity identified during the development of this work are listed below. Regarding the search carried out: a systematic literature review using various search engines presents the need to control the studies that are indexed in various sources and to select the version of the latest revision if this occurs. This aspect was addressed by using a control by index after the result of the search string at the end of phase 1 and until phase 4, even when the selection by title and abstract was made.

Regarding the included studies: we have sought to ensure the validity of the data sent in this review based on the quality of the set of articles included. According to the approach presented in good practice for conducting reviews, observational studies tend to be more susceptible to bias than experimental studies; the conclusions that can be drawn from them are necessarily more tentative and often generate hypotheses, highlighting areas for future research [15]. This approach was adopted for quality assurance criteria by Kitchenham and Charters to minimize bias and maximize internal and external validity. Using these quality assurance tools for each study, it was possible to obtain a quality measure of the set of studies to address this aspect of validity.

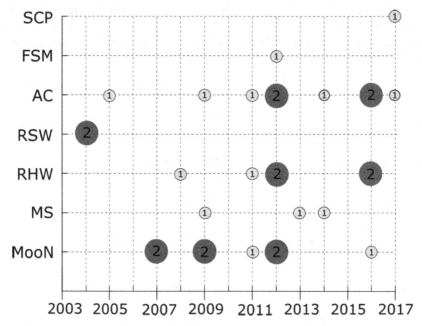

Fig. 4. Grouping of primary studies by architecture and year of publication.

6   Conclusions

In this work, an SLR focused on software architectures and their application in critical systems was presented. Therefore, the search and selection methods of the primary studies were defined, in order to obtain the state of the art of the approaches. The research criteria were defined, the method used to carry out the search and the selection criteria of the primary studies were presented and the report was made.

The results indicate that there is a broad development of software architectures in various industrial domains. A majority of the automotive domain and the domain of security in industrial equipment are evident. A study distribution per year, platform, technology and architecture in the design was reached. It was also sought to determine the integral security level treated in each architecture, in this sense, there is an important distribution on SIL 3 and SIL 4 levels in the set of studies analyzed. References to standards that regulate each process implemented as a security function delegated to the software were also found.

From this study, we can conclude that the implementation of software architectures in critical systems requires a comprehensive evaluation that includes the technologies to be used, the existing standards that provide a framework on which the development cycle must be adapted, the level of security that the functions implemented by the software must fulfill, the technology and development platform chosen to limit the failure rate, within what is allowed by the required level of security.

In general terms, software architectures that can meet high levels of SIL were evidenced. In this regard, proof was found that software architectures with a layered design predominate. Regarding the regulations that the developments present in the studies try to comply with, it was evidenced that the use of the IEC 61508 standard is presented in most of the studies, but its compliance must be presented in conjunction with domain-specific standards.

Regarding the sections of technology used and development platforms, a trend was identified to use specific solutions, although there are certified hardware solutions that allow greater control throughout the life cycle of the project. Most studies use their own hardware definitions and software definitions at source code level or libraries that make use of the established physical support, with frameworks intended for the validation of the functions implemented by software.

Regarding the section of reported activities, there is no single definition to follow for the development of architectures, but there are clear and standardized processes to establish modules, test each software element and control by simulation its interaction with the hardware, which, in many evidenced cases, means submitting the required level of security.

To summarize, the SLR results presented in the previous sections allow us to affirm that there is a strong trend to implement secure functions through software, this trend is growing, and it spans several domains of the industry.

Acknowledgment. This development was carried out from the research project PI 17F017 and 17F018 of the Secretaría General de Ciencia y Técnica de la Universidad Nacional del Nordeste.

References

1. International Electro-technical Commission IEC: IEC 61508: Functional safety of electrical/electronic/ programmable electronic safety-related systems (1998)
2. International Organization for Standardization (ISO): ISO26262 Road vehicles – Functional safety (2011)
3. Radio Technical Commission for Aeronautics (RTCA): DO-178B, Software Considerations in Airborne Systems and Equipment Certification (1992)
4. Gurbuz, H., Tekinerdogan, B.: Model-based testing for software safety: a systematic mapping study. Softw. Qual. J. **26**(4), 1327–1372 (2017). https://doi.org/10.1007/s11219-017-9386-2
5. Queiroz, P.G.G., Braga, R.T.V.: Development of critical embedded systems using model-driven and product lines techniques: a systematic review. In: 2014 Eighth Brazilian Symposium on Software Components, Architectures and Reuse, pp. 74–83 (2014)
6. Antonio, E.A., Ferrari, F.C., Fabbri, S.C.P.F.: A systematic mapping of architectures for embedded software. In: 2012 Second Brazilian Conference on Critical Embedded Systems, 2012, pp. 18–23 (2012). https://doi.org/10.1109/CBSEC.2012.22

7. Acevedo, J., Lezcano, A., Irrazábal, E.: Revisión sistemática de la literatura sobre implementación de arquitecturas software para sistemas críticos. In: XXVI Libro de actas del Congreso Argentino de Ciencias de la Computación (CACIC), pp. 350–359, 5 al 9 de octubre de 2020. ISBN: 978-987-4417-90-9. Modalidad virtual
8. Kitchenham, B.A., Charters, S.M.: Guidelines for performing Systematic Literature Reviews in Software Engineering|Request PDF[1]. https://www.researchgate. https://www.researchg ate.net/publication/302924724_Guidelines_for_performing_Systematic_Literature_Revi ews_in_Software_Engineering. Accessed 23 May 2020
9. Saldaña, J.: The Coding Manual for Qualitative Researchers. SAGE Publications Inc. (2015)
10. Crabtree, B.F., Miller, W.L.: Doing Qualitative Research. SAGE Publications Inc. (1999)
11. The Cochrane Collaboration, Cochrane Handbook for Systematic Reviews of Interventions (2019)
12. SAE: Surface vehicle recommended practice—Taxonomy and definitions for terms related to driving automation systems for on-road motor vehicles (2018)
13. ISO/DIS 7637–2, SO7637–2 Road vehicles - Electrical disturbances from conduction and coupling. International Organization for Standardization (2011)
14. Hashemi, R.R., De Agostino, S., Westgeest, B., Talburt, J.R.: Data granulation and formal concept analysis. In: Annual Conference of the North American Fuzzy Information Processing Society - NAFIPS, 2004, vol. 1, pp. 79–83 (2004). https://doi.org/10.1109/nafips.2004.133 6253
15. Centre for Reviews and Dissemination, Systematic Reviews: CRD's guidance for undertaking reviews in health care. York Publishing Services Ltd. (2009)

A Case Study to Validate Feasibility of Risk Proposal in the Deployment Process of Software Systems

Felipe Ortiz[1,3]([✉]) [iD], Marisa Panizzi[1,2,3] [iD], and Rodolfo Bertone[2,3] [iD]

[1] Master's Program in Information Systems Engineering, Technological National University at Buenos Aires, Buenos Aires, Argentina
[2] Department of Information Systems Engineering, Technological National University at Buenos Aires, Buenos Aires, Argentina
pbertone@lidi.unlp.edu.ar
[3] School of Information Systems – Computer Science Research Institute LIDI (III-LIDI), National University of La Plata, La Plata, Argentina

Abstract. Deployment is the process by which a software system is transferred to a business client. A risk is defined as the likelihood for a loss to occur. In a software project, a risk might imply decreased quality of the software product, increased costs, a delay in project completion or a flaw, among others. A case study is developed with the aim to refine the set of risks. Furthermore, procedures are proposed for their prevention, mitigation and/or transfer for the software system deployment process. This article presents the results of a case study which analyzed the documentation related to deployment of functionalities in a bank's Human Resources Portal conducted by an Argentina based software Small and Medium Enterprise (SME (Presidencia de la Nación. (2018). https://www.argentina.gob.ar/noticias/nuevas-categorias-para-ser-pyme. Last updated on 09/05/2018.)).

Keywords: Software system deployment · Risk management · Case study

1 Introduction

There are various factors that can affect software projects, such as modifications in priorities and inadequate planning [1]. One of the most important factors might be unmanaged risks. A risk is the probability for a loss to occur. In a software project, such loss might take the form of decreased quality of the software product, increased development costs, a delay in project completion or a flaw [2]. A prevailing condition for the growth of the software industry is that companies offer higher quality products that satisfy customer demands and requirements, but above all that generates confidence at the time of use [3]. This is achieved through the application of internationally recognized risk management models and methodologies. However, according to the 2019 annual report published by the Permanent Observatory of the Software and Information Services Industry (OPSSI) [4], in Argentina, the Software Industry is mainly made up of small and medium-sized companies (SMEs), which represent almost 80% of the sector (this

© Springer Nature Switzerland AG 2021
P. Pesado and J. Eterovic (Eds.): CACIC 2020, CCIS 1409, pp. 123–140, 2021.
https://doi.org/10.1007/978-3-030-75836-3_9

constitutes them as a fundamental link in the country's economy), but in this kind of companies it's difficult to implement this type of models and methodologies because it involves a large investment in money, time and resources. At the international level, the same reality is reflected regarding SMEs make up a large portion of the software industry [5]. These organizations have realized that it is crucial for their business to improve their processes and working methods, but they lack the knowledge and resources to do this. The only way to contribute to the success of projects, therefore, is to define, implement and stabilize the development processes [6].

A large number of projects lack formal approaches for risk management. The identification thereof usually depends, at an informal level, on the abilities and level of experience of software managers [7]. Although software risk management plays a key role in successful project management, it is usually not properly implemented in real world software projects, particularly in SMEs in Argentina [8].

Software system deployment is the phase of the development life cycle in which the software product is transferred to the client. The deployment process entails practices which tend to pose problems, such as the lack of components (generally external), incomplete downloads and faulty installations [9].

Software deployment is usually conducted in distributed and heterogeneous environments, which add complexity, thus causing time consumption and additional costs [10]. Deployment entails a series of changes at several levels: processes, working methods, technology and organizational structure [11].

According to Reascos Paredes et al. [12], the main causes of technological risks include heterogeneous and incompatible infrastructure, SMEs' poor technological capabilities and competences, the complexity of these systems, and bad data quality and safety. Forbes et al. [13] argue that the results of non-standardized and inadequate deployment practices are reflected in the information systems, which are difficult to maintain and operate.

This work presents the results of a case study aimed at refining (if necessary) the set of risks, as well as the procedures for their prevention, mitigation and/or transfer defined for the deployment process of software systems SMEs' in Argentina. Through this case study, the set of risks proposed for each of the tasks for the deployment process of software systems presented in CACIC 2020 [14] has been validated.

This article is organized as follows: related works are described in Sect. 2; Sect. 3 presents the set of risks for the deployment process; Sect. 4 addresses the case study; and finally, Sect. 5 presents the conclusions and future works.

2   Related Works

A Systematic Mapping Study (SMS) was performed to build the state of the art on risk management for the deployment process of software systems [15]. After analyzing 100 primary studies, it was found that the most commonly used methodologies, methods and standards addressing risk management are CMMI [16], PMBOK [17] and SOFTWARE RISK EVALUATION [18].

To complement the SMS, a comparative analysis of the previously mentioned methodologies, methods and standards was conducted based on the DESMET method characteristics [19]. MAGERIT [20] was added to the comparison since it is one of the pioneering risk management methodologies.

The comparative analysis for the deployment addressed three dimensions: "Process", "Person" and "Product" [21]. After this comparative analysis, it was concluded that in the "Process" dimension all the methodologies, methods and standards analyzed address the risks for the deployment process. In the "Product" dimension, SOFTWARE RISK EVALUATION as well as PMBOK and MAGERIT include the risks of the deployment process while CMMI does not. Finally, in the "Person" dimension, none of the methodologies, methods or standards evaluated address the risks of the deployment process.

3   Risks of the Deployment Process

The activities and tasks considered for the definition of the risks of the deployment process are those stated in the technical process called "Transition" of the ISO/IEC/IEEE 12207:2017 standard [22]. This standard was chosen because it is internationally recognized.

For a better structuring of the solution, as well as so that its application in the industry can be carried out in a systematic way in different deployment projects, it is decided to define a coding for it. The proposal of Runeson et al. [23] that proposes guidelines for the design of a coding scheme for the analysis and interpretation of the data in the case studies. These guidelines are detailed below:

– Code as much as possible.
– Codes must be prioritized as follows:

  • High-level codes, based on research questions.
  • Mid-level codes, based on code groupings: code categories.
  • The low-level code is your interpretation of the text (in the Comments field).

The resulting coding for the activities and tasks of the deployment process are detailed in Table 1.

The risk classification used is the one proposed in [7], with adjustments made considering the evolution of software engineering in the last few decades and the deployment process of software systems. For risk weighting, the proposal established in the ISO/IEC 31010:2009 standard [24] is adopted, since it is one of the main international references in terms of risk management for the software industry.

The definition of risks was established considering a three-dimensional approach, given by the "Process" dimension, the "Person" dimension and the "Product" dimension [21].

4   Description of the Case Study

This section presents a detailed account of the case study following the guidelines proposed in [23].

Table 1. Activities and tasks of the technical process "Transition" [22].

Activities	Tasks
A1 Preparation for deployment	T1 Identify technological restrictions
	T2 Obtain access to the environments, systems or services enabled
	T3 Analyze existing policies and standards
	T4 Define unit testing policies
	T5 Define deployment priorities in order to support the data and software migration and transition
	T6 Identify restrictions in the deployment strategy
A2 Deployment execution	T7 Develop or adapt software elements according to the deployment strategy
	T8 Record requirement compliance evidence
	T9 Adapt hardware elements and software services
	T10 Staff training
A3 Deployment results management	T11 Record the results and anomalies found
	T12 Keep traceability
	T13 Provide key artifacts
	T14 Document fulfillment of expectations and capabilities
	T15 Evaluate the need or opportunity for improvement

4.1 Case Study Design

The main objective is to examine the feasibility of the application of a set of risks, as well as the procedures for their prevention, mitigation and/or transfer in the deployment process of software systems in a real environment with the aim to refine them (if necessary). According to Robson's classification [25], case studies fall under the scope of exploratory studies. We worked with documentation related to the deployment of capability deliverables for a bank's Human Resources Portal performed by an Argentina-based software SME.

4.2 Research Questions

In order to address the objective of this study, the following research questions (RQ) are posed:

RQ1: How were risks managed during the activities of the software system deployment process (identification, analysis and severity)?

This question is intended to provide information about the risks encountered during the execution of the deployment process and the treatment provided by the consulting company in order to compare them with the proposal made.

RQ2: How can the software system deployment process be strengthened in this company?

This question is intended to determine the way in which the consulting company can enhance its deployment process. For this purpose, the identification of a set of risks is proposed, along with the procedures for their prevention, mitigation and/or transfer.

4.3 Case and Unit of Analysis

This section describes the context, the case and the unit of analysis of the case study. According to Yin's classification [26], it is a holistic single-case study.

Context: the case study was conducted in a software SME located in the Autonomous City of Buenos Aires, with a total of 430 employees. This company develops customized information systems for clients of different industry sectors, including finance, automotive, pharmaceutical and banking. Its software projects combine agile practices with iterative life cycle development methodologies. Access was granted to the documentation of the project subject to an agreement not to disclose the name of the company and a commitment to inform about any findings and recommendations to be considered for deployment process risk management.

Case: deployment of deliverables for a Human Resources Portal conducted at a bank based in Argentina. It consisted in adding new capabilities, using a modular strategy. These were: integration with a new data source, publication of Application Programming Interfaces (APIs), integration with a distance learning portal, modification of the final user interface, new employee management alerts and notifications, appearance modifications to the application organigram, and modification to approval flows.

Unit of analysis: documentation related to the deployment of deliverables for a Human Resources Portal.

4.4 Preparation for Data Collection

A third-degree technique was used combined with an independent method according to the classification proposed in [27]. A template with a coding scheme made up of 3 groups was used. Each group coincides with the 3 activities of the technical process called "Transition" of the ISO/IEC/IEEE 12207: 2017 Standard [22] (A1 Preparation for deployment, A2 Deployment Execution and A3 Deployment Results Management).

Table 2 shows the traceability of the documents analyzed and the risks associated with each of the dimensions.

Table 2. Traceability of the documents analyzed for the case study.

Documents/activities	A1	A2	A3
Risk monitoring spreadsheet	RProc6, RPers3 and RProd1	RProc10	RProd15
Progress report	RPers4	RProc7 and RProd9	RPers13
Deliverable 1 - closing report	RProd4	RProc8 and RPers9	RProc14, RPers15 and RProd13
Deliverable 1 - deployment report		RProd8	RProc15 and RPers12
Deliverable 1 - deployment summary		RPers8	RProc11 and RProd12
Deliverable 1 - deployment tests guide	RProc4, RPers2 and RProd5	RProd10	
Deliverable 1 - deployment Test cases	RProc4, RPers2 and RProd3		
Deliverable 1 – installation scripts	RPers1 and RProd2		RProc12
Deliverable 1 – work plan	RProc5 and RPers5	RProd7 and RPers10	
Deliverable 1 – installation requirements	RProc1 and RProd6	RProc9 and RPers7	
Deliverable 1 - deployment completion report	RProc2 and RPers6	RProd9	RProc13, RPers14 and RProd14
Deliverable 2 - closing report	RProd4	RProc8 and RPers9	RProc14, RPers15 and RProd13
Deliverable 2 - deployment report		RProd8	RPers12
Deliverable 2 – deployment summary		RPers8	RProc11, RProc15 and RProd12
Deliverable 2 - deployment tests guide	RProc4, RPers2 and RProd5	RProd10	
Deliverable 2 - deployment test cases	RProc4, RPers2 and RProd3		
Deliverable 2 – installation scripts	RPers1 and RProd2		RProc12
Deliverable 2 – work plan	RProc5 and RPers5	RPers10 and RProd7	
Deliverable 2 – installation requirements	RProc1 and RProd6	RProc9 and RPers7	
Delivery 2 - deployment completion report	RProc2 and RPers6	RProd9	RProc13, RPers14 and RProd14
General documentation	RProc3		RPers11 and RProd11

Table 3 shows the resulting risk weighting for the "Process" dimension in the case study.

Table 3. Risk weighting of the "Process" dimension for the case study.

Activity	Risk	Weight	Result
A1	RProc1	[Probability (H) * Impact (H)] =	VH
	RProc2	[Probability (M) * Impact (H)] =	H
	RProc3	[Probability (L) * Impact (L)] =	L
	RProc4	[Probability (H) * Impact (VH)] =	VH
	RProc5	[Probability (VH) * Impact (VH)] =	VH
	RProc6	[Probability (L) * Impact (H)] =	H
A2	RProc7	[Probability (L) * Impact (VH)] =	VH
	RProc8	[Probability (L) * Impact (M)] =	M
	RProc9	[Probability (M) * Impact (H)] =	H
	RProc10	[Probability (L) * Impact (H)] =	H
A3	RProc11	[Probability (L) * Impact (M)] =	M
	RProc12	[Probability (H) * Impact (H)] =	VH
	RProc13	[Probability (H) * Impact (VH)] =	VH
	RProc14	[Probability (M) * Impact (H)] =	H
	RProc15	[Probability (L) * Impact (L)] =	L

The risk weighting of the "Person" dimension is presented in Table 4.

Table 4. Risk weighting of the "Person" dimension

Activity	Risk	Weight	Result
A1	RPers1	[Probability (H) * Impact (H] =	VH
	RPers2	[Probability (L) * Impact (H)] =	H
	RPers3	[Probability (M) * Impact (H)] =	H
	RPers4	[Probability (L) * Impact (H)] =	H
	RPers5	[Probability (H) * Impact (VH)] =	VH
	RPers6	[Probability (H) * Impact (H)] =	VH
A2	RPers7	[Probability (H) * Impact (H)] =	VH
	RPers8	[Probability (ML) * Impact (H)] =	M
	RPers9	[Probability (L) * Impact (H)] =	H
	RPers10	[Probability (M) * Impact (H)] =	H
A3	RPers11	[Probability (L) * Impact (M)] =	M
	RPers12	[Probability (H) * Impact (H)] =	VH
	RPers13	[Probability (L) * Impact (H)] =	H
	RPers14	[Probability (H) * Impact (H)] =	VH
	RPers15	[Probability (H) * Impact (VH)] =	VH

The risks weight of the "Product" dimension is presented in Table 5.

Table 5. Risk weighting of the "Product" dimension

Activity	Risk	Weight	Result
A1	RProd1	[Probability (L) * Impact (H)] =	H
	RProd2	[Probability (M) * Impact (H)] =	H
	RProd3	[Probability (M) * Impact (H)] =	H
	RProd4	[Probability (L) * Impact (VH)] =	H
	RProd5	[Probability(H) * Impact (H)] =	VH
	RProd6	[Probability (MH) * Impact (H)] =	VH
A2	RProd7	[Probability (M) * Impact (M)] =	M
	RProd8	[Probability (H) * Impact (M)] =	H
	RProd9	[Probability (M) * Impact (H)] =	H
	RProd10	[Probability (H) * Impact (H)] =	VH
A3	RProd11	[Probability(H) * Impact (M)] =	H
	RProd12	[Probability(H) * Impact (H)] =	VH
	RProd13	[Probability (L) * Impact (H)] =	H
	RProd14	[Probability (M) * Impact (H)] =	H
	RProd15	[Probability (H) * Impact (VH)] =	VH

4.5 Analysis and Interpretation of Results

The results of the research questions defined for the case study are presented below:

RQ1: How were risks managed during the activities of the software system deployment process (identification, analysis and severity)?

Based on the documentation analyzed, it was possible to find flaws in the risk management proposed for the activities of the deployment process:

- Activity 1 (A1) – Preparation for Deployment: The deployment progress reports showed that, due to the few investments in technology made in recent years, the resources (hardware and basic software) assigned to the production environment did not comply with the minimum requirements requested by the consulting company to carry out the deployment in accordance with the established work plan. According to the deployment reports analyzed, the technicians (bank employees) did not have the knowledge and skills necessary for the correct deployment of scripts and monitoring of the guides sent by the consulting company. This is because the technicians who participated in the original deployment left the organization and were replaced by personnel with little technical or functional experience. The general documentation of the project shows that the bank does not have an adequate personnel retention policy, which generates frequent rotation.

- Activity 2 (A2) – Deployment Execution: according to the progress reports of the deployment project, the technical flaws mentioned in the previous stage (separation of technical personnel with experience in the technologies involved and greater complexity of the product) generated friction between the consulting company and the managers of the bank. This was due to non-compliance with the deadlines established in the work plan, which ended up activating a penalty clause against the consulting company.

  During the documentary analysis, incomplete test plans and inadequate deployment metrics were found. According to the deployment completion reports, the consulting company had to face cost overruns for not having the document management procedures required by the bank in the contract and in corporate policy. In addition, it was necessary to add technical resources from the consulting company to address the lack of technical expertise of the bank's employees, who had to be trained to carry out future deployments.

  These technical drawbacks, added to a very demanding work schedule for internal reasons and needs of the bank (shown in the closing reports), were some of the causes that produced very important delays and friction between different sectors of the organization that even considered the cancellation of the deployment project on several occasions.

- Activity 3 (A3) - Deployment Results Management: problems with the software repositories (lack of necessary permissions, previous versions, lack of components, etc.), in addition to the low commitment and inexperience of the bank's technicians, generated multiple drawbacks during the deployment. These technical drawbacks strongly impacted on the quality of the final product and the satisfaction of the users who saw their productivity affected due to failures in the application's capabilities once the deployment was complete.

  In the deployment completion reports, it was also evidenced that there was a wrong dimensioning of the deliverables and that the necessary security tests were not carried out. This gave end users access to sensitive human resource information.

RQ2: How can the software systems deployment process be strengthened in this company?

Proper risk management minimizes drawbacks in the deployment process. The following recommended procedures has been presented to the software consulting company in order to prevent, mitigate and/or transfer each of the risks associated with the "Process", "Person" and "Product" dimensions. Table 6 shows the procedures associated with the risks of the "Process" dimension.

Table 6. Procedures associated with the risks of the "Process" dimension.

Risks (RProc)	Procedures (PProc)
RProc1 Few investments in technology	PProc1 Accurate software measurements are the best prevention method for this type of risk. The methodology is based on adequately managing costs, deadlines, and other quantitative and qualitative factors associated with deployment projects
RProc2 Friction between the software management and senior executives	PProc2 Once friction is generated between the top executives and the software management, it is not easy to continue the project properly. Some of the approaches to control introduce radical changes, such as outsourcing software management and reducing the size of deliverables during deployment
RProc3 Void or non-existent corporate regulations	PProc3 Having an adequate corporate policy allows for clear and unambiguous objectives during the deployment project, forcing the use of rules and procedures
RProc4 Poorly drawn test plans	PProc4 One of the methods to prevent this type of risk is to prepare the deployment test plan during the analysis and design phase, thus anticipating the necessary requirements. The software testing methodology will depend on the one used for the project management
RProc5 Reduced schedule or work plan	PProc5 There are several estimation methods for deployment projects with the aim of mitigating these types of risks, such as expert opinion, the use of estimation models, the decomposition of the work plan and the comparison by analogy with other similar projects among others
RProc6 Cancellation of the deployment process	PProc6 The most effective prevention method is planning and estimating the deployment project. That is, well-defined goals and appropriately assigned tasks. Fluid communication must also be maintained between all participants
RProc7 Friction between the client and the software company	PProc7 In order to minimize the likelihood of friction between clients and contractors and the consequences that this may bring to the deployment project, it is advisable to have legal personnel trained in the software domain, so that they can comply with the contractual terms if necessary
RProc8 Inadequate metrics	PProc8 Analogies with metrics use in other projects is one of the most effective methods of preventing inadequate metrics during deployment. The larger the number of analog projects (not less than 25), the more effective the result will be
RProc9 Cost overruns	PProc9 as the project progresses, it is more difficult to control the associated costs. Cost overruns can occur for various reasons. The best form of mitigation is detailed monitoring of the deployment project. Any excess of time or resources used can generate cost overruns. In particular, the use of overtime for staff may be a factor that triggers the risk
RProc10 Inadequate training plans	PProc10 Each and every one of the necessary aspects of education and training for all the members of the deployment project, including technicians and end users, must be covered sufficiently in advance. Each one of the trainings carried out must be registered and its level of compliance must be evaluated according to the needs of the project

(continued)

Table 6. (*continued*)

Risks (RProc)	Procedures (PProc)
RProc11 Inadequate deployment management tools and methods	PProc11 The most effective approach to preventing the use of inappropriate software engineering tools during the deployment project is to conduct surveys and generate metrics for the tools most used by the software industry
RProc12 Inadequate repositories	PProc12 One of the most effective preventive steps for unsuitable configuration control of the repositories to be used during the deployment of the software product is to carry out a complete analysis of all the types of components that were produced, how they are connected and how often they are updated
RProc13 Inaccurate estimation of deliverables	PProc13 The most effective prevention methodology for estimation errors is the accurate measurement of the sizes of all deliverables and the resources required to produce them. The use of metrics during their deployment is also recommended
RProc14 Low user satisfaction	PProc14 User satisfaction is a complex and multifaceted issue. Some of the seemingly effective preventive steps include user experience specialists. In addition, user satisfaction surveys are the basic monitoring mechanism to guarantee it during deployment
RProc15 Ambiguous improvement goals	PProc15 Establishing a formal software measurement program and adopting functional metrics are effective preventative measures to eliminate ambiguous goals during software deployment

Table 7 shows the procedures associated with the risks of the "Person" dimension.

Table 7. Procedures associated with the risks of the "Person" dimension.

Risks (RPers)	Procedures (PPers)
RPers1 Lack of specialization in the technologies and processes involved	PPers1 A method of prevention and/or mitigation of this type of risk is to create an inventory of the skills of employees within the company and to establish specialization criteria and training study plans according to the deployment project
RPers2 Users without adequate access permissions	PPers2 In order to avoid delays and drawbacks during the deployment, it is recommended that all necessary access permissions for all the members of the deployment project, including technicians and end users, be analyzed and requested in advance according to the methodologies established by the Organization

(*continued*)

Table 7. (*continued*)

Risks (RPers)	Procedures (PPers)
RPers3 Inadequate staff retention policy	PPers3 The most effective approach to prevent the loss of resources during the deployment project is for the organization to have an adequate human resources policy that includes extra incentives for meeting project milestones not only economic but also based on other professional aspects
RPers4 Functional or business inexperience on the part of the users in charge of the tests	PPers4 In order to minimize this risk, the members of the deployment project should be carefully selected according to their role within the organization, their commitment and functional knowledge of the business. Another important aspect is to achieve proper communication between the members of the project
RPers5 Constant changes in priorities	PPers5 Having adequate management and monitoring of the deployment project is the best way to prevent this risk. Frequent follow-up meetings must be held in which the feasibility of the proposed changes and the impact they have on the project times are analyzed
RPers6 Additional efforts and/or resources	PPers6 Having an agile and structured induction plan during deployment reduces the drawbacks associated with this risk. New staff must be able to join in and assume their responsibilities transparently
RPers7 Little experience in present systems	PPers7 All platforms and interfaces that will be part of the deployment project must be analyzed and documented, and expert technicians must be selected in order to mitigate this risk. If training on any of them is necessary, it must be carried out in advance
RPers8 Lack of expertise	PPers8 It is recommended that the human resources assigned to the deployment project have technical and business expertise in order to ensure the correct operation of each of the deliverables. Each of the tasks must be properly documented
RPers9 Bad professional practice	PPers9 One of the most effective preventive steps to mitigate this risk is to establish a deployment plan based on expert opinion in each of the components involved (hardware and software services) in order to adapt them for proper deployment

(*continued*)

Table 7. (*continued*)

Risks (RPers)	Procedures (PPers)
RPers10 Significant drop in resources assigned to the project	PPers10 Clear policies must be established within the Organization so that the resources assigned to the deployment project are not reallocated to other tasks. Similarly, at a legal level, it is recommended that the need to maintain the quantity and technical level of the assigned resources be established with the contractors
RPers11 Document management inexperience	PPers11 One of the best practices to reduce or mitigate this risk is to train the resources assigned to the deployment project on the best practices of the document management methodology selected for the deployment project. Sometimes it is advisable to outsource this task to specialized personnel
RPers12 Various criteria or interpretations	PPers12 It is recommended that a standard traceability model be defined for the entire deployment process that includes the project participants, the sources (documents and models) and the objects or artifacts to be traced. These elements and their evolution must be explicitly identified in each flow of the deployment project
RPers13 Low productivity	PPers13 Proper monitoring of the tasks assigned to each of the members of the deployment project is the best way to minimize low productivity. To carry out adequate documentation and periodic follow-up meetings is recommended in order to resolve deviations or delays
RPers14 Lack of collaboration from end users	PPers14 To mitigate this risk, it is important that the top management of the organization embrace and disseminate the importance of carrying out the functional tests of the software product to the personnel affected by the deployment project so as to avoid operational drawbacks
RPers15 Low commitment	PPerso15 The most effective methodology is to work from different perspectives (technical, human, etc.) so that all the members of the deployment project (client and contractors) feel the project as their own and challenging

Table 8 shows the procedures associated with the risks of the "Product" dimension.

Table 8. Procedures associated with the risks of the "Product" dimension.

Risks (RProd)	Procedures (PProd)
RProd1 Novel technology or with little use	PProd1 It is recommended that new technology be used, but with enough maturity and local support to avoid problems during the deployment project. If possible, an analysis of similar projects should be carried out to verify its adaptability to the necessary capabilities
RProd2 Incompatibility with existing infrastructure	PProd2 to mitigate this risk, it is essential that a thorough analysis of compliance with the basic hardware or software requirements needed for the deployment be carried out in advance. All tasks must be properly documented and validated
RProd3 Lack of adaptation to new technologies	PProd3 Given the emergence of new technologies, such as DevOps and/or continuous deployment, it is necessary to adapt the organization's policies and/or procedures to the one selected for the deployment project. If necessary, it is recommended that external consulting be added to carry out this task adequately
RProd4 Lack of components	PProd4 It must be ensured that all components linked to the deliverables are available at the time of deployment. The best way to do this is through the proper traceability thereof
RProd5 Incompatible data format	PProd5 in order to prevent this risk, data sets must be selected for each of the technologies affected by the deployment process in order to validate their compatibility during their import into the new technology. These tests must be documented and supervised
RProd6 Little flexibility	PProd6 Defining the deployment strategy clearly and concretely will make it possible to choose the best technology for the software project so that it has the capacity to adapt to the changes that may arise during the deployment
RProd7 Greater complexity	PProd7 It is recommended that the capabilities and scope to be fulfilled by the software product be defined and properly documented in order to avoid increasing costs and time during the deployment project
RProd8 Flaws or Errors in operation	PProd8 A methodology should be used to record the fulfillment of all the capabilities of the product during the deployment, establishing reviews with the objective of guaranteeing that all technical and functional aspects were covered
RProd9 Loss of characteristics and/or functions	PProd9 to comply with all the necessary hardware requirements to avoid adapting the product due to technical incompatibility during deployment and to carry out a check-up in advance together with specialists is recommended
RProd10 Lack of knowledge of the capabilities of the product	PProd10 Fully documenting all the capabilities of the software product in an end user manual makes it possible to take full advantage of its features and ensure its correct deployment
RProd11 Scarce documentation	PProd11 Having a knowledge base allows recording of the results and anomalies found during deployment. They serve to detect recurring problems and improve the process continuously

(*continued*)

Table 8. (*continued*)

Risks (RProd)	Procedures (PProd)
RProd12 Inconsistencies in product versions	PProd12 Controlling the different versions of all analysis and design documentation, disseminating the latest versions as soon as possible and alerting the entire team is one of the best ways to prevent and/or mitigate this risk during deployment
RProd13 Incomplete capabilities	PProd13 the configuration parameters of key artifact components should be determined in advance (for example: Libraries, Shell Scripts parameters, among others). Completeness of all components within software repositories must be guaranteed during deployment. Additionally, the requirements on the workstations (plugins, active X components, etc.) must be identified
RProd14 Low quality	PProd14 Compliance with all capabilities of the software product should be thoroughly reviewed and recorded to ensure quality during deployment. It is recommended that a list previously defined in collaboration with the key users of the project be used
RProd15 Security tests not performed	Prod15 It is recommended that cybersecurity methodologies be applied during the deployment project in'accordance with the best market practices and procedures defined by the Organization

4.6   Threats to Validity

To analyze the validity of the study, the factors proposed in [27] were considered:

Construct validity. The results were obtained based on the documentary analysis of a set of risks for the process of deployment of software systems in a real context. This allowed us to answer the defined research questions, determining their relevance and suitability for the case.

Internal validity. The documentation used refers to a real case, a deployment of new deliverables for a Human Resources Portal performed in a bank in Argentina. In order to achieve greater precision and validity of the studied process, the need to combine the data source (project documentation) with other types of sources, such as interviews and/or focus groups to guarantee "data triangulation (source)", is recognized. Furthermore, the qualitative data collected and analyzed could be combined with quantitative data resulting from the project, thus ensuring a "Methodological Triangulation".

External validity. Carrying out a single case study may limit the generalizability of the results. However, a preliminary case study was conducted in [21]. These two experiences allow us to present results, which can be used by other researchers to carry out more studies with the same principles.

Reliability. The study data was collected and analyzed by the research group.

4.7   Lessons Learned

• Method selection: a validation of a set of risks, as well as the procedures for their prevention, mitigation and/or transfer, for the process of deployment of software systems, was needed in a real environment, in order to refine them (if required).

The results obtained allowed us to analyze the application of the set of risks defined in a real environment. Therefore, the method used is considered to have yielded the expected results.

- Data collection: although the documentation of the software system deployment process has been reviewed in order to analyze how the risks were managed, it is considered that the case could be strengthened if the data collected were complemented by another source or by quantitative data.
- Selected coding. The coding scheme selected for the design of the data collection and analysis template was adequate and allowed the systematic recording of risk information.
- Results report: Although the case is made up of two research questions, it is considered that the work carried out took into account an adequate level of detail for understanding the phenomenon under study.

5 Conclusions and Future Work

The results of a case study were presented to determine the feasibility of applying a set of risks, as well as the procedures for their prevention, mitigation and/or transfer for the process of deploying software systems in a real environment. It consisted of the risk analysis of the deployment of new deliverables for a Human Resources Portal carried out by a software SME in a bank in Argentina. After conducting the case study, it is concluded that:

- The first question allowed us to identify shortcomings in risk management through documentary analysis. These shortcomings include the lack of specialization of project personnel, mixed interests between the intervening areas and non-compliance with requirements of the installation environment.
- The second question allowed us to design a set of recommended procedures (presented in Sect. 4.5) for the company to improve its deployment process and to introduce good risk management practices for future software system deployments.

The lessons learned from the case showed that the research method was adequate to validate the proposal.

The following are identified as future works: (a) to validate the risk proposal for the software deployment process in different case studies in order to refine it. (b) To propose the use of the risks defined for the deployment of software systems, as well as the procedures for the prevention, mitigation and/or transfer thereof, by other professionals in the industry.

References

1. Charette, R.: Why software fails [software failure]. IEEE Spectr. **42**(9), 42–49 (2005)
2. Dhlamini, J., Nhamu, I., Kaihepa, A.: Intelligent risk management tools for software development, pp. 33–40 (2009)

3. Cámara de Software y Servicios Informáticos - CESSI. Anuario de la Industria Argentina de TI 2007/2008. Accessed 02 Dec 2008

4. Reporte anual 2018 sobre el Sector de Software y Servicios Informáticos de la República Argentina. OPSSI (2018). https://www.cessi.org.ar/opssi. Accessed April 2019

5. Abushama, H.M.: PAM-SMEs: process assessment method for small to medium enterprises. Softw. Evol. Process **28**, 689–711 (2016)

6. Ianzen, A., Mauda, E.C., Paludo, M.A., Reinehr, S., Malucelli, A.: Software process improvement in a financial organization: an action research approach. Comput. Stand. Interfaces **36**, 54–65 (2013)

7. Jones, C.: Assessment and Control of Software Risk. Yourdon Press, New Jersey (1994)

8. Liu, D., Wang, Q., Xiao, J.: The role of software process simulation modeling in software risk management: a systematic review. In: Proceedings of the 3rd International Symposium on Empirical Software Engineering and Measurement. Empirical Software Engineering and Measurement, pp. 302–311 (2009)

9. Jansen, S., Brinkkemper, S.: Definition and validation of the key process of release, delivery and deployment for product software vendors: turning the ugly duckling into a swan. In: IEEE International Conference on Software Maintenance, ICSM, art. no. 4021334, pp. 166–175 (2006)

10. Subramanian, N.: The software deployment process and automation. CrossTalk **30**(2), 28–34 (2017)

11. Tyndall, J.: Building an effective software deployment process. In: Proceedings of the 40th Annual ACM SIGUCCS Conference on User Services, pp. 109–114 (2012)

12. Reascos, I., Carvalho, J., Bossano, S.: Implanting IT applications in government institutions: a process model emerging from a case study in a medium-sized municipality. In: Proceedings of the 12th International Conference on Theory and Practice of Electronic Governance, pp. 80–85 (2019)

13. Forbes, J., Baker, E.: Improving hardware, software, and training deployment processes. In: Proceedings of 19th International Conference on Software Maintenance, pp. 377–380. IEEE, The Netherlands (2003)

14. Ortiz, F., Panizzi, M., Bertone, R.: Risk refinement in the deployment process of software systems: a case study. En las Actas del XXVI Congreso Argentino de Ciencias de la Computación - CACIC 2020. Universidad Nacional de La Matanza, 5 al 9 de Octubre. ISBN 978-987-4417-90-9

15. Ortiz, F., Davila, M., Panizzi, M., Bertone, R.: State of the art determination of risk management in the implantation process of computing systems. In: Botto-Tobar, M., León-Acurio, J., Díaz, C.A., Montiel Díaz, P. (eds.) Advances in Emerging Trends and Technologies. Advances in Intelligent Systems and Computing, vol. 1066, pp. 23–32. Springer, Cham (2019). https://doi.org/10.1007/978-3-030-32022-5_3. ISNB 978-3-030-32022-5

16. CMMI Institute: Capability Maturity Model Integration. https://cmmiinstitute.com. Accessed 24 June 2020

17. Project Management Institute. https://www.pmi.org/pmbok-guide-standards. Accessed 24 June 2020

18. Software Engineering Institute: Software Risk Evaluation Method (1999). https://resources.sei.cmu.edu/asset_files/TechnicalReport/1999_005_001_16799.pdf

19. Kitchenham, B., Linkman, S., Law, D.T.: DESMET: a method for evaluating software engineering methods and tools. Keele University (1996)

20. Portal de administración electrónica: MAGERIT v.3: metodología de análisis y gestión de riesgos de los sistemas de información 2012. Accessed 24 June 2020

21. Ortiz, F., Panizzi, M., Bertone, R.: Risk determination for the implantation process of software systems. En las Actas del XXV Congreso Argentino de Ciencias de la Computación - CACIC 2019. Universidad Nacional de Río Cuarto, 14 al 18 de Octubre, pp. 817–825 (2019). ISBN 978-987-688-377-1

22. ISO/IEC/IEEE 12207:2017. Systems and software engineering—software life cycle processes (2017)

23. Runeson, P., Höst, M., Rainer, A., Regnell, B.: Case Study Research in Software Engineering: Guidelines and Examples. Wiley Publishing, Hoboken (2012)

24. International Organization for Standardization: ISO/IEC 31010:2009. https://www.iso.org/standard/51073.html. Accessed 24 June 2020

25. Robson, C.: Real World Research, 2nd edn. Blackwell, Oxford (2002)

26. Yin, R.: Case Study Research: Design and Methods, 5th edn. Sage Publications, California (2014)

27. Lethbridge, T., Sim, S., Singer, J.: Studying software engineers: data collection techniques for software field studies. Empir. Softw. Eng. **10**(3), 311–341 (2005)

Data Evaluation Model Using GQM Approach

Julieta Calabrese⬛, Silvia Esponda(✉)⬛, Ariel Pasini⬛, and Patricia Pesado⬛

Computer Science Research Institute LIDI (III-LIDI),
School of Computer Science, National University of
La Plata, 50 y 120, La Plata, Buenos Aires, Argentina
{jcalabrese,sesponda,apasini,ppesado}@lidi.info.unlp.edu.ar

Abstract. Current organizations handle great amount of data. Nowadays, being able to better and keep their quality is one of the main goals that such organizations deal with. For this purpose, there exist standards defined by ISO that measure the data quality based on a group of characteristics which are inherent and dependent to the system. MED is presented, a data evaluation model that measures characteristics proposed by ISO/IEC 25012 through GQM approach (Goal, Question, Metric). Such approach is applied in an evaluation design, which will be subsequently carried out with the structure defined in ISO/IEC 25040.

Keywords: Data quality · ISO/IEC 25012 · ISO/IEC 25040 · GQM

1 Introduction

During the last years, the importance of data in an organization is more notorious. The digital progress is influencing in all sectors and it has turned data into the most powerful resources and in a key aspect for the decision-making process; however, these sectors do not tend to have accessible resources that assess the amount of their data.

It is very common to notice that data can be affected by negative factors: noise, lost values, inconsistencies, a very big size in any dimension (number of attributes and instances), among others. It has been shown that a low data quality leads to a low knowledge quality. Therefore, the lack of quality data can produce important consequences in the organization when companies seek to stand out of the rest in the current business and to provide an improved service that fulfils the demands of the clients.

Most of the companies are aware of the situation that the use of information generates a more competitive advantage when offering services and products according to the needs. Therefore, companies count on the support of the use of regulations and standards.

This context focuses our attention on standards defined by ISO. ISO/IEC 25000 family (mostly known as SQuaRE: Software Product Quality Requirements and Evaluation) starts in 2005 to cover the current needs of the organizations. Their goal is to create a common working framework to assess the quality of a software product from

Computer Science Research Institute LIDI (III-LIDI) - Partner Center of the Scientific Research Agency of the Province of Buenos Aires (CICPBA).
J. Calabrese, S. Esponda, A. Pasini, P. Pesado—Fellow UNLP.

P. Pesado and J. Eterovic (Eds.): CACIC 2020, CCIS 1409, pp. 141–154, 2021.
https://doi.org/10.1007/978-3-030-75836-3_10

different aspects. Within ISO/IEC 25000 family, the study is focused on ISO/IEC 25012 - "Data Quality Model" [1], which is defined by a group of characteristics that assess the data quality, and ISO/IEC 25040 - "Evaluation process" [2], that defines the evaluation process that will be carried out.

It is of utmost importance to be able to measure the characteristics defined in the ISO/IEC 25012, since that leads to obtain better quality data by focusing on their improvement in any scope. In this context, it is interesting to provide a solution in order to measure such characteristics by using the GQM (Goal, Question, Metric) approach [3].

The GQM approach is a method that strives for a way to measure certain goal through the use of questions. It is developed by the identification of one or more quality goals and by making questions with details of such goals in the most complex way. Subsequently, the way of measurement are defined, which will have a unique result based on the answers of such questions in order to identify the level of acceptance according to the defined goal. Finally, validation mechanisms and results analysis are developed.

The aim of this paper is to give a tool prototype called MED (Modelo de Evaluación de Datos - Data Evaluation Model) in order to design and carry out a quality evaluation defined in ISO/IEC 25012 and the GQM approach. The main goal is focused on knowing the data state of an organization through the level of a group of characteristics related to such data.

In the following section, the ISO/IEC 25012 and ISO/IEC 25040 regulations structures are described, stressing the characteristics associated to data. In the third section, GQM and their principles are defined. In the fourth section MED is presented, the data evaluation model that carry out the design of an evaluation by using the characteristics defined in ISO/IEC 25012 and GQM model. Subsequently, a data evaluation based on ISO/IEC 25040 using the defined design and finally, conclusions and bibliography are presented.

This paper is an extension of "Modelo de Evaluación de Datos utilizando el enfoque GQM" [7] published in Argentine Congress of Computer Science 2020 (CACIC 2020).

2   ISO/IEC 25000

The ISO/IEC 25000 (SQuaRE) family suggests a group of regulations whose goal is to create a common working framework to assess the quality of a software product from different aspects. Software developing companies that implement SQuaRE standards guarantee the quality of the shipped product, optimizing the shipping time, the resources used and the staff cost.

The group of regulations of ISO/IEC 25000 family are grouped in five divisions clearly defined:

- ISO/IEC 2500n family regulations determine common models, terms and definitions for the rest of the other regulations of 25000 families.
- The group of ISO/IEC 2501n regulations present a quality model where internal, external and in-use quality are included.

- The group of ISO/IEC 2502n regulations present a reference model to measure the quality of a software product, based on the definitions of quality measures (external, internal and in-use) and how they can be applied.
- The third division is composed of the ISO/IEC 25030 regulation, which specifies quality requirements that can be used in the elicitation of quality requirements of the product to be developed or in an evaluation process entrance.
- The regulations of the ISO/IEC 2504n family provide requirements, recommendations and guides to carry out the evaluation product of the software product.

In this paper, it is important to highlight the ISO/IEC 25012 e ISO/IEC 25040 regulations for their analysis and implementation.

2.1 ISO/IEC 25012 – Data Quality Model

The data quality is a key factor in any organization, since they represent the information in a formal and appropriate way for communication, interpretation or processing. ISO/IEC 25012 defines a quality general model for those data which are represented in a structured format within a computing system and their goal is to present an integrated vision to guarantee the systems interoperability. The regulation is composed of a group of fifteen characteristics, which are classified in two big groups:

Inherent Data Quality: with this grade, the characteristics have the power to satisfy the established needs when data are used under specific conditions. From the inherent point of view, the data quality makes reference to:

- Data values for the domain and their possible restrictions (e.g. Business rules with the quality required by the characteristics in an application)
- Relations among data values (e.g. Consistency)
- Metadata (e.g. autor, format, etc.)

System-dependent data quality: with this grade, the data quality is achieved and preserved through a computing system when data are used under specific conditions. From this point of view, the data quality depends on the technological domain in which data are used, and this is achieved through the capacity of the computing system components, such as: hardware devices (e.g. backup in order to get recoverability) and software (e.g. migration tools in order to get portability). Computer systems technicians tend to be in charge of this point. Table 1 shows the classification of the characteristics:

The group of characteristics that define the *Inherent Data Quality* are formed by: **Accuracy** (Semantics y Syntax), specifying the grade in which data represent the desired value properly in a specific context; **Completeness**, where compulsory data is expected to be complete; **Consistency**, referring to data free of contradiction, coherent data in a specific context; **Credibility**, including the concept of authenticity, that defines the grade in which certain data are considered as true and credible in a specific context; and **Actuality**, which defines the grade in which data are updated.

On the other hand, the characteristics that define *Inherent and System-dependent data* refer to **Accessibility**, where it is specified the grade in which data can be achieved

Table 1. Classification of characteristics defined in ISO/IEC 25012.

Característic	Inherent	System-dependent
Accuracy	X	
Completeness	X	
Consistency	X	
Credibility	X	
Actuality	X	
Accesibility	X	X
Acceptance	X	X
Confidenciality	X	X
Efficiency	X	X
Precision	X	X
Traceability	X	X
Comprenhension	X	X
Availability		X
Portabililty		X
Recoverability		X

in a specific context (e.g.: people who need support technology due to disability); **Acceptance**, where it is checked that the corresponding data fulfil the current standard and regulations; **Confidentiality** (it is associated to information safety) where it is guaranteed that data are only obtained and interpreted by specific and authorized users; **Efficiency**, where the level in which data can be processed and provided with the expected levels of efficiency; **Precision**, where data require exact values or with discernment in a specific context; **Traceability**, where it is analyzed whether data suggest a register of the events that modify them or not; and **Comprehension**, where data are expressed using appropriate languages, symbols and unities and can be read and interpreted for any kind of user.

Finally, the characteristics that form the *System-Dependent Data Quality* emphasize **Availability**, that define the level of data to be obtained by users or authorized applications; **Portability**, where it is analyzed whether data can be copied, replaced or eliminated or not, when there is a change from one system to another preserving the level of quality; and **Recoverability**, where it is proved that data keep and preserve a level of operations in case of failure [5].

Being able to measure the characteristics presented is one of the most complex steps at the moment of carrying out an evaluation. Measurement is a key element in any engineering process and, particularly, in SQuaRE, the measures are used to assess the quality of the software products from different points of view, and to understand their associated characteristics in detail.

There is a group of ways of measurement that carry out the measurement of data quality in terms of defined characteristics. Such ways of measurement are defined in ISO/IEC 25024 [4] and they will not be of interest for the goal in this paper.

2.2 ISO/IEC 25040 – Evaluation Process

ISO/IEC 25040 defines the process to carry out the evaluation of a software product through a reference model, considering the necessary entries, restrictions and resources to obtain the corresponding exits. The process to carry out the evaluation has five activities:

Activity 1: To establish the evaluation requirements. This activity consists of detailing the basic requirements for the evaluation:

1.1: Establish the purpose of the evaluation: it is pointed out the purpose through which an organization wants to assess the quality of a software product and from which aspect the focus of the evaluation will be pointed out.
1.2: Obtain the requirements of the product quality: the interested parties in the product are identified (developers, possible purchasers, users, suppliers). Moreover, the product quality requirements are described using a quality model (e.g. the one defined in ISO/IEC 25012).
1.3: Identify the parts of the product that must be assessed: the parts of the software product that are included in the evaluation are identified and recorded. The kind of product to be assessed depends on the phase in the life cycle in which the evaluation is carried out.
1.4: Define the thoroughness in the evaluation: the thoroughness of the evaluation is defined according to the purpose. Different types are taken as reference, such as, safety risks, financial risks or environmental risks.

Activity 2: To specify the evaluation. This activity lies in the specification of evaluation modules (ways of measurement, tools and techniques) as well as the decision criteria to be used.

2.1: To select the evaluation module: the ways of measurement for quality, techniques and tools are selected. They must cover all the evaluation requirements. Such ways of measurements must be able to be compared with the defined criteria to be able to take decisions.
2.2: To define the decision criteria for the ways of measurement: the decision criteria are defined, which are numeric thresholds that can be related to quality require-ments and evaluation criteria, in order to decide the product quality from the corresponding aspect.
2.3: To define the decision criteria for the evaluation: the criteria are defined for the different assessed characteristics. These results, in a higher level of abstraction, can carry out the evaluation of the product quality in a general way.

Activity 3: To Design the evaluation. In this activity, the plans with the tasks that must be carried out in the evaluation are defined.

3.1: To plan the activities of the evaluation: the activities of the evaluation are planned, having in mind the availability of the human resources and necessary materials, the Budget, the methods of evaluation and adapted standards, the evaluation tools, among others.

Activity 4: To carry out the evaluation. Activity that carries out the evaluation activities, obtaining the quality ways of measurement and using the decision criteria.

4.1: To carry out the measurements: the corresponding measurements are carried out to obtain the values of the ways of measurement selected and indicated in the evaluation plan. All the results must be registered.
4.2: To employ the decision criteria for the ways of measurement: the criteria for the ways of measurement are employed on the values obtained in the measurement of a product.
4.3: To employ the decision criteria of the evaluation: the decision criteria of the evaluation are employed, giving as a result the level in which the product fulfils the established quality requirements.

Activity 5: To conclude the evaluation: In this last activity the evaluation quality finishes, with a final results and conclusions report based on the obtained values.

5.1: To check the evaluation results: the assessor and the client (if there is any) are in charge of checking the results obtained in the evaluation. The goal is to make a better interpretation and better error detection.
5.2: To create the evaluation report: after the result analysis, an evaluation report is produced, showing the requirements, the results, the limitations and restrictions, the assessor staff, among others.
5.3: To check the evaluation quality: the assessor is in charge of checking the results of the evaluation and the validity of the process, the indicators and the ways of measurement employed. On this basis, a feedback is obtained, which must be useful to better the evaluation process.
5.4: To handle the evaluation data: the assessor must handle data according to what was agreed with the client, returning them, modifying them or keeping them, among others.

3 GQM (Goal Question Metric)

GQM is a method oriented towards the creation of a way of measurement that measures a goal in a determined way through the use of questions. It provides a useful way to define measurements, both the process and the results of a project.

It is focused on a measurement that can be more satisfactory if it is designed having in mind the goals, and the questions help to measure if the defined goal is being achieved. This is to improve the quality and reliability by reducing costs, risks and time [6].

GQM defines a goal, it establishes a group of questions based on it and it generates ways of measurement based on the answers of the questions. Likewise, it can be used by the individual members of a project team to focus their job and to determine their progress towards the achievement of their specific goals. The measurement must be carried out, in all the cases, oriented towards a goal.

The GQM measurement model has three levels:

- Conceptual Level (Goal): what is aimed at products, processes or resources is identified; as regards several quality models, from several points of view and related to a particular environment.
- Operational Level (Question): a group of questions from the goal is polished in order to verify their fulfilment. The questions seek to characterize the measurement object (product, process or resource) as regards a matter of selected quality, and to determine its quality from the selected point of view.
- Quantitative Level (Way of Measurement): a group of data for each question, formulating ways of measurement, is merged in order to give an answer in a quantitative way. Data can be objective (if it only depends on the object that is measured, not on the point of view that it is caught) or subjective (if it depends on both, the object that is measured and the point of view that it is caught).

For the same goal, there can be several defined questions and, at the same time, one question can be linked to multiple goals. For each question, there can be one or more ways of measurement. A way of measurement can be used for more than one question. Figure 1 defines the GQM Measurement Model.

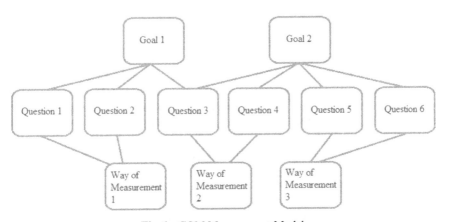

Fig. 1. GQM Measurement Model.

GQM could be specified as a series of steps that start to identify a quality and/or productivity goal, at a corporative level, of division or project (Step 1). From that goal, questions are made to define the goal in the most complete way (Step 2). The measures that must be taken in order to answer those questions and to do a monitoring of the approval of the product with the goal are specified (Step 3).

Step 1 – To establish the goals. The business goal and/or measure are identified. The goal is the exit of step 1 in GQM, making reference to conceptual and non-quantitative aspects. Such goal is quantified by its relation with the questions and the ways of measurement.

Step 2 – Question Creation. The goal is classified and polished by being moved from a conceptual to an operational level by making questions.

Questions that must be made in order to catch several perspectives to achieve the goal are identified. Goal meaning perspectives are provided in such environment, making questions and answering with their ways of measurement.

If the questions are very abstract, the relation between the questions and the ways of measurement will be hard to visualize. If the questions are very detailed, it is harder to obtain a clear interpretation of the goal. This step must be followed responsibly to make sure that the level of questioning is enough in order to handle properly the identification of ways of measurement.

Step 3 – Measurement Specification. The goal must move from a qualitative level (or operating level) to a quantitative level). It is necessary to define ways of measurement that provide all the quantities information to answer the questions in step 2 in a satisfactory way. Those which are directly linked with the goal must be linked either in the identification of ways of measurement step and in the identification of questions.

4   MED: Data Evaluation Model

As it was mentioned previously, one of the key elements in any engineering process is measurement and, particularly in SQuaRE, measures are employed to analyze the level of different characteristics associated to what it will be assessed.

From this context, the goal of this paper is to propose a new measurement model based on the use of ways of measurement defined, by using the GQM approach. In this way, a group of questions must be answered in order to obtain the corresponding value of the ways of measurement associated to the group of characteristics that are expected to be measured.

With this aim, the prototype of a tool is defined, and it will include the model of measurement proposed and that its goal is to facilitate the design and execution of an evaluation based on ISO/IEC 25040, using the quality model defined in ISO/IEC 25012 and measuring under the GQM approach.

The tool prototype has two phases that are clearly distinguished:

- Evaluation Design, which, at the same time, is divided into:

  - Design for general characteristics
  - Design for attributes

- Evaluation execution

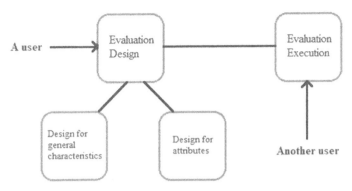

Fig. 2. Tool prototype.

4.1 Evaluation Design

The goal of the evaluation design phase is to define all the necessary/corresponding information for the setup of a quality evaluation that will be carried out later. In our case, the goal will be focused on giving an interested party the chance to create their own group of questions that can measure the attributes[1] of their data based on the defined characteristics in ISO/IEC 25012. For that purpose, the tool will present two sections: design for characteristics and design for attributes.

4.1.1 Design for Characteristics

This design section is focused on creating a group of questions in order to measure the characteristics defined in ISO/IEC 25012. Based on this goal, the tool will let the interested party load each of the questions, their allowable answers and the setup of a formula in order to obtain the final ways of measurement. Figure 3 defines the process of design and it lately details each of their phases.

The process is composed of:

- **Selection of a characteristic:** a characteristic from the group of characteristics presented by ISO/IEC 25012 must be selected. Since each characteristic makes reference to a particular aspect, such aspect will be taken as the goal to be measured (outlined previously in Step 1 of the GQM model). *For instance: we will select "Actuality" and "Completeness" characteristics.*
- **1..N Question entry:** a group of questions associated to the goal of the selected characteristic will be created (outlined previously in Step 2 of the GQM model). The tool will allow the entry of the questions. *Following the example, questions associated to the "Actuality" characteristic could be: (Q1) were data updated over the last 6 months? (Q2) Are data used in the development environment updated weekly along with data used in production? Questions associated to the "Completeness" characteristic could be: (Q3) what percentage of all data can be completed approximately?*

---

[1] *Attribute: it makes reference to a characteristic of an entity in data base.*

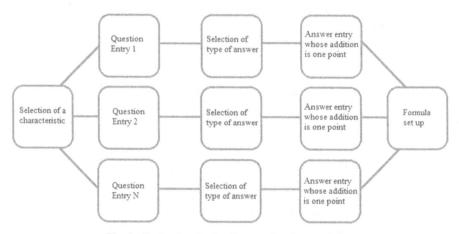

Fig. 3. Evaluation Design Process for characteristics.

In order to facilitate the question loading task and encourage the recycling of information, this section will suggest and allow the use of different questions that have been previously created by other assessors. This will extend, even more, the measurement possibilities before the different characteristics of the used model.

- **Selection of type of answer:** the type of answer associated to the question must be indicated. The types can be: YES/NO, numeric, the selection of a value from values ranking, multiple choice, among others. It is important to highlight that the answer must be quantifiable.

  Following with the example, the type of answer for both questions associated to the "Actuality" characteristic will be "YES/NO". The type of answer for the question associated to the "Completeness" characteristic will be "Numeric".

- **Answer entry whose addition is one point**: when the question and the type of answer is defined, the expected answer must be indicated, so that it has the same influence in the formula for the final way of measurement. This can implicate the total coincidence with an expected value or a higher/lower value to the one expected. In case the answer given by the person that carry out the evaluation is not what it was expected, it will not have any influence in the final formula whatsoever. *Following the example, the answer that will have influence on the formula is YES for both questions associated to Actuality. For the question associated to Completeness, an answer higher than or equal to 80% is the one that will have influence (value established by the person in charge of the evaluation design).*

- **Formula set up:** the final formula must be specified (for the setup of the way of measurement) having in mind all the questions made. The result of the formula will be able to create a value between 0 and 1, being 1 the highest value and 0 the lowest value.

Following the example, the formula for the "Actuality" characteristic will be:

$$0 \leq (P1 + P2)/QUANTITY\ OF\ QUESTIONS \leq 1$$

The formula for the "Completeness" characteristic will be:

$$0 \leq P3 \leq 1$$

On the basis of the answers to the questions (answered in the evaluation execution) a value for the formula will be obtained. The obtained value in the formula will determine the value of the way of measurement (outlined previously in Step 3 of the GQM model). Subsequently, in the evaluation it will be indicated and analyzed which is the expected value for each of the characteristics.

4.1.2 Design for Attributes

Usually, there are cases where there is a will to assess a characteristic for a specific attribute from a table of database. As an example, a person can be interested in measuring the "Precision" characteristic from the attribute -price- from a table, but not from the attribute -name- from the same table. Therefore, this second section of design (unlike the first one) is able to associate the questions to a specific attribute.

By adapting the process presented in the first section within the evaluation design, by selecting the characteristic, each of the attributes that want to be measure through questions for such characteristic must be uploaded. Subsequently, the process works in a similar way to the one presented in the first section.

Following the example, specific questions will be created in order to measure the "Completeness" characteristic, particularly from -ID- and -EIN (Employer identification Number)- attributes.

(Q4) What estimated percentage of ID numbers is complete? | Type of answer: numeric | Answer with one point: $\geq 90\%$
(Q5) What estimate percentage of EIN numbers is complete? | Type of answer: numeric | Answer with one point: $\geq 60\%$
Formula:

$$0 \leq (P4 + P5)/QUANTITY\ OF\ QUESTIONS \leq 1$$

4.2 Evaluation Execution

At the moment of finishing the evaluation design, it can be carried out immediately. An assessor will be in charge of performing the process and of completing each section of the structure of evaluation defined below, which is based and adapted under ISO/IEC 25040. The tool will include all what was defined in the design phase at the moment of carrying out the measurement.

To this effect, the example presented in the design will be used again and a group of test data defined in Table 2 will be taken into account.

Establish the Evaluation Requirements. Firstly, the evaluation purpose is defined.

Table 2. Affiliates data.

ID	EIN	Last name	First name	Address	Phone
36111555	27361115554	DIAZ	ALEJANDRA	16–1616	
12546548	20125465488	GARCIA	LUIS	18–1201	13–6422
	23456584541	FERNANDEZ	PEDRO	14–5675	
37394444		RODRIGUEZ	SOFIA	13–5456	45–7865
	20342581659	PEREZ	CAROLINA		67–5698

The evaluation purpose is to determine how updated and how complete data are, making reference to ID and EIN numbers of the members.

Based on the purpose, the characteristics of interest for the evaluation are selected, defined in the ISO/IEC 25012 regulation.

The ISO/IEC 25012 characteristics selected for the evaluation will be: Completeness and Actuality.

To Specify the Evaluation. In this evaluation phase, it is necessary to define decision criteria[2] for each one of the characteristics and for the final evaluation. To do so, the considered values (always between 0 and 1) for each characteristic must be defined. The values rankings will be as follows: unacceptable, slightly unacceptable, goal ranking ad it exceeds the requirements. Later, the considered values for the final evaluation must be indicated. Table 3 *defines the decision criteria of each of the assessed characteristics.*

Table 3. Decision Criteria of the Characteristics.

	Characteristic: Actuality	Characteristic: Completeness
Exceeds the requirements	$0.8 \leq$ value < 1	$0.9 \leq$ value < 1
Goal ranking	$0.4 \leq$ value < 0.8	$0.6 \leq$ value < 0.9
Slightly unacceptable	$0.2 \leq$ value < 0.4	$0.4 \leq$ value < 0.6
Unacceptable	$0 \leq$ value < 0.2	$0 \leq$ value < 0.2

To Design an Evaluation. At the moment of designing the evaluation, it must be specified if the evaluation will be carried out with a specific amount of users answering the questions or if the questions will be answered only by a user.

The questions will be answered only by a person, who has access to the test data.

---

[2] *The values rankings classified as follows: unacceptable, slightly unacceptable, goal ranking ad it exceeds the requirements.*

To Carry Out the Evaluation. This phase will present all the questions previously defined in the design phase. There will not be any favoritism on the characteristic that it is being assessed, on the contrary, they will have to be answered completely to perform the measurement.

(Q1) Were data updated during the past 6 months?
A: YES (equivalent to 1 in the formula according to the design)
(Q2) Are data used in the development environment updated weekly with the data used in production?
A: NO (equivalent to 0 in the formula according to the design)

(Q3) What estimate percentage of all data are complete?
A: 80% (equivalent to 1 in the formula according to the design)

(Q4) What estimate percentage of ID numbers are complete?
A: 60% (equivalent to 0 in the formula according to the design)

(Q5) What estimate percentage of EIN numbers are complete?
A: 80% (equivalent to 1 in the formula according to the design).

End of the Evaluation. Once all questions were answered, the tool will obtain the answers and will carry out the corresponding formulas showing the results for each one of the characteristics assessed. Therefore, the answer of the user, the formula specified in the evaluation design and the decision criteria are taken into account in order to define the value of the final way of measurement and to see if such value is what it was expected.

This information tend to be useful for the developers, who will be able to improve their future developments, to avoid creating and storing low quality data in their systems.

ACTUALITY – Results
Formula:

$$(P1 + P2)/QUANTITY\ OF\ QUESTIONS = (1 + 0)/2 = 0{,}5 ==> Goal\ ranking$$

COMPLETENESS – Results
General Sub formula (F1):

$$P3 = 1$$

Attributes Sub formula (F2):

$$(P4 + P5)/QUANTITY\ OF\ QUESTIONS = (0 + 1)/2 = 0{,}5$$

Formula:

$$(F1 + F2)/QUANTITY\ OF\ SUBFORMULAS = (1 + 0{,}5)/2 = 0{,}75 ==> Goal\ ranking$$

5 Conclusions

MED was presented, a data evaluation model based on the GQM approach, made on the basis of the characteristics defined in the ISO/IEC 25012 regulation. GQM starts with a concrete goal and then it creates questions related to such goal and, through the combination of their answers, a formula that creates the associated way of measurement is obtained.

MED tackles the data quality evaluation in a very simple and flexible way, by allowing an organization to know the state of their data, obtaining, this way, more reliable information.

A data quality evaluation was carried out based on ISO/IEC 25040, using the evaluation design that was defined in the model, and taking as an example two characteristics: "Actuality" and "Completeness". For the answers to the defined questions, a group of example data were taken as a reference. They were useful to support the evaluation performance.

Currently, the chance to extend the data evaluation model to another type of evaluation with a similar structure is still under discussion, but having the development of a usable tool by any type of user as primary focus; therefore, facilitating the task to design and carry out quality evaluations.

References

1. ISO/IEC 25012:2008. Software engineering – Software Product Quality Requirements and Evaluation (SQuaRE) – Data quality model
2. ISO/IEC 25040:2011. Systems and software engineering – Systems and software Quality Requirements and Evaluation (SQuaRE) – Evaluation process
3. Basili, V.R., Caldiera, G., Rombach, H.D.: The goal question metric approach. In: Encyclopedia of Software Engineering, vol. 1, pp. 528–535 (1994)
4. ISO/IEC 25024:2015. Systems and software engineering – Systems and software Quality Requirements and Evaluation (SQuaRE) – Measurement of data quality
5. Calabrese, J., Esponda, S., Pasini, A., Boracchia, M., Pesado, P.: Guía para evaluar calidad de datos basada en ISO/IEC 25012. In: Congreso Argentino de Ciencias de la Computación - CACIC 2019
6. Muñoz, R., Calabrese, J.: Asistente para la evaluación de calidad de producto de software según la familia de normas ISO/IEC 25000 utilizando el enfoque GQM. Tesina de Licenciatura en Sistemas (2018)
7. Calabrese, J., Esponda, S., Pasini, A., Pesado, P.: Modelo de evaluación de datos utilizando el enfoque GQM. In: Congreso Argentino de Ciencias de la Computación - CACIC 2020

Databases and Data Mining

Performance Analysis in NoSQL Databases, Relational Databases and NoSQL Databases as a Service in the Cloud

Luciano Marrero[✉], Verena Olsowy, Fernando Tesone, Pablo Thomas, Lisandro Delia, and Patricia Pesado

Instituto de Investigación en Informática LIDI, Facultad de Informática, Universidad Nacional de La Plata, La Plata, Argentina

{lmarrero,volsowy,ftesone,pthomas,ldelia,
ppesado}@lidi.info.unlp.edu.ar

Abstract. Non-Relational Database Management Systems (NoSQL) arise as an alternative solution to problems not efficiently solved by traditional Database Management Systems (DBMS). NoSQL, unlike the relational model, does not respond to a Data Base type, but represents a set of Database types, with different implementations and characteristics to represent the information. This work represents the continuation of previous studies and aims to compare and analyse 4 local NoSQL Database engines, 2 NoSQL Database as a Service engines in the cloud and a Relational Database engine, using different schemas and under large data volume.

Keywords: Relational Database Management Systems · NoSQL Database · Cloud computing · Key-Value Storage · Documental storage · Column Family Storage · Graph-Oriented Storage

1 Introduction

Nowadays, most of applications are multiplatform. Developments in digital communication, constant access to information and the increase in the use of mobile technology causes these applications to be commonly used by millions of users at the same time. The Codd relational model (1970) [12], which gave rise to Relational Database Systems is, without a doubt, the predominant model of information storage. However, the idea of considering that a single data model can efficiently adapt itself to all requirements has been called into question, and this has given rise to a set of alternatives that aim at storing information in a non-structured manner. As a result, other database engines are born, which have their own non-relational implementations and are called NoSQL (Not only SQL) Databases. These Databases are suitable for their scalability and are prone to use flexible consistency models in order to achieve higher performance and availability [2–4, 12]. There is a wide variety of NoSQL Database engines that can be classified into one of the following 4 categories.

Centro Asociado Comisión de Investigaciones Científicas de la Provincia de Buenos Aires.

© Springer Nature Switzerland AG 2021
P. Pesado and J. Eterovic (Eds.): CACIC 2020, CCIS 1409, pp. 157–170, 2021.
https://doi.org/10.1007/978-3-030-75836-3_11

Key-Value Storage. Easily implemented, they store data as sets of Key-Value pairs. The Key represents a unique identifier that can generate an object named Value. Some examples of well-known database engines with Key/Value storage are: Redis, Amazon DynamoDB, Memcached, among others. [20, 21].

Documental Storage. The main concept of this type of storage is the document. A NoSQL Documental Database stores, retrieves and manages document data. These documents encapsulate and encode data or information under some type of standard format. (XML, YAML, JSON, BSON). Some examples of well-known Database engines with document storage are: MongoDB, Cloud Firestore, among others. [5, 8, 17, 22].

Column Family Storage. In this type of storage, data is sorted by columns, not by rows. In these By Column Database, there is a column for each entry; therefore, the data of each entry is organized one below the other (not side by side, as in the row-oriented variant). The goal of this type of storage is to more accurately access the information needed to answer a query. In addition, it eliminates the need to explore and discard unwanted data on a row. For example, Apache Cassandra and Apache HBase, among others, use this type of storage [8, 9, 19, 23].

Graph-Oriented Storage. This type of storage represents Database under the concept of a Graph. It allows information to be stored as nodes of a graph and their respective relations (edges) with other nodes. It applies graph theory and it is very useful to storage information in models that have multiple relations among their data. For example, Neo4j y OrientDB, among others, implement this type of storage [11, 24].

Just as ACID properties (Atomicity, Consistency, Isolation and Durability) are present in the Relational Database, NoSQL Database present BASE properties (Base Availability, Soft State, Eventual Consistency). Availability is the main pillar of these properties. The system will basically be available all the time (BA), will not necessary be consistent (S), although at some point it will be, and eventually it will be in a known state (E). BASE properties differ from ACID properties, while ACID is more rigid and forces consistency, BASE allows for a flexible consistency state. This allows for large levels of scalability [4, 7, 10, 13].

This paper represents a continuation of [1] and [25], and focuses on a comparative performance analysis for 6 case studies, implemented in 7 different database engines, 4 locally installed and configured NoSQL (Cassandra, MongoDB, Neo4j y Redis), 2 NoSQL as a cloud service (Cloud Firestore y MongoDB Atlas) and one Relational Database engine (MySQL). A set of queries was developed for each case study and for each Database engine. 10 consultations were made for MySQL, 7 for MongoDB, 8 for Cassandra, 8 for Neo4j, 2 for Redis, 3 for Cloud Firestore and 3 for MongoDB Atlas. A total of 41 queries were tested using a large volume of information for the locally installed and configured database engines (Redis, MongoDB, Cassandra, Neo4j and MySQL). As regards NoSQL Database engines, as service in the cloud (Cloud Firestore and MongoDB Atlas), were used taking into account the restrictions they have in the free version. Each case study has its characteristics in order to compare the performance of different engines of Database in a variety of scenarios.

From Sect. 2 this paper is organised as follows: an introduction to cloud Database services is provided. In Sect. 3 and Sect. 4 general characteristics of the selected database engines are explained; in Sect. 5 and Sect. 6 the case studies are presented, in Sect. 7 and Sect. 8 the results obtained are analysed, in Sect. 9 the conclusions are presented, and finally, in Sect. 10, the future lines of work are presented.

2   Database as a Service in the Cloud

Nowadays, Relational and Non-Relational Database providers offer alternative implementations of cloud storage, similar to those that can be downloaded and installed on a local server. This allows an almost linear migration from a local environment to a cloud environment. Nevertheless, it is important to take into account the advantages and disadvantages of both alternatives (local and in the cloud) to be able to evaluate which one will be the alternative that best adapts to the business needs. There are differences to consider between a local Database implementation and a cloud Database service. Among the most important, we can find:

- Limitations: Databases in the cloud, in their free versions, generally show limitations in the benefits they offer, such storage space limitations, the number of readings and writings in a period of time, the number of simultaneous connections, among others. Alternatively, they offer various payment plans to extend these limitations, according to the client's needs.
- Servers' location: when configuring a Database in the cloud, the geographical location of the cluster. This allows the server and its replicas to be located closer to the client is usually selected. This allows the server and its replicas to be located closer to the client.
- Monitoring tools: some implementations incorporate, from its free version, tools that allow monitoring the number of connexions in a given moment, the physical space, both occupied and available, the number of operations in a given rage of time, among others.
- Less control over infrastructure: hardware and its infrastructure will be in the control of the service provider; as a consequence, this reduces the workload of database administrators and, in return, control over resource management is lost.

Database technologies in the cloud have changed and restructured the tasks to be performed by Database administrators. There are certain routine characteristics, in local Databases, that are not of a great concern now. Some of the tasks that are performed when a local Database engine is installed change themselves when using a Database engine in the cloud, thus resulting in other tasks closer to the application domain and to the incorporation and use of specific tools that each provider makes available to its users.

3   Local Database Engines Used

To carry out the experimentation presented in this work, the following Database engines were selected and installed locally: MySQL (Relational Storage), MongoDB (Document Storage), Apache Cassandra (Column Family Storage), Neo4j (Graph-Oriented Storage) and Redis (Key-Value Storage). The chosen NoSQL database engines are the most popular in their categories [14].

MySQL. It is one of the most recognized and popular relational Database systems on the market with dual license (general public license and commercial license). It is used by numerous companies worldwide, including Facebook, Twitter, YouTube, GitHub, Booking.com, Spotify [15, 16].

MongoDB. It is the most popular Documentary NoSQL Database, it is open source and multiplatform. Different companies such as Telefónica, Facebook, Nokia, among others, use MongoDB [5, 6, 17, 18].

Apache Cassandra. It is the most popular NoSQL database with storage in Column Family. It is multiplatform, designed to work in a distributed way with large volumes of data. Companies such as Instagram, Netflix, GitHub, among others, use Cassandra [19, 21].

Neo4j. It is the most popular Graph Oriented Database (GODB), written in JAVA and has a dual license (commercial and AGPL). It is based on graphs to represent data and the relations among them. Companies such as Walmart, Ebay and Cisco use Neo4j [11].

Redis. It is the most popular Key-Value Database. Redis is a database that operates its data structures in primary memory, offers high performance, has optional persistence and has a BSD Free Software license. It is used by different companies, Stack Overflow, Twitter, GitHub, among others [20].

4 Database Engines Used as a Service Cloud

With the aim of complimenting the experimentation presented in this paper, 2 Database engines were selected and configured, which offer services in the cloud, Cloud Firestore and MongoDB Atlas.

Cloud Firestore, in its Free Version. Firebase is a platform in the cloud that Google offers for Web and mobile applications development. Among the services and tools offered, Cloud Firestone is one of the most important, a Database engine in the NoSQL cloud, with documental storage. This Database is one of the most popular on the market [14, 26].

MongoDB Atlas in its Free Version. This is a Database as a service in the cloud, provided by MongoDB; in other words, the user receives a Database that is operated and maintained by MongoDB. The MongoDB Atlas service automatically includes the configuration of the servers and the whole environment for the database. In addition, it is compatible with different cloud service providers, such as: Amazon Web Services (AWS), Google Cloud Platform (GPC) and Microsoft Azure. MongoDB Atlas, like MongoDB, it is a NoSQL database engine with document storage [27].

5   Case Studies with Database Engines Locally Installed

For each case study, the Conceptual Data Model was previously created using an Entity Relation Diagram. Subsequently, the derivation to the physical corresponding schema was made to each Database engine used.

In MySQL the relational model was generated.

In MongoDB the entities are represented by means of BJSON document collections; the relations are expressed through embedded documents [1, 2, 17].

In Cassandra, the data are not stored in terms of entities, but are represented in terms of queries, therefore, it is important to define the queries to be made [1, 2, 9, 19].

In Neo4j, the data are represented through nodes and the relations are the edges between them [2, 24].

In Redis, being a main memory Database (RAM), the set of keys that would be necessary to have in force according to the queries to be performed were taken into account [2, 20].

The performance of tests for these Database engines was done using the same memory and operating system (4GB de RAM, Ubuntu version 18.04). In MongoDB version 4.0, in Cassandra version 3.11, in Neo4j version 4.1 and in Redis version 4.0. For each case study the volume of data used was randomly generated.

In the first 3 cases of study it was not possible to evaluate Redis due to the fact that the huge data volume used cannot be properly managed in main memory.

Next, the cases studies for these Database engines are shown. As an example and in order not to exceed the number of pages, only for the first of them the physical schemas and the code of the queries are shown. Nevertheless, in all the cases the DER and the results obtained are expressed.

5.1   Study Case 1

A outline for the inbox of an internal messaging system is presented. A total of 30,000,000 messages, corresponding to 6,000,000 different users, have been randomly generated. The DER of the problem in question is presented (see Fig. 1).

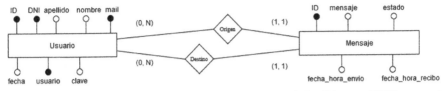

Fig. 1. Conceptual outline expressed by means of an Entity Relation Diagram (DER) expresado mediante un Diagrama Entidad Relación (DER).

Next, the resulting Relational model is shown for MySQL (sea Fig. 2).

```
Usuario = (id, DNI, apellido, nombre, mail, fecha_alta, usuario,
clave)
Menaje = (id, mensaje, estado, fecha_hora_env, fecha_hora_rec,
usuario_orig(FK), usuario_dest(FK))
```

Fig. 2. Relational outline expressed for MySQL.

Next, documental structure for MongoDB is shown (see Fig. 3).

```
Mensaje = {id, mensaje, estado, fecha_hora_env, fecha_hora_rec,
           usuario_origen = {'dni','nombre','apellido',
           'mail','usuario'},
           usuario_destino = {'dni','nombre','apellido',
           'mail','usuario'}}
```

Fig. 3. Documental outline for MongoDB.

In Cassandra, the physical outline is expressed according to the queries to be done. Next, the physical outline resulting for this case study is shown (see Fig. 4).

```
Mensajes_por_usuario = ((usuario_orig, usuario_dest,
fecha_hora_env)PK, mensaje, fecha_hora_rec, estado);
```

Fig. 4. Physical outline for Cassandra.

The following is a fragment of the Graph storage proposed for Neo4j. The green nodes represent users, while the grey ones represent messages. (See Fig. 5).

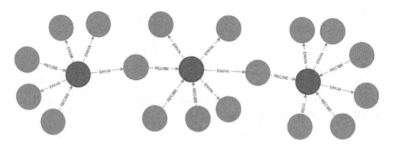

Fig. 5. Fragment of Graph (in *Neo4j*) created for this first case study.

Listed below are 3 queries to evaluate performance in this case study.

"Q1: Messages between two specific users"
"Q2: Search for a string of characters in the messages of a specific user"
"Q3: Messages received and unread by a specific user"

Each query was implemented in the 4 Database engines, MySQL, Cassandra, MongoDB and Neo4j (sea Fig. 6, 7, 8 and 9).

```
SELECT mensaje, fecha_hora_env, estado
FROM mensaje m INNER JOIN usuario o ON (o.id=m.usuario_orig) INNER
JOIN usuario d ON (d.id=m.usuario_dest) WHERE (o.usuario = 'user256'
AND d.usuario = 'user1') OR (o.usuario = 'user1' AND d.usuario =
'user256') ORDER BY m.fecha_hora_env DESC
```

Fig. 6. Implementation of Q1 in MySQL.

```
SELECT mensaje, fecha_hora_env, estado
FROM mensajes_por_usuario
WHERE usuario_orig IN ('user256','user1') AND usuario_dest IN
('user1', 'user256') ORDER BY fecha_hora_env DESC
```

Fig. 7. Implementation of Q1 in Cassandra (CQL).

```
SELECT mensaje, fecha_hora_env, estado
FROM mensajes_por_usuario
WHERE usuario_orig IN ('user256','user1') AND usuario_dest IN
('user1', 'user256') ORDER BY fecha_hora_env DESC
```

Fig. 8. Implementation of Q1 in MongoDB.

```
MATCH (u1:Usuario)-[r1]-(m:Mensaje)-[r2]-(u2:Usuario)
WHERE ID(u1) = 34000550 AND ID(u2) = 34000805
RETURN u1.usuario, r1, m, r2, u2.usuario;
```

Fig. 9. Implementation of Q1 in Neo4j.

Table 1 shows the execution time of each query expressed in seconds.

Table 1. Results of the first case study in seconds.

Consultas	MySQL	MongoDB	Cassandra	Neo4j
Q1	0,33	385	0,35	0,24
Q2	259	178	9	0,15
Q3	20	166	72	0,24

5.2 Case Study 2

This case study represents a monitoring centre that records and processes events from different sources. A total of 40,000,000 events have been randomly generated. The DER of the described problem is shown below (see Fig. 10).

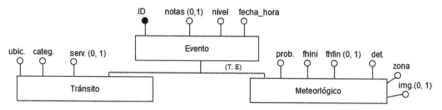

Fig. 10. Conceptual outline expressed by means of an Entity Relation Diagram.

Listed below are 3 queries to evaluate performance in this case study.

"Q1: Meteorological events exceeding a certain probability of occurrence"
"Q2: Traffic events with a certain category in a period of time"
"Q3: Number of events of a given priority level (High, Medium or Low)"

Table 2 shows the execution time of each query expressed in seconds for this second case study.

Table 2. Results of the second case study expressed in seconds.

Consultas	MySQL	MongoDB	Cassandra	Neo4j
Q1	200	119	123	360
Q2	233	117	120	134
Q3	81	106	200	288

5.3 Case Study 3

In this third case, a outline of flights belonging to different airlines is presented. The information of 40,000,000 flights between 10,000 different airports has been randomly generated. The DER of the problem in question is presented below (see Fig. 11).

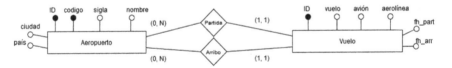

Fig. 11. Conceptual outline expressed by means of a Relation Entity Diagram.

Listed below are 2 queries to evaluate performance in this case study.

"Q1: Direct flights between a specific origin and destination"
"Q2: Fights with one stopover between a specific origin and destination"

Table 3 shows the execution time of each query expressed in seconds for this third case study.

Table 3. Results of the third case study expressed in seconds.

Consultas	MySQL	MongoDB	Cassandra	Neo4j
Q1	18	166	1	0,1
Q2	3720	–	1,5	0,4

5.4 Case Study 4

The fourth and last case study regarding engines locally installed and configured shows a outline chosen to specifically evaluate the Redis NoSQL Database engine in comparison to the MySQL Relational Database engine. For this purpose, a cache of recent searches is represented. Redis, although it offers the possibility of persistence, stands out for having its data structures in main memory. For this case study, 100,000 users and 10,000,000 searches in total have been generated. The following is the DER of the issue to be analysed. The "Search" entity has a mixed identifier, composed of the user identifier plus the date and time of the search (see Fig. 12).
    Listed below are 2 queries to evaluate performance in this case study.

"Q1: The most recent 5 searches for a specific user"
"Q2: The most frequent 5 searches for a specific user"

Table 4 shows the execution time of each query expressed in microseconds for this fourth case.

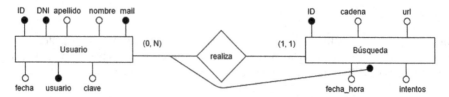

Fig. 12. Conceptual outline expressed by means of a Relation Entity Diagram.

Table 4. Results for the fourth case study expressed in microseconds.

Consultas	MySQL	Redis
Q1	580000	0,48
Q2	550000	0,53

6 Analysis of Results for the Case Studies in the Database Engines Evaluated Locally

6.1 Analysis of Case Study 1

In this first case study, Neo4j gets the best performance. Nevertheless, due to the fact that the number of "messages" nodes presents an exponential growth, its performance may degrade.

Regarding query 1, Cassandra and MySQL get times similar to Neo4j. This is due to the characteristic of the fields used in the query filter.

MongoDB achieves higher execution time than the other 3 Database engines. Queries involving fields that belong to embedded documents may affect its performance.

Regarding querying 2, Cassandra gets better time spans/uptimes than mejor MySQL and MongoDB, but needs the implementation of an index to perform relative searches. MongoDB gets better performance than MySQL; the relative searches and the use of JOINs affect the performance in MySQL.

Regarding querying 3, MySQL gets better performance than MongoDB and Cassandra. Making queries that involve columns that do not belong to Primary Key or Clustering Key affect its performance.

6.2 Analysis of Case Study 2

In this case study, none of the 4 Database engines obtains the best performance for all the queries proposed.

In queries 1 and 2, MongoDB achieves the best performance. In these queries, the outline proposed for MongoDB does not use embedded documents and does not require storing optional fields, avoiding null comparisons. In MySQL operations JOIN affect its performance. In Cassandra, the queries proposed involve fields that are not present in the Primary Key or Clustering Key, which affect its response time. In Neo4j the outline belonging to the case study is not suitable for Graph Storage, since there are not relations among the nodes of the graph.

In query 2, MySQL optimizes the COUNT aggregation function, thus improving its response time compared to the other 3 Database engines.

6.3 Analysis of Case Study 3

In this case study, Neo4j gets the best performance for the queries proposed. This is due to the fact that these queries are solved efficiently in the Graph Storage.

Cassandra obtains better execution time than MySQL and MongoDB, due to the fact that the physical schema in Cassandra is shaped in terms of queries. In MySQL the performance decline between query 1 and query 2 is due to the JOINs needed to solve each query.

6.4 Analysis of Case Study 4

In this case study 2 queries were performed for Redis and MySQL. Redis gets the best performance. This is due to the fact that Redis defines its structures integrally in RAM memory where it operates the data, while MySQL distributes its processing between RAM memory and secondary memory.

7 Cases Study with Database Engines as Service in the Cloud

In order to evaluate Database engines (Cloud Firestore and MongoDB Atlas), the case study shown in Sect. 5.2 was applied, where a monitoring centre that records and process events from different sources is represented.

For each Database engines, the free versions were evaluated.

The data volume generated is smaller compared to that used in Database engines locally installed, this is due to the amount of readings and writings that are allowed in a period of time. A local application was generated and a remote connection was established with both Database engines, achieving the insertion of approximately 150,000 documents.

Table 5 shows the execution time of each query expressed in seconds for this case study.

Table 5. Results for this case study expressed in seconds.

Consultas	Cloud Firestore	MongoDB Atlas
Q1	39	19
Q2	3	3
Q3	2	4

8 Analysis of Results for the Case Study in the Database Engine as Cloud Service

In this case study, none of the two Database engines gets the best performance regarding the 3 queries proposed; moreover, being Database engines in the cloud, the network connection resource and the transfer of documents affect the performance of each execution.

Regarding the first query (Q1) high time spans are obtained in both database engines, this is due to the fact that the result obtained for the evaluated query requires the transfer of a large number of documents.

In the case of query Q2, no differences are seen in the performance obtained by both Database engines.

It is worth noting that, in the case of Cloud Firestore, it was necessary to resort to the creation of an index.

To apply the required filtering in the query. In this aspect we find a point in common with Cassandra, where, for efficiency reasons, it is not possible to execute any type of query.

In the case of the third query (Q3), the results obtained are similar in both Database engines. In this case we have not found any observation regarding the query and the result obtained.

9 Conclusions

9.1 Conclusions for the Case Studies in Database Engine Locally Installed

A comparative analysis was performed among 5 Database engines (4 NoSQL and 1 Relational) locally installed, in 4 different case studies. The 4 case studies proposed show different information outlines and for each one a set of specific queries was defined, resulting in 35 queries. For the first of them a complete development is presented; in other words, the DER outline, the physical outline and the code for each query. In the remaining 3 cases DER was presented.

The results obtained in each of the 4 case studies have been analysed in order to justify why a given engine performers better than other in each case.

Finally, we can conclude that if a large volume of information is available, no Database engine can achieve the best performance to satisfy all the queries proposed.

As the volume of data increases, it is necessary to evaluate which storage alternative; in other words, which Database engine is suitable to use with the aim of providing better performance.

9.2 Conclusions for the Case Studies in Database Engine as Cloud Service

A comparative analysis was performed between 2 NoSQL Database engines as service in the cloud (Cloud Firestore and MongoDB Atlas), both with Documental storage and is free version.

One of the four case studies applied previously was used, but with a smaller data volume; this is due to the restrictions in the free version that offer both Database engines. A set of 6 queries was performed.

In both Database engines, transference of a huge number of documents and the state of the connexion at the moment of the query may affect the performance of its response time.

10 Future Work

As a future line of work, it is planned to incorporate new tests and reinforce existing ones with alternative Relational and Non-Relational Database engines as well as incorporating new evaluations for different Database engines in the cloud. Besides, we will seek to explore the capacity of horizontal scalability of NoSQL Databases and Relational Databases.

Finally, it is planned to experiment with NewSQL Database and Temporal Series Databases.

References

1. Mabel, P.P., et al.: Un estudio comparativo de bases de datos relacionales y bases de datos NoSQL. XXV Congreso Argentino de Ciencias de la Computación (CACIC 2019). Universidad Nacional de Río Cuarto, Córdoba, 14 al 18 de octubre de 2019. https://sedici.unlp.edu.ar/handle/10915/91403. ISBN 978-987-688-377-1
2. Aspectos de la Ingeniería de Software, Bases de Datos Relacionales y Bases de Datos No Relacionales para el desarrollo de Sistemas de Software en Escenarios Híbridos. XXII Workshop de Investigadores en Ciencias de la Computación (WICC 2020, Universidad Nacional de la Patagonia Austral, El Calafate, Santa Cruz, Argentina)
3. Aspectos de ingeniería de software y bases de datos para el desarrollo de sistemas de software en escenarios híbridos. XXI Workshop de Investigadores en Ciencias de la Computación (WICC 2019, Universidad Nacional de San Juan, San Juan, Argentina). https://sedici.unlp.edu.ar/handle/10915/77088. ISBN 978-987-3619-27-4
4. Singh, A., Ahmad, S.: Data Modeling with NoSQL Database (2019). ISBN 978-1072978374
5. Kumar, J., Garg, V.: Security analysis of unstructured data in NOSQL MongoDB database. In: International Conference on Computing and Communication Technologies for Smart Nation (IC3TSN) (2017). https://ieeexplore.ieee.org/document/8284495
6. Jose, B., Abraham, S.: Exploring the merits of nosql: a study based on MongoDB. In: International Conference on Networks & Advances in Computational Technologies (NetACT) (2017). https://ieeexplore.ieee.org/document/8076778
7. Replicación de bases de datos NoSQL en dispositivos móviles. https://sedici.unlp.edu.ar/handle/10915/48085
8. Bajpayee, R., Sinha, S.P., Kumar, V.: Big data: a brief investigation on NoSQL databases. Int. J. Innov. Adv. Comput. Sci. (IJIACS) 4(1) (2015). ISSN 2347
9. Vohra, D.: NoSQL Web Development with Apache Cassandra. Cengage Learning (2015). ISBN 9781305576773
10. NoSQL: modelos de datos y sistemas de gestión de bases de datos. XX Workshop de Investigadores en Ciencias de la Computación (WICC 2018, Universidad Nacional del Nordeste). https://sedici.unlp.edu.ar/handle/10915/67258

11. A Performance Optimization Scheme for Migrating Hive Data to Neo4j Database. Publicado en 2018 International Symposium on Computer, Consumer and Control (IS3C). https://iee explore.ieee.org/document/8644938. ISBN 978-1-5386-7036-1

12. Batini, C., Ceri, S., Navathe, S.B.: Diseño Conceptual de Bases de Datos, un enfoque de entidades-interrelaciones. Addison-Wesley/Díaz de Santos (1994). ISBN 0-201-60120-6

13. Flexibilidad en bases de datos NoSQL sobre ambientes web mining. https://sedici.unlp.edu.ar/handle/10915/59099

14. Ranking de bases de datos según su popularidad. https://db-engines.com/en/ranking. Accedido en julio 2020

15. MySQL. https://www.mysql.com/. Accedido en julio 2020

16. Clientes de MySQL. https://www.mysql.com/customers/. Accedido en julio 2020

17. MongoDB. https://www.mongodb.com/. Accedido en julio 2020

18. Empresas que utilizan MongoDB. https://www.mongodb.com/who-uses-mongodb Accedido en julio 2020

19. Apache Cassandra. https://cassandra.apache.org/. Accedido en agosto 2020

20. Redis. https://redis.io/. Accedido en agosto 2020

21. Amazon DynamoDB. https://aws.amazon.com/es/dynamodb/. Accedido en julio 2020

22. Apache CouchDB. https://couchdb.apache.org/. Accedido en julio 2020

23. Apache HBase. https://hbase.apache.org/. Accedido en julio 2020

24. Neo4j. https://neo4j.com/. Accedido en julio 2020

25. Marrero, L., Olsowy, V., Tesone, F., Thomas, P., Delia, L., Pesado, P.: Análisis de performance en Bases de Datos NoSQL y Bases de Datos Relacionales. XXVI Congreso Argentino de Ciencias de la Computación (CACIC 2020). Universidad Nacional de La Matanza, Buenos Aires, 5 al 9 de octubre de 2020. ISBN 978-987-4417-90-0

26. Cloud Firestore (Google Cloud). https://firebase.google.com/?hl=es. Accedido en Febrero 2021

27. MongoDB Atlas. https://www.mongodb.com/cloud/atlas. Accedido en Febrero 2021

Smart Grid Optimization with the Advanced jSO Algorithm

Fabricio Loor[1][(✉)], M. Guillermo Leguizamón[1], and Efrén Mezura-Montes[2]

[1] Laboratorio de Investigación y Desarrollo en Inteligencia Computacional (LIDIC), Universidad Nacional de San Luis, 5700 BPB San Luis, Argentina
{faloor,legui}@unsl.edu.ar
[2] Artificial Intelligence Research Institute, University of Veracruz, 91000 Xalapa, Veracruz, Mexico
emezura@uv.mx

Abstract. This paper presents an extended empirical comparison of the Advanced jSO (AJSO), an algorithm adapted to solve smart grid optimization problems. An additional algorithm was considered for comparison purposes and a suitable statistical test validation was also added. Furthermore, a convergence analysis was included to give insights about the on-line behavior of the compared approaches. The test beds proposed for the WCCI/GECCO 2020 competition for Smarts Grids were solved by the compared algorithms. The overall results indicate a highly competitive performance provided by AJSO.

Keywords: Optimization · Smart grids · Metaheuristics · Differential Evolution

1 Introduction

Optimization problems require minimizing or maximizing a measure according to a given configuration of values. If the possible permutations or combinations in those configurations are really vast, thinking of exhaustive methods or brute force becomes an impractical alternative. Motivated by the above mentioned, approximated search algorithms such as metaheuristics have been widely used to solve complex search problems. In particular, Differential Evolution (DE) [12] is a stochastic algorithm that has proven to be a simple but highly competitive approach. DE considers three parameters: a mutation factor (F), a probability of crossover (CR) and a population size (N). Currently, DE-based algorithms are highly competitive to solve different complex optimization problems [4,10,15].

In what follows, a summary of the previous works is presented. Such proposals are related with the AJSO algorithm, which is indeed based on DE.

- 2005, FADE [8], Fuzzy Adaptive Differential Evolution, where fuzzy logic controllers are used to control F and CR DE parameters.
- 2005, SaDE [11], Self adaptive differential Evolution. Parameters F and CR are updated in each generation by using Normal distributions.

© Springer Nature Switzerland AG 2021
P. Pesado and J. Eterovic (Eds.): CACIC 2020, CCIS 1409, pp. 171–181, 2021.
https://doi.org/10.1007/978-3-030-75836-3_12

- 2006, jDE [1], where the values of F and CR are given by uniform distributions.
- 2009, JADE [16], introduces a new mutation strategy *"current-to-pbest/1"* and adds an archive of less efficient solutions.
- 2013, SHADE, [13], which is based on JADE and proposes a memory to store good F and CR values. This algorithm was placed in third place in the CEC (Congress on Evolutionary Computation) 2013 competition on real parameter single-objective optimization.
- 2014, L-SHADE [14], uses SHADE and introduces a linear population decreasing mechanism. It was the winner in the CEC 2014 competition on real parameter single-objective optimization.
- 2016, iL-SHADE [2] is an improvement over L-SHADE. This algorithm introduces changes in the initialization and memory update. It also features a new mechanism to update the F and CR parameters, varying between the current and maximum generation. It was ranked fourth in the CEC 2016 competition on real parameter single-objective optimization.
- 2017, jSO [3], uses the *"current-to-pbest-w/1"* strategy and introduces modifications according to the search period on the mutation factor. It earned the second place in the CEC 2017 competition on real parameter single-objective optimization.
- 2019, HyDE-DF [6] is a self-adaptive DE algorithm that incorporates a perturbation of the best individual and a decay function in its mutation phase. In our proposal we use one of these improvements and we adapt it to solve a high-dimensional problem applied to intelligent energy distribution.
- 2020, AJSO was presented in [9], and is a new jSO-based metaheuristic that adopts different mutation strategies and updates the memory values for CR and F in a novel way. In this paper we present an extended experimental study in order to highlight the benefits of our approach, mainly based on its self-adaptive capability, compared to some of its predecessors.

The rest of the paper is organized as follows. In Sect. 2, we describe AJSO by showing its main features and specific details. In Sect. 3, we present the experimental design and the framework where AJSO and the compared algorithms have been tested. This section also contains a discussion regarding the results achieved and the corresponding statistical validation by the non-parametric Wilcoxon test. Finally, in Sect. 4, the conclusions reached and some future research paths are summarized.

2 Our Approach: AJSO (Advanced JSO)

In this section we detail AJSO [9], which is a a self-adaptive algorithm for solving single-objective real parameter optimization problems and its general pseudocode is shown in Algorithm 1. AJSO is an enhanced version based on SHADE [13] and jSO [3], two well-known algorithms based on DE. SHADE preserves two population structures, the first one keeps the current population and the other one (an archive) contains the replaced individuals throughout the search process. It also incorporates a recently successful parameter values memory to guide the generation of new values for both, crossover and mutation operators.

Unlike SHADE, AJSO has three structures to maintain different type of solutions. The first one is the main population P_g, the second one maintains an *Archive* of useful recent generated solutions, and the last one preserves the history of best individuals found at each generation (A_g). The Population (P_g) and *Archive* structures have a fixed N size, while the third one (A_g) grows dynamically at each generation. The process to update the control parameters is different with respect to SHADE and it will be detailed later in this paper.

Before entering the main loop, the population P_g in AJSO is initialized with solutions generated at random with uniform distribution, and *Archive* includes at this time the same initial population P_g. AJSO also has a memory for parameter values and it is initialized with random values that follow a Normal distribution. These values in turn will be the mean for future CR and F values. After initialization, the algorithm enters the evolutionary stage. The parameter $sF \in [0,1]$ (described in [13]) controls the magnitude of the differential mutation operator and will be explained later in this paper. This stage continues until the stop criterion is reached, in our case given by a maximum number of evaluations. Within each generation, the population is evaluated with two different mutation strategies, to subsequently carry out *length_phase* evaluations with the best strategy (*length_phase* is an input value of the algorithm).

2.1   Mutation and Crossover Operators

The SHADE algorithm [13] builds a mutant vector $\vec{v}_i$, according to the "*current-to-pbest/1*" strategy as shown in Eq. 1:

$$\vec{v}_{i,g+1} = \vec{v}_{i,g} + sF * (\vec{v}_{pbest} - \vec{v}_{i,g} + \vec{v}_{r1} - \vec{v}_{r2}) \tag{1}$$

where v_{pbest} is a randomly selected solution from the top $N * p$ ($p \in [0,1]$) members at generation g. Indices i, $r1$ and $r2$ are randomly selected from $[1,N]$ such that they differ from each other ($i \neq r1 \neq r2$).

Regarding AJSO (our algorithm), it incorporates two ways to mutate solutions by following two different strategies. To do this, an element of the population or elements of the archive are part of the strategies according to the need of the moment. The first strategy uses elements of the population ($\vec{v}_{r1}$ and $\vec{v}_{r1}$) to generate an individual i of generation $g + 1$ as in Eq. 2:

$$\vec{v}_{i,g+1} = \begin{cases} \vec{v}_{pr} + sF * (\vec{v}_{r1} - \vec{v}_{i,g}) + jF * (\vec{v}_{r1} - \vec{v}_{r2}), & \text{if } rand(0,1) < \vec{CR}_i. \\ \vec{v}_{i,g}, & \text{otherwise,} \end{cases} \tag{2}$$

where sF is a scalar obtained from applying a Normal distribution to random values in memory. jF is half the value of sF and, v_{pr} is a randomly chosen vector among the best B elements of the previous population. The second strategy is stated as in Eq. 3:

Algorithm 1: AJSO

---

1 //Initialization phase
2 $g = 1, N_g = N_{init}$;
3 Initialize population $P_g = (x_{1,g}, ..., x_{N,g})$ randomly;
4 Set all values in M_{CR}, M_F following a Normal distribution with $\mu_{CR} = I_{CR}$ and
   $\sigma_{CR} = 0.05$; $\mu_F = I_F$ and $\sigma_F = 0.1$;
5 $Archive = P_g$;
6 // Main loop
7 **while** *The termination criterion is not met* **do**
8 | Sort and select the best B individuals;
9 | Obtain a vector of values with CR and sF;
10 | From sF get jF;
11 | Generate two new populations with two different strategies;
12 | Control limits and evaluate;
13 | Select the best strategy S;
14 | // Exploitation phase
15 | **for** *i = 1 to length_phase* **do**
16 | | Sort and select the best B individuals;
17 | | Obtain a vector of values with CR and sF;
18 | | From sF get jF;
19 | | Generate a new population with the best strategy from 13;
20 | | Control limits and evaluate;
21 | | Update Archive;
22 | | Update Memory Parameters;
23 | | **if** $nsp = 0$ **and** $B_g = BSF$ **and** $nfes > I\_evalmax * 0.4$ **then**
24 | | | add in the Archive one of the best global past (A_g);
25 | | **end**
26 | **end**
27 **end**

$$\vec{v}_{i,g+1} = \begin{cases} \vec{v}_{pr} + sF * (\vec{v}_{r1} - \vec{v}_{i,g}) + jF * (\vec{v}_{r3} - \vec{v}_{r4}), & \text{if } rand(0,1) < CR_i. \\ v_{i,g}, & \text{otherwise.} \end{cases} \quad (3)$$

where vectors $\vec{v}_{r3}$, $\vec{v}_{r4}$ are randomly selected elements from $Archive$ and different each other ($r3 \neq r4$), while vectors $\vec{v}_{i,g}$ and $\vec{v}_{r1}$ are extracted from the population and $\vec{v}_{r1}$ is randomly chosen.

2.2   Selecting the Best Strategy

After checking that the mutated solutions are within the allowed boundaries of the decision variables, the algorithm proceeds to evaluate those solutions. When the evaluation concludes, a selection process is carried out to obtain the best strategy between the two used in the previous step. The selection criterion is based on the new population generated by each strategy. The one with more better solutions with respect to the previous population is preferred.

2.3   Updating the Historical Memory

In this section we describe the memories M_F and M_{CR} update process. The elements of the historical memories, similar to those used in SHADE, are updated in the exploitation stage (lines 14 to 26 in Algorithm 1). For this purpose, in each generation two values are computed: (1) nsp (number of successful parameters), which is the number of offspring that were better with respect to their corresponding parent, and (2) nfp (number of failed parameters), which is the number offspring that were not better with respect to their corresponding parent.

If more than a half of the individuals in a generation improved the previous population ($nsp > nfp$), Eq. 4 is applied to update $m_i \in Memory$, which is used as explained before for future values of control parameter F:

$$m_i = \begin{cases} 1.5 * avg(goodF) - 0.5 * m_i & \text{within limits } (0,1]. \\ m_i, & \text{out of limits } (0,1] \end{cases} \quad (4)$$

where avg calculates the average of a list of numbers and $goodF$ is a list of sF values which have generated a better offspring with respect to its parent.

If the number of offspring in a generation that improved their corresponding parent does not exceed half of the population ($nsp \leq nfp$) the Memory is updated as in Eq. 5:

$$m_i = \begin{cases} m_i + 0.2 * (0.5 * avg(goodF + BadF) - 0.8 * m_i) & \text{within limits } (0,1]. \\ m_i, & \text{out of limits } (0,1], \end{cases} \quad (5)$$

where $BadF$ is a list of sF values that were not able to generate a better offspring with respect to its parent.

The procedure for updating memory elements that store CR values (M_{CR}) is analogous to that described in this subsection.

3   The Problem and Results

3.1   Problem Definition: Optimization Applied to Energy Distribution

Energy distribution has many stages from its generation to its consumption. In smart grids, the distribution of energy is optimized for both, consumers and suppliers, then it is highly desirable to find a good balance between demand and supply. This balance can be modeled as an objective function where the input variables to the function have certain restrictions. Due to space issues, in this reference [7] interested readers can find a more detailed description of the objective functions adopted in this work.

3.2   The Benchmark

AJSO performance assessment was carried out by solving the IEEE WCCI/GECCO 2020 benchmark "*CEC-C4 Evolutionary Computation in the Energy Domain: Smart Grid Applications*". This benchmark has two test beds. The first one aims at optimizing energy resources management for day-to-day use in smart grids under uncertain environments. 500 scenarios with a high degree of uncertainty are used. The second test bed is concerned with a two-tier optimization of end-user bidding strategies in local energy markets (LM). These two levels represent a complex problem where competitive agents at the one level try to maximize their profits by modifying a price. On the other hand, an agent tries to minimize costs. The number of variables of Test Bed 1 and Test bed 2 are 3408 and 432, respectively. The competition rules indicate 50,000 evaluations as the termination condition for the algorithms that solve each test bed.

A solution in test bed 1 is evaluated in the objective function Eq. 6:

$$f_1(\vec{X}) = Z + \rho \sum_{i=1}^{N_c} max[0, g_i] \tag{6}$$

where $\vec{X}$ is a solution. In this case, g_i is the value of the i-th constraint (equality or inequality) and ρ is a configurable penalty factor (usually, a high value is considered). The function considers uncertainty in some parameters that modify the value of the fitness function according to different scenarios generated by Monte Carlo simulation. The fitness function value is modified by a perturbation as in Eq. 7:

$$F_S(\vec{X}) = f_1(\vec{X} + \delta_S) \tag{7}$$

where δ_S is the disturbance of variables and parameters in scenario S and $F_S(\vec{X})$ the fitness value associated to the S Monte Carlo sampling. Therefore, an expected mean value for a given solution over the set of considered scenarios can be calculated as in Eq. 8:

$$\mu FS(\vec{X}) = \frac{1}{N_S} \sum_{s=1}^{N_S} f_1(\vec{X} + \delta_S) \tag{8}$$

where N_S is the number of scenarios.

Similarly, the standard deviation of a solution over the set of scenarios can be calculated by using Eq. 9:

$$\sigma FS(\vec{X}) = \sqrt{\frac{1}{N_S} \sum_{s=1}^{N_S} (f_1(\vec{X} + \delta_S) - \mu FS(\vec{X}))^2} \tag{9}$$

Solutions in testbed 2 should be evaluated in an objective function that returns the mean average profit of all agents plus the standard deviation Eq. 10:

$$f_2(\vec{X}) = mean(profits) + std(profits) \tag{10}$$

where $mean(profits)$ and $std(profits)$ are functions that compute the average and standard deviation (respectively) of the profits that all agents obtained considering the bids/offers encoded in the individual. The negative sign in the first term is used to transform the profits maximization problem into a minimization one. The less the value in Eq. 10, the better the mean profits achieved by all agents.

3.3   Extended Study

In this section, we highlight the differences that AJSO has in terms of performance compared to other recently developed algorithms.

For all compared algorithms the population size was 10. For DE, the value for F was established as 0.5 and CR was 0.9. For SHADE, the initial mutation factor (M_F) was 0.5, the initial crossover (M_{CR}) was set to the value of 0.5 and the best selection rates was 0.1. For HYDE-DF the mutation factor (F) was 0.5 and the crossover value (CR) was 0.5. For AJSO the initial mutation factor (I_F) was 0.8, the initial crossover constant (I_{CR}) was 0.5, B was 0.1 and $length\_phase$ was set for these tests with the value of 8.

Table 1 (Test bed 1) and 2 (Test bed 2) contain statistical values and classification positions following the criteria of the WCCI 2020 competition of four compared algorithms, DE (a basic version), HYDE-DF[1], SHADE, and AJSO. The value that summarizes the corresponding performance in Table 1 is represented by $RankingIndex$. This value is calculated by Eq. 11:

$$RankingIndex = \frac{1}{20} \cdot \left[\sum_{i=1}^{20} (\mu FS(\vec{X}_i\_T1) + \sigma FS(\vec{X}_i\_T1)) \right] \qquad (11)$$

where $\mu FS(\vec{X}\_iT1)$ and $\sigma FS(\vec{X}_i\_T1)$ are Eq. 8 and 9 for the trial i across the 500 considered scenarios. In Table 1, the values $PAvgFit$, $PstdFit$ and $PminFit$ correspond to a summary (after applying the average) of the 20 independent performances of the mean, the standard deviation the minimum value of all the evaluations made by the algorithm in each run.

Table 2 shows the results for the fitness function on test bed 2. This function acts as a black box, only two resulting values are known, fit and $profit$. The first value is about minimizing and the second about maximizing. The value that is taken as a reference for the ranking is fit.

Based on the results reported in Table 1 and 2 it is clear that AJSO outperformed the compared algorithms in both test beds.

To further analyze the performance of the compared approaches, Figs. 1 and 2 show the box plots from 20 independent runs for test bed 1 and test bed 2, respectively. Figure 1 includes $AvgFit$ and $stdFit$ for test bed 1, while Fig. 2 considers Fit and $Profit$ for test bed2.

---

[1] This algorithm is taken as a baseline for the competition http://www.gecad.isep.ipp.pt/ERM-competitions/2021-2/.

Table 1. Results obtained by DE, HYDE-DF, SHADE and AJSO in Test Bed 1

Algorithm	RankingIndex	PAvgFit	PstdFit	PminFit
DE	**442.64**	329.09	23.38	286.53
SHADE	**370.81**	267.03	27.63	217.93
HYDE-DF	**342.15**	233.35	30.86	168.53
AJSO	**311.11**	214.68	24.07	182.50

Table 2. Results obtained by DE, HYDE-DF, SHADE and AJSO in Test Bed 2

Algorithm	Fit	Profit
DE	**3.03**	−4.98
HYDE-DF	**2.95**	−4.88
SHADE	**2.49**	−4.04
AJSO	**2.28**	−3.60

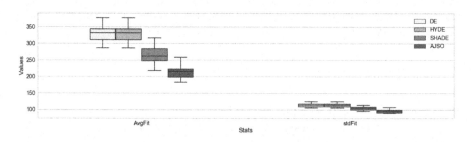

Fig. 1. Results obtained by each compared approach in 20 independent runs in Test Bed 1.

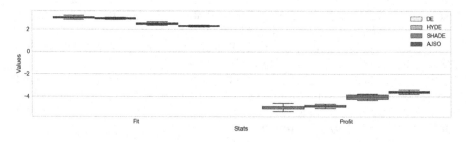

Fig. 2. Results obtained by each compared approach in 20 independent runs in Test Bed 2.

Figures 1 and 2 indicate that AJSO provided the best values and was also more robust in the two test beds when compared with HYDE-DF, DE and SHADE.

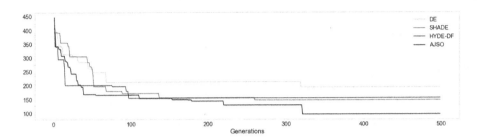

Fig. 3. Convergence graphs of the compared algorithms for minimum values of fitness function in Test Bed 1

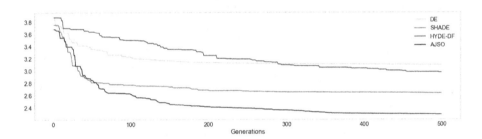

Fig. 4. Convergence graphs of the compared algorithms for Fit values in Test Bed 2

Figures 3 and 4 present the convergence plots of the tested algorithms in both test beds. Such plots indicate that AJSO was able to find better results faster than the other three compared approaches while keeping the maximum number of evaluations required by the competition.

3.4 Statistical Tests

To validate the differences observed in the results reported in the previous section, the 95%-confidence Wilcoxon signed-rank test [5] was calculated with the samples of 20 runs per each algorithm. This is a nonparametric test frequently used to compare pairs of algorithms. In this work, we have taken the score given by the competition as a reference. Therefore, the vectors that have been evaluated were the mean ($AvgFit$) and the standard deviation ($stdFit$) for test bed 1 and only Fitness (Fit) for test bed 2.

The p-values obtained by the Wilcoxon test can be seen in Table 3. It is worth remarking that a p-value below 0.05 indicates significant differences between the compared algorithms. Based on such table, in all cases, there are significant differences between AJSO and the compared algorithms. Therefore, we can conclude that this proposed algorithm provides a better performance in both testbeds solved.

Table 3. p-values returned by the Wilcoxon Test between AJSO and each compared algorithms. A value below 0.05 indicates significant differences and they are remarked in boldface.

Comparison	Test Bed 1	Test Bed 2
AJSO vs DE	**2.0361e−5**	**8.8575e−5**
AJSO vs HYDE-DF	**3.1545e−4**	**8.8575e−5**
AJSO vs SHADE	**0.0019**	**8.8575e−5**

4   Conclusions and Future Work

In this paper we have extended the performance assessment of the Advanced jSO (AJSO) algorithm to solve smart grid optimization problems related with the WCCI/GECCO 2020 competition. AJSO, inspired by SHADE and jSO algorithms, combined two DE strategies (to favor exploration and exploitation in the search), an archive of solutions to better explore the search space and also a memory of parameter values to self-adapt them. Regarding the extended performance analysis, an additional algorithm was considered for comparison purposes, the online behavior (convergence plots) of the compared algorithms was analyzed and the statistical validation by using an non-parametric test was calculated.

AJSO was able to provide statistically significant better results when compared to those of DE, SHADE and HYDE-DF. Moreover, the results obtained by AJSO were more robust and the convergence analysis showed its ability to find better solutions faster than the compared approaches.

As part of the future work, a deeper analysis will be performed by varying the Population and Archive sizes. Currently, AJSO has very few parameters to calibrate, but it may be possible to incorporate more self-adaptive techniques to control, as an example, the memory update.

References

1. Brest, J., Greiner, S., Boskovic, B., Mernik, M., Zumer, V.: Self-adapting control parameters in differential evolution: a comparative study on numerical benchmark problems. IEEE Trans. Evol. Comput. **10**(6), 646–657 (2006)
2. Brest, J., Maučec, M.S., Bošković, B.: iL-SHADE: improved L-SHADE algorithm for single objective real-parameter optimization. In: 2016 IEEE Congress on Evolutionary Computation (CEC), pp. 1188–1195 (2016)

3. Brest, J., Maučec, M.S., Bošković, B.: Single objective real-parameter optimization: algorithm jSO. In: 2017 IEEE Congress on Evolutionary Computation (CEC), pp. 1311–1318 (2017)
4. Brest, J., Maučec, M.S.: Population size reduction for the differential evolution algorithm. Appl. Intell. **29**(3), 228–247 (2008). https://doi.org/10.1007/s10489-007-0091-x
5. Gibbons, J.D., Chakraborti, S.: Nonparametric statistical inference. In: Lovric, M. (ed.) International Encyclopedia of Statistical Science, pp. 977–979. Springer, Heidelberg (2011). https://doi.org/10.1007/978-3-642-04898-2_420
6. Lezama, F., Soares, J.A., Faia, R., Vale, Z.: Hybrid-adaptive differential evolution with decay function (HyDE-DF) applied to the 100-digit challenge competition on single objective numerical optimization. In: Proceedings of the Genetic and Evolutionary Computation Conference Companion, GECCO 2019, New York, NY, USA, 2019, pp. 7–8. Association for Computing Machinery (2019)
7. Lezama, F., Vale, Z., Soares, J.A., Bruno, C.: Evolutionary computation in the energy domain: smart grid applications. CEC Competitions
8. Liu, J., Lampinen, J.: A fuzzy adaptive differential evolution algorithm. Soft Comput. A Fusion Found. Methodol. Appl. **9**(6), 448–462 (2005). https://doi.org/10.1007/s00500-004-0363-x
9. Loor, F., Leguizamón, G., Mezura-Montes, E.: Smart grids challenge: a competitive variant for single objective numerical optimization. In: XXVI Congreso Argentino de Ciencias de la Computación CACIC, La Matanza (2020)
10. Mallipeddi, R., Suganthan, P., Pan, Q., Tasgetiren, M.: Differential evolution algorithm with ensemble of parameters and mutation strategies. Appl. Soft Comput. **11**(2), 1679–1696 (2011). The Impact of Soft Computing for the Progress of Artificial Intelligence
11. Qin, A.K., Suganthan, P.N.: Self-adaptive differential evolution algorithm for numerical optimization. In: 2005 IEEE Congress on Evolutionary Computation, vol. 2, pp. 1785–1791 (2005)
12. Storn, R., Price, K.: Differential evolution: a simple and efficient adaptive scheme for global optimization over continuous spaces. J. Global Optimiz. **23** (1995)
13. Tanabe, R., Fukunaga, A.: Success-history based parameter adaptation for differential evolution. In: 2013 IEEE Congress on Evolutionary Computation, pp. 71–78 (2013)
14. Tanabe, R., Fukunaga, A.S.: Improving the search performance of shade using linear population size reduction. In: 2014 IEEE Congress on Evolutionary Computation (CEC), pp. 1658–1665 (2014)
15. Wu, G., Shen, X., Li, H., Chen, H., Lin, A., Suganthan, P.: Ensemble of differential evolution variants. Inf. Sci. **423**, 172–186 (2018)
16. Zhang, J., Sanderson, A.C.: JADE: adaptive differential evolution with optional external archive. IEEE Trans. Evol. Comput. **13**(5), 945–958 (2009)

Sequential Representation of Suffix Trie: An Empirical Evaluation

Darío Ruano, Norma Herrera$^{(\boxtimes)}$, Jésica Cornejo, and Paola Azar

Departamento de Informática, Universidad Nacional de San Luis, San Luis, Argentina
dmruano@unsl.edu.ar, nherrera@unsl.edu.ar

Abstract. A *suffix trie* is a full-text index that can efficiently answer queries in a text database. However, this index uses much more space than the text itself. In practice, a suffix trie requires from 10 to 20 times the size of T. In this work, we present an exhaustive experimental evaluation of a sequential representation of suffix trie (ST_s) consisting of storing each component of a suffix trie in a separated array. We analyze *count* and *locate* time, construction time, and space usage for three versions of ST_s: the original one and two later improvements.

Keywords: Text databases · Full-text indexes · Suffix trie

1 Introduction

Traditional databases are built around the concept of exact searching over structured data, that is, to search by equality over records each one having comparable fields. At present, a large portion of the information available in electronic form is in text form, that is, sequences of symbols representing not only natural language but also ADN or protein sequences, program code, MIDI pitch sequences, etc. Organizing text in records and fields is impossible and treating the whole text as an atomic value does not is useful in a real application. New technologies are needed to manage text databases.

A text database is a system that maintains a large text collection and provides fast and accurate access to it [24]. Without loss of generality, we will assume that the text collection is a unique text T over an alphabet Σ. T may be stored in one or more files and it is not necessarily natural language text, just a sequence of characters.

The simplest query to a text database is the pattern matching query: given a string P (called the pattern) find all the positions of T where P occur. The pattern matching query can be answered using two different approaches: sequential and indexed search. Sequential searching assumes that it is not possible to preprocess the text T, so only the pattern P is preprocessed and then the whole text T is sequentially scanned [2]. Indexed searching, on the other hand, preprocesses the text T to build a data structure or index over it, which can be used later to speed up searches. Building an index is usually a time and memory-demanding

© Springer Nature Switzerland AG 2021
P. Pesado and J. Eterovic (Eds.): CACIC 2020, CCIS 1409, pp. 182–196, 2021.
https://doi.org/10.1007/978-3-030-75836-3_13

task, so indexed searching is the choice when the text is so large that sequential scanning is too expensive. In a text database, indexed searching is the most suitable approach.

In this paper, we are interested in *suffix trie*, an index that can answer pattern matching query in time proportional to the length of P, independently of the length of T. However, this index uses much more space than the text itself. In practice, a suffix trie requires from 10 to 20 times the size of T. This means that even when we may have enough main memory to hold a text, we may need to use the disk to store the index.

In [28] a sequential representation of the suffix is proposed; this representation is suitable for a later paging process on secondary memory. In [29] and [6] the authors present improvements in space usage and query time, respectively, of this sequential representation.

In this work, we present an experimental evaluation of these three versions of the suffix tries. This article is a revised and extended version of the previous paper presented at [27]. We include an exhaustive experimental evaluation using the dataset provided in the Pizza&Chili Corpus. (http://pizzachili.dcc.uchile. cl).

The remainder of the paper is organized as follows: Sect. 2 presents some useful concepts. Section 3 describes the suffix trie data structure and Sect. 4 describes the sequential representation of this index. Section 5 gives the experimental evaluation and analysis of results. Finally, Sect. 6 presents the conclusions and discusses possible extensions for this work.

2   Previous Concepts

A text $T = t_1 \ldots t_n$ is a sequence of symbols over an alphabet Σ of size $|\Sigma| = \sigma$. A substring of T is denoted by $T_{ij} = t_i \ldots t_j$. A *prefix* of T is a substring of the form T_{1i} and a *suffix* is a substring of the form T_{in}. Any position i in T uniquely identifies a suffix of T namely T_{in}. We will call *suffix offset* to i.

The search pattern $P = p_1 \ldots p_m$ will be any sequence of symbols over Σ; we will suppose that m is much smaller than n. In order to ensure that each suffix occurs exactly once in the text, we will assume that the last text character of T is $t_n = \$$, a special end-marker symbol that belongs to Σ but does not appear elsewhere in T nor P, and that is lexicographically smaller than any other symbol in Σ.

As we explained in the previous section, the indexing approach is the most suitable for a text database. This means that an index is built to speed up searches. An index built on T will support at least the following two queries:

- *count(P)*: counts the number of occurrences (*occ*) of pattern P in T
- *locate(P)*: locates the positions of all *occ* occurrences of P in T.

Many different indexing data structures have been proposed in the literature for text searching. The main problem with these indexes is their large space requirements.

Each possible match point in T is referred to as an *index point*. The index points are the positions of T which will be retrievable. The storage requirements of an index are proportional to the number of index points in T. Consequently, we can reduce the storage requirements by restricting the number of index points and, therefore, the kinds of queries that can be answered. Reducing space is important because it gives the chance to keep the index in the main memory

A **word-oriented index** restricts matches to whole words, thus a word-oriented index search for $P = in$ will not return the occurrences inside *finding* or *internal*. In some word-oriented indexes, the matches of P are restricted to start a word. In these cases, the word index can return the occurrence of *in* at *internal* but not in *finding*. The well-known inverted index is a word-oriented index that only permit word and phrase queries on natural language texts [1,16].

Natural language excludes symbol sequences of interest in many applications, like bioinformatic and multimedia databases, and some important human languages. In these cases, the database T is just an arbitrarily long sequence of symbols and the index for these types of texts must be able to search any substring. These indexes capable of finding matches of P starting at any character of T are called **full-text indexes**. In a full-text index, each suffix offset is an index point. Many different full-text indexes have been proposed in the literature for text searching, most notably suffix arrays, suffix trees and suffix tries [5,10,20,30]. As we mentioned, the main problem with these indexes is their large space requirements They need between 4 to 20 times the text size (plus text) to achieve a reasonable efficiency.

Several attempts to reduce the space requirements of text indexes were made in the past giving rise to the **succinct indexes** concept. A succinct index is an index that provides fast search functionality using a space proportional to that of the text itself (say, two times the text size). The succinct indexes exploit the compressibility of T, then their size is a function of the compressed text length [7, 8,14,19,25,26]. This concept has evolved into **self-indexes**, which furthermore contains enough information to reproduce any text portion [12,13,21,22]. A self-index replaces the text and supports a fast search for arbitrary patterns.

However, there are cases where even the compressed self-index is too large to fit in the main memory. In these cases, it is necessary to have an index paging process that assures efficiency at query time.

3   The Suffix Trie Data Structure

In this paper, we are interested in suffix trie, a full text index that can answer the *count* search in $O(m)$ time, independent of n and occ, and *locate* search in $O(m+occ)$. Below, we describe this index and the classical representations for it.

A trie is a type of digital search tree that stores a set S of n strings over an alphabet Σ. It can support the search for a string in the set in time proportional to the length of the string, independently of n. In a trie, each edge is labeled with a character from the alphabet Σ. The maximum number of children for each trie node is σ and sibling edges must represent distinct symbols. The trie

Text:

1	2	3	4	5	6	7	8	9
a	b	c	c	a	b	c	a	$

Suffix Trie:

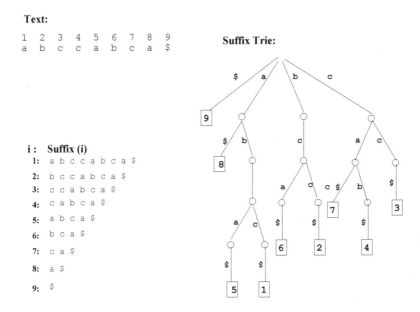

i : **Suffix (i)**

1: a b c c a b c a $

2: b c c a b c a $

3: c c a b c a $

4: c a b c a $

5: a b c a $

6: b c a $

7: c a $

8: a $

9: $

Fig. 1. A text T, its suffix set, and its suffix trie. In this example, $\Sigma = \{a, b, c, \$\}$ and $\sigma = 4$.

has exactly n leaves, each corresponding to a distinct string of S. A trie also can be used for prefix searching, that is, to find every string in S prefixed by some sequence P.

Notice that all occurrences of a pattern P in T are prefixes of some suffix of T, thus finding all the occurrences of P in T is equivalent to finding all suffixes of T that start with P.

A **suffix trie** [9] is a trie built over all the suffixes of text T. The pointers to the suffixes (suffix offsets) are stored at the leaf nodes. Each leaf represents a suffix and each internal node represents a substring of T that can appear more than once. In practice, the suffix trie is pruned at a node if there is only a unary path from this node to a leaf. An example of a suffix trie is shown in Fig. 1. In this example, leaves are indicated by squares containing the suffix offsets.

Using the suffix trie, the occurrences of P in T can be found by starting at the root and following matches down the trie edges until P is exhausted, or up to the point where we reach an external node. If the end of P is encountered, then any leaf in the subtree rooted at the last node visited is a match. If a leaf is encountered before the end of P, then the remainder of the pattern must be checked against the appropriate suffix.

To improve space utilization, the number of edges in the suffix trie can be reduced by collapsing unary paths (i.e. paths where each node has just one child) into a single edge. In each internal node, an indication of which character of the query is to be used for branching is stored. This value, well-known as **skip value**, may be given by an absolute position or by a count of the number of characters

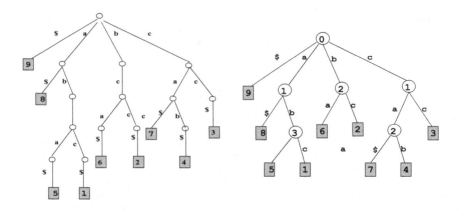

Fig. 2. The original suffix trie (left) and their version with skip values (right).

to skip. Figure 2 shows this representation for the same text T given in Fig. 1; in this example, the skip value is given as absolute position. At query time, the skip value must be considered to choose the branch the search must be following.

Because the search algorithm can skip the inspection of some characters of P, the search has to make one more final comparison. If the search finalizes at a leaf node, then pattern P must be compared to the leaf suffix to see if it matches. If the end of P is encountered before a leaf, then a suffix from the current subtree must be chosen and compared against P.

The classical representations of suffix trie require the use of pointers and suffix index. In a straightforward implementation, each node has pointers to all its child nodes together with the information about the edge label. These child pointers can be represented as an array, as a linked list or as a hash table [18].

If σ is small, the child node pointers can be represented in form of an array of size σ. Each i-th entry in this array represents the child node whose label is the i-th character in the ordered alphabet. This is very useful for tree traversals since the corresponding child can be located in constant-time.

For large alphabets, an array representation of children is impractical and can be replaced by a linked list representation. However, at query time, it requires additional time at each internal node in order to locate the corresponding child. Furthermore, since the position of a child in a list does not reflect the edge label, we need to store an additional byte representing this character.

Another possibility is to represent child pointers as a hash table. This representation preserves constant-time access to each child node and is more space-efficient than the array representation. An extension of this storage scheme was proposed by Kurtz [17]. In this optimization, the pointers to sibling nodes are not stored because the sibling nodes are placed consecutively in memory. Each node stores only the start position of its leftmost child. As before, each node may store an additional byte representing the edge label. At query time, it needs to make a binary search to find the corresponding child. This is the most space-efficient suffix tree representation known for main memory that uses pointers [18].

4   An Sequential Representation of Suffix Trie

As we saw in the previous section, most of the existing proposals explicitly maintain the tree shape with pointers, which can be physical (main memory addresses) or logical pointers (positions of an array). In [28] the authors present a sequential representation of a suffix trie based on techniques proposed in [15]. This representation allows to reduce the index size while keeping the functionality of the *count* and *locate* search. Besides, this representation is suitable for a later paging process on secondary memory.

Note that the information stored in the suffix trie can be classified into four categories: the tree shape, the skip values in the internal nodes, the edge labels and the suffix offsets in the leaves. In this representation, each one of them is stored in separated arrays.

Tree Shape. The tree shape is encoded using *balanced parentheses* representation instead of full pointers. This encoding is building from a preorder traversal of the tree. When visiting a node x for the first time, an opening parenthesis is written. After visiting its subtree, a matching closing parenthesis for x is written.

In this way, each node x is represented by a pair of parentheses: "(" (encode by 1) and ")" (encoded by 0). The x node is identified by its opening parenthesis. The nodes of a subtree of x are stored contiguously, then the size of its subtree is given by the beginning and ending points of the encoding.

Parentheses encoding of a general tree of n nodes requires $2n$ bits of space and support the core operations necessary for traversing the tree [23].

Edge Labels, Skip Values, and Node Degrees. Three arrays are used for this purpose, one for each one of these values. The elements in the arrays are ordered by a preorder traversal of the tree. During the downward traversal, the array position for the current node can be computed by tracking the number of nodes in each left subtree that is skipped.

Leaves and Suffix Offset. In this case, an array is used too but the suffix offsets have to be ordered from left to right. This ordering allows computing the array position of the first leaf of the current node.

In order to perform the search using this representation, the searching algorithm over parentheses encoding [23] is adapted to move over the five arrays. The operations of moving up or down the tree requires to make the following operations:

- *findclose(i)*: find the position of the closing parenthesis that matches the open parenthesis in position i.
- *findopen(i)*: find the position of the open parenthesis that matches the closing parenthesis in position i.
- *excess(i)*: find the difference of the number of open parentheses and the number of closing parentheses from de beginning to position i.

4.1 Improving the Storage Requirements

In [29] the authors present a space improvement of sequential representation. They propose to reduce the space requirements using Directly Addressable Codes (DACs codes) [3] for skip values and node degrees. Below, we briefly explain this encoding.

Given a sequence of k codes $C = C_1, C_2, \ldots, C_k$, we split the bits needed to represent each C_i into blocks of b bits. A first sequence A_1, will contain the least significant chunks of b bits (i.e., rightmost bits) of each C_i. A second one A_2, will contain the second chunks of each C_i that needs more than b bits. A third one A_3, will contain the third chunks of each C_i that needs more than $2b$ bits. This process continues until all the bits of the longest code are completed.

For each A_j sequence there is a bitmap B_j that indicates which C_i continues in A_{j+1}, that is: $B_{ji} = 1$ if C_i needs more that jb bits. The C_i code can be access found their b bits in each A_j sequence. This can be done using rank queries [11] on the B_j bitmap. A more detailed discussion of this can be found in [3].

Note that the number of chunks assigned to C_i depends on the magnitude of C_i. This means that smaller integers obtain shorter codes. In skip values and node degrees arrays, most of values are small, but some can be larger [4]. Hence, DAC is a good option to represent these sequences of integers.

4.2 Improving the Query Time

In [6] the authors present a new version of sequential representation that reduces the time needed to answer *count* and *locate* queries. More specifically, an array (called *ParentClose*) is added in order to improve the performance of *findclose* operations making over the parentheses encoding.

Let x the root of suffix trie, for each son y of x (level 1) *ParentClose* stores three values: the position of closing parenthesis of y, the number of nodes in the subtree rooted at y, and the number of leaves in the subtree rooted at y. These values have to be ordered by taking sons of x from left to right, allow navigation over the suffix trie.

ParentClose can be maintained in each level of the suffix trie, but this will considerably increase the space usage. Furthermore, in practice, the node degrees decrease as we go down the suffix trie. Therefore, in some level l it will be more efficient to compute *findclose* directly over the parentheses encoding instead of maintaining *ParentClose*. This level l must be experimentally determined.

5 Experimental Results

In this section, we present the results obtained with the three versions of sequential representation. We have measured and compared the time/space performance of these three versions.

It should be noted that this work is part of a larger project whose main objective is to achieve an efficient implementation on secondary memory of suffix trie. The paging process consists of partitioning the index into parts, each of which fits on a disk page. Each page will itself be a tree and can be stored using the representation explained in the previous section. At query time, one page (subtree) is loaded in the main memory, the search is carried out over this subtree, and the next one is loaded if necessary. Then, the searches in the main memory will be performed on small parts of suffix trie. For this reason, the experiments showed in this section have been carried out on small texts.

5.1 Experimental Setup

We will denote by:

- ST_s: the original sequential representation of suffix trie.
- ST_{sd}: the sequential representation of suffix trie that uses DAC code.
- ST_{sdp}: the sequential representation of suffix trie that uses DAC code and *ParentClose* array.

We have used datasets from the Pizza&Chili corpus (http://pizzachili.dcc. uchile.cl). They cover a representative set of application areas where the problem of full-text indexing is relevant. Specifically, we perform tests with:

- DNA: this file contains gene DNA sequences. Each of the 4 bases is coded as an uppercase letter A, G, C, T.
- PROTEINS: in this case, the file is a sequence of newline-separated protein sequences. Each of the 20 amino acids is coded as one uppercase letter.
- SOURCES: this file is formed by C/Java source code obtained by concatenating the .c, .h, .C and .java files of the linux-2.6.11.6 and gcc-4.0.0 distributions.
- XML (structured text). this file is an XML that provides bibliographic information on major computer science journals and proceedings.
- PITCHES (MIDI pitch values): this file is a sequence of pitch values (bytes in 0–127, plus a few extra special values) obtained from a myriad of MIDI files freely available on internet.

For each type of text, pieces of size 10, 20, 30, and 40 MB have been taken and indexed using a suffix trie represented with ST_s, ST_{sd}, and ST_{sdp}. We made *count* and *locate* queries for 500 patterns of length m, with $m = 5, 10, 15$, randomly chosen from the indexed texts.

The experiments have been carried out in two phases. The first one was aimed to determine the most appropriate value of l for ST_{sd}. In the second one, the most competitive ST_{sdp} variant was compared against ST_s and ST_{sd}. We measured query times, memory usage and index construction time. Because of space reasons, we will include only the most relevant graphics.

5.2   Results and Discussion

Choosing the *l* Value

Figure 3 shows the results obtained for DNA text, making *count* queries for patterns of length 5, 10, 15. The *l* values used in these experiments are represented on the *x*-axis, while the *y*-axis represents the average time to solve a *count* query.

As can be seen, the average time for *count* decreases as we increase the *l* values. Between the first two levels, a remarkable improvement is obtained saving around 70% of *count* time. If we compare levels 1 and 4, the improvement is around 90% approximately. From level 4, the curves tend to stabilize. Regarding the pattern length, the curves are similar, this implies that the pattern length does not affect the performance of ST_{sdp}.

The same behavior is observed for *locate* queries. This can be seen in Fig. 4 that shows the results for DNA text, making *locate* queries with patterns of length 5, 10, 15.

If we analyze the space usage, we can observe that with little additional space the improvements mentioned are achieved. Table 1 shows the space usage for DNA text. For each size text (first column), we give the total size of ST_{sdp} (second column) and the size of *ParentClose* array for each *l* value used (columns 3 to 8). In general terms, the table shows that the improvement of *count* and *locate* time is achieved with only 0.01% additional space approximately.

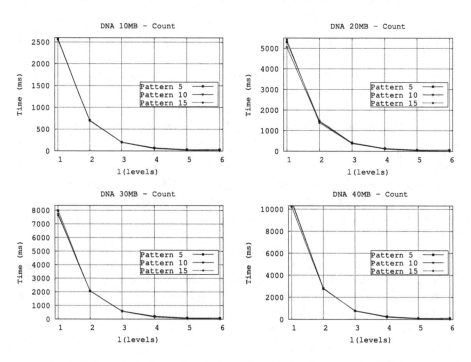

Fig. 3. Effect of number of levels *l* of ST_{sdp} in *count* time, using DNA text

Table 1. ST_{sdp}: Space usage for DNA Text. The values are expressed in MB.

Text size	ST_{sdp} size	$l = 1$	$l = 2$	$l = 3$	$l = 4$	$l = 5$	$l = 6$
10	69.21	0.00008	0.0004	0.001	0.004	0.01	0.06
20	139.38	0.0001	0.0006	0.002	0.005	0.01	0.06
30	209.05	0.0001	0.001	0.004	0.01	0.02	0.07
40	278.91	0.0001	0.001	0.004	0.01	0.02	0.07

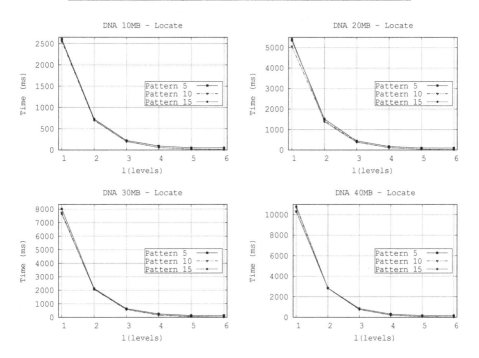

Fig. 4. Effect of number of levels l of ST_{sdp} in *locate* time, using DNA text

The behavior of ST_{sdp} with the other texts was similar. We can conclude that 4 and 5 are the most suitable values for l. These values were used to run the experiments in the next phase.

Count and Locate Time

Having defined the values for l, the next step was to compare the querie times for ST_s, ST_{sd} and ST_{sdp} (using 4 and 5 levels for *ParentClose*). Figure 5 shows the average time for *count* queries using patterns of length 10. The x-axis is the text size, and the y-axis is the average time (in logarithmic scale). We only show this pattern length, as the others yield similar conclusions.

It can be seen that ST_{sdp} outperforms the other versions saving between 80% and 90% of query time. This improvement is more notable in PROTEINS and PITCHES texts, where time savings reach 95%.

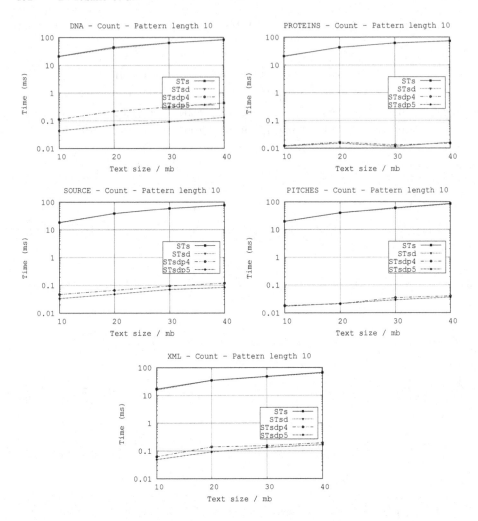

Fig. 5. Average time for *count* queries using ST_s, ST_{sd} and ST_{sdp} ($l = 4$ and $l = 5$).

Between $l = 4$ and $l = 5$, there is not a significant difference. This implies that level 4 is also a good option for ST_{sdp}.

Also, we can observe that ST_s and ST_{sd} have similar behavior with a small-time advantage for ST_s. This is because ST_{sd} needs to process the DAC codes in order to rebuild the node degree and the skip value.

Regarding *locate* time (Fig. 6), we can observe this same behavior.

Space Usage and Construction Time
Figure 7 summarizes construction time of ST_s, ST_{sd} and ST_{sdp} (levels 4 and 5) using texts of 40 MB. We only show results for this text size; the others yield similar conclusions.

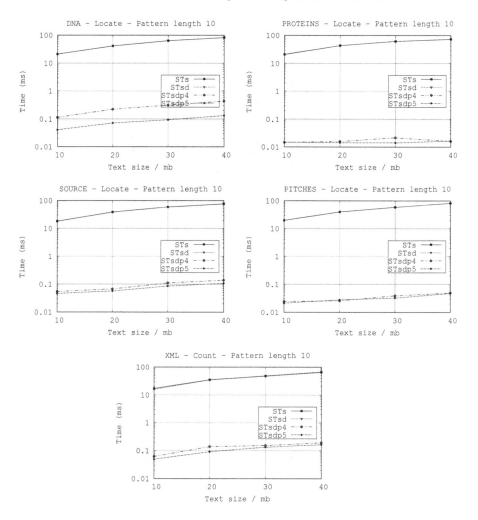

Fig. 6. Average time for *locate* queries using ST_s, ST_{sd}, and ST_{sdp} ($l = 4$ and $l = 5$).

It can be seen that ST_s builds faster than ST_{sd} and ST_{sdp}. This result was expected because ST_{sd} must build DAC codes and ST_{sdp} must build DAC codes and *ParentClose* array. This implies the use of 10% more time in the index construction.

However, this additional construction time will be amortized by saving time to answer *count* and *locate* queries. Furthermore, ST_{sd} and ST_{sdp} overcome to ST_s in the index size. This can be clearly see in Fig. 8: ST_s needs much more space to store the index, around 50% more than the other versions.

Notice that ST_{sdp} is not a succinct index, nevertheless, its space usage in some texts is around 7 times the size of T.

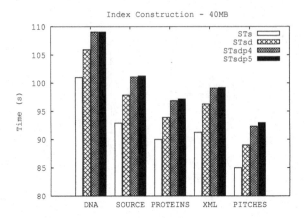

Fig. 7. Construction time of ST_s, ST_{sd} and ST_{sdp} ($l = 4$ and $l = 5$), using texts of 40 MB.

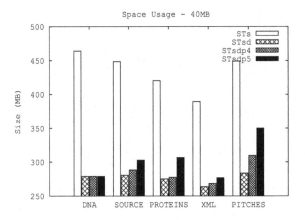

Fig. 8. Index Size of ST_s, ST_{sd} and ST_{sdp} ($l = 4$ and $l = 5$), using texts of 40 MB.

6   Conclusions and Future Work

In this paper, we have presented an exhaustive experimental evaluation of three versions of sequential representation of suffix trie: ST_s, ST_{sd} and ST_{sdp}. In the experimental results, we have observed that:

- In query time, ST_{sdp} outperforms the other versions, saving between 80% and 90% of time; ST_s and ST_{sd} have similar behavior.
- In space usage, ST_{sd} is the better option and ST_s is the worst. Nevertheless, ST_{sdp} uses a little more additional space than ST_{sd} and considerably improves the query time.
- In construction time, ST_s is the most competitive option, but not significantly.

We can conclude that ST_{sdp} is the most competitive version, achieving a balance between space usage and query time.

As future work, we are interested in achieving an efficient version of ST_{sdp} in secondary memory. To make it, an efficient paging process is needed to assure the index performance. We are currently working on this topic.

References

1. Baeza-Yates, R., Ribeiro-Neto, B.: Modern Information Retrieval. Addison-Wesley, Boston (1999)
2. Boyer, R.S., Moore, J.S.: A fast string searching algorithm. Commun. ACM **20**(10), 762–772 (1977)
3. Brisaboa, N.R., Ladra, S., Navarro, G.: Directly addressable variable-length codes. In: Karlgren, J., Tarhio, J., Hyyrö, H. (eds.) SPIRE 2009. LNCS, vol. 5721, pp. 122–130. Springer, Heidelberg (2009). https://doi.org/10.1007/978-3-642-03784-9_12
4. Clark, D., Munro, I.: Efficient suffix tree on secondary storage. In: Proceedings of the 7th ACM-SIAM Symposium on Discrete Algorithms, pp. 383–391 (1996)
5. Cole, R., Kopelowitz, T., Lewenstein, M.: Suffix trays and suffix trists: structures for faster text indexing. In: Bugliesi, M., Preneel, B., Sassone, V., Wegener, I. (eds.) ICALP 2006. LNCS, vol. 4051, pp. 358–369. Springer, Heidelberg (2006). https://doi.org/10.1007/11786986_32
6. Cornejo, J., Ruano, D., Herrera, N.: Una mejora en tiempo del trie de sufijos. In: Congreso Argentino de Ciencias de la Computación, Rio Cuarto, Córdoba, Argentina (2019)
7. Ferragina, P., Manzini, G.: Indexing compressed text. J. ACM **52**(4), 552–581 (2005)
8. Gagie, T., Navarro, G.: Compressed indexes for repetitive textual datasets. In: Sakr, S., Zomaya, A.Y. (eds.) Encyclopedia of Big Data Technologies. Springer, Cham (2019). https://doi.org/10.1007/978-3-319-77525-8_53
9. Gonnet, G.H., Baeza-Yates, R.: Handbook of Algorithms and Data Structures. Addison-Wesley, Boston (1991)
10. Gonnet, G.H., Baeza-Yates, R., Snider, T.: New Indices for Text: PAT Trees and PAT Arrays. Prentice Hall, Hoboken (1992)
11. González, R., Grabowski, Sz., Mäkinen, V., Navarro, G.: Practical implementation of rank and select queries. In: Poster Proceedings Volume of 4th Workshop on Efficient and Experimental Algorithms (WEA), Greece, pp. 27–38. CTI Press and Ellinika Grammata (2005)
12. González, R., Navarro, G.: Compressed text indexes with fast locate. In: Ma, B., Zhang, K. (eds.) CPM 2007. LNCS, vol. 4580, pp. 216–227. Springer, Heidelberg (2007). https://doi.org/10.1007/978-3-540-73437-6_23
13. González, R., Navarro, G., Ferrada, H.: Locally compressed suffix arrays. ACM J. Exp. Algorithmics **19**(1) (2014). Article 1
14. Roberto GROSSI and Jeffrey Scott VITTER: Compressed suffix arrays and suffix trees with applications to text indexing and string matching. SIAM J. Comput. **35**(2), 378–407 (2006)
15. Herrera, N., Navarro, G.: Árboles de sufijos comprimidos en memoria secundaria. In: Proceedings of the XXXV Latin American Conference on Informatics (CLEI), Pelotas, Brazil (2009)

16. Konow, R., Navarro, G.: Dual-sorted inverted lists in practice. In: Calderón-Benavides, L., González-Caro, C., Chávez, E., Ziviani, N. (eds.) SPIRE 2012. LNCS, vol. 7608, pp. 295–306. Springer, Heidelberg (2012). https://doi.org/10.1007/978-3-642-34109-0_31

17. Kurtz, S.: Reducing the space requirement of suffix trees. Softw. Pract. Exp. **29**(13), 1149–1171 (1999)

18. Thomo, A., Barsky, M., Stege, U.: A survey of practical algorithms for suffix tree construction in external memory. In: Software: Practice and Experience (2010)

19. Mäkinen, V., Navarro, G.: Succinct suffix arrays based on run-length encoding. Nord. J. Comput. **12**(1), 40–66 (2005)

20. Manber, U., Myers, G.: Suffix arrays: a new method for on-line string searches. SIAM J. Comput. **22**(5), 935–948 (1993)

21. Moura, E., Navarro, G., Ziviani, N., Baeza-Yates, R.: Fast and flexible word searching on compressed text. ACM Trans. Inf. Syst. (TOIS) **18**(2), 113–139 (2000)

22. Munro, J.I., Navarro, G., Nekrich, Y.: Fast compressed self-indexes with deterministic linear-time construction. Algorithmica **82**(2), 316–337 (2020). https://doi.org/10.1007/s00453-019-00637-x

23. Ian Munro, J., Raman, V.: Succinct representation of balanced parentheses and static trees. SIAM J. Comput. **31**(3), 762–776 (2001)

24. Navarro. Text Databases, pp. 688–694. Idea Group Inc., Pennsylvania (2005)

25. Navarro, G., Mäkinen, V.: Compressed full-text indexes. ACM Comput. Surv. **39**(1) (2007). Article 2

26. Navarro, G., Sadakane, K.: Compressed tree representations. In: Kao, M.-Y. (ed.) Encyclopedia of Algorithms, pp. 1–7. Springer, Heidelberg (2015). https://doi.org/10.1007/978-3-642-27848-8_641-1

27. Ruano, D., Herrera, N., Cornejo, J., Azar, P.: Representación del trie del sufijo: Una evaluación empírica. In Congreso Argentino de Ciencias de la Computación, Buenos Aires, Argentina, pp. 318 (2020)

28. Ruano, D., Herrera, N.: Representación secuencial de un trie de sufijos. In: XX Congreso Argentino de Ciencias de la Computación, Buenos Aires, Argentina (2014)

29. Ruano, D., Herrera, N.: Indexando bases de datos textuales: Una representación compacta del trie de sufijos. In: Congreso Nacional de Ingeniería Informática / Sistemas de Información, Buenos Aires, Argentina (2015)

30. Weiner, P.: Linear pattern matching algorithm. In: Proceedings of the 14th IEEE Symposium Switching Theory and Automata Theory, pp. 1–11 (1973)

Hardware Architectures, Networks, and Operating Systems

Extended Petri Net Processor and Threads Quantity Determination Algorithm for Embedded Systems

Luis O. Ventre[(✉)] [iD] and Orlando Micolini [iD]

Depto. Computación, Lab. de Arquitectura de Computadoras, Facultad de Ciencias Exactas Físicas y Naturales - U.N.C, Córdoba, Argentina
{luis.ventre,orlando.micolini}@unc.edu.ar
https://fcefyn.unc.edu.ar/

Abstract. The evolution of technology and electronic devices, the widespread use of IoT, and the compliance with specific regulatory requirements of the industry have made the process of designing embedded systems more complex and challenging. These systems are generally multi-threaded, parallel, concurrent, reactive, and/or event-driven. In these systems, the data and events are heterogeneous and non-deterministic as they interact with the external environment. Extended Petri nets constitute an elective platform and system-independent modeling language, which makes it appropriate for modeling embedded systems. To take full advantage of the modeling efforts, it is desirable to use the built models to obtain part of the system implementation. This work presents the design and implementation of an Extended Petri Processor, its modular architecture and an algorithm for the automatic determination of the number of active and necessary threads or processes. This processor makes use of the extended state equation of Petri Nets, executing the model of the mentioned systems, aiming to mitigate the time needed for development, and reduce programming errors.

Keywords: Petri processor · Automatic thread determination · Petri Nets · Code generation · IoT · FPGA

1 Introduction

Nowadays, critical, reactive (RS) and event-driven embedded systems (EDA) [1] are in high demand, especially by Industry 4.0 [2]. The design of these systems must meet strict non-functional requirements since they are parallel, concurrent systems and interact with variables and events from the system itself and from the outside world, where the data and events are heterogeneous and non-deterministic [3]. This article presents the design and implementation of an extended Petri processor and its modular architecture, for the development of these types of systems. This processor aims to reduce development time and mitigate programming errors.

© Springer Nature Switzerland AG 2021
P. Pesado and J. Eterovic (Eds.): CACIC 2020, CCIS 1409, pp. 199–214, 2021.
https://doi.org/10.1007/978-3-030-75836-3_14

The design phases of an embedded system include the development of the model based on a set of requirements [4]. This model is the basis for other stages, including the application building stage [5].

Non-autonomous and extended PN is a general-purpose modeling language that supports the modeling of reactive, concurrent, and parallel systems regardless of the platform. In the design of RS and EDA, the transformation of the model into software implies a translation work that leads to interpretation and implementation errors. In order to mitigate these errors, this processor capable of running the model regardless of the platform has been developed.

As a precedent to this work, and as part of this same research project, a modular Petri Processor (PP) that executes ordinary PN can be found in [6], next an algorithm for the division of the Petri nets and its structural locality was developed in [7], then a method for the design and development of embedded systems with the PP in [8,9], the state equation of PN was extended in [10] and subsequently a modular extended PP (PPX) in [11]. The main advantage of the PPX is the expression capacity, which is like a Turing machine since it can execute models with different types of arms or guards. In the present article, the work in [11] has been extended including an algorithm for the automatic determination of the number of threads; all these research instances have the objective of automatic code generation from the system model.

According to our research documents, there is no history of an automatic code generation or a model execution performed by a processor, nor algorithms for determining the number of threads from the model of a PN. The innovation of this proposal includes the design and implementation of a modular heterogeneous architecture processor, which executes the extended state equation of PN [7], which has the expression capacity of a Turing machine. This processor keeps all the properties verified in the model, since the model is essentially not interpreted and/or transcribed in code, but rather executed. Furthermore, this article describes the application of an algorithm for the automatic determination of the number of active and necessary threads or processes. This algorithm applies to the use cases where the development methodology employed is described in [8]; where the authors detail a methodology for the design and development of embedded systems using a Petri processor. The core of the heterogeneous system architecture proposed by the authors consists of a PP and a General-Purpose Processor (PPG). In the PP the Petri net (PN) that models the system is loaded, immediately implementing, with it, all the logic of the system; the processor processes events and with this logic determines the future states, thus establishing the order of execution of the actions. In the PPG, the threads are implemented for the execution of these actions, thus decoupling the logic of the actions from the developed system. The algorithm here used is responsible for analyzing the RdP that the system models and determining the number of maximum active threads to be used in the PPG, as well as determi-ning the number of maximum threads required in the same PPG.

The following section sets out the objectives of this work; while in Sect. 3 a brief theoretical framework is presented. Then, in Sect. 4, the architecture of the PPX is described as the proposed solution. In Sect. 5, the results, the tests carried out and finally, the conclusions are exposed.

2 Objectives

The system's logic model contains the necessary information for implementing the software logic. The coding stage involves successive iterative efforts to refine, interpret, and transcript the model into code, detecting and correcting errors in the process. This entails an overload of effort and time in the development stages.

The main objective of this work is the design and implementation of a processor that executes the logic model as code, thus unifying the modeling and coding stages. As a secondary objective, a modular design and interconnection with a traditional processor is carried out.

3 Methodology and Tools

There are several modeling tools, among which are: UML diagrams [12] and PN [13,14]. UML diagrams provide the necessary characteristics, partially, but they essentially lack mechanisms for formal verification that strictly guarantee compliance with critical requirements, which are fundamental aspects to be implemented in the SR and EDA.

Since the extended, non-autonomous, PN [15] allows to model concurrency, local and global state, and parallelism, it is possible to verify them formally. They are executable [16] and scalable when expressed with the extended state equation [7]; they have been considered to be the most convenient formalism and have been selected as a modeling tool and a processor execution language.

The development tools and implementation of the PPX are explained and described in Subsect. 4.5.

3.1 Petri Nets

A marked PN, denoted as PN, is a quadruple [5] defined by:

$$PN = (P, T, I, M_0) \tag{1}$$

where:

- $P = p_1, p_2, \cdots, p_n$ is a finite, non-empty set of places.
- $T = t_1, t_2, \cdots, t_m$ is a finite, non-empty set of transitions.
- I is the incidence matrix that relates places with transitions and vice versa.
- M_0 is the initial markup of the PN.

3.2 S³PR

The main concepts needed to define S³PR PN are: S²P PN, which models simple sequential processes; S²PR PN, which models simple sequential processes with resources; and finally S³PR PN are the net composition of S²PR PN through a set of commonplaces (resources). A specific explanation of the various subclasses of PN can be found in [17].

S²P - We define the class of simple sequential processes (S²P) PN as:

$$N = (P \cup \{P^0\}, T, F) \tag{2}$$

Where:

1. $P \neq \varnothing$, $p^0 \notin P$ (p^0 called Idle Place);
2. N is a strongly connected machine state;
3. Each circuit of N contains the place p^0.

The third condition imposes a "termination" property on the work processes we are considering: if a process evolves, it will terminate.

Hence, it is extended to model resource usage, which is an S²PR class. In other words, a simple sequential process with resources (S²PR), is an S²P that needs the use of a unique resource in each state that is not the idle state. Due to the interactions with the rest of the processes in the system will be carried out by sharing the set of resources, it is natural to assume that in the idle state there is no interaction with the rest of the system and, therefore, no resources are used in this state.

S²PR - An S²PR is a PN that fulfills:

$$N = \langle P \cup \{p^0\} \cup P_R, T, F \rangle \tag{3}$$

where:

1. The subnet determinated by $X = P \cup \{p^0\} \cup T$ is an S²P.
2. $P_R \neq \varnothing$ y $(P \cup \{p^0\}) \cap P_R = \varnothing$
3. $\forall p \in P. \, \forall t \in \bullet p. \, \forall t' \in p \bullet. \, \bullet t \cap P_R = t' \bullet \cap P_R = \{r_p\}$
4. The following two statements must be verified:
   a) $\forall r \in P_R. \, \bullet \bullet r \cap P = r \bullet \bullet \cap P \neq \varnothing$
   b) $\forall r \in P_R. \, \bullet r \cap r \bullet = \varnothing$
5. $\bullet \bullet (p^0) \cap P_R = (p^0) \bullet \bullet \cap P_R = \varnothing$

P_R: set of resource places.
P: set of state places.

Given the previos S²PR definition, an acceptable initial marking for N m_0 is defined by:

1. $m_0(p^0) \geq 1$
2. $m_0(p) = 0, \, \forall p \in P$
3. $m_0(r) \geq 1, \, \forall r \in P_R$

S²PR - And, lastly, the class of simple sequential process systems with resources (S³PR) is defined by the net composition of S²PR through a set of common-places.

$$S^3PR = \{N = O_{n=1}^k N_i = (P \cup P^0 \cup P_R, T, F)\} \tag{4}$$

3.3 Synchronized or Non-autonomous PN

This type of PN introduces events into the model and it is an extension of autonomous PN [15,16]. Non-autonomous PNs model systems in which firings are synchronized with external discrete events. Events are associated with transitions, and the firing occurs when two conditions are met: the transition is enabled and the event associated with the transition had taken place.

External events correspond to changes in the state of the system's environment (including time) while internal events are changes in the state of the system itself. Synchronized PNs can then be defined as a triplet:

$$PN_{sync} = (PN, E, sync) \tag{5}$$

where:

- PN is a marked PN,
- E is a set of external events and
- $sync$ is the function that relates the transitions T with $E \cup \{e\}$, where $\{e\}$ is the null event, that is, those transitions that are automatically fired.

Perennial, Non-perennial and Null Events
There are different types of events. A detailed description can be found in [16].

Extended Equation of State
In order to mathematically represent the existence of the new inhibitor, reader and reset arms, a matrix is required for each type of arc. These matrices are similar to the matrix I. When the arcs have a weight equal to one, the terms of the matrix are binary. A transition can be enabled if it meets the following conditions: if it has an inhibitor arm that does not have a token in the associated place; if it has a reading arm, and the place associated has one or more tokens; if it has a guard and the guard value is equal to true; if it has an event associated, and one or more events were queued and if it has a label with a time interval, and the counter is in the valid time range.

So the extended equation of state is now defined as:

$$M_{(j+1)} = M_j + I * (\sigma \text{ and } Ex)\#A \tag{6}$$

In this expression Ex is the extended enabled vector, represented by:

$$Ex = E \text{ and } B \text{ and } L \text{ and } G \text{ and } Z \tag{7}$$

where E, B, L, G y Z are the enabled vectors of the different arcs. The details of the calculation of (6) and (7) are found in [7].

4 Architecture of the Solution

The hypothesis of this work is based on the fact that a model made with a non-autonomous PN is a set of instructions, equations and restrictions or rules to generate the I/O behavior of a system. That is, the model is described as state transitions and mechanisms to accept input trajectories and generate output trajectories depending on their state.

The defining, in terms of system specifications, has the advantage of a solid mathematical basis and unequivocally defined semantics. To specify a behavior, the model needs an agent. This is basically a computer system capable of executing the model. The same model, expressed in a formalism, can be executed by different agents, thus enabling portability and interoperability at a high level of abstraction.

In this project, the PPX is the agent in charge of executing the model by making use of (6), so that it can generate the desired behavior. Extended PNs allow to model systems of events or stimuli, states, logic, policy and actions, which means it can be decoupled and they manage the control and execution of the whole system.

4.1 Architecture of the PPX

The main blocks of the PPX implement (6) which are: matrix-program, calculation-state, queues, and policies.

4.2 PPX Modules

The Fig. 1 represents a synthesized version of the processor.

Matrix-Program Modules: Responsible for defining the processor program with the matrices and vectors of the state equation. They are represented in Fig. 1, identified with ∗, and they are: the matrices I, H, R, Rst, A and Time comparison window, and the vector of automatic firings.

Calculation-Status Modules: Responsible for calculating and maintaining the status of the PN. Its components are marked in Fig. 1 with #, which are: the state vector, the new state vector, L, B, V, E, G, S, the timers array, the vector of possible firings, the Adder and the Calculation-reset module.

Module: Responsible for storing the input and output events and communicating the results of the PN execution with the traditional processor, Microblaze (MCS) [18]. These components are marked in Fig. 1 with @ (the firing and exit request queues).

Policies Module: Responsible for selecting the transition with the highest priority from the vector of possible firings. Its components have been identified on the Fig. 1 with &, they are the Firing Policy Matrix and the highest priority Firing Vector.

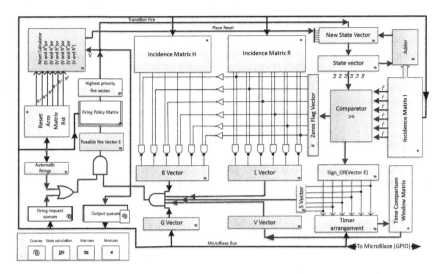

Fig. 1. PPX architecture.

4.3 Modules Description

The parts and functions of each component correspond to (6). They are consistent with the proposed modular structure and the main ones are:

Incidence Matrix I - array of integers. Its dimension is $|T| \times |P|$.
Inhibitor Arms Matrix H - binary matrix. Its dimension is $|T| \times |P|$.
Reader Arms Matrix R - binary matrix. Its dimension is $|T| \times |P|$.
Arm Matrix Reset Rst - binary matrix. Its dimension is $|T| \times |P|$.
Time Comparison Window Matrix - stores the alpha and beta values which correspond to the lower and upper time limits [5].
State Vector - vector of positive integers. Its dimension is $|P|$.
Vector L - binary vector. Its dimension is $|T|$. Inhibits the transition if the place is not marked.
Vector B - binary vector. Its dimension is $|T|$. Inhibit the transition if the place is marked.
Vector V - binary vector. Its dimension is $|T|$. Enable sensitive transition if your timer is in the window range (between alpha-beta).
Guardian Vector G - binary vector with the guard values. Its dimension is $|T|$.
Sensitized Vector S - binary vector, where each position corresponds to each column of the matrix of possible next states. Its dimension is $|T|$.
Timers arrangement - vector of integers. Its dimension is $|T|$. They are counters that are activated when the associated transition is enabled and are reset when it is disabled or fired.
Firing Request Queues - its interface exposes an input vector to the PPX, where each position of the vector corresponds to a transition.

Exit Queues - its interface exposes an output vector from the PPX, where each position of the vector corresponds to a transition.

Firing Policy Matrix - binary matrix of dimension $|T| \times |T|$. Its values indicate the relative priority between transitions.

Highest Priority Firing Vector - binary vector that represents the transition to be fired.

4.4   Processor Algorithm

Single-server semantics have been adopted in this work, so only one transition is fired at a time. Two cycles are required for each firing to determine and report the new status.

Cicle 1 - Calculations - In this cycle, the necessary calculations are performed to determine which transition to fire.

The tagging vector is compared with each column of the incidence matrix, denoted in Fig. 1 as I^i, to get the sign bit of each element of the array of possible next states. The results are binary columns where the i-th column contains the signs of the values of the next marking vector, in case the transition i is executed. This matrix contains only the signs of the possible next states; given a column, if any of the values is negative, it means that the next state will not be reachable by the PN (negative values in a tagging vector indicate that the transition is not enabled). To obtain this value, a logical disjunction is performed between all the elements of each column. The vector S is built using these values.

For each element of the state vector, a zero bit is determined. With these bits, the zeros flag vector is constructed. This indicates whether or not the place is marked and it is indicated in Fig. 1 as Zeros Flag. The vectors B y L are calculated with the product of the Zeros Flag vector and the matrices H and R, respectively.

The Guards Vector G is updated from the MCS processor, since it represents all the conditions that are external to the PPX processor.

The vector V indicates whether a transition is enabled (based on the values of the vector S), and if it is in the time window programmed in the Array of Timers.

The transitions that are possible to be fired are obtained from the logical conjunction between the vectors B, L, G, V and S. The logical disjunction between the Firing Request Queue vector and the Automatic Firings indicates the transitions that are requested to fire. Next, the logical conjunction between these last two vectors is carried out, which indicates the possible firings, noted as E in Fig. 1. This vector contains a value of 1 in the positions of the transitions that are possible to fire. Since single-server semantics have been adopted, it is necessary to determine the highest priority transition to fire. To achieve this, the Firing Policies Matrix is used. This returns the highest priority Firing Vector, which contains a value equal to 1 in the transition to fire. In this cycle it is also calculated if any place should be zeroed, so the internal product is performed between the columns R^i of the matrix of reset arms (Rst) and the highest priority Firing

Vector. This calculation is carried out by the module named Reset_calculator. If the value is one, the place reset bus sets the place value to zero.

Cycle 2 - Update - This is the cycle that computes the firing of the transition that was selected in the previous cycle. Here, the firing takes effect and the value of the marking vector is updated. To achieve this, the selected transition works as a column selector.

The adder, which is at the top of the Fig. 1, performs the sum of the marking vector with the matrix column I selected by the firing vector. The result of that sum is stored as the new marking vector. In this cycle, if applicable, the space indicated on the reset bus is reset. Additionally, the queues are updated; increasing the output queue counter and decrementing the input queue counter.

4.5   PPX, FPGA, and Microblaze MCS

The PPX solves the logic of the system so it operates with an associated processor [6,16] which executes the actions required. To achieve this, the PPX was interconnected with the MCS processor as shown in Fig. 2. It was implemented in a Spartan 6 FPGA from Xilinx (Atlys) [19], in which an IP-core MCS was installed since it is included in the ISE tool [20] and it has a low impact on the resources required for its implementation. A communications module (UART) was also installed in order to carry out the testing and a clock management module (DCM). This configuration has been selected to establish comparisons with the work carried out in [6].

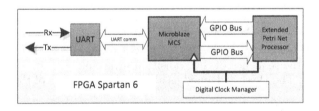

Fig. 2. Interconnection between processors.

4.6   Queues

The input and output queues of the PPX are configurable, each transition has an input queue and an associated output queue. A detailed description is found in [6].

4.7   Priorities and Conflicts Between Transitions

The PPX does not detect conflict states [15] between transitions, this is why it treats all enabled transitions as if they were in conflict (single server). This semantics, in conjunction with the priority policy module, also solves the problem of conflicts and makes it deterministic. The Firing Policies Matrix module determines the transition to fire, this module is configurable at runtime.

5   Threads Quantity Determination Algorithm

The algorithm here presented is responsible for analyzing the RdP loaded in the PPX. The PPX calculates the future states, therefore establishing the order of execution of the actions. This algorithm determines the number of maximum active threads to be used in the PPG, as well as the number of maximum threads required in the same PPG. Those threads that run in PPG execute the actions.

The present algorithm is applied to S^3PR [17] type networks, the steps of the algorithm will be described as follows:

5.1   Algorithm Steps

1. Construct A: The A set is defined as the places that are involved in the transition invariants. These places are the union of the sets:

$$A = \bigcup_{\forall t \in inv} \bullet t \cup \bigcup_{\forall t \in inv} t \bullet \tag{8}$$

2. Construct B: The B set is defined as the places in set A that are not restrictions or resources.

$$B = A - \{constraint/resourcePlaces\} \tag{9}$$

3. Construct C: The C set is defined as the places of B set excluding the IDLE places (initial/final buffers).

$$C = B - \{IdlePlaces(buffers)\} \tag{10}$$

4. Sort the set of places C: this set of places must be sort according to the evolution of the sequence of the transition invariant.
5. Construct D: The D set is defined as all possible markings of the set of places C.
6. Determination of the maximum number of simultaneous active threads in the invariant: of each possible marking of set D, perform the sum of the marks of each place in search of the maximum sum. This will be the maximum number of simultaneous active threads in that transition invariant.
7. Determination of the maximum necessary number of threads in the invariant:
   – Case 1: If the sequence of places of the transition invariant matches a place invariant and no places are part of a conflict, the number of threads for that subnet is equal to the value of the place invariant.
   – Case 2: The places crossed by a transition invariant, which participate in a conflict (since they are crossed by more than one invariant) divide the transition invariant into two segments. Thus, the invariant is segmented between conflict places. In the place conflict, for each exit arm of this place, a thread is required (one per transition invariant). The places that belong to the segment are assigned a number of threads equal to the sum of the maximum marks in this segment.

5.2   Algorithm Application Example

Next, the application of the algorithm will be analyzed with a simple example of an S^3PR network to understand the steps involved.

From the analisys of the S^3PR net in Fig. 3, the idle places are: idle = {P1, P6}.

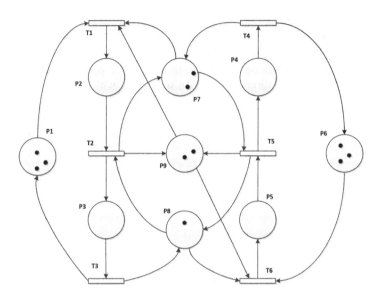

Fig. 3. S^3PR Petri net example.

The transition invariants of this S^3PR network are:
Inv_1 = {T1, T2, T3}, the firing sequence is T1, T2, T3.
Inv_2 = {T4, T5, T6}, the firing sequence is T4, T5, T6.

1. Construct A's:

A_{inv1} = {P1, P2, P3, P7, P8, P9}
A_{inv2} = {P4, P5, P6, P7, P8, P9}

2. Construct B's:

B_{inv1} = {P1, P2, P3}
B_{inv2} = {P4, P5, P6}

3. Construct C's:

C_{inv1} = {P2, P3}
C_{inv2} = {P4, P5}

4. Sort C's: The places in the C set are in firing order.
5. Construct D's:
6. From the analysis of P2 and its adjacent P3 (see Table 1), it is observed that they are marked simultaneously, therefore the thread should not be the same. From the analysis of each of the maximum marks of {P2, P3} that belong to D_{inv1}, it is observed that the mark of P2 is 2 simultaneously when the mark of P3 is 1. From the sum of the marks, it is determined that the maximum number of simultaneously active threads for invariant 1 is 3.
7. From the analysis of the place invariants, applying step 7-case1, it is observed that the transition invariant 1 crosses places that coincide with one of the place invariants; therefore, the maximum number of threads needed for that subnet is equal to the value of the place invariant, which is 3.

Table 1. C_{inv1} Possible markings

	D^1_{Cinv1}	D^2_{Cinv1}	D^3_{Cinv1}	D^4_{Cinv1}	D^5_{Cinv1}	D^6_{Cinv1}
P2	0	1	0	1	2	2
P3	0	0	1	1	0	1
Add	0	1	1	2	2	3

In this case, the maximum number of simultaneous active threads in invariant 1 is equal to the maximum number of threads necessary for the execution of actions binded to the places crossed by transition invariant 1.

An equivalent analysis can be carried out for invariant 2, determining that for this it is necessary: 3 maximum threads active simultaneously and 3 maximum threads for the execution of invariant 2.

To determine the maximum number of simultaneously active threads in the entire system modeled by this S^{3}PR network, the same analysis must be performed with both C_{inv} simultaneously. In this particular case C_{simult} is defined by $C_{inv1} \cup C_{inv2}$.

Table 2. C_{simult} Possible markings Part 1

	$D^1_{Csimult}$	$D^2_{Csimult}$	$D^3_{Csimult}$	$D^4_{Csimult}$	$D^5_{Csimult}$	$D^6_{Csimult}$	$D^7_{Csimult}$
P2	0	1	0	1	0	2	1
P3	0	0	1	1	0	0	0
P4	0	0	0	0	0	0	0
P5	0	0	0	0	1	0	1
Add	0	1	1	2	1	2	2

Table 3. C_{simult} Possible markings Part 2

	$D^8_{Csimult}$	$D^9_{Csimult}$	$D^{10}_{Csimult}$	$D^{11}_{Csimult}$	$D^{12}_{Csimult}$	$D^{13}_{Csimult}$	$D^{14}_{Csimult}$
P2	2	1	0	1	0	0	0
P3	1	0	1	0	0	0	0
P4	0	1	1	1	1	2	2
P5	0	0	0	1	1	0	1
Add	3	2	2	3	2	2	3

The maximum number of simultaneous active threads of the entire system is obtained by observing the maximum markings in Table 2 and Table 3, in the present case will be 3 threads; while the maximum number of threads required for the complete system is obtained by adding the maximum markings of each D_{inv} individual table (Table 1 and it's equivalent for D_{Cinv2}). In this case is 6 threads.

6 Results

With the PPX-MCS heterogeneous architecture, different application cases were executed to evaluate its performance. The successful executions of the cases were raised in [8] and [9]. The comparison of resources has been carried out taking into account the results obtained in [6]. For the purposes of this comparison, the configuration, FPGA and development tools selected were the same.

FPGA Resource Consumption - The processor was installed with different configurations of vector and matrix elements. Each configuration is expressed with a triplet of integers, which are: $P \times T \times Pa$, where P is the number of places, T the number of transitions, and Pa the length of the word that represents the weight of the arcs and the amount of tokens that a place supports. Multiple kernel syntheses were performed using different word-lengths (4-bit and 8-bit data). In Fig. 4 a) the amount of resources that were used from the FPGA is displayed for synthesized configurations. In Fig. 4 a) the exponential increase in the consumption of resources is observed, as the number of elements of the matrices and vectors increase. In Fig. 4 b) and Fig. 5 b) the consumption of resources of the PPX is compared to the PP, where the average increase of LUTs is 10% while the increase in register consumption is 18%. Overall, the impact of the MCS processor in resources is 12.72% for LUTs, and 21.09% for registers. These resources are the same for all the synthesized configurations of the PPX.

Frequency Analysis - The maximum theoretical frequencies for the different processor instances are shown in Fig. 5 a). Since optimizations have been made to the modules and interconnects, the PPX has achieved a substantial improvement in frequency over the PP. It is observed that for a configuration of $8 \times 8 \times 8$,

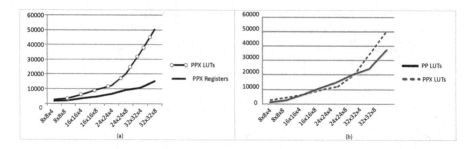

Fig. 4. a) Consumption of LUTs and PPX Registers. b) Comparison of the use of LUTs between PPX and PP.

the maximum frequency is 257 MHz while for $8 \times 8 \times 4$ it is 271 MHz; for a $16 \times 16 \times 8$ configuration the frequency is 190 MHz and for $16 \times 16 \times 4$ it is 216 MHz. It should be noted that the decrease in frequency, with respect to the length of the word, is 18% in average. On the other hand, if the length of the word is maintained and the number of places and transitions is increased, that is, the size of the PN, the difference in frequency is significantly larger, on average 30%.

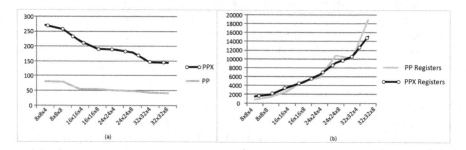

Fig. 5. a) Comparison of theoretical maximum frequencies between PPX and PP. b) Comparison of Records between the PPX and the PP.

7   Conclusion

In this project, a processor (PPX) was designed and implemented for executing the extended state equation, with a modular architecture. This processor extends the semantic capacity of the PP developed in [6]. The inclusions of different types of arcs, temporal semantics, and guards in the PPX give the PPX the expression capacity of a Turing machine without significantly increasing the necessary resources. Queue scheduling and support for different types of events have been maintained, as well as the communications module. The results show that the PPX is suitable, for the FPGA selected, for embedded systems that require up to 32 composite logical conditions, 32 logical variables, and 32 events that must be evaluated simultaneously. From the data obtained in the frequency analysis, the substantial improvement in the maximum theoretical frequency with respect to the PP stands out. The serial communication module has facilitated the configuration, debugging, and programming tests from a console. The modular implementation of the PPX implies a breakthrough for maintenance, scalability and future autoconfiguration.

The proposed algorithm is key to determine in the early stages of the system design the necessary resources for the implementation in an embedded system. The number of simultaneous active threads establish the degree of parallelism for each state of the system, thus facilitating the estimation of response times. This algorithm automates part of the design and code generation related to the sequences of system actions to be executed in the PPG according to the proposed architecture. Consequently, the model presented, where a PN is executed in the PPX together with this algorithm, mitigates the development times of embedded systems.

References

1. Halbwachs, N.: Synchronous Programming of Reactive Systems. Springer, Heidelberg (2013)
2. Schwab, K.: The Fourth Industrial Revolution. Currency (2017)
3. Munir, A., Gordon-Ross, A., Ranka, S.: Modeling and Optimization of Parallel and Distributed Embedded Systems. John Wiley (2015)
4. Zeigler, B.P., Muzy, A., Kofman, E.: Theory of Modeling and Simulation: Discrete Event & Iterative System Computational Foundations. Academic press (2018)
5. Diaz, M.: Petri nets: Fundamental Models, Verification and Applications. John (2013). https://doi.org/10.1002/9780470611647
6. Micolini, O., Daniele, E.N., Ventre, L.O.: In Argentine Congress of Computer Science, pp. 199–208. Springer. LNCS (2017)
7. Micolini, O., Ventre, L.O., Schild, M.I. (2016)
8. Micolini, O., Ventre, L.O., Ludemann, M., Viano, J.I.R., Bien, C.C.: In 2018 IEEE International Conference on Automation/XXIII Congress of the Chilean Association of Automatic Control (ICA-ACCA), pp. 1–7. IEEE (2018)
9. Micolini, O., Ventre, L.O., Ludemann, M.: In 2018 IEEE Biennial Congress of Argentina (ARGENCON), pp. 1–7. IEEE (2018)
10. Micolini, O., Cebollada, M., Ventre, L.O.: In XXI Congreso Argentino de Ciencias de la Computación, Junín 2015
11. Ventre, L.O., Micolini, O., Daniele, E.: In XXVI Congreso Argentino de Ciencias de la Computación (CACIC) (2020). http://sedici.unlp.edu.ar/handle/10915/114087
12. Selic, B., Gérard, S.: Modeling and Analysis of Real-Time and Embedded Systems with UML and MARTE: Developing Cyber-Physical Systems. Elsevier (2013)
13. Zhou, M., Wu, N.: System Modeling and Control with Resource-Oriented Petri nets, vol. 35. CRC Press (2018)
14. Siewert, S.: Real-Time Embedded Components and Systems. Charles River Media (2007)
15. David, R., Alla, H.: Discrete, Continuous, and Hybrid Petri nets, vol. 1. Springer (2010). https://doi.org/10.1007/978-3-642-10669-9

16. Micolini, O.: Arquitectura asimétrica multicore con procesador de petri. Ph.D. thesis, Universidad Nacional de La Plata (2015)
17. Liu, G., Barkaoui, K.: Information Sciences, vol. 363, p. 198 (2016)
18. P.D. Group, ATLAS. Xilinx, microblaze processor reference guide
19. Digilent, C.: Atlys spartan-6 fpga. https://store.digilentinc.com/
20. C.XILINX. Ise webpack design software. https://www.xilinx.com/products/design-tools/ise-design-suite/ise-webpack.html

Client-Server Architecture for High-Performance RTK Service

José H. Moyano[1,2(✉)] ⓘ, Karina M. Cenci[1,2], and Jorge R. Ardenghi[1]

[1] Laboratorio de Investigación en Sistemas Distribuidos, Bahía Blanca, Argentina
{jose.moyano,kmc,jra}@cs.uns.edu.ar
[2] Laboratorio de I+D en Ing. de Software y Sistemas de Información (UNS-CIC Provincia de Buenos Aires), Departamento de Ciencias e Ingeniería de la Computación, Universidad Nacional del Sur, Bahía Blanca, Argentina

Abstract. Global Navigation Satellite Systems (GNSS) standard accuracy varies between 2 and 10 m. This accuracy can be improved to centimeter-level in real time, using Real Time Kinematic (RTK). With RTK, a GNSS receiver with known position, a base station (BS), calculates errors and sends corrections to rovers, allowing the receiver to locate with centimeter-level accuracy. RTKLIB is an open source library, that can be included as part of software release in a device, to implement rovers or BSs. The purpose of this paper is to propose a low-cost implementation of a client-server architecture, to provide corrections in real time to rover devices, using RTKLIB and consumer-grade hardware.

Keywords: Real time kinematic · RTKLIB · Low cost · Client · Server

1 Introduction

Global Navigation Satellite Systems (GNSS) is the name given to the set of navigation satellite systems (SATNAV) in Earth orbit. These systems consist of space vehicles (SV) that transmit information using radio signals to receivers on Earth surface. With this information, the receiver calculates the geometric distance to each tracked SV, and using trilateration, can obtain its terrestrial location [12].

The error in the positioning is caused by uncertainty in the orbits and *clocks* of the SVs; signal delays caused by atmosphere [10]; and noise and *multipath* in the receiver [8]. For this reason, the horizontal accuracy achieved is between 6 and 10 m [26] for single constellation and single frequency receivers, and between 2 and 6 m for multiple constellation or multiple frequency receivers. This accuracy and precision is insufficient for topographic and geodetic tasks, so there are various augmentations [12] that improve performance.

Real Time Kinematic (RTK) is a GNSS augmentation that uses single and double differences on the phase measurements of the satellite signals captured

P. Pesado and J. Eterovic (Eds.): CACIC 2020, CCIS 1409, pp. 215–229, 2021.
https://doi.org/10.1007/978-3-030-75836-3_15

by two receivers, resolves carrier cycle ambiguity using algorithms like LAMBA, and obtains positions with centimeters [13,15,22] of accuracy in real time.

RTK requires the installation of a second GNSS receiver, with known position, that using the satellite information calculates error parameters in positioning, and generates correction information [9]. This receiver with know location is called base station (BS), or reference station (RS). The corrections are transmitted to a rover, which is the name used for objects of unknown position. The rover also has a GNSS receiver, but it needs the correction information to adjust its location for centimeter level accuracy and precision.

The information provided by a base station has a useful range bounded by atmospheric conditions. In practice, under mean ionospheric conditions, these errors can be neglected at distances between BS and rover up to 10 km [21]. The farther away the rover related to the base station, the corrections are less useful and less precision can be achieved. This is why it is desirable that the base station is not very far away from the rover, and also what motivates the installation of several BS to provide the service in a wide area.

Fixed base stations, which run continuously without interruption, are called Continuous Operation Reference Stations (CORS). These CORS provide RTK corrections to rovers close to their coverage area. Network RTK (NRTK) is the technique of using a CORS network, to provide rovers within the CORS coverage area with RTK information. Rovers require an internet connection, generally a GSM link, to request from a NRTK server the correction information of the closest CORS [4].

The price of acquiring a BS, the high costs of CORS services, or the cost and limited availability of high speed GSM communications to reach a NRTK provider, present an impediment to large scale and consumer grade use of high-precision positioning technologies, motivating the search for low-cost alternatives.

RTKLIB is a software library written in C language, licensed BSD2-clause [11], which offers the calculations of correction information, or the use of correction information to obtain solutions for centimeter-level positioning. This allows to implement a BS in the first case, or a rover in the second. Takasu and Yasuda [31] showed reasonable performance using a u-blox module and RTKLIB.

The use and interest in RTKLIB for scientific and industrial activities is proven and there are current attempts to exploit its capabilities as a low cost solution [7,27,35]. In Argentina, RTK is barely though as a surveying tool [20], with no public efforts to canalize this technologies for other location needs.

The objective of this work is to analyze the weaknesses in the design of RTK-LIB as a client-server solution, and propose improvements or adaptations that may be applied following the criteria of high performance client-server applications.

The current article continues the discussion cited in [18], updating analysis and results to the new version of RTKLIB (released the last days of 2020 [29]). This new release, named 2.4.3 b34, involves changes in 1064 files with respect to release 2.4.3 b33. This work also enrich the motivations to pursuit a low cost RTK solution, reformulates the analysis of RTKLIB as a software project to match the last beta release, and redo the tests in [18] with better conditions and understanding of the problem.

This proposal is presented as follows: Sect. 2 presents a summary of RTKLIB analyzed as Application Programming Interface (API), or library to be linked in a software project; Sect. 3 grasps the details considering the incorporation of RTKLIB in a high-performance client-server development; Sect. 4 delivers background to support the idea of RTK solutions for a large number of low cost devices; Sect. 5 proposes a possible architecture for low cost RTK service, and the first results achieved with generic commercial GPS modules; Sect. 6 presents analysis, explanations and future work in the light of current results.

2   RTKLIB Structure

RTKLIB offers functions to calculate high precision positioning with different techniques (PPP, DGPS, RTK), for single and double frequency receivers, in real time and post-processing, for the SATNAV constellations GPS, GLONASS, Galileo, QZSS, BeiDou, NavIC, SBAS [30]; writing software in C language, and adapted for POSIX and WIN32 systems.

Its utilities include programs to compile in Borland C++ for Windows systems. These applications allow post-processing with data from rover and BS, and with NTRIP services over the internet. Other tools allow to plot dots and routes with a map as background, and convert different message exchange formats.

RTK. From the set of tools included in RTKLIB, the RTK function is relevant for this work the RTK function, which is implemented in the source file `rtksvr.c`.

`rtksvr.c`, among its functions, it has two routines that perform the correction calculations: `rtksvrstart` and `rtksvrthread`. `rtksvrstart` uses system calls (*syscalls*) to create a thread that executes `rtksvrstart`.

`rtksvrthread` loops over the received satellite observations, and for each observation generates sequentially the correction information. Only the observations with a valid GNSS fix are used to generate corrections.

`rtksvr.c` requires other source files to implement the communications with devices, mathematical operations, logging support and mutual exclusion. To generate the corrected data, it requires `rtkpos.c`, which invokes the functions that implement the Extended Kalman filter and the MLAMBDA algorithm.

3   Analysis of RTK and RTKLIB as High-Performance service

As a high-performance client-server architecture, RTKLIB can be analyzed from two points of view: The strengths and weaknesses it presents as a service to clients, and the properties it has as a process that runs in a server.

3.1   Analysis as a Service

As a service provided by a high performance server [14], RTKLIB lacks a proper interface. The library only provides a thread of execution that, using the satellite observations, generates correction information or position solutions and leaves the information available in data structures internal to the library. Only a program compiled and statically linked to the library can access this information.

This implementation, although it has the ability to offer an open source solution to implement RTK, it does not advance on creating a high precision positioning service that can supply (provide) to more than one client, whether local or remote, without these clients incorporating the library as part of their source code, link to it, and have access to adequate hardware (like a GNSS receiver and some sort of transceiver) to generate and transmit corrections.

With the advent of mobile devices and IoT technologies, it is expected to implement a specific BS system, consisting of an embedded system, that replies to requests for correction information from more than one rover, being the rovers diverse mobile devices, such as mobile phones, tablets, tracking devices, wearables, sensors, IoT systems, etc.

It is therefore important to propose a superior management structure of requests and communications, which can take advantage of calculations and specialized hardware associated with a BS, to supply correction information efficiently and respecting real time constraints.

Communications: The classic simple base station implementation for precision positioning, consists of the BS with its GNSS antenna, and a connection to a radio transceiver. This implementation is limited to rovers that have radio receivers compatible with the transceiver.

Currently, radio communications are digital, internally supporting advanced network protocols such as TCP/IP. At the link layer level, the wireless standards IEEE 802.11 and 802.16 in all its variants, and the GSM @ standard, can be cited as examples.

In this scenario, a modern BS that intends to provide RTK service to a set of devices with various features, it will have a TCP/IP network link, which has the characteristic of being independent of the transmission medium, and can receive requests over wired or wireless networks.

It is expected then, that an RTK server implemented with RTKLIB, will have a TCP/IP interface, and the way that interface communicates with its clients depends on the communications hardware used by the device that acts as a server.

3.2   Analysis as Process

The thread `rtksvrthread`, processes each one of the rover observations, generating the RTK position with the `rtkpos` function. This processing is done in sequence, processing one observation after the other in sequence (Fig. 1).

```
 1  ....
 2  for (i=0;i<fobs[0];i++) { /* for each rover observation data
       */
 3      obs.n=0;
 4      for (j=0;j<svr->obs[0][i].n&&obs.n<MAXOBS*2;j++) {
 5          obs.data[obs.n++]=svr->obs[0][i].data[j];
 6      }
 7      for (j=0;j<svr->obs[1][0].n&&obs.n<MAXOBS*2;j++) {
 8          obs.data[obs.n++]=svr->obs[1][0].data[j];
 9      }
10      rtksvrlock(svr);
11      rtkpos(&svr->rtk,obs.data,obs.n,&svr->nav);
12      rtksvrunlock(svr);
13  ....
```

Fig. 1. Source code segment in `rtksvrthread` that process satellite observations in sequence

Since the observations can be adjusted independently of each other, the design of this algorithm does not consider taking advantage of the possibilities offered a multiprogrammed time-sharing system, such as a Windows system or Linux for which it is prepared, or the possibilities offered by the multi-core processors, which are available even in simple devices.

This implementation is built thinking of a thread of execution, which runs as part of a main program, which includes RTKLIB as part of its source code, and is also intended for offline processing (in the case of desktop programs), or with limited hardware (for implementations in embedded systems).

3.3 RTK Analysis

The RTK analysis is divided in client and server view.

- **Client:** The client of a BS is responsible for requesting the correction, processing it and generating the position solution with precision of centimeters. In a scenario where an area is covered with BSs to offer RTK service, the client must also choose the appropriate BS. This process involves determining available BSs in range, and choose the one that combines proximity, quality of information and have the lowest processing load.

  From the perspective of a client-server architecture, the rover is a fat client [34], which contains the business logic for the RTK service.
- **Server:** Analyzing current commercial RTK implementations:
  - The server (BS) never is a fat server. The responsibilities of the base station are limited to generating correction information from observations and its known position. Then this information is transmitted to rovers requesting it.
  - In the case of transmissions from the server, it is convenient to maintain a stateless link. The server doesn't need to have information about the rover, just answer its requests.

From the perspective of a client-server architecture, the rover is a fat client [34], which contains the business logic for the RTK service.

Server. Analyzing current commercial RTK implementations, the server (BS) never is a fat server. The responsibilities of the base station are limited to generating correction information from observations and its known position. Then this information is transmitted to rovers requesting it.

If the communication needs restrictions, as in the case of correction that is intended for a paid subscription, or for particular uses of an organization, it is necessary to encrypt communication and require credentials. In this case, stateless communication can be maintained with relative simplicity, with a rover sending its credentials altogether with the request.

4 Use Cases and Applications

4.1 Transport

Vehicle localization and tracking are relevant to many applications in transport. In several road zones (areas) there are no available connectivity and it is complex to locate and track an object. The utilization of an economical high precision system to locate an entity is beneficial to small and medium-sized companies [28].

Long distance train systems cross over several areas of a country, the localization of a train service is beneficial to improve the efficiency and precision of the system [16].

4.2 Internet of Things

Location information, and high precision location, is fundamental in several applications for Internet Of Things. The positioning of a system is fundamental input to context awareness algorithms [33]. Context awareness in IoT is discussed in [24], where GNSS information is presented as context information for IoT devices data. No matter which categorization is used in context information, position information is always present, and GNSS localization is commonly used.

IoT agriculture applications makes extensive use of GNSS devices [5]. IoT devices with location information involve also food processing industry, environmental monitoring, surveillance among others.

4.3 Security and Privacy

Chen et al. [2] cites GNSS positioning as the most privacy-preserving solutions for positioning. The user calculates its location without third party assistance.

However, there are NRTK architectures that require single positioning from the receiver to provide correction informations. In Virtual Reference Station (VRS) [32], the rover must provide its position to the Control Center. Multiple Reference Stations (MRS) doesn't have the same requirements, but demands high processing power in the rover. The latest developed architecture, Master-Auxiliary Concept (MAC) [1], also expects the rover to sends its position to the Control Center, to achieve maximum performance.

Even the CORS approach, like RAMSAC, provides correction through an Internet connection, exposing the user to localization based on IP address and GSM network positioning.

For a RTK solution to keep the same user privacy that the default GNSS provides, it is necessary for the user to have its own reference stations. This reason maintains current the interest in a low cost RTK solution.

5   High Performance Client Server Architecture Proposal for RTK positioning

The economical cost of using the RTK technique limits the range of applications that can use precision positioning. For industrial or big business, like precision agriculture industry [23], they can include in the production costs for the acquisition of a BS and compatible receivers, or the expenses of hiring a RTK service and paying for the GSM connection. However, to incorporate high precision localization for a commercial system, or an IoT system of low cost, requires reduction of RTK expenses.

Attempts to build low cost RTK setups can be found in the scientific, commercial and technology communities [23,31]. These attempts focus on the implementation of a BS that supports one or two clients, but they are not considering the needs of a system that can provide precision positioning to a large number of clients, such as IoT devices, and they do not consider client-server performance and communications requirements to implement those functions.

The purpose of this work, altogether with [18], is to address the next step in the implementation of an RTK solution, taking into consideration a high-performance client-server architecture, that can deliver reliable correction information to rovers, making adjustments as required by RTKLIB to improve its performance and support for multiple communication links.

5.1   Topology

Using RTK with single BS corresponds to a single client topology. This is the traditional methodology in surveying and geodesy, with an unique user and owner of the base station and GNSS receptor. The user is in charge of the installation and configuration of both elements.

As a BS can provide correction information to multiple rovers, but this method is used for only a single client, this topology results expensive in resources.

In contrast, an architecture with multiple clients [34] has a single BS as a server, and any number of rovers can connect to it to obtain the generated corrections.

Finally, the most suitable structure to implement the client-server RTK architecture, is to have multiple clients and multiple servers, designing the solution as a service with a coverage area. This coverage area matches the effective range of BS information validity, for all the available BS.

What this structure allows is the scalability of the service. The quality of correction data is limited by the distance between the rover and the BS. It is for this reason that to have a wider service coverage area, it is necessary to install servers that can provide correction information to close clients.

5.2   Tiers and Architecture

From the point of view of a client-server application, we define for RTK:

- **Application logic:** Determine the real-time position of a rover from the correction information.
- **Business logic:** If there is more than one BS, it consists of find and choose between the available BSs, the closest geographically, with the best quality of fixes; and establish the connection.
- **Data logic:** The BS service generating the information of correction valid for its area of influence.

For the reasons listed so far in this document, if a 2T architecture is implemented, it will delegate to the client the selection of the server. That is, the business logic must be necessarily on the client. To fulfil this responsibility, it is necessary to add the task of maintaining a list of RTK servers with their locations, to keep this list updated, and to determine which is the most suitable server to use.

These tasks are demanding on processing and communications. If we consider that the rover is a mobile device, running on batteries, possibly connected via a paid mobile data network, the 2T architecture is not the most suitable to provide an RTK service.

If a 3T architecture is implemented (Fig. 2), the client will communicates directly with a server that handles the business logic. This server will know the BS host, location and availability, and it would be possible to incorporate load balancing between them. In addition, it increases flexibility by being able to add new stations transparently to the customer, and facilitates implementation of stateful connections for more efficient transactions.

5.3   Implementation

At the data logic level, a correction information service is implemented in Linux, which compiles with RTKLIB, opening a TCP/IP communications port. For the business logic, a Linux service is created that connects to the correction service in each BS. The function of the client logic is to obtain corrections of the business logic and send them with an USB/RS232 interface to its own GNSS module. This module has support for fixes.

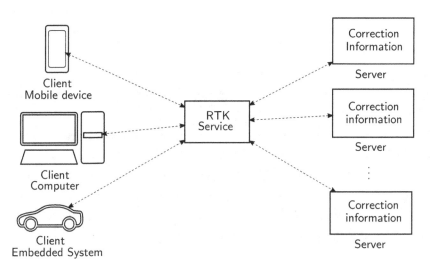

Fig. 2. Arquitectura 3T

Fig. 3. SmartGPS and validation

Platforms. Raspberry Pi 3 Model B+, with ARM Cortex A53 processor architecture, and Linux operative system, Raspbian Buster distribution.

The GNSS receivers are Smart GPS Revision 1.11 evaluation boards. The integrated circuit (IC) for GNSS support was desoldered and replaced by u-blox LEA-6T-0 of equal pinout with support for raw messages with proprietary ublox and RTCM format (left Fig. 3). The correct operation of the module was validated using the u-center software provided by the manufacturer, with correction information from the NTRIP service provided by RAMSAC [20] (right Fig. 3).

Two models of antennas were used, both active, Garmin GA25MCX and Taoglas AGGP .25F. For some measurements, a ground plane was added to antenna with an aluminum plate following U-Blox recommendations.

Source Code. It is written in C language version C89 [3], compiled for the combination of OS and processor, statically linked with RTKLIB `2.4.3 b34`.

Fig. 4. Setup at 38° 42′2.730 83″S 62° 16′7.923 81″W

Operating conditions. The tests were carried out with static baseline mode under bounded conditions. The current results attempt to improve the quality of the information provided by the measurements in [18]. This improvement is made using a know geodesic reference point used in Bahía Blanca, Buenos Aires, Argentina, at latitude 38°42′2.730 83″ South, longitude 62°16′7.923 81″ West; 41.651 mts. ellipsoidal height (Fig. 4). This point were determined by the Engineering Department, using VBCA reference station of the RAMSAC [20] network. The official reference frame for Argentina is POSGAR 07 [19].

6   Discussion

Initial tests were done with a PC acting as rover and Raspberry Pi working as a BS, running RTKLIB with static baseline mode. `htop` to verify process performance. The accuracy of the measurements was determined by measuring the geometric distance between antennas.

Accuracy. The accuracy obtained was between 1 and 4 m with 2 m of precision. This result is an improvement against previous tests done in [18]. However, it wasn't the accuracy or precision expected or obtained in other tests performed on RTKLIB [31]. These results may be tied to hardware and software adjustments. RTKLIB is presented as a generic RTK solution, and exposes to the final user a large amount of parameters, to adjust the software behavior with the GNSS module used. A more thorough analysis is needed. Future work will include the update of GNSS modules to latest versions like M8T or M8N (with multi constellation support), and compare the measured data with post-processing calculations obtained with commercial surveying-grade receptors. Adding ground planes to antennas (as suggested by the module manufacturer) didn't show any improvement in the signal reception.

Processing and Communications. Low processing requirements and communications. The load generated by the execution threads did not result significant to the operation of the system. The communication bandwidth was also low. In subsequent tests, it is necessary to simulate a high volume of requests, over a wireless link, to verify the effects of the communication interference.

6.1 Observed Problems

As a software project, RTKLIB doesn't make a clear distinction between the RTK library code, and the proposed Linux and Windows tools delivered by the RTKLIB author. The functionality related to high precision positioning (RTK, PPT, etc.) can be released as a separated component. For example, Dinamic-Link libraries (DLLs) for Win32 applications, or shared libraries for POSIX systems.

A *separation of concerns* between RTKLIB components [17] will allow different code bases, versioning and repository management. The RTKLIB codebase entangles RTK functionality, with a set of GUI and CUI tools proposed by Takasu. This situation causes that a modification in RTKLIB API or behavior, forces the release of new versions of the tools to keep consistency in the source code repository. This is not achieved in the last beta versions, where Qt GUI won't work if compiled.

RTKLIB does not implement a defined software architecture. It suffers from *code smells*: Too long source code files, functions with dozens of parameters, lines with multiple statements, conditional code, compilation with warnings. In many places in the code, variables with names composed of one or two letter, without intent. The authors of this work supposes that this naming policy aims to relate the implemented algorithms with their equations, such as the extended Kalman filter that smoothes the position, and the implementation of MLAMBA to resolve ambiguity. This one-letter variables designate covariance matrices, state update, prediction, observations, among others. The problem with this design is that the source code does not count with typographic resources that make these statements legible. They should be replaced with names that declare intent.

It is recommended to carry out a refactoring of the code, setting first test harnesses [6], and replace the type declarations by `stdint.h`. The verifications carried out in [31] were performed under a 32-bit architecture processor, while the implementations evaluated in this work use a processor with 64-bit architecture, generating uncertainties in the operation by not using standardized data types.

These modifications are difficult to make. RTKLIB has a battery of tests with limited coverage, which is difficult to evaluate due to the lack of a standard validation criterion. These tests are implemented as standalone C programs that run fragments of code and output the result.

6.2   Comments Related to the Latest Release

The last release of RTKLIB 2.4.3 b34 adds new features, functionality and support for GNSS services and their updates. However, no improvements have been made related to *code smells*.

It seems that there is an intention toward migrating C default data types to stdint.h use, replacing int declarations for proper intx_t data types. However, this wasn't implemented in the entire source code, neither is completely used in new code.

Versioning, at beginning understood as semantic versioning [25], is not complaint with this standard. It is not clear if the versioning follows any predefined criteria. Apparently, different releases receive random labels. The last release changes the API signature, replacing functions names and parameters, however, it was identified as b34. As a software project, proper RTKLIB versioning is important, if it expects to provide functionality in production environments, with different releases being running and in need of support.

Linux compilation shows warnings. Most warnings can be ignored, they are regarding declared variables and never used, variables used without initialization, or mixed declarations and code.

The existing Qt GUIs are not compatible with current changes introduced in version 2.4.3 b34. It seems that they will be dropped in the future. This represents an issue, because current running GUI applications depends on Embarcadero C++ Builder. A proprietary solution with limited access to free tools (only community editions of the company IDE). Being RTKLIB an open source project, used by the scientific community, the dependence of proprietary third party technology to build the applications is understood by the authors of this work as an unnecessary weakness.

7   Conclusions

The ubiquity of electronic and software systems in industrial, commercial and private activities is part of our current reality. From mobile devices (smartphones, tablets, smartwatches, etc.); until Internet of Things (IoT) systems that act and measure conditions for some purpose, such as detecting risk situations (pollution, fires), collect information (weather stations), or automate vehicles and machines. One of the frequent needs in these systems is to determine the location. If a service providing correction information is available, RTK technology offers centimeter-level accuracy for positioning and location in real time, using only a commercial GNSS receiver and antenna.

As shown in this work, it is possible to incorporate RTK to systems with GNSS, without a significant cost increase, with compatible alternative versions of the GNSS modules already used. However, this technology requires a correction information provider. Although there are private and government services providing NRTK, these services are often restricted, and aim at their use in surveying. They also suffer limitations of coverage, by the distance to the closest CORS, or by the absence of high speed internet connection.

RTKLIB allows to implement low cost devices that generate the correction information, with commercial grade hardware. RTKLIB is an active project, even when its developer and maintainer didn't release a final version in years, he keeps working improving performance and adding support for new signals and constellations. The changes observed in release 2.4.3 b34 shown an increased interest in improving RTKLIB as a software project, with structural changes. The weaknesses observed in previous releases remain, but the project is evolving, with bright future expectations.

In recent years, the low cost RTK-compatible hardware and RTKLIB evolution have sparked growing interest in the scientific and technological community with low cost RTK needs. This work starts the first steps for the implementation of a scalable RTK service with high availability, built in free software, that makes true the objective of high precision satellite positioning for IoT.

References

1. Brown, N., et al.: RTK rover performance using the master-auxiliary concept. In: Positioning 1.10 (2006)
2. Chen, L., et al.: Robustness, security and privacy in location-based services for future IoT: a survey. IEEE Access **5**, 8956–8977 (2017)
3. Computer and Business Equipment Manufacturers Association: ISO/IEC 9899:1990. Technical Report, International Organization for Standarization (1990)
4. Paolo D., et al.: Network real time kinematic (NRTK) positioning - description, architectures and performances. In: Satellite Positioning - Methods, Models and Applications, pp. 23–46, March 2015
5. Farooq, M.S., et al.: Role of IoT technology in agriculture: a systematic literature review. Electronics **9**(2), 319 (2020)
6. Feathers, M.C.: Working Effectively with Legacy Code. Robert C. Prentice Hall PTR, Martin (2004)
7. Garrido-Carretero, M.S., et al.: Low-cost GNSS receiver in RTK positioning under the standard ISO-17123-8: a feasible option in geomatics. Measurement **137**, 168–178 (2019)
8. Hauschild, A.: Basic observation equations. In: Teunissen, P.J.G., Montenbruck, O. (eds.) Springer Handbook of Global Navigation Satellite Systems. SH, pp. 561–582. Springer, Cham (2017). https://doi.org/10.1007/978-3-319-42928-1_19. Chapter 19
9. Henning, W.: User Guidelines for Single Base Real Time GNSS Positioning, April 2014
10. Hoblger, T., Jakowski, N.: Atmosferic signal propagation. In: Peter, J.G., Montenbruck, O. (eds.) Springer Handbook of Global Navigation Satellite Systems (2017). Chapter 19
11. Open Source Initiative. The 2-Clause BSD License (2020). https://opensource.org/licenses/BSD-2-Clause
12. Kaplan, E.D.: Introduction. In: Kaplan, E.D., Hegarty, C.J. (eds.) Understanding GPS/GNSS Principles and Applications. Artech House (2017). Chapter 1
13. Liu, J., et al.: Review of GNSS ambiguity validation theory. Geo-mat. Inform. Sci. (2014)
14. Loosley, C., Douglas, F.: High-Performance Client/Server. Wiley (1997)

15. Lou, Y., et al.: An algorithm and results analysis for GPS+ BDS inter-system mix double-difference RTK. In: Geodesy Geodyn (2016)
16. Marais, J., Beugin, J.: Evaluation method of GNSS-based positioning functions for safety applications in operational conditions. Proc.-Soc. Behav. Sci. **48**, 806–815 (2012)
17. Martin, R.C.: Components. In: Clean Architecture: a Craftsman's Guide to Software Structure and Design. 1st edn. Prentice Hall Press, Hoboken (2017). Chapter 12
18. Moyano, J.H., et al.: Arquitectura Cliente-Servidor de Alto Rendimiento para Servicio RTK. In: XXVI Congreso Argentino de Ciencias de la Computación (CACIC) (2020)
19. Instituto Geográfico Nacional. POSTGAR 07 (2021). https://www.ign.gob.ar/NuestrasActividades/Geodesia/Posgar07
20. Instituto Geográfico Nacional. Red Argentina de Monitoreo Satelital Continuo (2020). http://www.ign.gob.ar/NuestrasActividades/Geodesia/Ramsac
21. Odijk, D.: Positioning model. In: Teunissen, P.J.G., Montenbruck, O. (eds.) Springer Handbook of Global Navigation Satellite Systems. SH, pp. 605–638. Springer, Cham (2017). https://doi.org/10.1007/978-3-319-42928-1_21. Chapter 19
22. Odijk, D., Wanninger, L.: Differential positioning. In: Teunissen, P.J.G., Montenbruck, O. (eds.) Springer Handbook of Global Navigation Satellite Systems. SH, pp. 753–780. Springer, Cham (2017). https://doi.org/10.1007/978-3-319-42928-1_26. Chapter 26
23. Ouyang, F., et al.: Automatic delivery and recovery system of wireless sensor networks (WSN) nodes based on UAV for agricultural applications. Comput. Electron. Agric. **162**, 31–43 (2019)
24. Perera, C., et al.: Context aware computing for the Internet of Things: a survey. IEEE Commun. Surv. Tutor. **16**(1), 414–454 (2014)
25. Preston-Werner, T.: Semantic Versioning (2021). https://semver.org/
26. Renfro, B.A. et al.: An Analysis of Global Positioning System (GPS) Standard Positioning Service Performance for 2019. Technical Report The University of Texas at Austin, 14 May 2020
27. Romero-Andrade, R., et al.: Comparative analysis of precise point positioning processing technique with GPS low-cost in different technologies with academic software. Measurement **136**, 337–344 (2019)
28. Sun, Q.C., et al.: Pursuing precise vehicle movement trajectory in urban residential area using multi-GNSS RTK tracking. In: World Conference on Transport Research - WCTR 2016 Shanghai, Transportation Research Procedia, 10–15 July 2016, vol. 25 pp. 2356–2372 (2017)
29. Takasu, T.: RTKLIB. Ed. by GitHub, 29 December 2020. https://github.com/tomojitakasu/RTKLIB/tree/rtklib_2.4.3
30. Takasu, T.: RTKLIB: an Open Source Program Package for GNSS Positioning. (2020). http://www.rtklib.com/
31. Takasu, T., Yasuda, A.:Development of the low-cost RTK-GPS receiver with an open source program package RTKLIB. In: International Symposium on GPS/GNSS, January 2009
32. Wanninger, L.: Virtual reference stations (VRS). In: GPS Solutions 7.2, pp. 143–144, August 2003
33. Liu, W., et al.: A survey on context awareness. In: 2011 International Conference on Computer Science and Service System (CSSS), pp. 144–147, June 2011

34. Chandra Yadav, S., Kumar Singh, S.: An Introduction to Client Server Computing. New Age International Pvt. Ltd., Publishers, February 2009

35. Zhang, Y., et al.: Static and kinematic positioning performance of a low-cost real-time kinematic navigation system module. In: Advances in Space Research. Multi-GNSS: Methods, Benefits, Challenges, and Geosciences Applications vol. 63, no. 9, pp. 3029–3042 (2019)

Innovation in Software Systems

Emotion Recognition Through Facial Expressions Using Supervised Learning with Logistic Regression

Carlos Barrionuevo⬤, Jorge Ierache$^{(\boxtimes)}$⬤, and Iris Sattolo⬤

Instituto de Sistemas Inteligentes y Enseñanza Experimental de la Robótica, (ISIER) Secretaria de Ciencia y Tecnología (SECYT), Escuela Superior de Ingeniería, Informática y Ciencias Agroalimentarias, Universidad de Morón Cabildo, 134, Buenos Aires, Argentina
`{cabarrionuevo,jierache,isattolo}@unimoron.edu.ar`

Abstract. More than half of a message meaning is conveyed through facial expressions. Different studies have also shown that some of these expressions are considered universal. However, one of the most interesting characteristics of facial expressions is that they show emotion. This characteristic has led several areas to study them with different aims, and computing was no exception. Face detection and the main parts have been one of the major breakthroughs in computer vision. Together with the rise of machine learning in the last decade, it allowed the development of systems capable of detecting emotions through facial expression analysis. This paper shows the stages of development, training and testing of an algorithm based on logistic regression used for emotion detection, including specific details of the optimization process and the results in the training and test set.

Keywords: Facial expressions · Emotions · Computer vision · Machine learning · Logistic regression

1 Introduction

In the last century, improving the interaction between human beings and machines has become one of the main objectives of computing. Therefore, several lines of research have centered around new ways of interaction. Affective computing [1] is giving computers the ability of interpreting the user's emotional state. Analyzing facial expressions is one of the most efficient ways of showing an individual's emotional state. In his papers, Albert Mehrabian states the spoken word only conveys 7% of the meaning while the tone of voice conveys 38% and facial expressions convey the remaining 55% when communicating [2]. This paper is aimed at describing the process of building an emotion detection system capable of recognizing the seven emotional expressions considered universal in Paul Ekman's theory [3].

This paper further undertakes the initial research published in CACIC 2020 [4]. It specifically shows the stages of development, training and testing of an algorithm based on logistic regression used for emotion detection, including specific details of

P. Pesado and J. Eterovic (Eds.): CACIC 2020, CCIS 1409, pp. 233–246, 2021.
https://doi.org/10.1007/978-3-030-75836-3_16

the optimization process and the results in the training and test set. A new experiment with the use of Face++ service and a new CK+ data set is included. New comparative tests between the Microsoft "Face" service and the original tool are included. Lastly, the discussion of the results obtained in the tests are presented.

In Sect. 2, the facial image database used is described, and the extraction process of the characteristics needed for training a machine learning algorithm is detailed. In Sect. 3, the algorithm used is introduced and details about the optimization process are included. In Sect. 4 the tests carried out with the algorithm used in which their performance is compared with the one of similar services are shown. In Sect. 5, the discussion of the results obtained during the tests are presented and lastly, in Sect. 6, conclusions and futures lines of research are introduced. This paper is the result of a previous research [4] which has been expanded and improved particularly in Sect. 3.2 by detailing the normalization process of data obtained from the training and test sets for optimizing the execution of the proposed algorithm, by including a new comparative test in Sect. 4 -which includes the CK+ [5] face image bank and the API of facial expression recognition from the Face++ [6] platform, and by adding Sect. 5 of discussion where interpretation of the results obtained from the different tests carried out is presented.

2   Categorical Approach – Face Image Database

In the categorical approach, Paul Ekman introduces six universal facial expressions which exceed the scope of language and regional, cultural, and ethnic differences. He links them to six basic emotions anger, disgust, fear, happiness, sadness, and surprise. In his paper [3] Ekman then includes a seventh facial expression representing contempt. Figure 1 shows the seven images representing the seven universal facial expressions. They have been taken from Paul Ekman's webpage [7] with the pictures' titles.

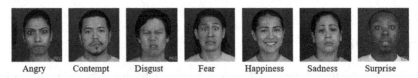

Angry   Contempt   Disgust   Fear   Happiness   Sadness   Surprise

Fig. 1. Seven universal facial expressions according to Paul Ekman's theory

The "RaFD" [8] face database created by Radbound University in Nijmegen (The Netherlands) was used in this research. It is comprised of face images of 67 models. The models were mainly Caucasian, men and women, adults, and children. According to the Facial Action Coding System -"FACS2– [9] created by Paul Ekman, each model in the set is photographed from five different angles (0°, 45°, 90°, 135° and 180°) and frontal pictures (90°) are taken as the individual looks in three different directions -left, front and right. This set includes the seven universal facial expressions previously defined and adds an eighth expression defined as "neutral". All these characteristics make the set fit for several research fields such as attention facial signs and facial expression processing. Even though other face databases exist like "Jaffe" [10] known as the "Japanese women image database" and the "Cohn-Kanade dataset" [5], "RaFD" was chosen because: a) of its high image quality and resolution (1024 × 681 pixels). Photo sessions were done in a highly controlled setting with optimal light conditions; b) of its range of model characteristics such as race, gender, and age; c) of its correct labelling of each of the pictures with the emotional facial expression in the file name; d) the photoshoot was directed and assisted by specialists certified in Facial Action Coding System [9]. Even though this characteristic is shared by several image sets, it is important and adds reliability to the research. In the file name of each image, the database name, the shooting angle, the model number, the race, the gender, the emotion displayed, and the looking direction can be found. For example, if the image name is "Rafd090_07_Caucasian_male_sad_left", it means that the picture was taken at 90° -front-, the model number is "07", the model is Caucasian, the gender is male, the emotion displayed is "sad" and the model is looking to the left. Since the set includes pictures from five different angles, we only used those taken at ninety degrees -front- with a total of 460 images. From this subset, 90% of the pictures -414- were set aside for training [11] of the logistic regression algorithm used for emotion recognition. The remaining 10% -46 pictures- was set aside for tests and prediction experiments [11]. This last set was chosen in such way that model numbers 16, 18, 23, 24, 25, 30, 32, 36, 38 and 54 were completely removed from the training set. Having introduced the face database used for the research, the following step was developing a routine allowing the extraction of the characteristics needed from each image of the set. The programming language chosen was "Python" because it includes the "dlib" [12] library which provides the necessary tools for development. The first task was getting the label from the emotion associated with it from the file name. Accordingly, a numeric code between one and eight was assigned. Thus, each emotion was uniquely represented. Table 1 shows the emotion codification used. As a result, a vector labelled "Y" of "K" dimensions was obtained in which "K" is the number of images used from the set to train the logistic regression algorithm. The final vector was saved in an ".txt" file. The following step was identifying the face region -also known as the "region of interest"- for each image which allowed the identification of characteristic points -also known as "landmarks". There is a wide range of face point detectors which vary in the number of "landmarks" which they identify; yet they often match in the localization of the mouth, eyebrow, nose, eye and face contour regions.

Table 1. Emotion codification.

Label	Anger	Contempt	Disgust	Fear	Happiness	Neutral	Sadness	Surprise
Code	1	2	3	4	5	6	7	8

The detector included in the "dlib" [12] library was used in this research. This detector is the execution of the algorithm created by Vahid Kazemi and Josephine Sullivan [13] which allows to get the "x" and "y"-axis coordinates of 68 characteristic face points. Their localization can be found in Fig. 2 [14].

Once landmarks are located, taking into consideration their pairs -x, y-, a total of 136 elements are found and a line for each image was created. Thus, the facial characteristics

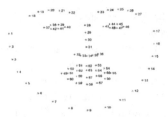

Fig. 2. Distribution of the characteristic face points.

of each image were represented by their corresponding tuple. Generally speaking, the process result is a matrix of "m" lines and "n" columns being "m" the number of training examples and "n" the number of characteristics. For this study case, "m" was equal to 414 (number of images used for the algorithm training) and "n" was equal to 136 as previously stated. This matrix was identified with the letter "X" and is known as "characteristic matrix". Like vector "Y", it was saved in a ".txt" file. Once both matrixes were described, it is important to mention that they were simultaneously created so the "i" line of the "X" matrix corresponds to the "i" element of the "Y" vector. After this process ends, we have the input necessary for training the supervised learning algorithm.

3 Supervised Learning Applied to Emotion Recognition

3.1 Logistic Regression Algorithm

This section was first presented in the original research [4] with the title "Emotion prediction using Logistic Regression". In this case, the section's name was changed to "Logistic regression algorithm" because all the execution details of an algorithm of said characteristics applied to emotion recognition are presented. Given a new image of a person's face, one of the possibilities for predicting which emotion is expressing is to use a supervised learning algorithm. It is called "supervised" because a data set previously labelled and classified [15] is needed for their training. On this data set known as "training data set", the algorithm will make predictions and compare them to the labels, and the error obtained, and through consecutive iterations the algorithm will adjust the model, thus gaining progressive learning. There is a great variety of algorithms with these characteristics such as lineal regression, logistic regression, neural networks, support vector machines, or k-nearest neighbours [15]. The use of these algorithms usually depends on the problem's dimensions [16]. For this research, a logistic regression algorithm [17] was chosen and its implementation was achieved with Octave [18] programming language. This algorithm helps calculate the probability of a new example belonging to a certain class by means of a classifier. Since a total of eight classes was obtained for this problem, a technique called "one vs all" [16] was applied. Thus, training eight classifiers was possible with this method, one for each of the emotions considered. Each classifier is represented by its corresponding hypothesis function. First, to simplify the explanation, we will define the "z" polynomial function, which is part of the hypothesis, according to Andrew Ng's proposition [16]:

$$z(x) = \theta^T.X \tag{1}$$

where "θ" is a matrix of "i" lines and "j" columns and "i" being the number of classes and "j" being the number of polynomial parameters. For the case study, "i" equals eight -the number of emotions- and "j" equals the number of characteristics -136- which make the "landmarks". Initially, all elements of this matrix were equal to 0 -zero. These parameters were adjusted through training to make predictions, where "X" is the characteristic matrix defined in the previous section. Once function "z" is defined, the hypothesis function expression for logistic regression [16] will be:

$$h_\theta^i(x) = \frac{1}{\left(1 - e^{(-z)}\right)} \tag{2}$$

in which "i" refers to the i-nth class. The previous function is using the sigmoid function on "z(x)". Thus, its result is a value between 0 and 1 which represents the probability of a new training example -in this case, the characteristics of a new face- belonging to the class -emotion- "i". The label of the classifier's emotion showing the highest probability will be the final output of the algorithm. Moreover, the penalty suffered by the algorithm when a probability value is calculated with the hypothesis function in which "y" is the label is called "cost". The cost for logistic regression is defined by the following expression [16]:

$$cost(h_\theta(x), y) = -y.\log(h_\theta(x)) - (1 - y).\log(1 - h_\theta(x)) \tag{3}$$

If y = 1, we calculate the probability of belonging to said class, so the cost representation will be the one shown in Fig. 3:

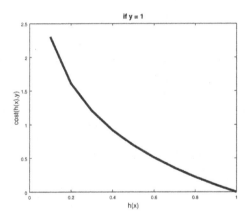

Fig. 3. Cost representation.

For example, when given a new image showing "anger" (y = 1), the following situations can arise: a) If the value calculated by the hypothesis function h(x) linked to the anger classifier calculates a value of 1–100% probability of the emotion shown being "anger"-, the cost suffered by the algorithm will be 0; b) If the value calculated by the hypothesis function h(x) linked to the "anger" classifier tends to 0 -0% probability of the emotion shown being "anger"-, the cost suffered by the algorithm will tend to infinity. Once the cost is defined, the cost function expression is [16]:

$$J(\theta) = -\frac{1}{m}\sum_{m}^{i=1}[y^{(i)}\log(h_\theta\left(x^{(i)}\right) + (1 - y^{(i)})\log(1 - h_\theta\left(x^{(i)}\right))] \qquad (4)$$

in which "m" equals the number of training examples, which is 414 faces in our case. As observed in expression 4, the cost function calculates the mean error among all the training set examples. As for the matrix "θ", all its elements will initially be equal to 0 - zero-, as previously mentioned. So, the aim is to find those "θ" parameters minimizing the cost function error. There are different techniques for this task. For example, the gradient descent was considered for this task, but, in the end, an advanced optimization function called "fminunc" -"function minimization unconstrained"- provided by "Octave" was chosen [19]. "fminunc" gets a function "f" pointer, an "x" parameter matrix, and a vector of additional key-value options among which the maximum iteration number is worth mentioning ("MaxIter" key). This function returns the "x" parameter matrix so that "f(x)" is a local minimum [20]. In this research, said function was parameterized with: a) a pointer to cost function, b) the "θ" parameter matrix and c) the "MaxIter" key defined with the value 1200 indicating the maximum iteration number on the dataset looking to meet at a local minimum of the cost function. The output of this function is the parameter matrix adjusted according to our training data.

3.2   Training Data Normalization

Based on the original research [4], which is part of this paper, the training data normalization process is detailed. Even though it was used in the original research, specifications about the techniques used are included in this paper. This process is used to accelerate the convergence in a local minimum of the cost function which should be achieved in the lowest iteration number possible on the training set. Thus, two techniques were used on the "x" matrix elements. These techniques are "Feature Scaling" and "Mean Normalization" [21]. Taking into consideration that each element of the "x" matrix belongs to one of the 136 characteristics -for the study case-, "Feature Scaling" consists of dividing each element by the range calculated for the corresponding characteristic elements. The range is defined as the difference between the maximum and minimum value of a certain characteristic [21]. For example, if the first element of the "x" matrix -line and column one- is taken into consideration, it corresponds to characteristic 1, so it will be divided by the range calculated among the 414 elements of characteristic 1. There is an alternative at this point which is dividing each element by the standard deviation instead of the range [21]. To simplify the programming, the last option was chosen for this research since "Octave" provides the "std" [22] function which calculates the standard deviation among a value set taken as parameters. "Mean Normalization" consists of subtracting the mean value among the elements of the corresponding characteristic to each element of the characteristic matrix. Using both techniques, each element will be represented through the expression 5 [21] formula:

$$x_i := \frac{x_i - \mu_i}{s_i} \qquad (5)$$

in which "μ_i" represents the mean value of all the "i" characteristic values; and "s_i" is the value or standard deviation range of the "i" characteristic [21] elements. Using the techniques mentioned, the result was that all characteristic matrix elements were found in the expression 6 range:

$$-5 < x_i < 5 \tag{6}$$

Table 2 compares the results obtained about the iteration in which the local minimum of the cost function is obtained with or without using the characteristic matrix techniques mentioned. In the first column, the emotion classifiers numbered according to what was defined in Table 1 are presented; in the second column, the results obtained with "Mean Normalization" and "Feature Scaling" are presented and finally, in the third column, the values without using these resources are presented:

Table 2. Performance comparison with "Mean Normalization" and "Feature Scaling".

Iteration in which the local minimum is achieved		
Emotion classifier	With M.N and F.S.	Without M.N. and F. S.
1 – Anger	615	1200
2 – Contempt	1044	1200
3 – Disgust	247	1200
4 – Fear	668	1200
5 – Happiness	341	1200
6 – Neutral	855	1200
7 – Sadness	811	1200
8 – Surprise	649	1200

In Table 2, it can be observed that the cost function minimum for the eight emotion classifiers is achieved by using these methods on the characteristic matrix while the iteration limit set is reached if they are not used. It is worth noting that an API called "fmincg" [23] identically set as "fminunc" [19] is used to collect the data mentioned, indicating in which interaction the local minimum of the cost function is achieved.

4   Test and Results Obtained

The test set used is comprised of 46 images, which correspond to the subjects -models- 16, 18, 23, 24, 25, 30, 32, 36, 38 and 54, as it was mentioned when describing the face database. Table 3 shows the test set description:

Table 3. Test set description.

Code	Description	Number of images	Models used
1	Anger	5	16, 18, 30, 32 y 36
2	Contempt	7	16(2), 18, 23, 25, 30 y 32
3	Disgust	7	18(2), 25, 30(2), 32 y 38
4	Fear	8	16(2), 18, 25(3), 30 y 32
5	Happiness	4	24, 25, 30 y 54
6	Neutral	4	24, 25, 30 y 32
7	Sadness	5	16, 18, 25 y 30(2)
8	Surprise	6	16, 25, 30, 32, 36 y 38

In Table 3, the emotion code used in this research -as defined in Table 1- is shown in the first column; the description of these codes -emotion name- is found in the second column; the number of images related to each emotion in the test set is shown in the third column; and the model number and, between brackets, the number of images -if there were more than one- are indicated in the last column named "Models used". Figure 4 shows a concept diagram of the experience sequence:

Fig. 4. Sequence used in the experiences.

As in the training stage, it was necessary to create the characteristic matrix for the test data set. The matrix comprised 46 lines -image number- and 136 columns -number of characteristics-. The resulting matrix was saved in a "txt" file. This task is performed by a routine developed in Python language as mentioned before. Once the "X" matrix was obtained, the following step was evaluating the 136 characteristics of each image in the hypothesis functions corresponding to the 8 emotion classifiers -predictive models. The result of this operation was an 8-line, 46-column matrix. The number of lines corresponds to the number of classifiers -of different emotions-, and the line number indicates the emotion code as defined in Table 1. Thus, the classifier outputs associated with the code-1 emotion -anger- will be included in line 1. The number of columns is equal to the number of test set images. For example, the outputs for the 8 classifiers of the first image were shown in column 1. The final algorithm output is the line number -as we have just mentioned, it corresponds to the emotion classifier number- for each image; so, the maximum probability value was calculated. The results obtained allowed for the confusion matrix construction [24] in Fig. 5. From the matrix shown in Fig. 5

and based on the number of images per emotion indicated in Table 3, it is possible to infer that the system developed in this research failed at: a) 3 images where the expected result was "contempt" -code 2- and the predicted value was the emotion "sadness" -code 7- in 2 occasions and the emotion "neutral" -code 6- in the remaining one. It was correct in the remaining four images for contempt for a total of 7 images -contempt; b) in an image where the expected result was "fear" -code 4-, the predicted value was "sadness" -code 7- for a total of 8 images -fear; c) in 2 images where the expected result was "neutral" -code 6-, the algorithm mistook them for the emotions "anger" -code 6- and "contempt" -code 2- for a total of 4 images -neutral; d) in an image where the expected result was "sadness" -code 7-, the predicted value was "anger" -code 1- for a total of 5 sadness images. The total was 7 wrong predictions and 39 correct predictions. Moreover, 3 different metrics which allow us to evaluate the performance of the proposed predictive model -logistic regression algorithm- were calculated with the predictions made. The first is called "Recall" [25] and measures, for each emotion class, what fraction of the total of available images for that class was correctly predicted. Taking the emotion "Contempt" as example and considering its related column in Fig. 5, we observed that, of 7 available images for said emotion, the algorithm correctly predicted 4 getting a "recall" of 0,57 (57%) for said emotion. The second metric calculated was "Precision" which indicates, for each of the 8 emotion classifiers, how many were correct of the number of predictions made by these classifiers. Taking the line related to the emotion "Sadness" -code 7- as example in Fig. 5, we observe that, of the 7 occasions in which the predicted value was this emotion, 4 were correct getting a precision of 0,57 (57%). Finally, the last metric calculated was "Accuracy" [25]. Unlike the other metrics, "Accuracy" measures the global algorithm performance and not the specific of each emotion. It is calculated as the total of predictions correctly made on the total of predictions made. As previously mentioned, the total of correct predictions in this test was 39 over 46 total predictions getting an "accuracy" of 85%.

		Actual Values								Precision
		Anger	Contempt	Disgust	Fear	Happiness	Neutral	Sadness	Surprise	
		1	2	3	4	5	6	7	8	
	1	5	0	0	0	0	1	1	0	0,83
	2	0	4	0	0	0	1	0	0	0,8
	3	0	0	7	0	0	0	0	0	1
Predicted	4	0	0	0	7	0	0	0	0	1
Values	5	0	0	0	0	4	0	0	0	1
	6	0	1	0	0	0	2	0	0	0,67
	7	0	2	0	1	0	0	4	0	0,57
	8	0	0	0	0	0	0	0	6	1
Recall		1	0,57	1	0,88	1	0,5	0,8	1	85%

Fig. 5. Confusion matrix built with the results obtained for the test with 46 images.

Once the tests were made with the data set, an independent test with external images was also carried out. In this case, the images shown in Fig. 1 were chosen from Paul Ekman's webpage [7] which include different subjects to represent the different emotions. For this test, the images were classified with the proposed system and a comparison was made with the artificial intelligence "Face" service from Microsoft [26], independently from the number of landmarks of each model, which also considers the same eight emotions proposed in this research. The results obtained are shown in Fig. 6, where the probability values calculated for the 8 emotion classifiers in both systems for each of the images can be observed. The first line shows the image titles, and, between brackets, the emotion code associated to the expected result. For each image of the first line, the results obtained by the "Face" service and the developed system proposed in this paper -S.P.- are included. The first column shows the emotion code with their name included in Table 1, which were used in this research.

	(1) anger		(2) contempt		(3) disgust		(4) fear		(5) happiness		(7) sadness		(8) surprise	
	Face	S.P.	Face	S.P.	Face	S.P.	Face	S.P.	Face	S.P.	Face	S.P.	Face	S.P.
1 - Enojo	0,472	0	0	0	0,006	0	0	0	0	0	0	0	0	0
2 - Desprecio	0,006	0	0,213	0,01	0	0	0	0	0	0,012	0	0,018	0	0
3 - Asco	0,001	0	0	0	0,993	0,043	0	0	0	0	0	0	0	0,02
4 - Miedo	0,038	0	0	0	0	0	0,991	0,153	0	0	0	0,001	0,006	0
5 - Feliz	0	0	0,004	0	0	0	0	0,001	1	0,465	0	0	0	0
6 - Neutral	0,089	0,056	0,772	0,007	0	0	0	0,071	0	0	0,124	0,005	0,017	0
7 - Tristeza	0,001	0,002	0,011	0	0	0	0,001	0,916	0	0	0,876	0,762	0	0
8 - Sorpresa	0,392	0	0	0	0	0,002	0,008	0	0	0	0	0	0,977	0,124

Fig. 6. Results obtained in the proposed system and Microsoft "Face" service.

As it can be shown in Fig. 6, the Microsoft system failed in predicting the emotion "contempt" while the predictive model developed failed in predicting the emotions "anger" and "fear". The final logistic regression algorithm output developed in this research is shown in Fig. 7:

```
Result:

Ordinal (1) Result: 6 - Neutral
Ordinal (2) Result: 2 - Contempt
Ordinal (3) Result: 3 - Disgust
Ordinal (4) Result: 7 - Sadness
Ordinal (5) Result: 5 - Happiness
Ordinal (6) Result: 7 - Sadness
Ordinal (7) Result: 8 - Surprise
```

Fig. 7. Final output of the proposed system for the test with the image set from Paul Ekman's webpage.

As a second independent test, one of the subjects from the initial test set with 46 photographs from the "RaFD" [8] face dataset was used. The model chosen was number 30 [11] because it included, at least, one image for each emotion -8 images in total- and a new comparison with the Microsoft service was made. The results obtained are shown in Fig. 8.

It can be observed in Fig. 8 that both the developed system for this research and the Microsoft service failed in the "contempt" image calculating the highest probability value in the emotion "neutral" -99,8% calculated by the "Face" service and 95,7% calculated by our system. Moreover, the Microsoft service failed in predicting "anger" and mistook it for the "neutral" expression, and "contempt" for "anger".

As an extension from the original research [4], a comparative test was added using eight images randomly chosen from the CK+ [5] face database. CK+ is an image bank

	(1) angry		(2) contemptous		(3) disgusted		(4) fearful		(5) happy		(6) neutral		(7) sad		(8) surprised	
	Face	S.P.	Face	S.P.	Face	S.P.	Face	S.P.	Face	S.P.	Face	S.P	Face	S.P.	Face	S.P.
1 - Enojo	0,291	1	0	0	0,66	0,005	0	0	0	0	0	0,074	0,006	0	0	0
2 - Desprecio	0,004	0,931	0,002	0,046	0,001	0	0,014	0,001	0	0	0	0,05	0,094	0	0	0
3 - Asco	0	0	0	0	0,339	0,999	0,225	0	0	0,085	0	0	0,013	0	0	0
4 - Miedo	0	0	0	0	0	0	0,679	1	0	0	0	0	0,016	0,354	0	0
5 - Feliz	0	0	0	0	0	0	0	0	1	1	0	0	0	0	0	0
6 - Neutral	0,704	0	0,998	0,957	0	0,004	0	0	0	0	1	0,993	0	0,1	0	0
7 - Tristeza	0	0	0	0	0	0	0,007	0,713	0	0	0	0	0,644	0,998	0	0,137
8 - Sorpresa	0,001	0	0	0	0	0	0,074	0,002	0	0	0	0	0,026	0	1	1

Fig. 8. Results obtained from the comparison between the proposed system and the Microsoft "Face" service in the test with subject number 30.

developed by the University of Pittsburgh -Pennsylvania, United States- and composed by 593 image sequences of 123 subjects. Each sequence starts with the neutral expression in the first frame and the target expression in the last. As target expression, it uses one of the seven universal face expressions defined by Paul Ekman [3]. Using this characteristic, it was possible to create a new test set with one image for each emotion including one related to the neutral expression -eight images in total- [11]. The comparison was once again made with the Microsoft "Face" service [26] and the web API of emotion recognition from the "Face++" [6] platform. Face++ identifies the 6 basic facial expressions defined in Ekman's theory [3] and the neutral expression allowing us to obtain the values calculated for each of the emotion classifiers. While this API does not identify the expression "contempt", we decided to use it since it was not possible to find another API that would identify the same eight facial expressions as the "Face" service and the original system and would allow to know the value calculated by the emotion classifiers. Figure 9 shows the results obtained in the comparative test. For a better display, all the values obtained are rounded to two decimal points. The expected results are shown in the first line while the emotion codes -as defined in Table 1- associated with the emotion classifiers are included in the first column. As previously stated, since the Face++ [6] service does not identify the expression related to the emotion "contempt", the image related to said emotion was not tested and the line related to the corresponding emotion classifier in this service was left blank.

	(1) Anger			(2) Contempt		(3) Disgust			(4) Fear			(5) Happiness			(6) Neutral			(7) Sadness			(8) Surprise		
	Face	F++	S.P.	Face	S.P.	Face	F++	S.P.	Face	F++	S.P.	Face	F++	S.P.	Face	F++	S.P	Face	F++	S.P.	Face	F++	S.P.
1	0,58	0,07	0,08	0	0	0,02	0	0	0,01	0	0	0	0	0	0	0	0	0	0,72	0	0	0	0
2	0,12	0	0	0,65	0,04	0,04	0	0	0	0	0	0	0	0	0	0	0	0	0	0	0	0	0
3	0	0,01	0	0	0	0,80	0,80	0,01	0,18	0	0	0	0	0	0	0	0	0	0	0	0	0	0
4	0	0	0	0	0	0	0	0	0,52	1,00	0	0	0	0	0	0	0	0	0	0	0	0	0
5	0	0	0	0,55	0	0	0	0	0	0	0	1,00	1,00	0,91	0	0	0	0	0	0	0	0	0
6	0,29	0,92	0,01	0,45	0	0,05	0,06	0	0	0,02	0	0	0	0	1,00	1,00	0,01	0	0	0,05	0	0	0
7	0,01	0	0	0	0	0,09	0,14	0,43	0	0	0	0	0	0	0	0	0	1,00	0,28	0,98	0	0	0
8	0	0	0	0	0	0	0	0	0,24	0	0	0	0	0	0	0	0	0	0	0	1,00	1,00	0,95

Fig. 9. Results obtained in the comparative test among Face, Face++ and the original system with the CK+ image set.

As for the results obtained, Fig. 9 shows that the proposed system based on logistic regression failed in predicting the emotion "disgust" by mistaking it for the emotion "sadness", and the emotion "fear" for the "neutral" expression. As for the Face++ [6] emotion recognition API, it failed in identifying the expression "anger" by mistaking it for "neutral", and "sadness" for "anger". Finally, the Microsoft "Face" only failed in predicting the emotion "contempt" by mistaking it for "happiness". Moreover, we experimented with the RaFD [8] image set for the model number 30 and the photograph set taken from Paul Ekman's webpage [7] with the web API from the Face++ [6] platform. The image for the emotion "contempt" was taken out from both image sets since, as previously mentioned, Face++ [6] does not identify it. With the RaFD [8] image set, there was a total of 5 successful tries over 7 total images failing in identifying the expressions related to "disgust" by mistaking it for "anger", and "fear" for "surprise". As for the image set from Paul Ekman's webpage [7], there were 4 successful tries over 6 total predictions failing in identifying the emotion "anger" by mistaking it for "surprise", and "sadness" for "neutral".

5 Discussion

Different types of test done to evaluate the prediction effectiveness on emotions with the original system were included in the previous section. The results obtained in the different comparative tests show that said system had a significant success rate similar to the ones from the other services compared. Table 4 shows a summary of the mistakes obtained in each system when testing the different test set images.

Table 4. Summary of the mistakes obtained in the comparative tests

Number of mistakes				
	RaFD Set	Ekman's Set	CK + Set	Number of mistakes
S.P.	1	2	2	5
Face	3	1	1	5
Face++	2	2	2	6[*]

[*]The Face+ + service was not tested for images of "contempt" since it does not identify it

As for the Microsoft "Face" service [26], it obtained a considerable number of mistakes when used with the RaFD [8] image set for model number 30. It obtained a high success rate in the other tests. However, it should be pointed out that the service failed in identifying the expression associated with the emotion "contempt" in every test. The web API from the Face++ platform [6] failed in predicting the emotions "anger" and "sadness" when tested with the Ekman [7] and CK+ [5] image sets but correctly identified the emotions associated with these expressions in the RaFD [8] test set. Finally, the original system -S.P.- did not generally face problems when identifying a particular emotion. It can be pointed out that it achieved predictions with higher success values in the tests done on the RaFD [8] and CK+ [5] test set images than with the ones from Paul Ekman's webpage [7]. This can be linked to picture resolution since it is considerably lower in the images from Paul Ekman's webpage [7] (360 x 360 pixels) than in the RaFD [8] (681 x 1024 pixels) and CK+ [5] (640 × 490 pixels) test sets. This situation results in "x" and "y" values from the facial landmarks from the test set images to be found in very different ranges to the landmark values obtained from pictures the system was trained with. Another possible cause is that race models not included in RaFD [8] -face database used for the training set-, in which models are predominantly Caucasian, are part of the images in Paul Ekman's webpage [7].

6   Conclusion and Future Lines of Research

According to the analysis made on the results obtained, we can conclude that the built system showed a good performance with both the training set images and the external images. There is an improvement margin that can be achieved by training the algorithm with a higher number of images, models with more characteristic diversity, or by modifying the characteristic extraction process by collecting the eye or mouth opening range. In future lines of research, the performance of other supervised learning techniques, such as neural networks or support vector machines, for emotion detection will be tested and a comparison with the built application in this research will be done. In addition, the integration in multimodal systems [27, 28] combined with different sensors -heartrate variation, skin conductance, egg-based brain-computer interfaces- will be considered, thus emphasizing the categorical emotion determination through face detection. This will allow the integration in different application domains of affective computing.

Acknowledgments. The authors acknowledge the support of Universidad de Morón and the National Agency for Scientific and Technological Promotion of the MINCyT (PICTO-UM-2019– 00005).

References

1. Picard, R.W., et al.: Affective computing (1995)
2. Mehrabian, A.: Communication without words. Psychol. Today **2**(4), (68)
3. Ekman, P., et al.: Universals and cultural differences in the judgments of facial expressions of emotion. J. Pers. Soc. Psychol. **53**(4), 712–717 (1987)
4. Barrionuevo, C., Ierache, J., Sattolo, I.: Reconocimiento de emociones a través de expresiones faciales con el empleo de aprendizaje supervisado aplicando regresión logística. In: CACIC: XXVI Congreso Argentino de Ciencias de la Computación, Universidad Nacional de La Matanza, San Justo, octubre 2020. ISBN 978-987-4417-90-9, pp. 482–491 (2020)
5. Lucey, P., Cohn, J.F., Kanade, T., Saragih, J., Ambadar, Z., Matthews, I.: The extended Cohn-Kanade dataset (CK+): a complete expression dataset for action unit and emotion-specified expression (2010)
6. Emotion Recognition, Face++. https://www.faceplusplus.com/emotion-recognition/. Accessed Dec 2020
7. Paul Ekman Group. https://www.paulekman.com/. Accessed June 2020
8. Langner, O., Dotsch, R., Bijlstra, G., Wigboldus, D.H.J., Hawk, S.T., van Knippenberg, A.: Presentation and validation of the radboud faces database. Cogn. Emot. **24**(8), 1377–1388 (2010). https://doi.org/10.1080/02699930903485076
9. Ekman, P., Friesen, W.V., Hager, J.C.: Facial Action Coding System: The Manual. Research Nexus, Salt Lake City (2002)

10. Lyons, M.J., Akamatsu, S., Kamachi, M., Gyoba, J.: Coding facial expressions with gabor wavelets. In: 3rd IEEE International Conference on Automatic Face and Gesture Recognition, pp. 200–205 (1998)
11. Conjuntos de imágenes de rostros usados para entrenamiento y pruebas. https://drive.google.com/drive/folders/1AhYfPoBoBp0oU4WBWgSmXeD8xTPKqXLJ?usp=sharing
12. Dlib. https://pypi.org/project/dlib/. Accessed June 2020
13. Kazemi, V., Sullivan, J.: One millisecond face alignment with an ensemble of regression trees (2014)
14. Facial landmarks with dlib, OpenCV, and Python. Pyimagesearch. https://www.pyimagesearch.com/2017/04/03/facial-landmarks-dlib-opencv-python/. Accessed June 2020
15. Tipos de Machine Learning. https://medium.com/soldai/tipos-de-aprendizaje-autom%C3%A1tico-6413e3c615e2. Accessed June 2020
16. Ng, A.: Machine learning. Coursera. https://www.coursera.org/learn/machine-learning. Accessed June 2020
17. La Regresión logística. https://www.analyticslane.com/2018/07/23/la-regresion-logistica/. Accessed June 2020
18. Octave. https://www.gnu.org/software/octave/. Accessed June 2020
19. Fminunc. https://octave.sourceforge.io/octave/function/fminunc. Accessed June 2020
20. Minimizers. https://octave.org/doc/v4.4.1/Minimizers.html. Accessed Sept 2020
21. Gradient Descent in Practice I – Feature Scaling. https://www.coursera.org/learn/machine-learning/supplement/CTA0D/gradient-descent-in-practice-i-feature-scaling. Accessed Dec 2020
22. Std. https://octave.sourceforge.io/octave/function/std.html. Accessed Dec 2020
23. Multi – class – classification and neural networks. https://www.coursera.org/learn/machine-learning/programming/Y54Zu/multi-class-classification-and-neural-networks. Accessed Dec 2020
24. Multi-Class Metrics Made Simple, Part I: Precision and Recall. Towards data science. https://towardsdatascience.com/multi-class-metrics-made-simple-part-i-precision-and-recall-9250280bddc2. Accessed June 2020
25. Confusion Matrix for Your Multi-Class Machine Learning Model. Towards data science. https://towardsdatascience.com/confusion-matrix-for-your-multi-class-machine-learning-model-ff9aa3bf7826. Accessed June 2020
26. Face, Microsoft. https://azure.microsoft.com/es-mx/services/cognitive-services/face/. Accessed June 2020
27. Ierache, J., Nicolosi, R., Ponce, G., Cervino, C., Eszter, E.: Registro emocional de personas interactuando en contextos de entornos virtuales. In: XXIV Congreso Argentino de Ciencias de la Computación (La Plata, 2018), ISBN 978-950-658-472-6, pp. 877–886 (2018)
28. Ierache, J., Ponce, G., Nicolosi, R., Sattolo, I., Chapperón, G.: Valoración del grado de atención en contextos áulicos con el empleo de interfase cerebro-computadora. In: CACIC 2019, ISBN 978-987-688-377-1, pp. 417–426 (2019)

Specification of the Schema of Spreadsheets for the Materialization of Ontologies from Integrated Data Sources

Sergio Alejandro Gómez[1,2]([⊠]) and Pablo Rubén Fillottrani[1,2]

[1] Laboratorio de I+D en Ingeniería de Software y Sistemas de Información (LISSI),
Departamento de Ciencias e Ingeniería de la Computación,
Universidad Nacional del Sur, San Andrés 800, Bahía Blanca, Argentina
{sag,prf}@cs.uns.edu.ar
[2] Comisión de Investigaciones Científicas de la Provincia de Buenos Aires
(CIC-PBA), La Plata, Argentina
https://lissi.cs.uns.edu.ar/

Abstract. In Ontology-Based Data Access (OBDA), a knowledge base known as an ontology models both the problem domain and the underlying data sources. We are concerned with providing with tools for performing OBDA with relational and non-relational data sources. We developed an OBDA tool that is able to access H2 databases, CSV files and Excel spreadsheets allowing the user to explicitly formulate mappings, and populating an ontology that can be saved for later querying. In this paper, we present a language for specifying the schema of the data in a spreadsheet data application, which then can be used to access the contents of a set of Excel books with the ultimate goal of materializing its data as an OWL/RDF ontology. We characterize the syntax and semantics of the language, present a prototypical implementation and report on the performance tests showing that our implementation can handle a workload of Excel tables of the order of ten thousand records. We also show a case study in which the ontology of an idealized university library can be defined using the our tool integrating both relational and spreadsheet data.

Keywords: Ontology-based data access · Ontologies · Relational databases · Spreadsheets

1 Introduction

Despite their simplicity and ubiquity, spreadsheets are still relevant because they provide a semi-structured, distributed way of representing the information of an organization when there is no formal database; even, many times, in spite of the existence of a centralized system, informal or operational information not covered by the main system is managed in spreadsheets. Although the spreadsheet

P. Pesado and J. Eterovic (Eds.): CACIC 2020, CCIS 1409, pp. 247–262, 2021.
https://doi.org/10.1007/978-3-030-75836-3_17

applications (such as MS Excel, Apache Open Office, or Libre Office) give the possibility of making totalizations and filters, these tools allow limited functionality and are difficult to integrate with the rest of the organization's information, having to resort to data mining and datawarehousing solutions that are not always straightforwardly useful for the layman.

Ontology-based data access [1] is a prominent approach to accessing the content of heterogeneous and legacy databases that has gained relevance in the past years in which the database schema along with the semantics of the business model they are exposed as an OWL ontology and the data as RDF triples in distributed form on the web that can be queried through SPARQL end-points.

In this research, we are interested in studying formal models and novel ways of performing OBDA, with the goal of providing concrete implementations. In this sense, in recent times, we have been developing a prototype that allows to export the schema of a relational database in H2 format as an OWL ontology and its relational instance as an RDF graph, also allowing the expression of mappings to define concepts from of complex SQL queries [2]. In this paper, we present an extension to our OBDA prototype that allows a user to specify a spreadsheet application using a schema definition language. This language allows a naive user to specify the format of the data in the tables contained in sheets of several books, indicating the orientation of the tables, format of columns and rows, cross-relations between tables and books. This allows the spreadsheets to be interpreted as databases and ultimately being integrated with the rest of the OBDA application. We assume that the reader has a basic knowledge of Description Logics (DL) [3], relational databases and the Web Ontology Language [4].

This work consolidates and extends results presented in [5]. As extension of that work, we now include a discussion of how the GF OBDA systema can be used to integrate and query information of a university library composed in terms of relational and spreadsheet data where public open data has to be machine processed.

The rest of the paper is structured as follows. In Sect. 2, we present a framework for conceptual modeling of spreadsheets as ontologies. In Sect. 3, we show an empirical evaluation of the performance of the prototype creating tables and ontologies from several Excel files of increasing size. In Sect. 4, we describe a possible solution for the publication on the Semantic Web of data from a hypothetical university library where its data comes from several heterogeneous sources. In Sect. 5, we discuss related work. Finally, in Sect. 6, we conclude and foresee future work.

2   A Framework for Representing Spreadsheets

Now we present a theoretical framework to represent the data of a spreadsheet application. Later, with this framework, we will define a language to describe the schema of the data. Such a schema will be used to access the contents of the spreadsheets, interpret them, generate an SQL script, create and populate an H2 database such script, and then materialize an OWL/RDF ontology with the contents of such a database. This ontology could then be queried via a SPARQL processor (see Fig. 1). We provide the syntax of the data description language in the spreadsheet application using a BNF grammar and give its operational semantics in terms of this framework. We will use a running example throughout the article to illustrate how to use it.

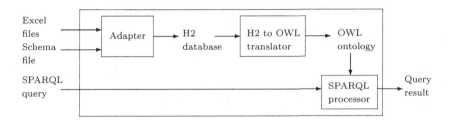

Fig. 1. Architecture of the system

A spreadsheet application data is a set of books. More formally:

Definition 1. *An spreadsheet application A is a pair (books, m) where books is a set of books and m is a map from a unique identifier into an object of the application.*

A book is basically a set of sheets along with further information. Formally:

Definition 2. *A book b is a tuple (id, path, sheets, sheetByID) where id is the identifier of the book, path is the absolute path of the Excel file defining the book, sheets is a list of sheets, and sheetByID is a map from sheet identifier into a sheet.*

A sheeet is composed by a set of tables. Formally:

Definition 3. *A sheet s is a tuple (id, name, tables, tableByID, container BookID) where id is the unique identifier of the sheet, name is the sheet's name in the container Excel book, tables is the set of tables contained in this sheet, tableByID is a map from unique table identifier into a table, and containerBookID is the identifier of the book containing the sheet.*

A table has a header, a set of records, and has an orientation (either horizontal or vertical). A cell range defines a rectangle of the data sheet specified by two cell references. Tables can contain references to other tables. Formally:

Definition 4. *A table t is a tuple (id, className, orientation, initialDataCell, finalDataCell, initialHeaderCell, finalHeaderCell, headerInfo, indexOfKeyField, crossReferences, containerSheetID, containerBookID) where id is the unique identifier of the table, className is the class in the target ontology defined by the table, orientation is either vertical or horizontal, initialDataCell is the*

top-left corner of the table's data, finalDataCell is the bottom-right corner of
the table's data, initialHeaderCell is the top-left corner of the table's header,
finalHeaderCell is the bottom-right corner of the table's header, headerInfo is a
map from integer i into a header datum object h_i, crossReferences is a set of
cross-references from this table into other tables, containerSheetID is the identifier of the sheet containing this table, and containerBookID is the identifier of
the book containing this table. A header datum is a tuple $(i, name, type)$ where i
is the 1-based index of the header datum in its container map, name is the name
of the field, and type is the type of the field, that can be one of string, numeric
(either integer or real), boolean, or date. A cell has a row (a positive number)
and a column (a 1-based positive number). A range is pair (c_i, c_f) composed of
an initial cell c_i and a final cell c_f. A cross-reference is a tuple (i, t, j) where i
is the index of the field in the source table, t is the identifier of the destination
table and j is the index of the field in the destination table.

2.1 Grammar for the Spreadsheet Description Language

We need a language for expressing the elements of this framework. Let us consider
the spreadsheet in Fig. 2 containing two tables representing people and their cell
phones. We will use that example in order to introduce the elements of our
language for describing the schema of the data in the spreadsheet with the goal of
materializing an ontology from it so it can be queried by means of SPARQL. We
now define the grammar for writing scripts for defining the structure of Excel
application data. We discuss each construct by giving its meaning, the BNF rules
that defines its syntax and an example describing its elements.

	A	B	C	D	E	F	G
1							
2		PersonID	Name	DateOfBirth	Checked	Weight	Status
3		1	John	1/1/1981	TRUE	100.5	heavy
4		2	Mary	2/2/1982	FALSE	60.5	light
5		3	Paul	3/3/1983	TRUE	80.5	heavy
6							
7							
8		CellID	1	2	3	4	
9		Brand	Samsung	Apple	Nokia	Samsung	
10		Model	S8	Iphone 11	1100	J7	
11		Owner	1	2	1	2	

Fig. 2. A spreadsheet named *Data* representing a set of people and their cell phones

A script is sequence of commands and is the start symbol of the grammar:

⟨script⟩ ::= ⟨command⟩*

There are several available commands to be used in the description of schemas
of Excel files.

⟨command⟩ ::= ⟨book-declaration⟩ | ⟨sheet-declaration⟩ | ⟨table-declaration⟩
  | ⟨table-header-declaration⟩ | ⟨table-data-declaration⟩ | ⟨table-field-declaration⟩
  | ⟨table-key-field-declaration⟩ | ⟨cross-ref-declaration⟩ | ⟨comment⟩

A book can be declared by giving it an identifier and a path. Identifiers are sorrounded by quotation marks and are composed in the usual way.

$\langle book\text{-}declaration \rangle ::=$ book $\langle id \rangle$ has-path $\langle path \rangle$

$\langle id \rangle ::=$ " $\langle identifier \rangle$ "

$\langle identifier \rangle ::= \langle letter \rangle.(\langle letter \rangle | \langle digit \rangle)$ *

$\langle letter \rangle ::=$ a | b | ...|z | A | B | ...| Z

$\langle digit \rangle ::=$ 0 | 1 | ...| 9

$\langle path \rangle ::=$ "... windows file path ... "

Example 1. Consider the piece of code that expresses that book b_1 has as its path the Excel file `book1.xlsx` located in the `Escritorio8` subfolder in the desktop folder: `book "b1" has-path "c:/users/sgomez/Desktop/Escritorio8/book1.xlsx"`.

A book has at least one data sheet. Each sheet has an identifier in this schema file, a name in the spreadsheet and it is located in a book.

$\langle sheet\text{-}declaration \rangle ::=$ sheet $\langle id \rangle$ name $\langle id \rangle$ in $\langle id \rangle$

Example 2. Consider the code: `sheet "s1" name "Data" in "b1"`. It expresses that the spreadsheet s_1 has been named *Data* and it is located in the book b_1.

Each spreadsheet can have several tables. Each table has an identifier, is contained in a certain spreadsheet, defines a class and has an orientation which either is horizontal or vertical.

$\langle table\text{-}declaration \rangle ::=$ table $\langle id \rangle$ in-sheet $\langle id \rangle$ class-name $\langle id \rangle$ orientation $\langle orientation\text{-}literal \rangle$

$\langle class\text{-}name \rangle ::= \langle id \rangle$

$\langle orientation\text{-}literal \rangle ::=$ horizontal | vertical

Example 3. Consider the commands: `table "t1" in-sheet "s1" class-name "Person" orientation vertical` and `table "t2" in-sheet "s1" class-name "Phone" orientation horizontal`. They define that there are two tables: t_1 and t_2, which are both located in sheet s_1. Table t_1 defines a class name *Person* while table t_2 defines a class named *Phone*. The orientation of t_1 is vertical but the orientation of t_2 is horizontal.

Every table defition is composed of header and data sections, with syntax:—

$\langle table\text{-}header\text{-}declaration \rangle ::=$ header $\langle id \rangle$ range $\langle range\text{-}specification \rangle$

$\langle table\text{-}data\text{-}declaration \rangle ::=$ data $\langle id \rangle$ range $\langle range\text{-}specification \rangle$

$\langle range\text{-}specification \rangle ::=$ " $\langle cell\text{-}spec \rangle : \langle cell\text{-}spec \rangle$ "

$\langle cell\text{-}spec \rangle ::= \langle letter \rangle^+ \langle digit \rangle^+$

Example 4. Consider the commands for defining the limits of tables t_1 and t_2: `header "t1" range "b2:g2"`, `data "t1" range "b3:g5"`, `header "t2" range "b8:b11"`, and `data "t2" range "c8:f11"`.

Fields are declared specifying the table to which they belong, an index, a name and a type. There is an special field called the key field:

⟨*table-field-declaration*⟩ ::= field ⟨*id*⟩ index ⟨*positive-integer*⟩ name ⟨*id*⟩ type ⟨*type-id*⟩

⟨*type-id*⟩ ::= integer | string | date | real

⟨*table-key-field-declaration*⟩ ::= key-field ⟨*id*⟩ index ⟨*positive-integer*⟩

⟨*positive-integer*⟩ ::= (1..9)⟨*digit*⟩*

Example 5. Consider the piece of code for defining the fields of tables t_1 and t_2:

```
field "t1" index "1" name "PersonID" type integer
field "t1" index "2" name "Name" type string
field "t1" index "3" name "DateOfBirth" type date
field "t1" index "4" name "Checked" type boolean
field "t1" index "5" name "Weight" type real
field "t1" index "6" name "Status" type string
key-field "t1" index "1"
field "t2" index "1" name "CellID" type integer
field "t2" index "2" name "Brand" type string
field "t2" index "3" name "Model" type string
field "t2" index "4" name "Owner" type integer
key-field "t2" index "1"
```

The table t_1 has 6 fields named *PersonID*, *Name*, *DateOfBirth*, *Checked*, *Weight* and *Status* of type integer, date, boolean, real and string, resp. The table t_2 has 4 fields named *CellID* and *Owner* both of type integer, and *Brand* and *Model* of type string. The key field of t_1 is *PersonID* while the key field of t_2 is *CellID*. Notice that no indications are given here if the contents of a cell is either a formula or a value and it is neither necessary. For instance the column *Status* is a formula of the form: =IF(F3>=80, "heavy", "light") indicating that if the weight of the person is greater than or equal to 80 kg, the person is considered as heavy, otherwise is deemed as light.

A table can have cross-references to other tables.

⟨*cross-ref-declaration*⟩ ::= cross-ref from ⟨*id*⟩ index ⟨*positive-integer*⟩ into ⟨*id*⟩ index ⟨*positive-integer*⟩

Example 6. The following piece of code defines a cross-reference from field number 4 of table t_2 into field number 1 of table t_1:

```
cross-ref from "t2" index "4" into "t1" index "1"
```

One-line comments are allowed in our scripting language and they begin with the hashtag character.

⟨*comment*⟩ ::= #⟨*character*⟩*

⟨*character*⟩ ::= any Ascii character excluding end of line

2.2   Semantics of Spreadsheet Constructors

The semantics of the empty spreadsheet application *create* is $(\{\}, \{\})$. The semantics of commands is given in terms of the function Sem from commands by spreadsheet applications into spreadsheet applications. The semantics of a book declaration is as follows:

Sem(sheet "*id*" name "*n*" in "*bid*", (*books*, *m*)) = (*books'*, $\{(id, s)\} \cup m$) where

$$books' = books - \{b\} \cup \{b'\}$$
$$b = m(bid) = (bid, p, sheets, sheetByID),$$
$$b' = (bid, p, \{s\} \cup sheets, \{(id, s)\} \cup sheetByID)$$
$$s = (id, n, \{\}, \{\}, bid)$$

The semantics of the declaration of a table *id*, in sheet *sid*, determining a class *c*, with orientation *o*, with *n* fields named $name_1, \ldots, name_n$ of types t_1, $\ldots, t_n$, key field *k*, *m* cross-references from fields i_1, ldots, i_m into foreign tables $tid_1, \ldots, tid_m$ and foreign fields with indexes $j_1, \ldots, j_m$, resp., header info in the range $h_1 : h_2$ and data info in the range $d_1 : d_2$ is given shown in Fig. 3.

Sem(*sec*, (*books*, *m*)) = (*books'*, $\{(id, t)\} \cup m$) where
  sec = (table "*id*" in-sheet "*sid*" class-name "*c*" orientation *o*⏎
    = header "*id*" range "$h_1 : h_2$"⏎
      field "*id*" index "1" name "$name_1$" type t_1⏎
      . . .
      field "*id*" index "*n*" name "$name_n$" type t_n⏎
      key-field "*id*" index "*k*"⏎
      data "*id*" range "$d_1 : d_2$"⏎
      cross-ref from "*id*" index "i_1" into "tid_1" index "j_1"⏎
      . . .
      cross-ref from "*id*" index "i_m" into "tid_m" index "j_m")
  s = *m*(*id*) = (*sid*, *name*, *ts*, *tableByID*, *containerBookID*)
  t = (*id*, *c*, *o*, d_1, d_2, h_1, h_2, *head*, *k*, *cross*, *sid*)
  s' = (*sid*, *name*, $\{t\} \cup ts$, $\{(id, t)\} \cup tableByID$, *containerBookID*)
  books' = *books* − $\{b\} \cup \{b'\}$
  b = (*bid*, *p*, *sheets*, *sheetByID*) = *m*(*containerBookID*)
  b' = (*bid*, *p*, *sheets'*, *sheetByID*)
  sheets' = $\{s\} \cup sheets$
  cross = $\{(i_1, tid_1, j_1), \ldots, (i_m, tid_m, j_m)\}$
  head = $\lambda i.(i, name, t_i)$, with $i = 1, \ldots, n$

Fig. 3. Semantics of table declaration commands

2.3   Generation of Databases and Ontologies from Spreadsheets

We now discuss the generation of OWL/RDF ontologies from spreadsheet applications. Given a book with mapping *m* of identifiers into objects, let *t* be a table such that $t = (id, c, o, d_1, d_2, h_1, h_2, head, k, cross, s)$, such that *cross* = $\{(i_1, tid_1, j_1), \ldots, (i_m, tid_m, j_m)\}$, and *head* = $\lambda i.(i, name_i, t_i)$, with $i = 1, \ldots, n$.

The SQL code in Fig. 4 represents the schema of table t, where second and sixth are the projectors of the second and the sixth components of a tuple, resp. Then this SQL code is used to materialize an H2 database, which in turn is used to materialize an OWL/RDF ontology using the methodology described in our previous work [6].

```
create table "c" (
    "name_1" t_1, ..., "name_k" t_k primary key, ..., "name_n" t_n,
    foreign key ("second(head(i_1))") references "second(m(tid_1))" ("second(sixth(m(tid_1))(j_1))"),
    ..., foreign key ("second(head(i_m))") references "second(m(tid_m))" ("second(sixth(m(tid_m))(j_m))") );
```

Fig. 4. SQL script for creating a generic table t

Example 7. The spreadsheet in Fig. 2 is represented by the SQL script in Fig. 5. Then, from this script, a database is created and the ontology materialized from that database has the following DL axioms (that are ultimately serialized as OWL/RDF): Person $\sqsubseteq$ $\exists$PersonID, $\exists$PersonID$^-$ $\sqsubseteq$ Integer, Person $\sqsubseteq$ $\exists$name, $\exists$name$^-$ $\sqsubseteq$ String, Person $\sqsubseteq$ $\exists$dateOfBirth, $\exists$dateOfBirth$^-$ $\sqsubseteq$ Date, Person $\sqsubseteq$ $\exists$checked, $\exists$checked$^-$ $\sqsubseteq$ Boolean, Person $\sqsubseteq$ $\exists$weight, $\exists$weight$^-$ $\sqsubseteq$ Real, Person $\sqsubseteq$ $\exists$status, $\exists$status$^-$ $\sqsubseteq$ String, Phone $\sqsubseteq$ $\exists$cellID, $\exists$cellID$^-$ $\sqsubseteq$ Integer, Phone $\sqsubseteq$ $\exists$brand, $\exists$brand$^-$ $\sqsubseteq$ String, Phone $\sqsubseteq$ $\exists$model, $\exists$model$^-$ $\sqsubseteq$ String, Phone $\sqsubseteq$ $\exists$owner $\exists$owner$^-$ $\sqsubseteq$ Integer, Phone $\sqsubseteq$ $\exists$ref_owner $\exists$ref_owner$^-$ $\sqsubseteq$ Person. The assertions for representing the first record of the class Person are: PersonID(Person#1, 1), name(Person#1, JOHN), dateOfBirth(Person#1, 1981-01-01), checked(Person#1, TRUE), weight(Person#1, 100.5), and status(Person#1, HEAVY).

```
create table "Person" (
    "PersonID" int primary key,      "Name" varchar(50), "DateOfBirth" date,
    "Checked" boolean, "Weight" real, "Status" varchar(50) );
create table "Phone" (
    "CellID" int primary key, "Brand" varchar(50), "Model" varchar(50), "Owner" int,
    foreign key ("Owner") references "Person" ("PersonID") );
insert into "Person" ("PersonID", "Name", "DateOfBirth", "Checked", "Weight", "Status")
    values (1, 'John', '1981-01-01', true, 100.5, 'heavy');
insert into "Person" ("PersonID", "Name", "DateOfBirth", "Checked", "Weight", "Status")
    values (2, 'Mary', '1982-02-02', false, 60.5, 'light');
insert into "Person" ("PersonID", "Name", "DateOfBirth", "Checked", "Weight", "Status")
    values (3, 'Paul', '1983-03-03', true, 80.5, 'heavy');
insert into "Phone" ("CellID", "Brand", "Model", "Owner") values (1, 'Samsung', 'S8', 1);
insert into "Phone" ("CellID", "Brand", "Model", "Owner") values (2, 'Apple', 'Iphone 11', 2);
insert into "Phone" ("CellID", "Brand", "Model", "Owner") values (3, 'Nokia', '1100', 1);
insert into "Phone" ("CellID", "Brand", "Model", "Owner") values (4, 'Samsung', 'J7', 2);
```

Fig. 5. SQL code obtained from the spreadsheet in Fig. 2

3   Experimental Evaluation

We now discuss some of the tests we have performed in order to test how our application handles increasing demands in database size. The performance of our system is affected mainly by the fact that we tables are metarialized as RDF triples and also by four factors: (i) the system is implemented in the JAVA programming language; (ii) the database management system that we use is H21, (iii) the handling of the global ontology is done via the OWL API [7], and (iv) the access to the Excel files is implemented using the Apache POI library [8]. Our tests were conducted on an ASUS notebook having an Intel Core i7, 3.5 GHz CPU, 8 GB RAM, 1 TB HDD, and Windows 10. They involved the creation of databases with single table extracted from Excel books containing only a sheet with a table containing 100 fields of numeric type filled with an increasing number of records. In Table 1, we can see the times for loading the Excel files and the size of the materialized ontologies. Therefore, we conclude that our application can only handle tables with a size of tens of thousands records and is not able of handling tables of a hundred thousand records.

Table 1. Running times for ontology generation from Excel files

Number of records	Excel file size [Megabytes]	Time for loading Excel file [seconds]	Time for creating ontology [seconds]	Size of ontology file [Megabytes]
10	0.012	0.901	0.276	0.115
100	0.033	1.774	0.359	0.910
1,000	0.255	5.825	1.067	8.951
10,000	2.640	29.703	4.253	90.951
100,000	26.742	Out of memory error		

4   Case Study: OBDA for Library Management

We contend that the approach for describing the schema of spreadsheet data described above can be used as the basis for the development of real-world OBDA applications allowing the publication of organization data as rich OWL/RDF ontologies. We try to validate our thesis by describing a possible solution for the publication on the Semantic Web of data from a hypothetical university library where its data comes from several heterogeneous sources.

University libraries often work with proprietary software, or spreadsheets, to represent their inventory. When the bibliographic inventory data are represented in a relational database, they can adopt ad-hoc codings representing domain peculiarities that are often difficult to extrapolate to other systems. The attention is often personal, which makes it impossible to search the literature for the material present in them as noted in [9–13].

The OBDA system called GF [2] that allows OWL/RDF ontologies to be materialized from data represented in the form of a relational database, CSV data sheet and now Microsoft Excel spreadsheet. We will use the system to establish mappings to retrieve subsets of the data from the database and to establish rich relationships between such data in the form of classes, subclasses and properties in an ontology. This ontology, together with other similar ones from other libraries, can be published on the internet and can be consulted through a SPARQL endpoint in an integrated way to search for the availability of bibliographic material, as well as on the status of their users. Thus the objective of this section is to show how an ontology like the one presented in Fig. 6 can be constructed from heterogeneous data sources containing ad-hoc encodings and then show how GF can deal with a combination of data specified as relational data and spreadsheet data.

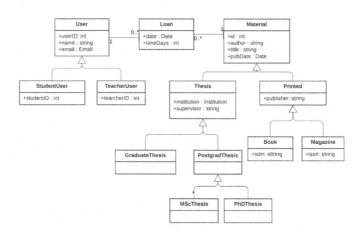

Fig. 6. Ontology for the university library

Suppose that the data of the bibliographic material, users and loans of a university library are stored in a relational database with the schema and instance as shown in Fig. 7. We see that the table that models the library loans reifies a many-to-many relationship between user and bibliographic material, which in turn is separated into 2 tables, namely, thesis and printed matter. Printed material is separated into books and magazines. The type of theses must encode variants such as graduate thesis, master's thesis and doctoral thesis. This type of simplification may, for example, need to use special values for ad-hoc encodings. For example, notice the D for codifying doctoral thesis and the M for Master Thesis, which, when querying the data using SQL, to search for doctoral thesis, requires resorting to low-level constructions such as: *select * from "Thesis" where type = "D"*.

We then will show how the use of OBDA technologies makes it possible to more naturally model the type of each document by referring to the classes and subclasses belonging to the semantics of the application domain. Ultimately all of the presented techniques can be implemented by a naive user in the GF framework of which a previous version was presented in [2] and references there in. To do this, suppose that the tables defined above are populated as in Fig. 7.

$User(\underline{userNo}, name, email, type)$
$Thesis(\underline{id}, author, title, pubDate, type, institution, supervisor)$
$Loan(\underline{userNo}, \underline{id}, date, timeDays)$

User

userNo	name	email	type
1	John	john@nosite.com	S
2	Peter	peter@nosite.com	T

Loan

userNo	id	date	timeDays
1	1	2020-09-01	40

Thesis

id	author	title	pubDate	type	institution	supervisor
1	Marie Curie	Recherches sur les substances radioactives	1903-01-01	D	Faculte des Sciences de Paris	Gabriel Lippmann
2	Claude Shannon	A Symbolic Analysis of Relay and Switching Circuits	1937-01-01	M	Massachusetts Institute of Technology	Vannevar Bush

Fig. 7. Relational instance of the library's database concerning Users, Theses and Loans

Consequently, when proposing a richer modeling of the domain, we are interested in defining two subconcepts of the Thesis concept called undergraduate thesis and postgraduate thesis. In turn, the postgraduate thesis concept will have two sub-concepts called MSc Thesis and PhD Thesis. Formally, we are interested in establishing the axioms in the ontology shown in Fig. 8.

$$UndergraduateThesis \sqcup GraduateThesis \sqsubseteq Thesis$$
$$UndergraduateThesis \sqcap GraduateThesis \sqsubseteq \bot$$
$$MScThesis \sqcup PhDThesis \sqsubseteq GraduateThesis$$
$$MScThesis \sqcap PhDThesis \sqsubseteq \bot$$

Fig. 8. Axioms for classifying theses

Then, it is necessary to establish the link between the data in the tables and the concepts and assertions of the ontology. This is achieved using mappings, which are SQL expressions that define the values of the ontology assertions in terms of the values of the relational instance. In the case of theses, the mappings are as shown in Fig. 9. The definition of such mappings can be done visually in the GF frame. The system allows you to define the name of the sub-concept, from which table the data is obtained, automatically computes the SQL filter and shows the records that fill the concept. It also allows you to automatically add the axioms as shown in Fig. 8.

$$PhDThesis(id) \leftarrow select\ "id\ from\ "Thesis"\ where\ "type" = 'D'$$
$$MScThesis(id) \leftarrow select\ "id"\ from\ "Thesis"\ where\ "type" = 'M'$$
$$UndergraduateThesis(id) \leftarrow select\ "id"\ from\ "Thesis"\ where\ "type" = 'T'$$

Fig. 9. Mappings for defining assertions from the table *Thesis*

Suppose we have the library magazines represented in a spreadsheet like the one shown in Fig. 10. In this case, we see that the magazines table has been represented horizontally instead of vertically as it is usuallly done as GF supports both representations.

	A	B	C	D
...				
3		Id	100	101
4		Author	Thomas G. Rokicki	James Willis
5		Title	An Algorithm for Compressing Space and Time	Build Your Own Turing Machine
6		PubDate	4/1/2006	4/1/1981
7		Issn	1044-789X	0360-5280
8		Publisher	UBM Technology Group	UBM Technology Group
9		Magazine	Dr Dobb's Journal	BYTE Magazine
10		Editor	Andrew Binstock	Wayne Green
11				

Fig. 10. Spreadsheet called *Magazine* for representing magazines

As shown in Sect. 2.1, it is necessary to define the schema of the data prior to its import into the OBDA system. In Fig. 11, we show the schema of the spreadsheet shown in Fig. 10. As implied by Fig. 1, the system generates a relational table, which is used to generate the OWL code to update the ontology. Additionally, the axiom *Magazine ⊑ Printed* indicating that a magazine is a type of printed matter must be included. In Fig. 12, we show, as an example, the definition of the *Editorial* property of the *Magazine* class. From this spreadsheet several DL assertions are produced such as: *Magazine*(101), *author*(101, James Willis), *editor*(101, Wayne Green), ... In Fig. 13, we show the OWL serialization of the magazine 101.

To query the data integrated in the ontology, it is necessary to use the SPARQL language [14]. For example, to find data about copies of BYTE magazine in the library, a query like the one shown in Fig. 14 can be used.

5   Related Work

XLWrap [15] constitutes an approach for generating RDF graphs of arbitrary complexity from various spreadsheet layouts, including cross tables and tables

```
book "b1" has-path "c:/users/john/Desktop/magazines.xlsx"
sheet "s1" name "Magazine" in "b1"
table "t1" in-sheet "s1" class-name "Magazine"
orientation horizontal
header "t1" range "b3:b10"
data "t1" range "c3:d10"
key-field "t1" index "1"
field "t1" index "1" name "id" type integer
field "t1" index "2" name "Author" type string
field "t1" index "3" name "Title" type string
field "t1" index "4" name "PubDate" type date
field "t1" index "5" name "issn" type string
field "t1" index "6" name "Publisher" type string
field "t1" index "7" name "Magazine" type string
field "t1" index "8" name "Editor" type string
```

Fig. 11. Data definition scheme for the Magazines spreadsheet

```
<owl:DatatypeProperty rdf:about="http://foo.org/Magazine#Publisher">
<rdfs:domain rdf:resource="http://foo.org#Magazine"/>
<rdfs:range rdf:resource="http://www.w3.org/2001/XMLSchema#string"/>
</owl:DatatypeProperty>
```

Fig. 12. Part of the OWL code for publishing magazines describing the Publisher property

```
<owl:NamedIndividual rdf:about="http://foo.org/Magazine/id=101">
<rdf:type rdf:resource="http://foo.org#Magazine"/>
<Magazine:Author rdf:datatype="http://www.w3.org/2001/XMLSchema#string">
James Willis</Magazine:Author>
<Magazine:Editor rdf:datatype="http://www.w3.org/2001/XMLSchema#string">
Wayne Green</Magazine:Editor>
</owl:NamedIndividual>
```

Fig. 13. Part of the OWL code for 101 magazine

```
prefix foo: <http://foo.org/>
prefix r: <http://foo.org/Magazine#>

select ?r ?author ?title ?publisher
where
{
        ?r r:Magazine "BYTE Magazine" .
        ?r r:Author ?author .
        ?r r:Title ?title.
        ?r r:Publisher ?publisher.
}
```

Fig. 14. SPARQL query to retrieve a BYTE journal.

where data is not aligned in rows. They provide a functionality similar to ours but relying in JSON for the description of data. Our approach features a simpler language geared towards naive users. *NOR2O* [16] can convert excel to Scovo and Data Cube Vocabulary but it is no longer maintained. *Excel2rdf* [1] is a Java-based command-line utility that converts Excel files into valid RDF files but as far as we know it is not possible to make precise definitions of the data contained nor export terminologies as done in our proposal. *RDBToOnto*[2] allows to automatically generate fine-tuned OWL ontologies from relational databases. A major feature of this full-fledged tool is the ability to produce structured ontologies with deeper hierarchies by exploiting both the database schema and the stored data. RDBToOnto can be exploited to produce RDF Linked Data. It can also be used to generate highly accurate RDB-to-RDF mapping rules (for D2RQ Server and Triplify). *Spread2RDF*[3] is a converter for complex spreadsheets to RDF and a Ruby-internal DSL for specifying the mapping rules for this conversion. Other solutions to the problem of wrapping Excel files into semantic technologies have migrated from the academic world to the commercial world. For example, *Open Anzo*[4] used to include both an open source enterprise-featured RDF quad store and a sophisticated service oriented, semantic middleware platform that provides support for multiple users, distributed clients, offline work, real-time notification, named-graph modularization, versioning, access controls, and transactions, giving support to applications based on W3C semantic technology standards like OWL, RDF and SPARQL. This project is no longer available it has turned into a company named *Cambridge Semantics*[5]. *TopBraid Composer*[6] can convert Excel spreadsheets into instances of an RDF schema. *TabLinker*[7] can convert non-standard Excel spreadsheets to the Data Cube vocabulary. Our work converts the contents of the records in Excel sheets to RDF but also allows to precisely define the schema of the data in OWL.

6   Conclusions and Future Work

We have presented a framework for the modeling of the schema and data of spreadsheet files by means of a description language. We have given a formal specification of the syntax of such a language with a BNF grammar and its formal semantics in terms of the framework of representation. We have shown an example of how it is used in order to explain its main components. We have also provided a prototypical implementation, showing how it is integrated into an ontology-based data access system with the aim of publishing such spreadsheets as freely available ontologies on the Semantic Web. We believe that this

---

[1] https://github.com/waqarini/excel2rdf.

[2] https://sourceforge.net/projects/rdbtoonto/.

[3] https://github.com/marcelotto/spread2rdf.

[4] https://www.w3.org/2001/sw/wiki/OpenAnzo.

[5] http://www.cambridgesemantics.com.

[6] https://www.topquadrant.com/knowledge-assets/faq/tbc/.

[7] https://github.com/Data2Semantics/TabLinker/wiki.

language provides a valid alternative to more technical options like JSON from which naive users can benefit while providing more control than WYSIWYG-type applications that provide similar functionality. Also, we have carried out experimental tests to determine what is the workload that our implementation can effectively handle, showing that it is viable for spreadsheets containing tables with thousands of records. We have presented a case study that shows that the approach presented in this paper can be used to integrate several data sources in heterogeneous formats to comprise a suitable alternative for the publication of data of an idealized university library.

As part of future work, we are interested in continuing to explore other types of NoSQL database models and thinking about integrating them into our ontology-based data access prototype with the aim of developing novel algorithms and techniques such as virtualization by query-rewriting to provide more flexibility in regards to volatile data than the one offered by the materialization approach.

Acknowledgments. This research is funded by Secretaría General de Ciencia y Técnica, Universidad Nacional del Sur, Argentina and by Comisión de Investigaciones Científicas de la Provincia de Buenos Aires (CIC-PBA).

References

1. Xiao, G., et al.: Ontology-based data access - a survey. In: Proceedings of the Twenty-Seventh International Joint Conference on Artificial Intelligence (IJCAI-18), pp. 5511–5519 (2018)
2. Gómez, S.A., Fillottrani, P.R.: Materialization of OWL ontologies from relational databases - a practical approach. In: Pesado, P., Arroyo, M. (eds.) Computer Science - CACIC 2019 selected papers, pp. 285–301. Springer International Publishing, Cham (2020). https://doi.org/10.1007/978-3-030-48325-8_19
3. Baader, F., Horrocks, I., Lutz, C., Sattler, U.: An Introduction to Description Logic. Cambridge University Press, Cambridge (2017)
4. Bao, J., Kendall, E.F., McGuinness, D.L., Patel-Schneider, P.F.: OWL 2 Web Ontology Language Quick Reference Guide (Second Edition) W3C Recommendation, 11 December 2012 (2012)
5. Gómez, S.A., Fillottrani, P.: A language for the specification of the schema of spreadsheets for the materialization of ontologies. In Mon, A., et al. (eds.) XXVI Congreso Argentino de Ciencias de la Computación (CACIC 2020), pp. 546–555, October 2020
6. Gómez, S.A., Fillottrani, P.R.: Towards a framework for ontology-based data access: materialization of OWL ontologies from relational databases. In Pesado, P., Aciti, C., (eds.) X Workshop en Innovación en Sistemas de Software (WISS 2018), XXIV Congreso Argentino de Ciencias de la Computación CACIC 2018, pp. 857–866 (2018)
7. Matentzoglu, N., Palmisano, I.: An Introduction to the OWL API. Technical report, The University of Manchester (2016)
8. Minh, N.H.: How to Read Excel Files in Java using Apache POI (2019)
9. Dilroshan, T.C.: Identification of problems faced by university libraries in the process of automation: with special reference to the libraries of moratuwa and colombo universities. Sri Lanka J. Librarianship Inf. Manage. 1(2), 82–98 (2009)

10. Malhan, I.: Challenges and problems of library and information education in India: an emerging knowledge society and the developing nations of Asia. Libr. Philos. Pract. **670** (2011). https://digitalcommons.unl.edu/libphilprac/670/

11. Mishra, A., Thakur, S., Singh, T.: Library automation: issues, challenges and remedies author. Times Int. J. Res. (Issue January 2015), 9–16 (2015). https://www.academia.edu/12808629/LIBRARY_AUTOMATION_ISSUES_CH ALLENGES_AND_REMEDIES

12. Pothumani, S., Sridhar, J.: Solving problems of library management system. Int. J. Innov. Res. Comput. Commun. Eng. **3**(7), 6466–6469 (2015). https://doi.org/ 10.15680/ijircce.2015.0307167

13. Raval, A.: Problems of library automation. Int. J. Res. Educ. **2**(2) (2013). http://www.raijmr.com/ijre/wp-content/uploads/2017/11/IJRE_2013_vol02_is sue_02_01.pdf

14. Harris, S., Seaborne, A.: SPARQL 1.1 Query Language for RDF W3C recommendation, 21 March 2013 (2013). https://www.w3.org/TR/rdf-sparql-query/

15. Langegger, A., Wöß, W.: XLWrap – querying and integrating arbitrary spreadsheets with SPARQL. In: Bernstein, A., Karger, D.R., Heath, T., Feigenbaum, L., Maynard, D., Motta, E., Thirunarayan, K. (eds.) ISWC 2009. LNCS, vol. 5823, pp. 359–374. Springer, Heidelberg (2009). https://doi.org/10.1007/978-3-642-04930- 9_23

16. Terrazas, B.V., Gomez-Perez, A., Calbimonte, J.P.: NOR2O: a library for transforming non-ontological resources to ontologies. In: ESWC 2010 (2010)

Signal Processing and Real-Time Systems

GPS Device for Monitoring Sports Performance

Luisina Santos[1,2], Marcelo Guiguet[1,2], Pablo Luengo[1,2(✉)],
Eduardo Alvarez[1,2], Carlos Di Cicco[1,2], Gustavo Useglio[1,2], Federico Gómez[1,2],
and Matías Capelli[1,2]

[1] Institute for Research and Technology Transfer (ITT), 1169 Sarmiento, Junín, Bs. As.,
Argentina
{luisina.santos,marcelo.guiguet,pablo.luengo,eduardo.alvarez,
carlos.dicicco,gustavo.useglio}@itt.unnoba.edu.ar
[2] National University of the Northwest of the Province of Buenos Aires (UNNOBA) Associated
Center, Commission for Scientific Research (CIC), Junín, Argentina
{fmgomez,mcapelli}@comunidad.unnoba.edu.ar

Abstract. This work uses GPS technology applied to sport to generate a training system that allows the monitoring of aspects of interest of the athlete's physical performance in a real context, facilitating sports improvement through the scientific analysis of the data obtained. An economic GPS prototype was developed that allows collecting the necessary data to calculate the physical performance parameters of an athlete, focusing on a strategy that is easy to manufacture and accessible to athletic and professional sports institutions that may occur in the national territory. The work is carried out at the Institute for Research and Technology Transfer, within the framework of the research project "Computing and Emerging Technologies" and "Technology and Applications of Software Systems: Innovation in processes, products and services", as counterpart the company Silamberts SRL financed by Dr. Manuel Sadosky Foundation and the UNNOBA.

Keywords: Global positioning system · IMU · Sports performance ·
Datalogger · Communication protocol

1 Introduction

After winning eight gold medals in the 1972 games in Munich, in 1976 Australia returned from Montreal without a single one. Five years later the government created the Australian Sports Institute (AIS) and in 1990 developed the Cooperative Research Centers (CRC) for the industrial, commercial and economic growth of the country. Shaun Holthouse and Igor van de Griendt, who led a team of CRC researchers dedicated to the application of emerging microtechnologies, began a project with AIS aimed at improving the physical performance of athletes through evidence based on science. Although monitoring in the laboratory allowed a detailed idea of the demands, the athletes did not make the same efforts as during the real competition. Therefore, to transfer the research to the real field, the CRC developed portable sensors. To commercialize the product, at the end of 2006, Holthouse and Griendt created Catapult, a global leader in the athletic

© Springer Nature Switzerland AG 2021
P. Pesado and J. Eterovic (Eds.): CACIC 2020, CCIS 1409, pp. 265–274, 2021.
https://doi.org/10.1007/978-3-030-75836-3_18

analysis [1]. Currently, only the wealthiest clubs can access Catapult in Argentina. Those who do not, use a GPS that collects simple data such as distances, times, intensities and frequencies. From the collected data, the physical trainer draws up reports that are used for the diagnosis and planning of individual training according to the period and duration of the competition, among other variables. Our challenge is to build a low-cost technology that is somewhere between the standard GPS and the advanced and very expensive Catapult to be able to answer both professional and amateur athletes.

In this context, the current work is the extension of the work presented at CACIC 2020, it describes the evolution of the original prototype and version 1 [2], which consists of the integration of the modules through a printed circuit board, the addition of an autonomous power supply and a container cabinet, data transmission via Bluetooth (also USB) and a Web App developed specifically for the project using it in a real space.

2   Context

The original prototype has a printed circuit board that reduces the device size, integrates the modules and eliminates the wiring errors due to false contacts.

This board was designed to provide a connection between the modules: Arduino (NANO), GPS (GY-GPS6MV2) IMU (MPU9250), microSD, RTC (DS3231), Battery charger (TP5100) [3], 2 lithium batteries of 3, 7 v [4], Bluetooth Module: HC-06. [5], Load balancer.

The original version developed uses two lithium cells as a power source. The board has a built-in battery charging and protection circuit, along with a battery charging circuit, power cut while the battery charging system is in operation. The assembly of the modules that provide independence to the device for its power supply, charging and control, did not adapt to what was expected due to the instability of the control circuit of the batteries (see Fig. 1).

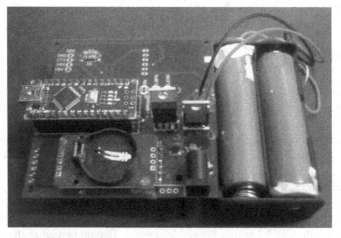

Fig. 1. First approximation of the prototype on a PCB.

The original prototype evolved to the version 1 prototype, intending to reduce its volume, giving it energy autonomy (and stability), and designing and implementing a command protocol of communication that allows the transmission of data safely and without errors (see Fig. 2).

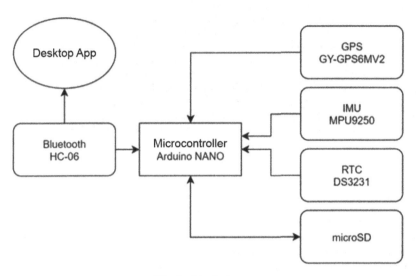

Fig. 2. Block diagram

Other problems detected in the original version such as excessive size and weight, unreliable charging module and heat dissipation of the 5v regulator, the results were found by creating a lithium cell with a charging and protection system integrated into a single module. In prototype version 1, the board can be used while the cell tent system is in operation. This is achieved by assembling a power selector using two diodes. Because each lithium cell has a voltage of 3.7v, it is necessary to use a voltage booster to reach the necessary 5v for the operation of the modules and the Arduino Nano platform.

The following components are used for the board power supply system: TP4056 charger with built-in protection, a 5v voltage switch, a 18650 lithium battery.

The improvements incorporated in prototype version 1, converged in a device with production possibilities since it can be used in the game field, located in a sports bra, which sizes are 4.52 × 3.34 × 1.18 inches and weighing 5.3 oz approximately (See Fig. 3). Complemented with the web interface described later in the next document.

Fig. 3. Photograph of the prototype version 1.

3 Communication Protocol

A protocol, that allows the transmission of data with a zero error rate, was developed. Each line sent from the device to the computer is retransmitted as many times as necessary, to ensure that it is received correctly [6].

This protocol is based on request/response commands, where the computer is the active component and is in charge of "asking" the device for each line stored. In the case of an error in the frame (CHECKSUM $\neq$ 0), the retransmission or automatic reconnection is requested. Knowing the format of the frame to be transmitted and focusing on the line-by-line incremental numbering of both files (GPS and IMU), it is used to recognize and control what data is being sent in the form of ACK.

Based on the expected reliability, a communication protocol was developed that behaves according to the state (see Table 1).

Table 1. Design of the communication protocol

Start	The computer starts the protocol through the command data, whose parameter will be the name of the file from which they must be extracted, given the nature of data prototype storage. Ex: data (IMU)
Error-free frame	If the computer receives the complete and error-free transaction (CHECKSUM = 0), then it will return an ACK with the last line number received. The prototype will send the next line
Incorrect frame	If it produces an error in the transmission (CHECKSUM $\neq$ 0), the ACK will not coincide with the one expected by the device, so it will go to the retransmission state
Retransmission	Knowing what the expected ACK is, then the prototype knows which line to transmit to the computer
Time-out	When the prototype sends the frame, a counter is started at 0 (zero) which is incremented by one unit per millisecond. If it reaches a certain specific value and does not receive a response from the computer, it is assumed that the connection was lost and the reconnection state passed
Reconnection	The connection is reestablished without losing the ACK of the last line received correctly and the data is sent from the loss forward
Finish	When the device recognizes that all the lines (n) were sent correctly, the communication ends, and it removes from the prototype memory the transmitted file

Figure 4 specifies the diagram of sequence that allows to identify the states in which the messages are.

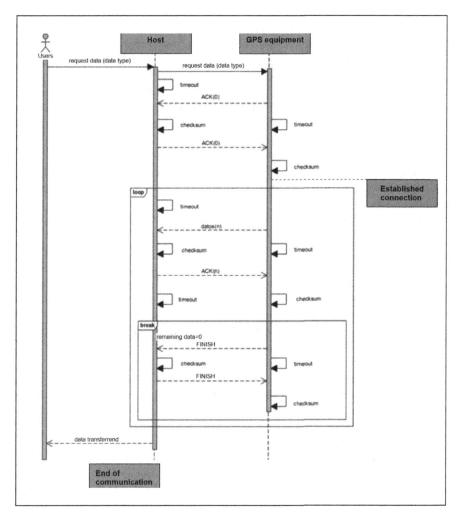

Fig. 4. Ideal sequence.

In addition to the code implemented in the version 1 prototype, an application developed in Python is necessary, on the computer side, to interpret the frames received through the serial port. This application is responsible for replicating the file stored in the microSD memory with an error rate equal to zero, from the active point of view or the beginning of communication.

4 Data Visualization

An application that automates the processing and analysis of the received data related to the athlete's physical performance in its real context was developed, to provide performance metrics of the athletes. The software developed takes as input the data generated by the hardware device, relates them to the profiles of the players, and their respective teams, and then stores them. Once this is done, the data is available to be processed and generate different types of reports, according to the needs of each operator [7].

The modules developed are the following: System configuration, allowing the loading of the club, teams, players, teachers and managers. Generation and loading of events, including games, walks, tests. Identifying mainly if they are of the indoor/outdoor type since those that are developed in closed environments are unable to use the GPS module for global positioning. Generation of profiles to work with load hierarchies and information analysis. Downloading of information from the data collection device and its processing. Generation of reports that allow the analysis of the data through reports, maps and graphics.

The data generated by the sensor are the date and time of the measurement, in UNIX timestamp format, latitude and longitude of the position.

Taking a satellite map as a base and defining a position error between 7.87 and 15.74 inches, two visualization modes are created, on the one hand, a map with markers that on the map shows an indicator of each registered position and on the other hand, a map of heat, which shows the locations and their frequency distribution on the map. To facilitate the analysis of the positions, controls are included to view the map in full screen, to zoom in and out as well as to enable and disable the two modes of graphics. Below each map, summary measures about the event are shown, including the duration of the event, the distance traveled and the average speed. For the IMU, it is only graphed in the reports section, the acceleration in the 3 axes (x,y,z) and as a function of time.

The reports section can be accessed through the main page. Once a team and an event have been selected, a list with all the players can be seen for whom there are files uploaded. This part of the application is one of the most important, as it allows users to view information about a player's performance in an event. By clicking on a player the reports corresponding to that player for that event can be seen. In this section two graphs can be displayed, one shows information from the IMU sensor and the other one about the GPS. It is worth mentioning that, in the case of indoor events, the IMU sensor graph is only available.

The development of a web application was decided, given the ease that it offers at the time of installation and the possibility of usage, not only from a PC but also from smartphones and tablets. The application has a responsive design, which allows adapting its content to the environment where the device is. The programming language selected for the development was Javascript, using the NodeJS [8] framework for the backend and React [9] for the frontend.

In regards to the database, it was decided to opt for a relational model and the database engine chosen was MySQL.

5   Results Obtained

Using prototype version 1, a test of the GPS module was carried out to check the correct operation of the registration and also several tests of transferring files through the USB port. They reflect a zero error rate with a transference time of 480 frames per minute approximately. It was necessary to adapt the prototype to be incorporated into a sports bra (see Fig. 5).

Fig. 5.   Sports bra.

Distancia recorrida: 1871.07m   Duracion: 7.57 minutos   Velocidad promedio: 4.12m/s

Fig. 6.   Web App clipping.

In December 2019 the prototype was tested in the city of Junín, with the collaboration of the UNNOBA women's soccer team. The battery duration did not cause any inconvenience throughout the test. The transfer of the sensed data was carried out via USB through the communication protocol designed and the data from a single-player were displayed as it is shown below (see Fig. 6) to simplify the view.

From the IMU, the acceleration in the 3 axes (x, y, z) is plotted for the sensed event as a function of time (see Fig. 7).

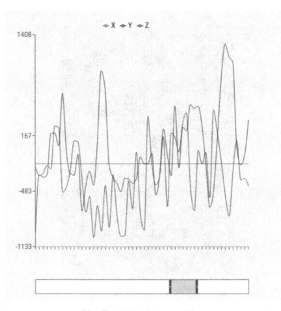

Fig. 7. IMU data graphics.

6   Progress in the Version 2 Prototype

After several tests performed with the version 1 prototype in different scenarios, it is decided to evaluate new platforms to implement version 2.

The chosen platform, after conducting corresponding research and evaluations, it is the NodeMCU ESP32 [10] board since it is superior to the Arduino Nano. Its operating voltage is 3.3 v which simplifies the auxiliary power electronics, has integrated WiFi 802.11b/g/n 2.4 GHz and Bluetooth 4.2-BLE.By using this board,it is possible to reduce the size and weight of the final motherboard.

Prototype version 2 is conceived with the idea of incorporating a cardiac sensor to measure the athlete's pulse. Another objective considered is to transfer the sensed data to the cloud in real-time. This would allow an ecosystem that is easy to understand and use and also obtain information for a fast decision-making process.

Regarding the cardiac sensor, it is necessary to have medical advice to know in detail the techniques used and to be able to define a protocol for performing tests that allow obtaining performance metrics of the sensor, and knowing what level of error it has and what its precision is. This is fundamental since it is a measurement that could be used to define some types of exercises and if a reliable value is not provided, it can cause injuries to the athletes.

The architecture proposed for prototype version 2 can be seen in Fig. 8.

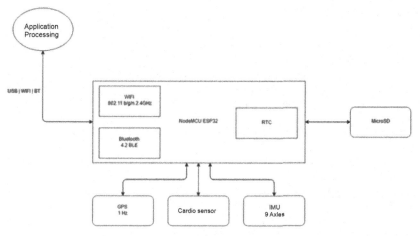

Fig. 8. Physical architecture.

7 Conclusions and Future Works

The reduction of the physical size and weight of the equipment is fundamental for safe use by athletes and this was achieved, among other things, with the use of a lithium cell with a loading and prospecting system integrated into a single module. The hardware obtained in the version I prototype allows adequate use in a sports bra, being its measurements: $4.52 \times 3.34 \times 1.18$ inches and weighing 5.3 oz approximately.

The development of a web application, automating the processing and analysis of the data received relative to the physical performance of the athlete in its real context, allowed to obtain performance metrics of the athletes and the decision-making of the different actors involved meditate the analysis of information sensed and visualized in a geo-referenced way.

The partial results obtained show that the Arduino Nano platform is not the one best choice to carry out the necessary processing. The RAM usage is about 98% (calculated based on stack pointers), which means that data cannot be processed or that the necessary functionalities cannot be implemented. As a result, it is impossible to use the IMU magnetometer due to not having enough memory to run the calibration routine.

Work continues on the version 2 prototype, conceived with the idea of incorporating a cardiac sensor to measure the athlete's pulse. The objective of achieving automatic transfer in real-time of the sensed data to the cloud is taken into account, to achieve an ecosystem that is easy to understand and use, allowing information to be obtained to allow fast decision-making.

Another point to be developed is the definition of additional tests to validate both prototypes in different environments and under different conditions and with the feedback of athletes, technical directors, medical specialists, etc.

References

1. Igor Van de Griendt Net Worth, Catapult. https://es.wallmine.com/asx/cat/officer/1654428/igor-van-de-griendt. Accessed 1 Feb 2021
2. Santos, L., et al.: GPS device for monitoring sports performance. In: 2020 XXIVI Congreso Argentino de Ciencias de la Computación CACIC2020, La Matanza, pp. 590–598 (2020)
3. Datasheet TP5100 - Dual battery charger. https://voltiq.ru/datasheets/TP5100-datashhet.pdf. Accessed 1 Nov 2019
4. Lithium batteries. https://es.wikipedia.org/wiki/Bater%C3%ADa_de_ion_de_litio. Accessed 1 Nov 2019
5. Datasheet HC-06 –Bluetooth Module. https://www.olimex.com/Products/Components/RF/BLUETOOTH-SERIAL-HC-06/resources/hc06.pdf. Accessed 1 Nov 2019
6. Wikipedia contributors. (s.f.). Communication protocol. https://es.wikipedia.org/wiki/Protocolo_de_comunicaciones. Accessed 1 Oct 2019
7. Capelli, M., Gómez, F.: GPS applied to sport. In: Junin, Argentina: National University of the Northwest of the Province of Buenos Aires, School of Technology (2020)
8. NodeJs Documentation. https://nodejs.org/es/. Accessed 18 June 2020
9. React. https://es.reactjs.org/. Accesed 08 Jan 2020
10. Datasheet ESP32-WROOM-32 - 32bit MCU & 2.4 GHz Wi-Fi & BT/BLE SoCs. https://www.alldatasheet.com/datasheet-pdf/pdf/1148023/ESPRESSIF/ESP32.html. Accessed 21 Feb 2021

Idle Time Administration on FreeRTOS Using Slack Stealing

Francisco E. Páez[1]([✉]) [iD], José M. Urriza[1] [iD], and Javier D. Orozco[2,3] [iD]

[1] Depto. de Informática, Fac. de Ingeniería,
Universidad Nacional de la Patagonia San Juan Bosco,
Puerto Madryn, Argentina
fpaez@unpata.edu.ar, josemurriza@unp.edu.ar
[2] Depto. de Ingeniería Eléctrica y Computadoras,
Universidad Nacional del Sur, Bahía Blanca, Argentina
[3] CONICET, Buenos Aires, Argentina

Abstract. The need to enrich and maximize the performance of embedded systems have led to the integration of tasks with dissimilar temporal requirements. Several techniques have been developed for scheduling this heterogeneous task sets, using the idle time left by the execution of critical real-time tasks. One of such methods is Slack Stealing, which allows exact or approximate calculation of the available idle time. In this work we present an implementation of an exact variant of this technique on the FreeRTOS real-time operating system that requires minor modifications to its kernel. This allows to give priority execution to non-real-time tasks without compromising the critical real-time tasks deadlines, when scheduled under the Rate Monotonic or Deadline Monotonic priority assignments. Evaluations done on an mbed LPC1768 development board shows that the computational costs overheads introduced to the default context-switch are not significant for utilization factors up to 80%.

Keywords: RTS · Slack stealing · RTOS

1 Introduction

Nowadays, there exists an increasingly need to maximize the performance of embedded systems, especially in fields like Internet of Things (IoT). To accomplish this without increasing the development costs, an efficient administration of the system resources is a must. Nevertheless, it is common to find that many embedded systems have their hardware design over-provisioned. As result, resources like the CPU lie idle, instead of being used to satisfy other requirements. Furthermore, if no energy saving techniques are employed, then a large amount of power is wasted.

In the last decades, several methods and techniques have been developed to address the jointly scheduling of critical real-time tasks ($RTTs$) and tasks with other kind of requirements [1,2]. This heterogeneity of tasks requires that the

© Springer Nature Switzerland AG 2021
P. Pesado and J. Eterovic (Eds.): CACIC 2020, CCIS 1409, pp. 275–289, 2021.
https://doi.org/10.1007/978-3-030-75836-3_19

scheduler manages at less two distinct task sets: $RTTs$ and non-real-time tasks ($NRTTs$) which likely must satisfy some Quality of Service (QoS) requirements, like priority attention or fault-tolerance. The system scheduler must do its best effort to satisfy the QoS of the $NRTTs$, without compromising the execution of the $RTTs$. This requires an efficient administration of the idle time, which appears when the $RTTs$ do not saturate the microprocessor. In consequence, classical schedulers like a cyclic executive are not adequate to fulfill the complex requirements of this kind of heterogeneous task-sets.

The simplest technique to handle the $NRTTs$ is to simply execute them when no $RTTs$ are ready to execute, known as a *background scheduling*. Nevertheless, this technique could not satisfy any QoS for the $NRTTs$. The most known technique for this is the use of servers. In general, a server is implemented as a periodic task which uses it execution budget to run $NRTTs$. This server task is usually configured with the maximum possible priority, and the size of its budget is calculated offline. Example of these technique are the Priority Exchange Server [19], the Deferrable Server [23], the Extended Priority Exchange [23], the Sporadic Server [20], or the Total Bandwidth Server [21], among others. A different strategy is presented in [5], using a multilevel scheduler.

Another technique is Slack Stealing (SS), which have online and offline variants, of exact or approximate precision. It uses the execution predictability of the Rate Monotonic (RM) [10] and Deadline Monotonic (DM) [8] priority assignments to bring forward a portion of the future idle time, without compromising the temporal constraints of the critical $RTTs$. It calculates at a time t the future idle times of a task i before the deadline of its next activation. This calculation assumes the task's worst-case execution time ($WCET$) [27], but it is possible to reclaim any gained time after its execution. This idle time is called the *available slack of the task i at time t*, denoted $AS_i(t)$. The lowest of these values among all the $RTTs$ is called the *system available slack at time t*, denoted $AS(t)$. This is the maximum amount of time that can be used at time t to execute $NRTTs$ whilst preserving the temporal constraints of all $RTTs$. The available slacks calculated when all the tasks demand execution at the same time (known as *critical instant*, usually at $t = 0$ when no jitter or offset is considered) is denoted K_i, as is the same value calculated at [16].

The first SS algorithm was proposed in [7,18] by Lehoczky and Ramos-Thuel. A drawback of these works is the requirement of memory vectors in the order of the system hyperperiod, limiting it use to task sets with a short one. Later, Davis presented in [3,4] a substantial enhancement, which reduces the memory requirements to the order of the number of tasks, but still with a large computational cost. In a later work, Tia et al. [24] presented a new SS algorithm, not feasible for online use given its large memory requirements. The contribution of that work was two theorems that proven that no online algorithm could apply a uniform optimization criterion that minimizes the response time of all $NRTTs$ nor can be their mean response time minimized either. More recently, [26] proposed several enhancements that significantly reduce both temporal and spatial costs, allowing the exact calculation of the available slack to be performed online.

In this work we present an implementation of *SS* methods on the FreeRTOS[1] real-time operating system (*RTOS*) to facilitate the scheduling of heterogeneous real-time systems (*RTS*). FreeRTOS was chosen based on its popularity, excellent portability among many different architectures, well documented source code and open-source license that allows to introduce modifications. Moreover, FreeRTOS has a small footprint and low memory and processing requirements.

This work is organized as follows: Sect. 2 present previous and related works. Section 3 describes the system's design and implementation. Section 4 shows an example execution. The evaluations performed and their results are presented on Sect. 5. Finally, the conclusions and future work are presented Sect. 6.

2   Previous and Related Works

This work improves the implementation presented on [17]. The *SS* support is added into the kernel without modifications to existing code, the application programmer interface is simplified and new tests and evaluations are presented.

Previous works about implementations of *SS* methods could be found in the literature. For example, approximate slack algorithms are implemented for MarteOS [15], LejosRT [14] and the Real-Time Specification for Java [11–13]. Implementation of an exact *SS* method is presented on [6]. Other works like [9] implements *SS* algorithms on the Linux kernel.

The major contribution of this work is the implementation of an *exact* and *low-cost SS* method on an popular *RTOS* for embedded systems with modest hardware resources.

3   Implementation

All the new functions and data structures are logically organized in one module, exposing only a minimum set of functions to the application programmer. Since version 10, FreeRTOS allows developers to include their own functions and data structures, through a file named `freertos_task_c_additions.h` which is included into the kernel source. Although only two kernel functions need to be replaced, all the auxiliary functions and data structures are implemented in this file for performance reasons. The prototypes of the functions used by the application programmer were added into a separated `slack.h` header file. The Fig. 1 illustrates the design.

3.1   Task Model

The tasks are organized as *RTTs*, *NRTT* and background-tasks (*BTs*).

---

[1] https://www.freertos.org.

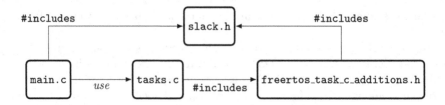

Fig. 1. Implementation on FreeRTOS using the *task additions* header file.

Table 1. *RTT* attributes.

Attribute	Description
Task type	*RTT* o *NRTT*
i	Unique numerical identifier
T_i	Period
D_i	Relative deadline
C_i	*WCET*
R_i	worst-case response time (*WCRT*)
K_i	Available slack at time $t = 0$
d_i	Absolute deadline
l_i	Release time of the current instance
$c_i(t_c)$	Current instance executed time at time t_c
n_i	Release counter
$AS_i(t_c)$	Available slack of the task at time t_c

The *RTTs* are those that have critical time constraints, so the time at which the results are expected is as critical as its correctness [22]. The *RTTs* should follow the model presented in [10], of periodic and independent tasks. Each *RTT* generates an infinite series of instances (also known as *releases*), being $j_{k,i}$ the k-th instance of the *RTT* i. The *RTTs* must be scheduled using the *RM* or *DM* static priority assignments. Table 1 shows the additional attributes required for each *RTT*.

The *NRTTs* have no expected model as is application dependent and should execute if and only if there is enough available slack. The *BTs* are those that executes with the lowest priority and are not accounted on the available slack calculation.

3.2   FreeRTOS Configuration

To support the execution of the *SS* method, the following configuration options of FreeRTOS must be enabled:

- Thread Local Storage (*TLS*): to add additional properties to each task.
- Tasks Additions: to include new functions into the kernel and invoke additional initialization code at the scheduler start.

The application programmer could also configure the following configuration parameters:

- configUSE_SLACK_METHOD: the slack method to use. Two methods are provided: the low-cost exact method presented on [26] (default) and Davis [4].
- configMIN_SLACK_SD: the lower threshold of available slack. The *NRTT* will be executed if and only if the amount of available slack is higher than this value. The default value is 1.
- configMAX_SLACK_PRIO: how many priority levels are reserved for the *NRTT*. The default the value is 1.

3.3 Additional Data Structures

Extended Task Control Block. The task's type (*RTT* or *NRTT*) and the properties defined in the task model are specified in a data structure called SsTCB. Each task has an instance of this structure added to its Task Control Block (*TCB*) using the *TLS* functionality.

New Task Lists. Three new task lists are required. They are implemented using the FreeRTOS List_t data type so that they could be accessed with the list API provided by FreeRTOS. Each list element has an attribute xItemValue, used to order the element inside the list and a pointer pvOwner, that references the object represented by the element, in this case the *TCB* of a task. The new task lists are:

- xSsTaskList: contains references to all the *RTTs* and is used to simplify the calculation of the available slack.
- xDeadlineTaskList: contains the absolute deadline of each *RTT*, ordered by the most recent deadline first. It is used for the online deadline verification.
- xSlackDelayedTaskList: contains references to all the *NRTT* whose execution is suspended because of insufficient available slack. These tasks will be moved to the ready task list when the system available slack is greater than the configured threshold. It is called the *slack delayed* list.

3.4 Kernel Modifications

The available slack calculation is performed at the scheduler first execution, and then at the finalization of each task instance. Moreover, the available slack is updated periodically using the counter system described in [4].

The following kernel functions were modified:

- vTaskDelayUntil(): this function is used to implement strict periodicity of tasks. As it is invoked to finish a task's instance execution, it was modified to perform the available slack calculation.

- xTaskIncrementTick(): this function is called by the FreeRTOS portable layer each time a clock interrupt occurs. It manages the tick count and the activation of tasks. It was modified to update the slack counters and to perform the deadline verification.
- vTaskSchedulerStart(): this function start the execution of the scheduler. The initial slack calculation was added using a *hook*.

vTaskSchedulerStart(). To avoid modifications to this function, the FreeRTOS macro FREERTOS_TASKS_C_ADDITIONS_INIT() was used to call the function vSlackSchedulerSetup() which executes the following actions:

- Calculates the *WCRT* of each *RTT*, using the method presented on [25].
- Verify that the *RTT* set is schedulable based on the *WCRT* values.
- Calculates the initial available slack (K) for each *RTT*.

vTaskDelayUntil(). As the slack calculation should be performed atomically (otherwise, the calculated available slack would be erroneous) and the execution of this function could not be preempted by higher priority tasks, it is the best place it. The actions added are:

- Update the absolute deadline of the task as the absolute deadline of its following release.
- Calculate the available slack. This is the costliest operation.
- Add any gained time to the slack counters of the lower priority *RTT* and update the available slack of the system.
- Resume the execution of the *NRTT* if the available slack of the system is greater than the configured threshold.
- Reset the accumulated execution time of the task.

xTaskIncrementTick(). This function was modified to perform the following actions:

- Perform the deadline verification of all *RTTs* ready to execute or suspended.
- If a new instance is released, increment the instance counter of the task.
- Increment the execution counter of the current task.
- Reduce the available slack counters.
- Suspend the execution of all the *NRTT* if the available slack of the system its lesser than the configured threshold or resume their execution if its greater.

The Fig. 2 shows when the modified functions are invoked:

The previous kernel functions are replaced by the modified versions using the *wrap* option of the GCC compiler. This option instructs the linker to replace all references to a function with the specified one when linking the application binary.

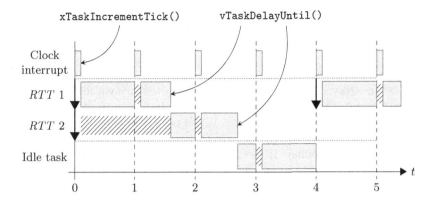

Fig. 2. Example execution of two RTT showing when the available slack is calculated and when the counters are updated.

3.5   Supporting Functions

The following support functions are provided to update the slack counters and move $NRTTs$ from one task-list to another:

- `vSlackDecrementTaskSlack(i, n)`: Reduces by n ticks the slack counter of the $RTTs$ with higher priority than i.
- `vSlackDecrementAllTasksSlack(n)`: Reduces by n ticks the slack counter of all the $RTTs$.
- `vSlackGainSlack(i, n)`: Add n ticks to the slack counters of the $RTTs$ with lower priority than i.
- `vSlackUpdateAvailableSlack()`: Updates the system-wide available slack.
- `vTaskSlackSuspend()`: Moves all the ready-to-execute $NRTTs$ from the ready task list into the slack delayed list.
- `vTaskSlackResume()`: Moves all the RTT tasks from the slack delayed list into the ready task list.

3.6   Application Programmer Interface

The application programmer must call the `vSlackSetTaskParams()` function to set the additional parameters required for each task: type (RTT or $NRTT$), $WCET$, period and deadline. Also, a macro `pvSlackGetTaskSsTCB()` is defined to retrieve the `SsTCB` associated with a task.

The application programmer needs to provide a implementation of the function `vApplicationNotSchedulable()`, which is called when the schedulability test fails. Note that the scheduling evaluation do not consider the context switch costs and is only used as a validation of the RTT model.

3.7   Scheduling

The FreeRTOS scheduler uses, by default, a preemptive *FIFO* with priorities scheduling policy. The scheduler guarantees that the highest ready priority task at any given time is *always* chosen for execution. The ready task list is implemented as an array of lists. Given m priorities, the array's first element (at index zero) contains the lowest priority tasks list, and the last element (at index $m - 1$) contains the highest priority list. When two or more tasks with the same priority are ready to execute, by default they will share processing time using a Round Robin (*RR*) policy. If the application writer turned preemption off a *FIFO* policy is used instead.

The ready task list is modified as follows. The n highest priorities are reserved for the *NRTTs*. These tasks will be ready to execute (that is, they will be present on the ready task list) if and only if there is enough available slack on the system. If this is not the case, the *NRTTs* are moved into the slack delayed list. The remaining priority range $(m - n, 1]$ is assigned to the *RTTs*, with the restriction of only one task per priority. The Fig. 3 illustrates the organization.

This way, if a *NRTT* is ready to execute and there is enough available slack, it has priority over any *RTT*. This is a *greedy* use of the available slack for scheduling.

The lowest priority tasks are only executed when no *NRTTs* or *RTTs* are ready to execute. These *BTs* are not accounted on the available slack calculation.

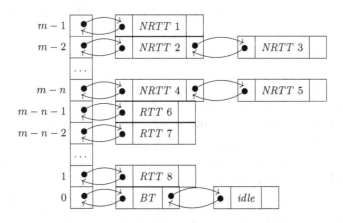

Fig. 3. Ready task list organization.

4   Example Execution

The following example illustrates the scheduling of a heterogeneous *RTS* using *SS*. For clarity purposes large periods and execution times were used. The system is composed of 4 *RTTs*, with periods of 3, 4, 6 and 12 s, and *WCET* of 1 s each.

The actual run-time of each task instance is random. These $RTTs$ are scheduled using RM along with two aperiodic $NRTTs$, TA1 and TA2, that have random execution times of at most 2 s. Figure 4 shows the graphical trace of the execution on a *mbed* LPC1768 development board, generated with Tracealyzer v3.1.2[2].

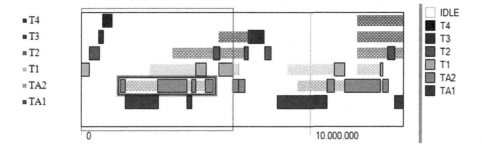

Fig. 4. Example execution trace generated with Tracealyzer.

The trace shows how the first instance of TA2 is preempted by the first two instances of TA1. Also, both $NRTTs$ have priority over the second instance of T1. But when the system available slack is depleted, the execution of TA2 is suspended and the second instance of T1 is executed, as it cannot longer be postponed or otherwise its deadline could be missed. As the actual run-time of T1 was less than its $WCET$, the gained time is added to the system available slack, and as result TA2 execution can be safely resumed. It can be seen too that at time $t = 12$ all the $NRTTs$ are postponed by the execution of the third instance of TA2.

The Fig. 5 shows the joint scheduling of 4 $RTTs$ and one $NRTT$, along with the variation of available slack of the system. It can be seen at time $t = 6$ how the available slack is consumed by the execution of the $NRTT$ until it is depleted.

5   Performance Evaluation

To measure the costs introduced by the proposed modifications, several evaluations were performed on a *mbed* LPC1768 development board (ARM Cortex-M3 at 96 Mhz and 32 Kbytes of RAM) using FreeRTOS v10.4.2. The test program on the board receives the tasks parameters from the computer through the serial port, create the tasks, and launch the scheduler. When the execution finish, it sends back the data to the computer. The board is then restarted, and the next task-set is transmitted.

A set of 900 RTS was evaluated, divided in ten groups of 100 RTS for each utilization factor (UF) from 10% to 90% in steps of 10%. Each task-set is composed of 10 $RTTs$, which periods follow a uniform distribution between 25

---

[2] https://percepio.com/tracealyzer/.

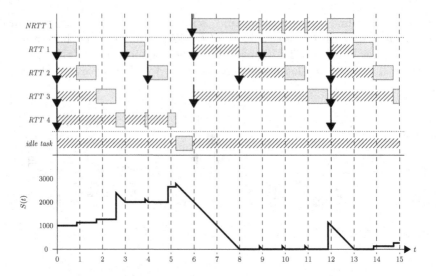

Fig. 5. Variation of the system's available slack at execution time.

and 1000 ticks. The *WCET* of each task follows a uniform distribution up to 50% of its period. For all the tasks the relative deadline is equal to its period ($T_i = D_i$). The tasks were scheduled using *RM* and the exact *SS* method proposed in [26] was used.

To evaluate the computational cost overhead added to the context switch, the amount of CPU cycles elapsed since the invocation to `vTaskDelayUntil()` until the next ready-task is fully loaded was measured. The CPU cycles were counted using the Clock Cycle Counter (*CYCCNT*) provided by the Data Watchpoint and Trace (*DWT*) interface of the Cortex-M3. The first 30 instances of each task were measured. The clock interruption was configured at 1 ms, so the time slice between two clock interrupts is of approximate 96000 CPU cycles. The test was performed under three configurations:

- FreeRTOS without modifications, used for reference.
- Performing the available slack calculation at each task instance finalization.
- At each instance finalization of a *RTT i*, update its available slack counter with K_i. This way the cost of the modifications is measured independently of the *SS* algorithm used. This is also an approximate slack algorithm.

5.1   Results and Discussion

The Table 2 resumes the results of the evaluations and the Fig. 6 shows the context switch costs grouped by *UF* when performing the available slack calculation.

The results shows that the mean slack calculation cost increases with the *UF* in a similar way that the simulations performed on [26]. Even for a *UF* of 90%, the mean cost of the available slack calculation is below the 3% of a time slice.

Table 2. Context-switch cost as CPU cycles for each test configuration and *UF*.

UF (%)	Online			Counters			FreeRTOS		
	Mean	Best	Worst	Mean	Best	Worst	Mean	Best	Worst
10	1348.2	596	3783	575.6	511	601	558.4	495	578
20	1478.6	596	5111	574.9	511	601	557.7	495	578
30	1605.8	596	6713	574.2	511	601	557.1	495	578
40	1712.9	596	7162	573.9	511	601	556.7	495	578
50	1825.1	596	8461	573.5	511	601	556.2	495	578
60	1967.6	600	13523	572.6	511	601	555.4	495	578
70	2070.2	596	13859	571.6	511	601	554.4	495	578
80	2219.6	600	21305	570.3	511	601	553.2	495	578
90	2411.5	596	24675	566.6	511	601	550.3	495	578

Context-switch cost with slack calculation

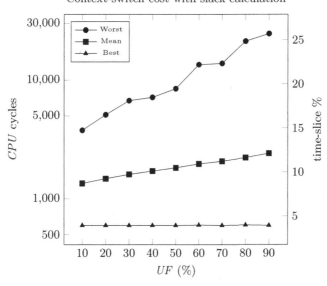

Fig. 6. Context-switch cost as CPU cycles when performing the available slack calculation.

The cost of the context switch without performing the online available slack calculation remained bounded between constants values and in the same order of magnitude that the FreeRTOS context-switch.

If we look instead at the worst-case execution times, the cost increases notably. Nevertheless, the mayor contributor are the slack calculations performed by the lower priority *RTTs*. Figure 7 shows that tasks 7, 8, 9 and 10 have calculations that have a cost of more than the 5% of the time-slice.

Slack calculation cost as % of the time-slice

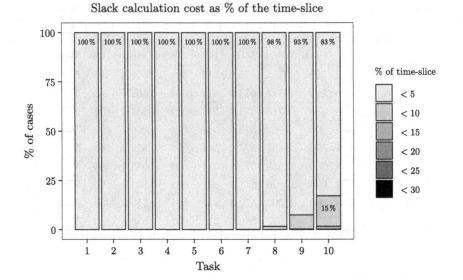

Fig. 7. Slack calculation cost as a percentage of the time-slice per task.

Even for the lowest priority *RTTs*, the worst costs only appear on task-sets with a high *UF*. Although for a 90% *UF* the context switch cost can be as much as 30% of the time-slice, in the tests only 1% of the slack calculations incurs in this cost. Moreover, in the tests only a 5% of the calculations on task-sets with a 90% *UF* have a cost higher than the 10% of the time slice (Fig. 8).

Cost as % of the time-slice for tasks 6 to 10

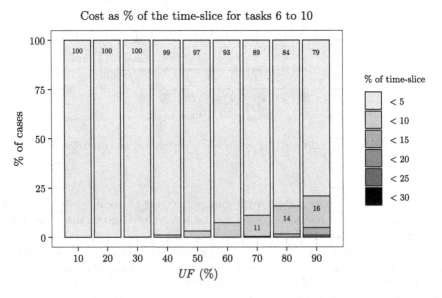

Fig. 8. Slack calculation cost as a percentage of the time-slice for tasks 6 to 10 per *UF*.

As the slack calculation is performed when a RTT instance finish its execution, it can be easily added as part of the task $WCET$.

6   Conclusions

Many systems do not use to the fullest the available CPU time, and this idle time could be used to satisfy other requirements. To accomplish this heterogeneous scheduling an efficient administration of the idle time is needed. Although the use of a $RTOS$ relieves the application programmer of the burden of activities like scheduling or inter-task communications, they offer limited scheduling policies options to handle this kind of systems. To solve this, an exact idle time administration using SS methods on FreeRTOS was presented. The evaluations shows that the costs overheads introduced to the context switch are not significant.

In future works, we will implement and evaluate new lower-cost SS algorithms and study how they could be used to solve specific problems, like fault-tolerance, energy saving or imprecise computing, among others.

The source code, examples and the test code and data can be downloaded from: https://github.com/unpsjb-rtsg/slack-freertos.

References

1. Burns, A., Davis, R.I.: A survey of research into mixed criticality systems. ACM Comput. Surv. **50**(6), 82:1–82:37 (2017). https://doi.org/10.1145/3131347
2. Buttazzo, G.C.: Research trends in real-time computing for embedded systems. SIGBED Rev. **3**(3), 1–10 (2006). https://doi.org/10.1145/1164050.1164052
3. Davis, R.I.: Approximate slack stealing algorithms for fixed priority preemptive systems. University of York, Department of Computer Science (1993)
4. Davis, R.I., Tindell, K., Burns, A.: Scheduling slack time in fixed priority preemptive systems. In: Proceedings of the Real-Time Systems Symposium, Raleigh-Durham, NC, December 1993, pp. 222–231 (1993). https://doi.org/10.1109/REAL.1993.393496
5. Davis, R.I., Wellings, A.J.: Dual priority scheduling. In: Proceedings of the 16th IEEE Real-Time Systems Symposium, Palazzo dei Congressi, Via Matteotti, 1, Pisa, Italy, 4–7 December 1995, pp. 100–109. IEEE Computer Society (1995). https://doi.org/10.1109/REAL.1995.495200
6. Díaz, L.A., Páez, José, F.E., Urriza, J.M., Orozco, J.D., Cayssials, R.: Implementación de un Método de Slack Stealing en el Kernel de MaRTE OS. In: Proceeding XLIII Jornadas Argentinas de Informática e Investigación Operativa (43 JAIIO) - III Argentine Symposium on Industrial Informatics (SII), pp. 13–24 (2014)
7. Lehoczky, J.P., Ramos-Thuel, S.: An optimal algorithm for scheduling soft-aperiodic tasks in fixed-priority preemptive systems. In: Proceedings of the Real-Time Systems Symposium - 1992, Phoenix, Arizona, USA, December 1992, pp. 110–123. IEEE Computer Society (1992). https://doi.org/10.1109/REAL.1992.242671
8. Leung, J.Y.-T., Whitehead, J.: On the complexity of fixed-priority scheduling of periodic, real-time tasks. Perform. Eval. **2**(4), 237–250 (1982). https://doi.org/10.1016/0166-5316(82)90024-4

9. Lin, C., Brandt, S.A.: Improving soft real-time performance through better slack reclaiming. In: Proceedings of the 26th IEEE Real-Time Systems Symposium, RTSS 2005, Miami, FL, USA, 6–8 December 2005, pp. 410–421. IEEE Computer Society (2005). https://doi.org/10.1109/RTSS.2005.26

10. Liu, C.L., Layland, J.W.: Scheduling algorithms for multiprogramming in a hard-real-time environment. J. ACM **20**(1), 46–61 (1973). https://doi.org/10.1145/321738.321743

11. Masson, D., Midonnet, S.: Slack time evaluation with RTSJ. In: Wainwright, R.L., Haddad, H. (eds.) Proceedings of the 2008 ACM Symposium on Applied Computing (SAC), Fortaleza, Ceara, Brazil, 16–20 March 2008, pp. 322–323. ACM (2008). https://doi.org/10.1145/1363686.1363769

12. Masson, D., Midonnet, S.: Userland approximate slack stealer with low time complexity. In: RTNS 2008, pp. 29–38, Rennes, France, October 2008. https://hal-upec-upem.archives-ouvertes.fr/hal-00620349

13. Masson, D., Midonnet, S.: Handling non-periodic events in real-time Java systems. In: Higuera-Toledano, M., Wellings, A. (eds.) Distributed, Embedded and Real-time Java Systems, pp. 45–77. Springer, Boston (2012). https://doi.org/10.1007/978-1-4419-8158-5_3

14. Midonnet, S., Masson, D., Lassalle, R.: Slack-time computation for temporal robustness in embedded systems. Embed. Syst. Lett. **2**(4), 119–122 (2010). https://doi.org/10.1109/LES.2010.2074184

15. Minguet, A.R.E.: Extensiones al Lenguaje Ada y a los Servicios POSIX para Planificación en Sistemas de Tiempo Real Estricto. Ph.D. thesis, Universidad Politécnica de Valencia (2003)

16. Orozco, J., Santos, R., Santos, J., Cayssials, R.: Taking advantage of priority inversions generated to improve the processing of non-hard real-time tasks in mixed systems. In: The 21st IEEE Real-Time Systems Symposium WIP, pp. 13–16 (2000)

17. Páez, F.E., Urriza, J.M., Orozco, J.D.: Administración del Tiempo Ocioso Mediante Slack Stealing en FreeRTOS. In: XXVI Congreso Argentino de Ciencias de la Computación - CACIC 2020. Libro de actas, pp. 629–638 (2020)

18. Ramos-Thuel, S., Lehoczky, J.P.: Online scheduling of hard deadline aperiodic tasks in fixed-priority systems. In: Proceedings of the Real-Time Systems Symposium, Raleigh-Durham, NC, December 1993, pp. 160–171 (1993). https://doi.org/10.1109/REAL.1993.393504

19. Sprunt, B., Lehoczky, J.P., Sha, L.: Exploiting unused periodic time for aperiodic service using the extended priority exchange algorithm. In: Proceedings of the 9th IEEE Real-Time Systems Symposium, RTSS 1988, Huntsville, Alabama, USA, 6–8 December 1988, pp. 251–258. IEEE Computer Society (1988). https://doi.org/10.1109/REAL.1988.51120

20. Sprunt, B., Sha, L., Lehoczky, J.: Aperiodic task scheduling for hard-real-time systems. Real-Time Syst. **1**(1), 27–60 (1989). https://doi.org/10.1007/BF02341920

21. Spuri, M., Buttazzo, G.C.: Scheduling aperiodic tasks in dynamic priority systems. Real-Time Syst. **10**(2), 179–210 (1996). https://doi.org/10.1007/BF00360340

22. Stankovic, J.A.: Misconceptions about real-time computing: a serious problem for next-generation systems. Computer **21**(10), 10–19 (1988). https://doi.org/10.1109/2.7053

23. Strosnider, J., Lehoczky, J., Sha, L.: The deferrable server algorithm for enhanced aperiodic responsiveness in hard real-time environments. IEEE Trans. Comput. **44**(1), 73–91 (1995). https://doi.org/10.1109/12.368008

24. Tia, T.-S., Liu, J.W.-S., Shankar, M.: Algorithms and optimality of scheduling soft aperiodic requests in fixed-priority preemptive systems. Real-Time Syst. **10**(1), 23–43 (1996). https://doi.org/10.1007/BF00357882

25. Urriza, J.M., Páez, F.E., Ferrari, M., Cayssials, R., Orozco, J.D.: A new RM/DM low cost schedulability test. In: 2017 Eight Argentine Symposium and Conference on Embedded Systems (CASE), pp. 1–6 (2017). https://doi.org/10.23919/SASE-CASE.2017.8115368

26. Urriza, J.M., Paez, F.E., Cayssials, R., Orozco, J.D., Schorb, L.S.: Low cost slack stealing method for RM/DM. Int. Rev. Comput. Softw. **5**(6), 660–667 (2010)

27. Wilhelm, R., et al.: The worst-case execution-time problem - overview of methods and survey of tools. ACM Trans. Embed. Comput. Syst. **7**(3), 36:1–36:53 (2008). https://doi.org/10.1145/1347375.1347389

Innovation in Computer Science
Education

Applying Augmented Reality to Learn Basic Concepts of Programming in U-Learning Environment

Denis Acosta⬤, Margarita Álvarez$^{(\boxtimes)}$ ⬤, and Elena Durán⬤

Research Institute in Informatic and Information System, Faculty of Exact Science and Technology, National University of Santiago del Estero, Santiago del Estero, Argentina
{alvarez,eduran}@unse.edu.ar

Abstract. Learning the basic concept of programming, such as control structures, is considered difficult due to their complexity and require a high level of students' abstraction. Faced with this problem and taking advantage of ubiquitous learning that allows learning without being limited to a specific space or time, developing a ubiquitous learning app that helps students learn these concepts more tangible for them has been considered challenging. For this reason, we developed a software application (App) that, through augmented reality techniques, shows an object to the student, who must move in search of it. As a result, the App generates a program with the actions carried out. This article presents the ubiquitous learning App and the principal modules' development: the compilation module and the 3D manager module. The first one allows translating the student's cell phone's geographical coordinates into a programming language's instructions. The second one allows the student to visualize the objects using augmented reality. The tests carried out on both modules are also shown, demonstrating the feasibility of translating the actions and displaying the objects.

Keywords: Ubiquitous learning · Augmented reality · Control structure · Geo-localization

1 Introduction

By ubiquitous learning (UL) can be understood, one that is not limited to a specific context or is conditioned by a particular space, but the acquisition of new knowledge can occur in any situation in which the subject is, regardless of the moment and place [1]. The UL allows students to access all kinds of information through interaction with the objects surrounding it, whether physical or virtual [2]. Encourage collaboration, connect formal, non-formal, and informal spaces; and, relocates the location of learning, both inside and outside the classroom, and adapts the contents, presentations, and activities to the students' characteristics and context.

On the other hand, augmented reality (AR) is the technology that improves and enriches users' perception and interaction with the physical world by complementing it with virtual 3D objects that seem to coexist in the physical world [3]. This technology

© Springer Nature Switzerland AG 2021
P. Pesado and J. Eterovic (Eds.): CACIC 2020, CCIS 1409, pp. 293–307, 2021.
https://doi.org/10.1007/978-3-030-75836-3_20

is generally used with ubiquitous and mobile technologies and has found a vibrant application in education. Thus, the combination of mobile and portable devices, AR and UL, provide immersive learning, enriched, situated, and fluid learning experiences [4].

The learning activities associated with programming are recognized that present a high degree of difficulty. Several studies have determined that the causes that generate this problem are related to specific characteristics that occur in the classroom and with particular cognitive skills relevant to learn the fundamentals of programming. Among them are abstraction capacity, an excellent logical-mathematical aptitude, and the facility for solving algorithmic problems [5].

Given the problems raised and taking advantage of UA and AR provide, we considered the challenge to develop an App supporting students in learning the basic programming concepts. This App shows the student the algorithms he/she performs when he/she moves in a particular environment, using the microlearning approach, which proposes learning with relatively short efforts and takes little time [6]. Thus, the App shows an object that the student must obtain using AR techniques. The student walks to the thing, and as a result, the App generates a program with the actions carried out. In [7], we present the App's architecture, which provides a compilation module. It takes inputs from the student's cell phone sensors, and then they are manipulated and processed by the sensor module. It translates them into a program written in the language designed to such an end. This last represented a significant challenge, as there is currently no tool to make this translation possible. In [7], we also present the development and validation of the compilation module. The App also consists of a 3D manager module that allows inserting and manipulating objects with AR, a user interface module, and the main module. In this paper, we present in detail these modules.

The interaction with the App provides the student with an immediate response, favoring the student experimentation in the real world and quickly forming a mental model thanks to the tool's answers.

In the following sections, we cite antecedents of related works, present the architecture, and design and develop the App modules. Finally, we have shown the tests carried out and expressed some conclusions regarding the work carried out and future actions.

2 The Background

This section presents the background of software applications for teaching the basics of AR-based programming; and some antecedents of works related to the learning of informatics and computational issues through UL.

In [8], the authors present a flexible U-learning mobile application for students to access the material. The authors adopted computational thinking (PC) to help students develop practical computing skills. They chose three classes of first-year students for the empirical study. They were divided into three groups: two experimental groups (UL&PC group and PC group) and a control group. Based on this study results, students who received UL treatment might have significantly better computer skills using PowerPoint and Word than those who did not. However, PC's treatment did not result in better development of the students' computer skills in this investigation.

In [9], a customized UL support system based on multiple information sources is proposed to encourage college students to take computer programming courses. It includes a new technique that integrates student learning problems, knowledge level, and learning style to personalize learning paths that offer students their programming concepts.

In [10], the requirements necessary to support UL with existing software tools for teaching and learning computer programming to children between 4 and 10 years of age are identified. Twenty-two tools were analyzed and contrasted with UL's five known characteristics: permanence, accessibility, immediacy, interactivity, and awareness of the context. On a final note, they recommend adding UL features in kids' programming tools.

Boonbrahm et al. [11] developed a tool to learn the primary flow of commands and control structures, including sequence, selection, and iteration structures. Using the tool, students construct a program flow diagram using AR markers. The developed software captures the image of the flow chart that the student has built, processes the program, and shows the result of the command's execution. The tool identifies the command, the variable value, and the Boolean operator. Then, the software simulates each command's result, and thus the student can check if the program's logic is correct.

In [12], educational material has been developed using AR to teach basic programming concepts. The theme developed was Control structures, and AR exploration activities were carried out using previously printed markers. It was also evaluated by the teachers of the first-year chairs related to the teaching of programming.

In work presented by Tan and Lee [13], they argue that using AR in teaching basic programming concepts is very appropriate. The article analyzes a survey of students enrolled in computer programs at Sunway University in 2016. The results indicate that students have moderate participation when traditional methods are used to teach programming concepts. Moreover, the results were determined, too, that 80% of the students agreed that the AR learning method is useful because it provides more fun, interest, and a basic understanding for students to learn to program.

Da-Ren Chen et al. [14] study show the use of AR technology to create virtual objects for mobile devices. This study provides students with contextual information related to the outdoor learning environment. The ubiquitous system developed is for the tourism area. Context-awareness was used to allow students to follow learning activities along a predetermined path, using AR features. The goal is to provide students with a friendly, interactive interface and engaging means to stimulate intrinsic motivation and learning performance.

In the background review carried out, we did not find works presenting UL experiences with AR in programming concepts or software applications for this purpose.

On the other hand, although there are applications that translate geographic coordinates, no antecedents have been found for converting such units to a programming language such as the one proposed in this work.

3   U-Learning App

3.1   App Description

The purpose of the App is to support the teacher in introducing programming concepts related to basic control structures: sequential, selection, and iteration, and to allow the student to transition to the development of more complex algorithms.

For the design of the App, the microlearning approach has been considered [6]. To this end, we divided into three levels the teaching of basic control structures in such a way as to introduce a basic control structure at each level, increasing the level of complexity of the exercises that the student can perform. In level 1, simple activities are carried out to learn the concept of instruction and instruction sequence. In level 2, exercises are included where the conditional structure gives rise to instructions to turn right and left to avoid obstacles. At level 3, the activities introduce the concept of repetition [7].

3.2 App Architecture

The App's objective is for the student to walk to where the virtual object is located. The App returns to the student a program formed by a set of atomic instructions with steps that he carried out until he found the object. To achieve this goal, we design the App architecture consisting of five main modules. In Fig. 1, the modules and the interrelationships between them are shown.

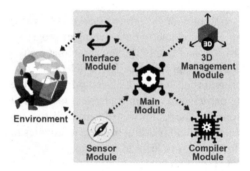

Fig. 1. App architecture

The **interface module** takes care of the student's communication with the App. It determines the complexity level to offer the learning activities according to it and finally shows the student the resulting program using representative symbols.

The **sensor module** is responsible for sensing the environment of the device. With the help of GPS, it can obtain geo-referential data (latitude and longitude). On the other hand, the gyroscope and accelerometer work together to carry out the tasks of anchoring the object found in the real environment (calculating the X, Y, and Z axes) and relocating it in case of moving (left, right, up, or down) in the environment (calculating the axis of rotation).

The **main module**: When starting the App, this module downloads all the data necessary for the App's operation: object database, level register, and initial settings. It is also in charge of coordinating all the tasks with the other modules and facilitating the interaction between them, providing support for the App's operation. As the main task, it sends all the data collected throughout the activity to the compiler to translate it and gives the algorithm (program) obtained on the way to reaching the object as a result.

The **3D management module**, with the help of the ARCore tool, renders the object to be viewed and adapts it based on the graphic capabilities of the user's device, providing a three-dimensional model of the object ready to be processed on the screen.

The **compilation module** contains the three parsers' tasks (lexical, syntactic, and semantic) to translate geographic locations. These locations are the product of collecting information that the main program performs from the student's actions. These actions may or may not be optimized based on the complexity of the task accomplished, granting fully customized algorithms.

3.3 Sequence Diagram of the App

The user's interaction, the mobile device, the App's modules, and sensors are model in the sequence diagram (Fig. 2).

When the user starts the App, the GPS determines which is the user's current location. Based on this data, the system can determine if a geo-referenced object is close to its location displayed on the map during the activity. In proximity to it, the user can select it and start sensing the context to obtain information from the environment and anchor the object in the real world. Previously, the App performs the task of rendering the object's three-dimensional model. The data obtained from the environment mapping

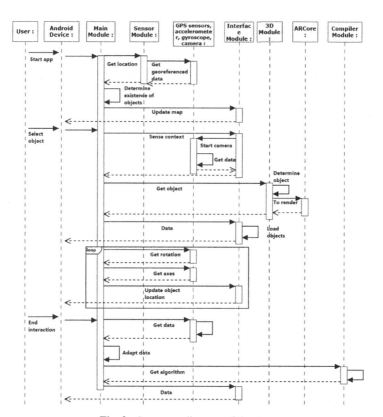

Fig. 2. Sequence diagram of the App

(axis values) can be anchored and updated in movement events. Finally, when the user ends the activity, all the data obtained throughout the experience is collected and adapted to the compiler to return the representative algorithm to the activity carried out.

4 Design and Development of the Modules

4.1 Compilation Module

The methodology followed for the compiler's design and development consisted of the following steps: Definition of the source and object languages, Design and construction of the analysis phases: lexical analysis, syntactic analysis, and semantic analysis. Then, the synthesis phase was developed: the code generator.

Source Language and Object Language. Since a compiler is a program that reads a program written in a source language and translates it into an equivalent program in an object language, both languages are defined in this section.

We design source language with a simple syntax so that the rest of the modules do not require a complicated interface to communicate with the compiler. In this way, we guarantee a completely modular and independent design of the App.

The compiler's input data are each of the geographic locations (latitudes and longitudes) obtained by the different devices capable of sensing the geographic context (GPS, Accelerometer, and Gyroscope). Therefore, the source language is composed of the user level and the set of geographic points.

The program resulting from the compilation is write in the object language. The characteristics considered for selecting the object language's instructions or sentences are expressed in [7]. In this case, the object language consists of the following atomic instructions: move forward (represents a forward step made by the student on his or her walk to the object), backward (represents a backward step that the student performs to meet the objective of the exercise), turn left and turn right (they allow to deviate from the linear path), if there is an object then (represents the fork when an obstacle is presented or not) and repeat (with this instruction the student visualizes a repetitive control sentence).

Construction the Compiler Phases. The lexical components and the patterns or regular expressions that these components generate have been defined for constructing the lexical analyzer. The specified lexical components are punctuation symbols and numeric constant.

For the Syntactic Analyzer phase, context-free grammar is defined using the BNF notation, which is the input to the ANTLR generator.

```
start:
  LLAVE_A
    CORCHETE_A nivel CORCHETE_C
    CORCHETE_A puntos CORCHETE_C
  LLAVE_C;
nivel: NUMERO;
puntos: tupla (COMA tupla)*;
tupla: PARENTESIS_A latlong COMA latlong PARENTESIS_C;

latlong: NUMERO PUNTO NUMERO;
```

In the semantic analysis phase, type verification is performed on the numeric constants to determine if they are of the latitude type or the longitude type.

Object Program Generation. The procedure described in Fig. 3 is carried out for the object program's generation. It applies three algorithms: the relationship algorithm, the classification algorithm, and the ranking algorithm.

Relationship and classification algorithms have been developed to determine the relationship between two pairs of geographic points to determine whether the student has stepped forward, backward, or turned in some direction.

Each time two consecutive elements are stored (the process that the parser executes when it traverses the abstract syntax tree), a comparison is made to determine the relationship between them (vector). The relationship is classified according to its equivalent in atomic instructions.

A vector in the plane is an ordered pair of real numbers (a, b) belonging to the space R^2 [15]. In this case, "a" is considered a set of latitudes, and the component "b" is the set of longitudes. They are the input to the Relationship Algorithm, and the results indicate the different directions that a vector can have. From the vectors obtained, the classification algorithm is applied, which establishes the relationship between said vectors. The results presented after classifying a pair of vectors are divided into two categories: parallel and orthogonal.

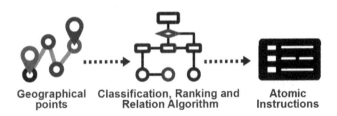

Geographical   Classification, Ranking and   Atomic
points   Relation Algorithm   Instructions

Fig. 3. The process to obtain the program

To determine when a pair of vectors belong to one set or another, we considered [15]:

The parallelism of vectors. Let u and v be non-zero vectors of R^2, the vector u is parallel to the vector v if and only if there is a non-zero scalar c such that

$$u = c.v. \tag{1}$$

Orthogonality. Let u and v be non-zero vectors of R^2; it is said that u is orthogonal to v if and only if the scalar product of u and v is equal to zero,

$$c.v = 0 \tag{2}$$

Angles between vectors. Let u and v be non-zero vectors of R^2 and let the scalar product then there exists and is unique an α [0, π] such that:

$$\cos(\alpha) = \frac{u.v}{\|u\|\|v\|} \tag{3}$$

For the classification of vectors, we apply the following rules:

- If both calculated vectors are parallel, we assumed that the user advanced in a straight line, and we consider the direction of the vectors to determine whether he advanced or retreated,
- If the vectors are perpendicular, the intersection between them is calculated to obtain the angle that joins them. If the angle is close to 90°, it is assumed to be a change of direction.
- If the upper vector has a left direction, we assume that the user has turned to the left.
- If the upper vector has the right direction, we assume that the user has turned to the right.

Finally, each of the rules is mapped with the equivalent atomic instruction (Table 1).

Table 1. Mapping relationships to atomic instructions.

Relation	Sense	Atomic instruction
Parallels	Upward	ADVANCE
	Downward	GO BACK
Orthogonal	Left	TURN LEFT
	Right	TURN RIGHT

As the last stage, the compiler will adapt the set of atomic instructions based on the student's level. The ranking algorithm is applied to do this, which takes the atomic instruction set as input data and returns an adapted set based on its level as a response. This adaptation produces a reduction of instructions or addition of new ones, such as "*repeat*" and "*if there is an obstacle then*". For the conditional statement, the compiler, when detecting the tuple $(0, 0)$, infers an obstacle. For example, if there are three points as input: $(-64.25139158964157, -27.80154927681387)$, $(0, 0)$, $(-64.25133660435677, -27.801606219132715)$, the App deduces that between point 1 and point 3, there is an obstacle.

4.2 Interface User Module

This module allows communication with the student to request the App's operation's data and show him the tool's results. To begin the execution, the student must log in to the application to obtain their data (Fig. 4a).

The user interface then enables options that allow access to the user profile and object registry. The first option shows the student information about previous activities (for example, the current level of knowledge, level of experience, traveled kilometers, number of steps, number of found objects, and a record of the date on which the student started using the App (Fig. 4b)). The second option permits the student to access objects found in previous sessions (Fig. 4c).

When the exercise begins, this module displays an interactive map on the main screen. The map will update based on the user's location. When the student is close to

| (a) Login interface | (b) User profile | (c) Object registration |

Fig. 4. User interfaces.

the object, the interface module prompts him to sense the current context through his device's camera and identifies a surface on which to anchor and insert the object on the map. The map contains two markers. A blue one indicates the user's current position, and a red one indicates the presence of an interactive object (Fig. 5a).

The interface module shows, as a result, a screen where the image of the object, the geographical position where it was found, the resulting algorithm, and the object with AR (Fig. 5b) are displaying.

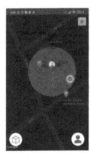

| (a) Marker map | (b) Result interface |

Fig. 5. Result interfaces.

4.3   3D Management Module

The 3D management module selects from the object database the object that it will show to the student. We classified the objects into three categories based on the level of knowledge. Then, the user can visualize particular objects based on the level of experience or knowledge they have.

Each object has associated an occurrence probability. The module defines a number randomly for selecting objects, and chose that one close to said value will be. Also, it performs a check to determine that the student in previous sessions has not found the object. In case this had not happened, the module will be executed again to prevent the user from encountering repeated objects.

Once the object has been downloaded and the student is within the visibility radius, the module will see a 3D object marker on the map. The user can touch it and display a dialog that will indicate that she is about to enter RA mode to project the object in context.

Finally, the 3D management module coordinates with the sensor and interface modules to determine the anchor point based on the device's rotation axes and update it in case of user movement.

5   Implementation

For the interpreter program's construction, we use the ANTLR tool (ANother Tool for Language Recognition). It is a generator of analyzers to read, process, execute or translate structured text. The regular expressions of the defined lexical components and the context-free grammar generated by the described language have been entered into ANTLR.

For the development of the 3D management module, the ARCore tool, developed by Google, was used to build AR applications. This tool allows files with extension FBX, SFB, GLT, GLTF, OBJ. It uses three technologies to integrate, through the phone camera, virtual content with the real world. They are position tracking relative to the real world, environmental understanding for detecting the size and location of flat surfaces such as the floor or a table, and light estimation, which allows the phone to estimate the current lighting conditions of the environment).

We developed the interface module with the XML language, typical of Android Studio. It is a tag language that matches each meta-tag with an internal Android class. In this way, it is possible to control what elements are inserted into the user interface and manipulate them during execution. It has the advantage that each label is adaptable to each device's screen, complying with the property of a responsive interface design.

We developed the sensor module with the Java language, also typical of Android Studio, which contains specialized libraries to access the internal components such as GPS, accelerometer, and gyroscope.

Finally, we developed the main module under the structural facade design pattern. It allows structuring several subsystems or modules, minimizing communication and dependencies between them, providing a single communication interface through the main module.

6 Tests

6.1 Compiler Module Test

We conducted tests for all levels of complexity.

Table 2 shows a test carried out for the level of complexity 1. In (Fig. 6a), we can observe the set of latitudes and longitudes captured by the App when the student makes the journey towards the object. Also, the output of the compilation module, the resulting program, and finally, the interface presented to the student is shown.

Table 3 shows a test carried out for the level of complexity 2. The student may encounter an obstacle on his path (Fig. 6b), so the resulting program introduces a conditional structure concept.

Table 4 shows a test carried out for the level of complexity 3. When the student performs the same operation several times, for example, moving forward (Fig. 6c), the resulting program contains the sentence repeat, thus introducing the concept of the repetitive control structure.

Table 2. Test performed for complexity level 1.

Input	Output	Interface

{
[1]
[(-64.25157129764557,-27.801613336920475),
(-64.25148211419582,-27.80157715482788),
(-64.25138555467129,-27.8015510562618),
(-64.25134532153606,-27.801586645213977),
(-64.25128899514675,-27.80155639460536),
(-64.25122663378716,-27.80151843304538),
(-64.25117500126362,- 27.80154868366457)]
}
	{
	[ADVANCE,
	ADVANCE,
	TURN RIGHT,
	ADVANCE,
	ADVANCE,
	TURN RIGHT]
	}	

Table 3. Test performed for complexity level 2.

Input	Output	Interface

{
[2]
[(-64.25157129764557,-27.80161570951628),
(-64.25148278474808,-27.801581306871892),
(-64.25139158964157,-27.80154927681387),
(0,0),
(-64.25133660435677,-27.801606219132715),
(-64.25126284360884,-27.801596728748322),
(-64.2511984705925,-27.801581306871892)]
}
	{
	[ADVANCE,
	ADVANCE,
	IF THERE IS OBJECT
	THEN,
	TURN RIGHT,
	ADVANCE,
	TURN LEFT]
	}	

Table 4. Test performed for complexity level 3.

Input	Output	Interface

{
  [3]
  [(-64.25157062709332,-27.801612150622535),
  (-64.2514868080616,-27.801581306871892),
  (-64.25141505897044,-27.801553428858966),
  (-64.25135537981987,-27.8015231782411),
  (-64.25130508840084,-27.801555801456097),
  (-64.25124809145927,-27.801533854930724),
  (-64.25118573009968,-27.801497079662074)]
}
	{
	[REPEAT 3,
	ADVANCE,
	TURN RIGHT,
	REPEAT 2,
	ADVANCE]
	}	

(a) Walkthrough for level 1.   (b) Walkthrough for level 2.   (c) Walkthrough for level 3.

Fig. 6. Student journey of the tests performed.

6.2 3D Management Module Tests

We tested the 3D Management Module for portability, and visual distinction [16] in different environments, with have varying lighting levels, various objects, and different platforms and devices.

1. **Portability Test:** since the users of the App are the students, and they use a wide variety of devices, then the 3D management module was tested with different operating systems, versions, and devices.

   We carried out 32 tests with Android versions that allow the ARCore library: Android 7.0 (Nougat), 8.0 (Oreo), 9.0 (Pie), and 10. We carried out tests with the following range devices: Samsung, Xiaomi, Huawei, and Motorola (each with different OS versions and models). From the tests carried out, we can conclude that the rendering of the different 3D objects is useful thanks to each device's hardware characteristics and the support of Google ARCore Services installed by default in the mentioned devices and complements the rendering. There is no current support for devices with Android versions less than the above mentioned because they do not meet the hardware conditions to run the Google ARCore tool.

2. **Visual Distinction:** AR applications can lose visual distinction based on the physical world in which they operate. We carried out the following tests:

   a) *In an environment with intense light:* we carried out two tests, one outdoor in broad daylight (Fig. 7a) and the other indoor with harsh lighting (Fig. 7b).
   b) *In an environment with low or intermediate lighting:* we carried out a test at night (Fig. 8a) and another indoors at night and with little lighting (Fig. 8b).

From the tests carried out, we can conclude that:

(a) Outdoor, daylight   (b) Indoor, with lighting

Fig. 7. Visual distinction tests in bright light.

- It has been possible to carry out tests in scenarios with different lighting characteristics, which is a primary factor when rendering a virtual object in the real environment.
- The anchorage of objects and their three-dimensional characteristics such as height, width, and depth have been precisely maintained.

(a) Outdoor, at night   (b) Indoor, at night, and low
                                   lighting

Fig. 8. Visual distinction tests with low or intermediate lighting.

7 Conclusions

In this work, we present a UL App for teaching the basic concepts of programming to overcome the learning problems of the ideas that include the control structures.

We describe the main modules, such as the compilation module and the 3D manager module. The compilation module allows translating the recorded geographical locations of the student's activities in the ubiquitous environment. The tests carried out on the compiler show that it is feasible to have a UL App that accurately converts coordinates into instructions in a language, which students can then use to program. The compilation module is useful, novel, and widely applicable since there is no history of this type of translation from geographic location to program instruction. It can also be displayed graphically and extend to generate more complex instructions later.

The 3D manager module is a complete and efficient subsystem that will allow the rendering and manipulation of three-dimensional models. These models can be viewed on any Android device compatible with the implemented technology, leaving the possibility of working not only with objects but with more complex scenarios totally in 3D thanks to the development of the said module.

As future work, we will carry out the App integration tests and tests in real contexts to evaluate students' learning in programming courses. In this way, both geolocation and UA and AR result in powerful tools that enable more prosperous and motivating learning spaces.

References

1. Burbules, N.C.: Ubiquitous learning and the future of teaching. Encounters **13**, 3–14 (2012)
2. Martínez, L.V., del Moral Pérez, M.E.: Geolocalización y realidad aumentada para un aprendizaje ubicuo en la formación inicial del profesorado. @tic revista d'innovació educativa **21**, 40–48 (2018)
3. Azuma, R., Baillot, Y., Behringer, R., Feiner, S., Julier, S., MacIntyre, B.: Recent advances in augmented reality. IEEE Comput. Graphics Appl. **21**(6), 34–47 (2001). https://doi.org/10.1109/38.963459
4. Bozkurt, A.: Augmented reality with mobile and ubiquitous learning: immersive, enriched, situated, and seamless learning experiences, January 2017. https://doi.org/10.4018/978-1-5225-1692-7.ch002
5. Insuasti, J.: Problemas de enseñanza y aprendizaje de los fundamentos de programación. Revista Educación y Desarrollo Social **10**, 234–246 (2016)
6. Salinas, J., Marín, V.I.: Pasado, presente y futuro del microlearning como estrategia para el desarrollo profesional. In: Campus Virtuales, Huelva, España, vol. III, no. 2, pp. 46–61 (2014)
7. Acosta, D., Álvarez, M., Durán, E.B.: Compilador para traducir ubicaciones geográficas en instrucciones atómicas en una aplicación de aprendizaje ubicuo de programación. In: XXVI Congreso Argentino de Ciencias de la Computación (CACIC) (Modalidad virtual, 5 al 9 de octubre de 2020), pp. 650–659 (2020)
8. Tsai, C.-W., Shen, P.-D., Tsai, M.-C., Chen, W.-Y.: Exploring the effects of web-mediated computational thinking on developing students' computing skills in a ubiquitous learning environment. Interact. Learn. Environ. **25**(6), 762–777 (2017)
9. Chookaew, S., Wanichsan, D., Hwang, G.-J., Panjaburee, P.: Effects of a personalised ubiquitous learning support system on university students' learning performance and attitudes in computer-programming courses. Int. J. Mob. Learn. Organ. **9**(3), 240–257 (2015)
10. Hosanee, Y., Panchoo, S.: The analysis and the need of ubiquitous learning to engage children in coding. In: Fleming, P., Lacquet, B., Sanei, S., Deb, K., Jakobsson, A. (eds.) ELECOM 2018. LNEE, vol. 561, pp. 268–276. Springer, Cham (2019). https://doi.org/10.1007/978-3-030-18240-3_25
11. Boonbrahm, S., Boonbrahm, P., Kaewrat, C., Pengkaew, P., Khachorncharoenkul, P.: Teaching fundamental programming using augmented reality. Int. J. Interact. Mob. Technol. (iJIM) **13**(07), 31–43 (2019)

12. Salazar Mesía, N.A.: Realidad Aumentada en la Enseñanza de Conceptos Básicos de Programación. Universidad Nacional de La Plata, Facultad de Informática (2015)
13. Tan, K.S.T., Lee, Y.: An augmented reality learning system for programming concepts. In: Kim, K., Joukov, N. (eds.) ICISA 2017. LNEE, vol. 424, pp. 179–187. Springer, Singapore (2017). https://doi.org/10.1007/978-981-10-4154-9_22
14. Chen, D.R., Chen, M.Y., Huang, T.C., Hsu, W.P.: Developing a mobile learning system in augmented reality context. Int. J. Distrib. Sens. Netw. 9(12), 594627 (2013)
15. Kolman, B., Hill, D.: Algebra Lineal, 8th edn, pp. 216–224. Pearson Educación, México (2006)
16. Scheibmeir, J., Malaiya, Y.K.: Quality model for testing augmented reality applications. In: IEEE 10th Annual Ubiquitous Computing, Electronics & Mobile Communication Conference (UEMCON), New York City, NY, USA, pp. 0219–0226 (2019). https://doi.org/10.1109/UEMCON47517.2019.8992974

Agile Framework for the Training of Entrepreneurs. A Proposal in Higher Education in ICT

Sonia I. Mariño[(⊠)] and Viviana R. Bercheñi

Departamento de Informática, Facultad de Ciencias Exactas y Naturales y Agrimensura, Universidad Nacional del Nordeste, 9 de Julio 1449, Corrientes, Argentina
msonia@exa.unne.edu.ar, viviana.bercheni@comunidad.unne.edu.ar

Abstract. The article presents an agile framework to establish entrepreneurial actions in students of the Computer Science discipline. The proposal was designed based on the experiences of articulation between the Applied Economics and the Final Degree Project in the 2019 and 2020 school cycles. As a result, the SCRUM foundations were adapted in the design of the framework, revealing how the different roles and artifacts. Also, the proposal defined the roles for the team responsible for the project: Responsible Scrum Team, Product Owner, Scrum Master. In order to achieve goals the functions of the work team were designed. In particular, the experiences with students in the 2019 and 2020 classroom cycles were associated with Sprint 4. Progress is made by quantifying some of the proposed indicators based on the analysis of different sources of information, which show the importance of contributing to the construction and strengthening of entrepreneurial actions in the training of university students.

Keywords: University training · Agility in education · Entrepreneurship

1 Introduction

Higher education in its duty towards the context promotes economic development through the fulfillment of missions that are related to the promotion of entrepreneurship, innovation and social commitment is responsible for the formation of the entrepreneurial potential of its students through significant changes and transversal in the interaction of their study plans.

Nowadays, in higher education, the training of students as potential entrepreneurs is faced, significant and transversal changes are designed in their study plans.

In accordance with this statement, we agree with [1] that changing attitudes, enhancing entrepreneurial skills, developing new values and personal training, cognitive and managerial skills have to be part of the Curriculum design so that students begin to realize that there are new job options within the university itself.

It is necessary to promote entrepreneurship in higher education, given that the more intensive the teaching of entrepreneurship, the more likely it is that students will make

© Springer Nature Switzerland AG 2021
P. Pesado and J. Eterovic (Eds.): CACIC 2020, CCIS 1409, pp. 308–318, 2021.
https://doi.org/10.1007/978-3-030-75836-3_21

the effort to start a new business and, in this way, contribute to the development of the economy [2].

From this perspective, it agrees with Bello [3] in the sense of considering that the new economy is transforming employment and the incidence of information and communication technologies in all human activities, and in this sense, they affect education and in particular to higher education. This is exposed to two forces: on the one hand, to the demands of adaptation to the demands of the new economy and the consequent modification of the requirements and qualifications of university professionals and, on the other, to the incidence of information technologies and communication about education.

This article presents an extended version with respect to the one presented at CACIC 2020 [4] referred to two articulation interventions between the subjects Final Degree Project and Applied Economics, carried out in the 2019 and 2020 school cycles with a view to strengthening the entrepreneurial spirit in technological developments. Different realization contexts conditioned by the COVID-19 pandemic were characterized, one face-to-face and the other mediated by synchronous and asynchronous ICTs. The results indicate the need to continue strengthening the proposed perspective aimed at strengthening the entrepreneurial spirit in undergraduate training.

SCRUM is an agile methodology to manage projects of various kinds applicable to this purpose. In this article the proposal is extended and explicit, introducing SCRUM practices implicitly treated previously, such as the roles that are assumed through four Sprints, where the articulation experiences are included in one of them.

Thus, this new proposal capitalizes -in an agile framework- the 2019 and 2020 experiences to promote the training of entrepreneurs, making the acquired expertise explicit. Also, it can be replicated in the 2021 school year, anticipating its virtual development based on an institutional decision made at the end of 2020.

1.1 Education for Entrepreneurship

Entrepreneurship in educational contexts, particularly from higher education implies a strong commitment of the university with the state, companies and organizations of various kinds.

The literature review indicates many experiences disseminated with a view to achieving awareness on these issues and appropriation from the university to society.

As expressed in [4] quoting [5] "In general, entrepreneurial education has contributed significantly to its environment and to the production of companies" especially in developing countries. This possibility is also addressed, as a strategy to overcome the problems of unemployment and exclusion. [2, 3] These approaches have been treated both in a public and private character [7].

Thus, targeted reviews of the literature were identified as described in [5]. In [9] a bibliometric investigation referring to the entrepreneurial intention of university students in the period 1996 to 2015 is summarized from data collected from the Scopus database. The bibliometric study around entrepreneurship topics related to "skills" or "knowledge" or "capacities" or "social development" located in the ISI Web of Science in the period 2000 to 2016 are reported in [10]. So, [12] applied systematic literature review in order to contribute on entrepreneurial intentions, located in Scopus in the period 2000 to 2018.

The relevance of entrepreneurship education and training for regional development were described in [11] in terms of systematic literature review/

These, like other experiences, account for the exponential growth and how other exhibitors are joining this relevant topic in the complex knowledge society. Another outstanding issue in university education around entrepreneurship is its transversal nature in the curriculum [5, 13] and mentioned in [4]. Also, is a topic commented in [14–16].

1.2 Agility in Educational Management

Agility is a premise in the knowledge society where efficient and effective solutions are required to constantly emerging. Thus, project management provides various methodologies focused on the definition and validation of results-oriented strategies. In the literature there are numerous agile methodologies such as SCRUM, XP, Kanban.

In order to provide a literature review on agility the authors "based on the study five categories of research streams were identified: papers focusing on agile software development, papers related to agile project management research, contributions to agility on the organization level, contributions to the application of hybrid approaches, papers discussing application of agile methods for innovation" [17].

The educational context is constantly being transformed and one of the relevant innovations addresses the use of SCRUM in educational management. Among the antecedents, the descriptions set out in previous paragraphs are mentioned.

In particular, the adaptation of SCRUM in educational contexts in the Bachelor's degree in Information Systems are mentioned in [18] to attend the expositions of subject work, in [19] who detail how they adapted SCRUM in a context of higher education, especially for the management of final graduation projects for a computer science degree. In [20] that incorporate SCRUM practices in an ADDIE instructional design model in a 2019 course.

1.3 Contextualization of the Experience

In undergraduate degrees, the design and development of a final and integrative production is required for the degree. In the case of the Bachelor's Degree in Information Systems from Faculty of Exact and Natural Sciences and Surveying, Northeast National University (FaCENA), this academic space is called Final Degree Project. In background paragraphs it was stated that the main objective of this research work was to complete the academic and professional training of the students, enabling the integration and use of the knowledge acquired during their years of study to solve problems of a professional, academic and scientific nature, aimed at strengthening your entrepreneurial profile.

Since 2016, different interventions have been carried out with previous subjects of the study plan to achieve an approach to the definition of the object of study that the students will address in the Final Degree Project (FDP). In particular, since 2018, articulations have been generated with the Applied Economics (AE) subject to reconvert the entrepreneurial project idea through the construction of a business plan dealt with in this subject, in the completion work. As expressed in [21] it is a product of knowledge and skills developed in the career and that can be rethought, deepened and updated in the final project.

At [4], the Applied Economics subject was characterized, remembering that it is taught in the first semester of the fourth year of the Information System's Degree career. Its general objective is to make the link between the technical knowledge that students acquire from the specific subjects of the Career, with the strategic objectives of the organizations, and of these with their environment. By passing the course, students are able to integrate information technology with the mission and vision of for-profit organizations.

2   Methodology

The proposed framework is based on agility for the development of entrepreneurial experiences based on the formation of interdisciplinary work teams where, once processes designed in previous experiences have been defined, a set of good training practices will be applied regularly to work collaboratively with students of both chairs, in order to obtain the best possible results.

The roles for the team responsible for the project that are proposed will be grouped into the following segments:

- Responsible Scrum Team: Designs and executes entrepreneurial training in the academic field of the Degree in Information Systems. It will have two well-defined functions, on the one hand, administratively manages the validation of the training (Resolution of the Academic Council) and, on the other, identifies limiting factors that could take away interest in the training of entrepreneurs. Moreover, they will be in charge of activities related to mentoring, coaching and facilitating synchronous and asynchronous meetings aimed at evaluating the development of the training process.
- Product Owner: This role will be assumed by the training organizers. His purpose is to identify and define exhaustively the list of main and accessory tasks and actions aimed at making the work of the training team more efficient. From an academic perspective, activities will be carried out that are linked to classroom planning, definition of the roles of teachers and construction of dynamic practical work so that students achieve meaningful learning. He is in charge of the work team developing its activities and responsibilities appropriately from the perspective of the initial objective set. So, to the development of its functions, they will be in charge of sharing in a Product Backlog, the progress related to the development of a business plan or idea.
- Scrum Master: The main task assets to this role will be linked to the elimination of obstacles that may prevent the team from reaching the sprint objective. The Scrum Master makes the defined rules fulfilled both in academic roles and in students. Regarding the role of the teacher, control will be in the hands of the teachers responsible for the subjects addressed. In the student role, the person in charge must be a leader agreed upon by their peers, empowering the group to make its maximum effort and to see the effort in the quality of the business plans presented.

For the development of the proposal, it was decided to divide the investigative process into the following phases to be addressed:

- Phase 1: Explicit background information that supported the development of the framework.
- Phase 2: Definition of objectives in relation to the university training of computer science students in practices consolidating their entrepreneurial talent.

Phase 3: Design of intervention activities to promote the entrepreneurial spirit, aimed at achieving significant learning to contribute to professional training in a context of agility.

3   Results

The results are presented considering the proposed framework and the Sect. 3.2. Particularly, the experiences with students in the 2019 and 2020 classroom cycles were associated with Sprint 4 and described in Sect. 3.2.

3.1   Adapting the Framework Proposed

Based on the framework proposed in the previous section, the functions of the work team were designed, related to:

- Management of the risk of deviations on a regular basis, through synchronous and asynchronous meetings with the members of the Scrum Team or organizing team. They will try to prioritize, estimate and consolidate training in entrepreneurship within the higher education sector.
- Planning Meeting: Organization of meetings for the planning and design of activities aimed at consolidating entrepreneurial training through the construction of business plans linked to technology-based companies. Presentations that reveal painstaking work and market research will be socialized in a Product Backlog.
- Defining the Sprint: Each version of the different business plans is built based on previous versions and validated based on the requirements of the responsible academic team. Duration of three weeks of interaction is estimated to obtain a product eligible for financing.
- Defining meetings. They will take place for the duration of the health emergency, synchronously and asynchronously using institutional platforms such as Moodle or Google Meet. Perhaps this strategy can be thought from now on, as definitive.
- Sprint Review: The responsible team (Scrum Team) will present the quantitative instruments defined "ex ante", to carry out the validation of the work presented. The Scrim Team and each responsible student team participate in these activities.

Sprint 1. Background Information that Supported the Proposal Framework

Applied Economics and Final Degree Project are subjects of the study plan with perspectives of developing entrepreneurial training with an emphasis on ICT's. These correspond to the fourth- and fifth- year of the degree respectively.

The articulation interventions aimed at entrepreneurship that contribute to professional training and with an emphasis on achieving significant learning that are described were specified in the period 2017 and 2018 in the subjects "Final Degree Project" and "Applied Economics". As immediate antecedents, the joint organization was reflected in the development of the seminars that were carried out simultaneously and were called "La Acción Emprendedora" [22–24].

In this context, as basic didactic resources, we can cite the organization of seminars aimed at fostering the entrepreneurial spirit in fourth- and fifth-year subjects and dictated by professionals from the corresponding Agentia's team [25]. These seminars are considered the triggering element for the construction of a business plan or to complete the idea-projects form, the basis for presentation in different programs to promote entrepreneurial initiatives [21].

Sprint 2. Definition of Approach Objectives in Relation to Entrepreneurship
Since it is an intervention from academic areas, the didactic objectives were defined. Thus, the inclusion of topics related to Entrepreneurship was aimed at providing skills and abilities related to professional practice and providing the student with a broader vision of their career and their potential contribution to the community from their own ability to self-generate business plans.

From this perspective, following what was stated in [4, 21, 26] are mentioned as objectives linked to the development of knowledge, attitudes and skills linked to this intervention.

In particular, the objectives that are related to technical and cognitive knowledge that is intended to be worked on during the proposal and include specific technical aspects of the subjects in which the activity is applied and reflected in individual plans –as mentioned in [4, 21], are mentioned below:

The development of specific skills (reading comprehension, evaluation of information, use of information and knowledge of experts, roles, decision-making and argumentation, anticipation of consequences, written and oral expression) among others.

The objectives linked to the development of attitudes try to get students to recognize actions that allow the application of the specific knowledge dealt with in the career in the space of a new company or in the process of creating it, and thus achieve effective entrepreneurial role. Those exposed in [21, 26, 27] are taken up, namely:

Sprint 3. Design of Intervention Activities to Promote the Entrepreneurial Spirit
In this Sprint, activities were planned as indicated in [4], aimed at achieving significant learning as a contribution to their professional training.

- Materials and equipment needed: they are adjusted to the circumstances. In the 2019 school year, it was carried out in person, considering the classroom and time in which the classes of the subjects are usually held. In the 2020 school year, synchronous and asynchronous virtual interventions were redefined in response to the Isolation decreed at the national level and to which the University adhered.
- Total duration of the activity: They were adapted to conditions in each school year.

- Schedule of the classes: in the 2019 school year, two interventions were planned, in the first and second semester. The results suggested feedback information for adjustment and development in the 2020 school year, precisely at the end of May 2020.
- Intervening teachers: Teaching speakers responsible for the subjects involved and in 2019 there was a referent on the subject belonging to the AGENTIA team.
- Defining special logistical needs: Development of the planned activities in the usual time and space in which the classes of the subjects involved take place, it should be clarified that one day of the week they coincide.
- Other clarifications:

  • A resolution of approval of the instance of articulation between subjects of the Bachelor is processed.
  • It is expected to replicate this activity in the next school years, including different subjects and adjusting according to the feedback information resulting from the analysis of previous implementations.

Also, implicates the definition and elaboration of a viable Business Plan. Carrying out the intervention the definition and elaboration of a viable Business Plan to carry out was addressed. It's constitutes a preliminary instrument that could potentially guide the student in defining a final degree project. Applied Economics was addressed with intervention of the subject Final Degree Project, the target audience being the students who take the first of these subjects.

Sprint 4. Evaluation of the Intervention
Once the activities were completed, the experiences were capitalized, that is, the generation of timely information for future interventions and decision making is relevant. The following metrics were defined since the interventions specified in the Applied Economics subject in relation to the Final Degree Project can be followed and measured over time; it is proposed to apply the following monitoring indicators based on the didactic strategies developed in the 2019 school cycles and 2020. Therefore, following what is stated in [21], the following will be determined:

- Number of business ideas specified or generated in end-of-degree projects.
- Number of projects related to business ideas presented to the corresponding agency of the university.
- Number of projects related to business ideas presented in the business incubator of the University
- Number of students of the Bachelor's degree in Information Systems who chose to take the Free Chair for University Entrepreneurs.
- Number of students who, attending these seminars, chose to take the Free Chair for University Entrepreneurs
- Number of business plans that obtained financing from different sources and are in execution.
- Number of students attending the workshop: financing alternatives for technology-based projects, organized by both subjects.

3.2 Experiences of the 2019 and 2020 Cycle to Define Sprint 4

The experiences developed in the 2019 and 2020 school cycles allowed establishing, as expressed in [4], approach strategies to strengthen the entrepreneurial profile in university students. In the 2020 school year, the articulating intervention between the aforementioned subjects was carried out in both semesters, and in virtual mode.

In the first four-month period of the 2019 cycle, a face-to-face meeting was held with the intervention of a specialist in the entrepreneurial subject and member of the AGENTIA'S team who discussed business plans in real contexts in a seminar. In addition, the question of the importance of how the ideas-projects to be elaborated in the framework of AE was installed can be considered as a preliminary sketch that could alternatively be reconsidered in the framework of the Final Degree Project, starting point for the document presented [4].

During the second semester, the students who presented their Business Plan in the AE subject were summoned. They were informed about lines of financing or non-refundable financial assistance available in the market to implement projects or technology-based business plans.

It was observed that very few students attend extra-curricular complementary activities, even though these would result in the construction and implementation of the FDP. This feedback information implied carrying out the articulation activity during AE subject, that is, in the first semester of the following year.

So, these results implied a redefinition of the actions. Educational environments were transformed into virtual mode. As reported in [4], a didactic strategy was planned that had to be modified due to the health emergency situation according to [28], the "Social, preventive and compulsory isolation" is established.

This is how the articulation strategy was reformulated and materialized through an intervention based on the use of synchronous and asynchronous tools. As an asynchronous tool, the virtual classroom was used where material composed of:

– Project ideas form.
– Guidance material to transform a business plan in the FDP. In the interface of the virtual classroom of the subject AE where the digital presentations elaborated by respective subjects are displayed, and triggers of the proposed activities.
– Project of articulation of both subjects. ·
– Enabling a forum to reflect on certain issues related to the concept of entrepreneurship that served as a trigger to reflect on the proposal.

Synchronous interventions were carried out through video-conferences via the Zoom tool. The potential to rethink the business plan presented as a requirement to regularize or promote Applied Economics was highlighted in an initial idea that could be reformulated or deepened for the development of the Final Degree Project, as presented in [4].

These experiences allowed us to rethink in the construction of this proposal, the potential of applying an agile work mechanism based on SCRUM. The contents developed during the articulation seminars were related to certain topics addressed by the Applied Economics subject and were linked to: characteristics of the entrepreneurs: Qualities and aptitudes. Entrepreneur and entrepreneurship concept. Identification of innovative ideas to satisfy unresolved needs. Identification of business ideas. Constituent elements of a Business Plan. Cash Flows. Income and Costs. Market Study and Marketing Mix.

Of the total number of students attending, 11% would be in a position to develop technology-based business projects. Therefore, these results would indicate a divergence between the characteristics of the entrepreneurial spirit in the Faculty and the main economic sectors of the City, so the curricular model proposes a series of spaces and strategies to facilitate a dialogue between the university and the regional context and an approach of the students attending to the realities and development needs of the context. It is estimated that said indicator would improve substantially when applying the proposed work methodology.

4 Conclusions

The article proposed an agile framework to establish entrepreneurial actions in students of the Informatics discipline with a view to improving the process of consolidation of the entrepreneurial profile in students of the Bachelor's degree in Information Systems.

For this, face-to-face interventions were carried out in the 2019 period and synchronous and asynchronous through video-conferencing via the Zoom tool and google meet during the 2020 period. This initial plan could be reformulated or deepened for the development of the FDP based on the work proposal presented at [4].

This experience allowed us to rethink in the construction of this agility proposal based on SCRUM applicable to the process of construction of technology-based business plans oriented towards the structure of a Final Degree Project. The contents developed during the articulation seminars were related to certain topics addressed by the Applied Economics and may be applied to define them.

From the experience analyzed, it appears that of the total number of students attending, 11% would be in a position to develop technology-based business projects. Therefore, these results would indicate a divergence between the characteristics of the entrepreneurial spirit in the Faculty and the main economic sectors of the City, so the curricular model proposes a series of spaces and strategies to facilitate a dialogue between the university and the regional context and an approach of the students attending to the realities and development needs of the context where the Scrum methodology can constitute a process that transversely consolidates the training of entrepreneurial talent in the computer science discipline, considerably improving the quantified indicators.

The methodology called Scrum was selected as it is a process in which a set of good practices are applied on a regular basis, -Final Degree Project's orientation to the development of technology-based business ideas, with contributions and accompaniment from heads of both chairs- to work collaboratively as a team, and obtain the best possible result in your final degree project. Given its specific characteristics, it is expected to be able to apply it in previous school cycles.

This way of working involves making progress deliveries of the business plan through partial and regular reports, prioritizing the relevant economic information based on the context and the chosen market, mostly local with global projection, so it will require the adaptability of the methodology to complex environments and it was required to obtain results in real time, where local and international contextual variables are highly sensitive, and where innovation, competitiveness, flexibility and productivity will be fundamental. The choice of this process served substantially during the 2020 period, to overcome the consequences of preventive and mandatory isolation on economic activity as a whole since it had enough flexibility to resolve situations of contextual volatility extended to the global market, and students were able to advance in their particular proposals, using online marketing tools in an almost exclusive way, operating from Information and Communication Technologies to supply and expand the chosen market segment.

Acknowledgements. The authors are part of the Project accredited by the General Secretariat of Science and Technology of the Northeast National University, PI 19F014, title is "Sistemas informáticos: modelos, métodos y herramientas". The support of the Secretariat is appreciated.

References

1. García, J.C.S., Caggiano, V., Sánchez, B.H.: Competencias emprendedoras en la educación universitaria. Int. J. Dev. Educ. Psychol. INFAD 3(1), 19–28 (2011)
2. Alvarez, R., De Noble, A., Jung, D.: Educational curricula and self-efficacy: entrepreneurial orientation and new venture intentions among university students in Mexico. In: International Research in the Business Disciplines, vol. 5, pp. 379–403 (2006). https://doi.org/10.1016/S1074-7877(06)05019-7
3. Bello, J.R.: La preparación emprendedora y la formación de graduados universitarios. Cuadernos Unimetanos (8), 2–9 (2006)
4. Mariño, S.I., Bercheñi, V.: Experiencias de articulación para formar emprendedores en los ciclos lectivos 2019 y 2020. In: XXVI Congreso Argentino de Ciencias de la Computación (CACIC), pp. 680–689, RedUNCI, La Plata (2020)
5. Sánchez García, J.C., Ward, A., Hernández, B., Florez, J.L.: Educación emprendedora: Estado del arte. Propósitos y Representaciones 5(2), 401–473 (2017)
6. Formichella M.: El concepto de emprendimiento y su relación con la educación, el empleo y el desarrollo local, Buenos Aires, Argentina (2004)
7. Ortiz García, J.M., Pensado Fernández, M.E., Ortiz Barradas, A.M.: La formación para el emprendimiento en las IES. Un estudio comparativo entre lo público y lo privado. en: Brizeida, H.-G., Hernández-Sánchez, E.R., Giuseppina M. (2019)
8. Brizeida, H.-G., Hernández-Sánchez, E.R., Cardella G.M., Sánchez-García, J.C. (eds.): Emprendimiento e Innovación: Oportunidades para todos, Dykinson, S.L. (ed.) (2019)
9. Valencia Arias, A., Montoya Restrepo, I., Montoya Restrepo, A.: Intención emprendedora en estudiantes universitarios: Un estudio bibliométrico. Intangible Capital 12(4), 881–922 (2016)
10. Ovalles-Toledo, L.V., Moreno Freites, Z., Olivares Urbina, M.A., Silva Guerra, H.: Habilidades y capacidades del emprendimiento: un estudio bibliométrico. Revista Venezolana de Gerencia 23(81) (2018)
11. Galvão, A., Ferreira, J.J., Marques, C.: Entrepreneurship education and training as facilitators of regional development: a systematic literature review. J. Small Bus. Enterp. Dev. 25(1), 17–40 (2018). https://doi.org/10.1108/JSBED-05-2017-0178
12. Dolhey, S.: A bibliometric analysis of research on entrepreneurial intentions from 2000 to 2018. J. Res. Mark. Entrepreneurship 21(2), 180–199 (2019). https://doi.org/10.1108/JRME-02-2019-0015

13. Contreras-Velásquez, J.C., Wilches-Duran, S.Y., Graterol-Rivas, M.E., Bautista-Sandoval, M.J.: Educación Superior y la Formación en Emprendimiento Interdisciplinario: Un Caso de Estudio. Formación universitaria **10**(3), 11–20 (2017)

14. FaCENA, UNNE Plan de Estudios de la carrera Licenciatura en Sistemas de Información. Resol. 1137/09 CS. UNNE (2009)

15. Resolución Ministerial N° 786/09. Ministerio de Educación de la República Argentina (2009)

16. Red UNCI. Documento de Recomendaciones Curriculares de la RedUNCI (2015). redunci. info.unlp.edu.ar

17. Soñta-Drączkowska, E.: From Agile Project Management to Agile Organization? – a Literature Review From Agile Project Management to Agile Organization? – a Literature Review. https://www.ceeol.com/search/article-detail?id=714851

18. Mariño, S.I., Alfonzo, P.L., Arduino, G.A.: Agilidad para gestionar proyectos educativos informáticos en educación superior. Eur. Sci. J. **16**(34), 123–137 (2020)

19. Mariño, S.I., Alfonzo, P.L.: Implementación de SCRUM en el diseño del proyecto del Trabajo Final de Aplicación. Scientia Et Technica **19**(4), 413–418 (2014)

20. Fernandez, M.G., Godoy Guglielmone, M.V., Mariño, S.I., Barrios, W.G.: Agility in instructional design. Strengthening of digital skills in incoming students at FaCENA-UNNE. In: Pesado, P., Arroyo, M. (eds.) CACIC 2019. CCIS, vol. 1184, pp. 124–136. Springer, Cham (2020). https://doi.org/10.1007/978-3-030-48325-8_9

21. Mariño, S.I., Bercheñi, V.R.: Propuesta de promoción del espíritu emprendedor en la disciplina Informática. Técnica Administrativa, vol. 19, núm. 2, [ISSUE:82a] (2020). https://www.cyta.com.ar/ta/article.php?id=190201

22. FaCENA, UNNE. Seminario Corrientes Emprende 2015. Res. 0207/15. FaCENA (2015)

23. FaCENA, UNNE. Seminarios "La Acción Emprendedora – Ciclo Lectivo 2017", Res. 1688/17 CD. FaCENA (2017)

24. FaCENA, UNNE. Seminarios "La Acción Emprendedora – Ciclo Lectivo 2018", Res. 191/18 D. FaCENA

25. AGENTIA. Agencia de Innovación y Desarrollo, dependiente de la Universidad Nacional del Nordeste (2020)

26. Mariño, S.I., Godoy, M.V.: Propuesta de un modelo de rol emprendedor en la asignatura Proyecto Final de Carrera. In: IX Congreso de Tecnología en Educación & Educación en Tecnología, pp. 75–82 (2014)

27. Braidot, N., Cesar, R.: Curso de Posgrado de Formación de Formadores en Competencias Emprendedoras, Curso, Universidad Nacional del Nordeste (2018)

28. Aislamiento Social PreventiVO y Obligatorio. Republica Argentina. Decreto 297/2020, DECNU-2020-297-APN-PTE. https://www.boletinoficial.gob.ar/detalleAviso/primera/227042/20200320

Computer Security

Exploring Internal Correlations in Timing Features of Keystroke Dynamics at Word Boundaries and Their Usage for Authentication and Identification

Nahuel González[1]([✉]) [ID], Germán M. Concilio[1] [ID], Jorge Ierache[1] [ID],
Enrique P. Calot[1] [ID], and Waldo Hasperué[2] [ID]

[1] Laboratorio de Sistemas de Información Avanzados, Facultad de Ingeniería,
Universidad de Buenos Aires, Buenos Aires, Argentina
{ngonzalez,gconcilio,jierache,ecalot}@lsia.fi.uba.ar
[2] Instituto de Investigación en Informática (III-LIDI),
Facultad de Informática, Universidad Nacional de La Plata,
Investigador Asociado – Comisión de Investigaciones Científicas (CIC),
La Plata, Argentina
whasperue@lidi.info.unlp.edu.ar

Abstract. The internal correlation of timing features inside word boundaries of free text sessions are studied, together with the classification performance in both authentication and identification tasks, using three publicly available datasets. Increasing distance between keystrokes was not found to be predictive of decreased correlation, even when individual users are considered and not the dataset as a whole. Considering five or more letter words, classification performance ranged 75%–90%+ for authentication and 60%–90%+ for identification tasks, with Random Forest classifier performing the best, and the simple k-nearest neighbours (k-NN) the worst. All the conclusions and observations generalised to the three datasets and its subsets, and particularly to both Spanish and English languages.

Keywords: Keystroke dynamics · Biometrics · User authentication · User verification · Second factor authentication · Information security · Man-machine interaction

1 Introduction

Keystroke dynamics is a subfield of behavioural biometrics and human—machine interaction, which has studied how typing rhythms can be used to discover or verify the identity of users since its inception in the late 70's [7]. A plethora of methods have been explored for feature extraction and later classification, both for static passwords and free text, as any recent review like [19] can show.

But its techniques are not restricted to authentication. Several behavioural and physiological states have been shown to modify, subtly but consistently and

© Springer Nature Switzerland AG 2021
P. Pesado and J. Eterovic (Eds.): CACIC 2020, CCIS 1409, pp. 321–333, 2021.
https://doi.org/10.1007/978-3-030-75836-3_22

in a detectable way, how users interact with the keyboard and other peripherals like computer mice [1]. Thus, the dominant hand [14], the latent progression of neurodegenerative diseases [20], and even the coarse emotional states of the user at the moment of typing can be identified [6], as well as whether the user is composing original text or copying it verbatim [15], and even their stance towards the entered text [2]. The reported accuracy of the latter classification tasks is much lower than when authenticating users, yet the fact that they can be performed, however limited, only with timing features and typing rhythms is already a remarkable feat. Recently, keystroke dynamics has proved useful to flag troll profiles spreading fake news about COVID-19 in social networks [17].

In this article a novel approach to keystroke dynamics analysis in free text is presented. Instead of extracting global features from the typing session, or splitting it in fixed-size letter arrangements—like n-grams—for further analysis, we propose splitting the timing feature vectors at word boundaries and training a set of classifiers based on individual words. To begin with, internal correlations in timing features at word boundaries are analysed. Then, the error rate for identification and classification tasks, based on the most frequent words for each length in characters, as found in the source datasets, is explored. With the objective of encouraging independent verification of our results, the word-split dataset LSIA used for the experiment was made publicly available at [12].

This paper extends the article *Exploración de las correlaciones internas de los parámetros temporales generados en dinámicas de tecleo*, presented at *IX Workshop Seguridad Informática* (WSI) of the *XXVI Congreso Argentino de Ciencias de la Computación* (CACIC 2020) [11], organised by Universidad Nacional de la Matanza. The supplementary contributions here presented include the evaluation of results for authentication and identification over two additional evaluation datasets, as well as the global characterization of growth with a word length of the average distance between letters of maximally correlated features.

The rest of the article is organised as follows. Section 2 states the problem that will be attacked and the chosen approach. Section 3 describes the experimental setup, datasets used, and data processing. Section 4 discusses the results and findings. Finally, Sect. 5 summarises the conclusions and suggests future lines of research.

2   Problem Statement and Approach

Free text keystroke dynamics analysis has classically been conducted using all the available information in a typing session, indiscriminately. For example, the A and R metrics of [3,8] weigh all n-grams equally and independently of their semantic context. However, pondering n-grams with a reasonable estimation of their uniqueness for the considered user has been proven to increase the classifier performance [9]. In particular, using semantic boundaries like word or sentence spans, inasmuch those created by punctuation marks, to split sessions and to weigh the contained n-grams accordingly seems like a natural strategy to follow.

The internal correlations in timing features inside word boundaries were studied by calculating the correlation matrices of hold times and flight times for each word in each dataset with at least ten observations, and extracting the position of the maximally correlated feature. Averaging over all the words of the same length, the growth of the average separation between letters of maximally correlated features with word length was determined.

Classification performance for authentication and identification tasks using individual words was evaluated. An *authentication task* is understood here as the verification of a user identity which is already known by other means; thus, we are corroborating that the user is who they claims to be. Authentication is a binary classification task where the two classes are legitimate and imposter. In contrast, an *identification task* intends to discover the identity of the user based on his typing behaviour without *a priori* knowledge. Thus, all enrolled users have to be considered as potential candidates and the classification task is no longer binary, but encompasses one class for each enrolled user.

Four different classifiers were compared (k-NN, Random Forest, SVM, and neural networks) for the tasks at hand. No special efforts were made to optimise the hyperparameters of the classifiers or for model selection, and as such the results should be considered as a lower bound that proves the worth of using words boundaries to split free text sessions for both authentication and identification tasks. The choice of classifiers was based on genericity, out of the box availability, and widespread use. Surely, a careful selection of classifiers together with hyperparameter optimization can further reduce the error rates but a detailed inquiry of the improvements that can be achieved with model selection is outside the scope of the present study.

3 Experimental Setup

3.1 Datasets

To ensure conclusions apply as generally as possible and not only for a handpicked set of data, three different datasets were used for the present experiment. All of them have been used in previous studies in keystroke dynamics and have been acquired in dissimilar environments, for different purposes, by non-mutually-collaborating sets of authors. Two different languages are represented, Spanish in LSIA and English in KM and PROSODY.

LSIA. For the present research, we employed a filtered subset of the dataset LSIA [4], used before to evaluate the error rates of finite context modelling for authentication [13], to replicate two well-known free text keystroke dynamics experiments [10], and to optimize the p parameter of Minkowski distance for verification [5]. It contains a large number of typing sessions, captured with conventional keyboards. Further details about the source data can be found in the aforementioned articles.

The most up to date version of our dataset includes free text entered during the course of the daily work of many typists, in the Spanish language. The sequence of virtual keys and timing parameters that comprise the session has been registered together with the identity of the user. Both hold times (the interval between a key down and the key up events for the same key) and flight times (the interval between successive key down events) were recorded with milliseconds precision, though sometimes they were rounded to the nearest multiple of eight milliseconds, or possibly other values, due to limitations in the recording tool. As the software used to capture the text runs on a web page, the web browser (as much as the platform of execution) restricts the precision with which the key events can be timestamped.

Free text sessions of 158 typists, both male and female, were captured during a time range spanning several years. To the best of our knowledge, our dataset is the only one where the effects of long term changes in the keystroke dynamics can be observed. The users were between 28 and 60 years old, and their typing proficiency varied from slow single finger typists to well-trained experts. Of course, their accuracy also varies wildly and surprisingly not in a way correlated with typing speed. The identity of the writers was verified before each session started using a passphrase and possibly a second factor authentication method in addition, thus rendering the chance of equivocal labelling very low. Typing sessions can be as short as 50 keystrokes but extend above the thousand rather often, with an average of around 250 keystrokes per session.

In comparison with a dataset captured in a quiet and predictable laboratory environment, this one was captured in a demanding real-world environment. Users moved around the organization, and as such, they might not necessarily be using the same keyboard for every session. They are subject to interruptions and distractions, and everyday stress. What is more, the text is not being copied but elaborated by the users. Thus, the noise introduced by a decision process while composing the text is added to the keystroke dynamics *per se*.

KM. The dataset KM was used to compare anomaly-detection algorithms for keystroke dynamics [15], and made publicly available. It contains sessions by twenty users of both free text composed on the fly and text transcribed verbatim, inasmuch typing errors and involuntary mistakes allow, from another source. The purpose of such distinction is to evaluate whether different typing tasks produce interchangeable profiles for later use to train a classifier. As volunteers find it easier to transcribe text than to come up with their own, and are more willing to engage in a transcription task than a composition one, using transcribed text as training seems to be a rewarding strategy.

The authors of [15] found that hold and flight times are two to three milliseconds slower on average during transcription session, enough to be statistically significant and to allow the determination of the task being performed. However, adding transcription sessions to the classifier training did not change evaluation results. In view of this, we merged the different groups in which the users were split into a single dataset for this study. The same filtering was used for dataset LSIA.

PROSODY. The dataset PROSODY, made publicly available by the authors of [2], was used to find cues of deceptive intent by analyzing variations in typing patterns. As in dataset KM, we also find free text composed on the fly and text transcribed verbatim, but the tasks are further subdivided with the objective of adding an emotional dimension. Three controversial topics were chosen (restaurant reviews, gay marriage, and gun control) and a set of 400 users was asked to write two short essays, against and in favour of the proposed idea, and to copy two other short essays, once again for and against.

As with dataset KM, the authors found variations in keystroke dynamics that are statistically significant between dissimilar tasks, and which also show differences based on the subjective reaction of the typist to the content being composed or transcribed. Yet, as our purpose in the present study is to evaluate classification errors and not the task being performed, we merged the different groups in which the users were split into a single dataset for this study. It is expected that in their everyday work and leisure tasks, any user will combine text transcription and creation, with topics they both approves or disapproves of; thus, a classifier used for authentication should be robust when trained with such diversity of data. The same filtering was used as for dataset LSIA.

3.2   Data Preprocessing, Cleaning, and Filtering

The three datasets LSIA, KM, and PROSODY, were preprocessed with a custom tool for keystroke dynamics experiments developed in-house, as each one comes in a particular non-standardised format which requires to be converted to a manageable unified format.

To reduce some sources of noise for this exploratory study, short typing sessions were filtered out in order to keep only those exceeding 150 keystrokes. Any timing parameter, whether hold time or flight time, exceeding 1500 ms was considered as a natural or artificial pause, and used to split the sessions so the classifiers would not be overwhelmed with values not representative of natural typing rhythms. As typical values for flight times usual fall in a range between 100 ms and 500 ms when typing naturally, and larger values generally indicate short pauses that must be considered as a part of a fluent typing streak, a second filtering stage was applied. In it, values exceeding three times the moving average of the latest values, even if below 1500 ms, were considered as pauses and used to split the sessions before finding individual words.

The resulting filtered sessions were split at word boundaries, using spaces and punctuation marks. Only alphabetic sequences were kept, discarding alphanumeric or combined sequences of keys like abc123 or #blue5ky. For each length, the most frequent word was found and each instance of it in every user session was extracted together with its timing parameters, hold time and flight time. The result was a set of tabular CSV files with a fixed number of columns containing, for each observation of the most frequent word of length n in each dataset, the user and $2n - 1$ timing parameters, n for hold times and $n - 1$ for flight times. We make these publicly available as part of this article at [12].

3.3   Data Processing

Training sets for authentication tasks were generated using, for each most frequent word of its length in each dataset, the instances of the user with the most instances, flagged as legitimate, and a random sample (without replacement) of the same size containing instances of all the other users, flagged as imposters. In this way, the binary classification problem remained, by design, balanced. To avoid dealing with the biases introduced by imbalanced classes in identification tasks, the number of instances for each most frequent word of its length was cut down so that every user had the same number of instances: as much as the one with the lesser amount.

The Python package *sklearn* [18] was used for the classification tasks, using a standard scaler and the cross-validation function `cross_val_score` with ten folds to evaluate the accuracy that is shown in the Tables 2 and 3.

4   Results

4.1   Internal Correlations Inside Word Boundaries

The general structure of internal correlations inside word boundaries is better illustrated with an example. Table 1 shows the correlation coefficients, in decreasing order, for the timing features of the word EVOLUCION (Spanish for "evolution"); flight time features have been labelled FT, together with a subindex denoting the corresponding key, while hold time features have been labelled HT. To avoid cluttering the table with spurious correlations, only those pairs with a correlation coefficient above 0.5 are shown. Even though this threshold value might seem too low, keystroke dynamics features are noisy and correlations between features are never as high as in other domains.

Table 1. Timing features with correlation coefficient > 0.5 for the word EVOLUCION

Feature 1	Feature 2	Correlation
HT_I	HT_{O_2}	0,693
HT_V	HT_C	0,681
FT_E	FT_U	0,591
HT_E	HT_C	0,551
HT_{O_2}	HT_N	0,549
HT_{O_1}	HT_U	0,526
HT_I	HT_N	0,524
HT_E	HT_V	0,510
FT_C	FT_{O_2}	0,507

Figure 1 shows this same information graphically, to emphasise maximally correlated features. Empty circles between letters represent flight times while the letter themselves represent their own hold time, and edges indicate to which feature of the lower row is the one the upper row maximally correlated. It is not surprising that the strongest correlations tend to appear between hold time features, as these tend to be more stable and more related to the average writing speed than to flight times or other hold times.

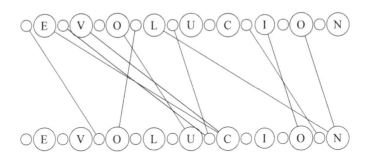

Fig. 1. Maximally correlated features inside the word EVOLUCION

In this particular example, whose observations will be seen to generalise, the influence of each feature is not necessarily local or restricted to adjacent features. Maximal correlations between features four or even five keystrokes away (as between E and C, or L and N) can be found. Thus, n-grams of size two or three will probably be insufficient to represent accurately the biometric signature of the user. Similarly, when using finite context modelling [9] the length of the contexts should be at least five to adequately model this specific word.

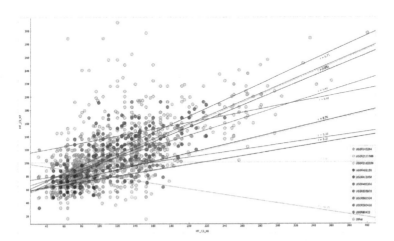

Fig. 2. Correlation between flight times for E and U in the word EVOLUCION, for several users

Strong correlations of features between non-adjacent keys are also apparent when the dataset is disaggregated. Figure 2 shows a scatter plot of flight times of keys E and U, where the vertical axis represents the flight time of E and the horizontal axis represents the flight time of U. For each user, the correlation coefficient and the regression line are shown. For example, user 400150 has an $r = 0.71$. Most users follow the same trend of positive correlation, but counterexamples exist as user 145264, with $r = -0.25$, reminds us.

The illustrated behaviour is not specific to the specific word considered above. When evaluating the dataset as a whole, the average separation between letters of maximally correlated features grows with word length as Fig. 3 shows for hold times and flight times. As we are considering this value as a random variable, the grey bands display a one standard deviation interval to better understand how it is distributed; missing bands in some of the last points are not a mistake, but an artifact due to the low number of samples.

4.2 Classification Performance for Authentication Tasks

Even though, as has been shown in the previous subsection, the two features introduced by each letter are not completely independent, it can be expected that the longer the word considered, the easier it will be for the classifier to correctly flag it as belonging to an imposter or to the legitimate user. As shown in Table 2, this anticipated behaviour is observed rather consistently throughout all datasets with a general trend for decreasing accuracy with decreasing word length. Following [16], the accuracy is considered a random variable and it is reported with a 95% binomial confidence interval because the number of word instances per user and the number of users who have typed that word varies significantly among the datasets.

The accuracy of the different classifiers is commensurable, with k-NN regularly scoring slightly lower than the rest and Random Forest more often than not leading by a small margin. Once again, this observation generalises to all datasets. It is interesting to note that although the training sets belonging to datasets other than LSIA contain a comparatively small number of instances, the classification performance is still comparable with those of the latter. This is encouraging, as it shows that the amount of free text needed to build a user profile does not need to be large, and deserves further consideration in later studies.

Last but not least, the accuracy for most individual words of length five or more is around 90% and higher, a promising exploratory result that can be improved with scrupulous model selection. For those scoring lower, all but one remain above 75%.

4.3 Classification Performance for Identification Tasks

Identification is a harder task than authentication, as the possible classes are more than just legitimate user and imposter. Thus, we expect the classification performance to be consistently lower than for the authentication tasks. Table 3

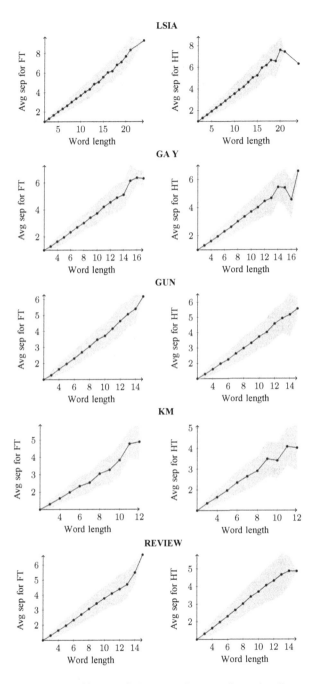

Fig. 3. Average separation (Avg sep) between letters of maximally correlated (max corr) features as word length grows for each dataset for hold (HT) and flight times (FT).

Table 2. Accuracy and confidence interval (CI) of k-NN, SVM, Random Forest (RFC) and ANN (Artificial Neural Networks) classifiers for authentication tasks for each word and dataset considered.

	Word	k-NN	CI	SVM	CI	RFC	CI	ANN	CI
LSIA	CARDIORRESPIRATORIA	96.4	94.9–97.6	97.7	96.5–98.6	98.8	97.9–99.4	96.8	95.4–97.9
	CARDIORESPIRATORIA	90.1	85.8–93.4	92.2	88.3–95.2	97.4	94.7–98.9	91.4	87.3–94.5
	HEMODINAMICAMENTE	95.9	95.0–96.6	97.0	96.3–97.6	97.4	96.7–98.0	96.8	96.1–97.5
	PARTICULARIDADES	95.3	92.2–97.4	93.7	90.3–96.2	96.5	93.7–98.2	95.3	92.2–97.4
	HIPOVENTILACION	92.8	90.8–94.5	91.7	89.6–93.5	93.7	91.9–95.3	90.6	88.4–92.5
	POSTOPERATORIO	99.0	98.6–99.3	99.2	98.9–99.5	99.3	99.0–99.6	99.2	98.8–99.4
	SEROHEMATICOS	98.9	98.6–99.2	98.8	98.5–99.1	99.0	98.8–99.3	98.9	98.6–99.2
	CONSULTORIOS	98.9	98.4–99.3	99.5	99.1–99.7	99.7	99.4–99.9	99.7	99.4–99.9
	LABORATORIO	95.2	94.7–95.7	95.3	94.9–95.8	96.5	96.1–96.9	95.4	94.9–95.9
	DEPRESIBLE	92.3	91.5–93.1	90.5	89.5–91.3	93.1	92.3–93.8	91.9	91.1–92.7
	EVOLUCION	93.5	92.5–94.3	92.1	91.1–93.1	96.7	96.0–97.3	96.2	95.4–96.9
	PACIENTE	87.9	87.3–88.5	86.7	86.0–87.3	89.6	89.0–90.1	88.7	88.1–89.3
	CONTROL	91.8	91.2–92.3	90.5	89.9–91.1	93.2	92.7–93.7	92.5	92.0–93.0
	BLANDO	90.8	89.8–91.6	88.3	87.3–89.3	93.6	92.8–94.4	93.8	93.0–94.5
	BUENA	91.3	90.6–92.0	88.8	88.0–89.5	92.5	91.9–93.1	92.2	91.6–92.9
	PARA	88.5	87.9–89.2	87.8	87.1–88.4	89.9	89.3–90.5	89.7	89.0–90.3
	CON	89.9	89.5–90.2	88.3	88.0–88.7	90.1	89.8–90.4	90.3	90.0–90.6
KM	WEARING	86.7	73.1–94.8	90.0	77.4–96.7	95.0	84.4–99.0	92.5	80.8–98.0
	THERE	82.5	68.5–91.9	95.0	84.7–99.0	92.5	81.1–97.9	92.5	81.1–97.9
	WITH	92.5	81.1–97.9	97.5	88.7–99.7	97.5	88.7–99.7	97.5	88.7–99.7
	THE	96.7	94.5–98.2	96.7	94.5–98.2	98.6	97.0–99.5	98.1	96.3–99.1
GAY	RELIGIOUS	80.0	63.6–91.1	80.0	63.6–91.1	83.3	67.5–93.2	83.3	67.5–93.2
	CHILDREN	87.5	73.7–95.4	89.2	75.9–96.3	91.7	79.2–97.6	97.5	88.0–99.8
	MARIAGE	86.1	76.8–92.6	87.3	78.3–93.5	90.5	82.3–95.7	88.8	80.0–94.5
	SHOULD	94.3	86.0–98.3	98.3	92.2–99.8	98.3	92.2–99.8	96.3	89.0–99.2
	THEIR	70.0	53.2–83.5	75.8	59.5–87.9	88.3	74.3–96.0	75.0	58.6–87.3
	THAT	79.9	71.0–87.0	87.3	79.6–92.9	81.9	73.3–88.6	85.1	76.9–91.2
	THE	76.0	69.1–82.0	71.7	64.5–78.1	86.8	81.1–91.3	79.0	72.3–84.6
GUN	GOVERNMENT	80.8	65.2–91.4	100.0	92.7–100.0	96.7	86.2–99.6	97.5	87.6–99.8
	CRIMINALS	93.3	77.8–98.9	88.3	70.9–96.9	93.3	77.8–98.9	91.7	75.4–98.3
	CITIZENS	74.2	59.1–85.8	75.0	60.0–86.5	92.5	81.1–97.9	72.5	57.3–84.5
	CONTROL	73.5	60.1–84.3	76.0	62.8–86.2	82.0	69.6–90.8	78.0	65.0–87.8
	PEOPLE	87.1	78.5–93.2	84.5	75.3–91.2	91.2	83.5–96.0	87.3	78.7–93.3
	RIGHT	77.0	63.3–87.4	76.5	62.7–87.0	85.5	73.1–93.5	79.5	66.1–89.2
	THAT	68.0	57.0–77.8	79.6	69.5–87.5	80.0	69.9–87.8	86.6	77.6–92.9
	THE	73.0	66.1–79.2	69.0	61.9–75.5	73.5	66.6–79.6	74.2	67.3–80.2
REVIEW	RESTAURANT	66.7	46.3–83.1	85.0	66.7–95.2	90.0	73.1–97.6	80.0	60.7–92.3
	ALWAYS	92.5	81.5–97.8	92.5	81.5–97.8	97.5	89.1–99.7	95.0	85.1–98.9
	PLACE	78.3	61.1–90.2	93.3	80.0–98.6	100.0	91.8–100.0	96.7	85.2–99.7
	THEY	73.5	59.8–84.5	60.5	46.2–73.5	80.5	67.6–89.8	82.5	69.9–91.3
	THE	85.8	79.7–90.6	69.8	62.3–76.5	84.0	77.6–89.1	84.5	78.2–89.5

shows that this is the case, with all classifiers performing worse for each word throughout every dataset.

A similar trend of decreasing accuracy with decreasing word length is evident also here, and for the same motives, but with a more pronounced downwards slope that is consistent with the added difficulty of identification. The comparative behaviour of classifiers is almost identical, with k-NN mostly underscoring

Table 3. Accuracy and confidence interval (CI) of k-NN, SVM, Random Forest (RFC) and ANN (Artificial Neural Networks) classifiers for identification tasks for each dataset and word considered.

	Word	Users	k-NN	CI	SVM	CI	RFC	CI	ANN	CI
LSIA	CARDIORRESPIRATORIA	11	87.4	84.9–89.6	89.7	87.4–91.7	91.7	89.5–93.5	86.9	84.4–89.2
	CARDIORESPIRATORIA	11	82.3	78.9–85.4	83.8	80.5–86.8	90.2	87.4–92.5	80.8	77.2–84.0
	HEMODINAMICAMENTE	107	77.2	76.4–77.9	79.9	79.1–80.6	84.7	84.0–85.3	76.6	75.8–77.3
	PARTICULARIDADES	26	71.8	68.5–74.9	75.7	72.6–78.6	83.4	80.6–85.9	71.1	67.9–74.3
	HIPOVENTILACION	38	78.1	76.5–79.7	80.5	78.9–82.0	85.6	84.2–86.9	79.0	77.4–80.6
	POSTOPERATORIO	24	94.6	93.7–95.3	96.4	95.7–97.0	97.2	96.6–97.8	95.4	94.7–96.1
	SEROHEMATICOS	12	97.8	97.3–98.1	97.9	97.5–98.3	98.1	97.7–98.5	97.6	97.2–98.0
	CONSULTORIOS	72	74.8	73.8–75.8	77.6	76.6–78.5	83.5	82.7–84.3	76.8	75.9–77.8
	LABORATORIO	91	80.5	80.0–81.1	81.0	80.5–81.5	85.9	85.4–86.3	82.6	82.1–83.1
	DEPRESIBLE	125	73.5	72.9–74.2	73.9	73.3–74.5	80.7	80.2–81.2	75.5	75.0–76.1
	EVOLUCION	172	67.2	66.5–67.8	70.1	69.4–70.7	76.6	76.0–77.2	74.5	73.8–75.1
	PACIENTE	244	67.0	66.6–67.3	66.6	66.2–67.0	74.2	73.8–74.5	70.8	70.4–71.1
	CONTROL	199	67.9	67.5–68.3	67.7	67.3–68.0	75.3	75.0–75.7	71.7	71.3–72.1
	BLANDO	153	54.2	53.7–54.8	51.6	51.0–52.1	64.4	63.8–64.9	59.2	58.6–59.7
	BUENA	211	51.5	50.9–52.0	48.2	47.7–48.7	58.7	58.2–59.2	56.0	55.5–56.5
	PARA	180	46.9	46.4–47.4	45.8	45.3–46.2	53.8	53.4–54.3	51.2	50.8–51.7
KM	WEARING	5	83.3	73.2–90.7	90.7	82.1–95.9	92.1	84.0–96.8	83.3	73.2–90.7
	THERE	15	73.3	67.0–79.0	72.9	66.6–78.6	76.3	70.2–81.7	61.7	55.0–68.1
	WITH	15	77.1	71.1–82.4	78.6	72.7–83.7	77.6	71.6–82.8	66.7	60.1–72.8
	THE	20	59.6	57.6–61.6	58.7	56.7–60.7	63.4	61.4–65.4	60.6	58.6–62.6
GAY	RELIGIOUS	2	100.0	91.8–100.0	100.0	91.8–100.0	96.7	85.2–99.7	96.7	85.2–99.7
	CHILDREN	10	84.8	77.6–90.4	89.9	83.6–94.4	95.0	90.0–97.9	82.4	74.9–88.4
	MARIAGE	202	49.6	47.8–51.3	56.5	54.8–58.3	66.3	64.7–68.0	52.6	50.8–54.4
	SHOULD	62	62.7	59.3–66.1	66.3	62.9–69.5	73.8	70.6–76.8	62.2	58.7–65.6
	THEIR	12	57.5	49.4–65.3	57.6	49.4–65.4	70.0	62.3–77.1	55.5	47.3–63.4
	THAT	202	29.8	28.3–31.5	29.5	28.0–31.2	39.2	37.5–40.9	34.6	32.9–36.3
	THE	373	15.0	14.3–15.8	13.7	13.0–14.4	21.3	20.5–22.2	18.2	17.4–19.0
GUN	GOVERNMENT	4	92.7	83.4–97.5	100.0	95.5–100.0	100.0	95.5–100.0	98.0	91.4–99.8
	CRIMINALS	2	100.0	89.3–100.0	100.0	89.3–100.0	100.0	89.3–100.0	100.0	89.3–100.0
	CITIZENS	2	93.3	80.3–98.6	93.3	80.3–98.6	100.0	92.0–100.0	96.7	85.5–99.6
	CONTROL	70	62.1	58.9–65.2	66.6	63.4–69.6	77.3	74.4–79.9	57.6	54.3–60.8
	PEOPLE	84	53.9	51.0–56.7	56.8	54.0–59.7	69.7	67.0–72.3	56.4	53.5–59.2
	RIGHT	22	57.6	51.6–63.4	57.9	51.9–63.7	66.1	60.3–71.6	49.6	43.7–55.6
	THAT	177	30.9	29.2–32.7	30.4	28.7–32.2	40.2	38.4–42.1	35.7	33.9–37.5
	THE	383	16.3	15.6–17.0	14.2	13.6–14.9	24.0	23.2–24.8	19.3	18.6–20.1
REVIEW	RESTAURANT	3	100.0	92.5–100.0	96.7	86.0–99.6	100.0	92.5–100.0	96.7	86.0–99.6
	ALWAYS	9	72.7	64.3–80.0	70.3	61.7–77.8	93.4	88.0–96.8	73.5	65.2–80.7
	PLACE	14	84.7	78.7–89.6	87.2	81.4–91.6	90.8	85.7–94.5	79.7	73.1–85.3
	THEY	57	33.9	30.4–37.4	34.4	31.0–38.0	41.8	38.2–45.5	33.0	29.6–36.5
	THE	490	11.5	11.0–12.0	10.3	9.8–10.8	17.1	16.4–17.7	13.7	13.1–14.2

and Random Forest leading, but with the differences between the best and the worst are more pronounced and neural network performing more erratically.

Once again, the accuracy for most individual words, although lower than for authentication, ranges from around 60% to 90% for words of length five or more. This is remarkable given the limited amount of information timing features of typing rhythms provide, and that the number of classes in not small. Conversely, the accuracy for shorter words like THE diminishes sharply. Some of the happiest results in Table 3 should be taken with a grain of salt, like RESTAURANT for the REVIEW dataset and CITIZENS for the GUN dataset; the very limited number of instances and different users contained in the training set does not reflect the real-world difficulty of the task in an environment with many users.

5   Conclusions

In the present study, the internal correlation of timing features inside word boundaries of free text sessions has been studied, together with the classification performance in both authentication and identification tasks, using a filtered subset from the dataset of [10] and two other publicly available and previously used datasets. It was observed that each feature shows a meaningful correlation with those of non-adjacent keys, ranging even further than the previously assumed n-gram length of three or four keys. Inside word boundaries, increasing distance between keystrokes was not found to be predictive of decreased correlation. This conclusion still applies when individual users are considered, and not only when a whole dataset is aggregated.

Classification performance using individual words turned out to be promising (mostly around 90% for authentication and 60%–90% for identification tasks) in spite of the reduced amount of timing features available and the generic, unoptimised classifiers that were used for the evaluation. As expected, longer words yielded better accuracy and identification was harder than authentication. Random Forest performed the best, while the simple k-NN performed the worst. All the conclusions and observations generalised to the three datasets and theirs parts, and particularly to both Spanish and English languages.

Acknowledgments. The authors acknowledge the support of Universidad de Buenos Aires through Proyecto de Desarrollo Estratégico PDE-44-2019, "Reconocimiento de patrones de teclado en ambientes web" (Strategic Development Project PDE-44-2019, "Recognition of typing patterns in web environments").

References

1. Ahmed, A.A.E., Traore, I.: A new biometric technology based on mouse dynamics. IEEE Trans. Dependable Secure Comput. **4**(3), 165–179 (2007)
2. Banerjee, R., Feng, S., Kang, J.S., Choi, Y.: Keystroke patterns as prosody in digital writings: a case study with deceptive reviews and essays. In: Proceedings of the 2014 Conference on Empirical Methods in Natural Language Processing, pp. 1469–1473. Association for Computational Linguistics, Doha (2014)
3. Bergadano, F., Gunetti, D., Picardi, C.: User authentication through keystroke dynamics. ACM Trans. Inf. Syst. Secur. (TISSEC) **5**(4), 367–397 (2002)
4. Calot, E.P.: Keystroke dynamics keypress latency dataset. Database (2015). http://lsia.fi.uba.ar/pub/papers/kd-dataset/

5. Calot, E.P.: Robustez de las métricas de clasificación de cadencia de tecleo frente a variaciones emocionales. Ph.D. thesis, Universidad Nacional de La Plata (2019). https://doi.org/10.35537/10915/76652. http://sedici.unlp.edu.ar/handle/10915/76652

6. Epp, C., Lippold, M., Mandryk, R.L.: Identifying emotional states using keystroke dynamics. In: Proceedings of the SIGCHI Conference on Human Factors in Computing Systems, pp. 715–724. ACM (2011)

7. Forsen, G.E., Nelson, M.R., Staron, R.J.J.: Personal attributes authentication techniques. Technical report, DTIC Document (1977). Final technical report. http://lsia.fi.uba.ar/papers/forsen77.pdf

8. Francesco Bergadano DGyCP: Identity verification through dynamic keystroke analysis. Intell. Data Anal. 7(5), 469–496 (2003)

9. González, N., Calot, E.P.: Finite context modeling of keystroke dynamics in free text. In: 2015 International Conference of the Biometrics Special Interest Group (BIOSIG), pp. 1–5 (2015). https://doi.org/10.1109/BIOSIG.2015.7314606

10. González, N., Calot, E.P., Ierache, J.S.: A replication of two free text keystroke dynamics experiments under harsher conditions. In: 2016 International Conference of the Biometrics Special Interest Group (BIOSIG), pp. 1–6. IEEE (2016)

11. González, N., Concilio, G., Ierache, J., Calot, E.P., Hasperué, W.: Exploración de las correlaciones internas de los parámetros temporales generados en dinámicas de tecleo. In: IX Workshop Seguridad Informática (WSI) of the XXVI Congreso Argentino de Ciencias de la Computación (CACIC 2020), pp. 717–725 (2020). ISBN 978-987-4417-90-9

12. González, N.: Dataset for exploring internal correlations in timing features of keystroke dynamics at word boundaries and their usage for authentication and identification. In: Mendeley Data V1 (2021). https://doi.org/10.17632/vx83444p8n.1

13. González, N., Calot, E.P.: Finite context modeling of keystroke dynamics in free text. In: 2015 International Conference of the Biometrics Special Interest Group (BIOSIG), pp. 1–5. IEEE (2015)

14. Idrus, S.Z.S., Cherrier, E., Rosenberger, C., Bours, P.: Soft biometrics for keystroke dynamics: profiling individuals while typing passwords. Comput. Secur. 45, 147–155 (2014)

15. Killourhy, K.S., Maxion, R.A.: Comparing anomaly-detection algorithms for keystroke dynamics. In: International Conference on Dependable Systems & Networks (DSN-09), Los Alamitos, California, Estoril, Lisbon, Portugal, 29 June–02 July 2009, pp. 125–134. IEEE Computer Society Press (2009)

16. Killourhy, K.S., Maxion, R.A.: Should security researchers experiment more and draw more inferences? In: CSET (2011)

17. Morales, A., et al.: Keystroke biometrics in response to fake news propagation in a global pandemic. arXiv preprint arXiv:200507688 (2020)

18. Pedregosa, F., et al.: Scikit-learn: machine learning in Python. J. Mach. Learn. Res. 12, 2825–2830 (2011)

19. Raul, N., Shankarmani, R., Joshi, P.: A comprehensive review of keystroke dynamics-based authentication mechanism. In: Khanna, A., Gupta, D., Bhattacharyya, S., Snasel, V., Platos, J., Hassanien, A.E. (eds.) International Conference on Innovative Computing and Communications. AISC, vol. 1059, pp. 149–162. Springer, Singapore (2020). https://doi.org/10.1007/978-981-15-0324-5_13

20. Van Waes, L., Leijten, M., Mariën, P., Engelborghs, S.: Typing competencies in Alzheimer's disease: an exploration of copy tasks. Comput. Hum. Behav. 73, 311–319 (2017)

Digital Governance and Smart Cities

IndiMaker - Open Data Linking Framework

Juan Santiago Preisegger⬤, Alejandro Greco⬤, Ariel Pasini(✉)⬤,
Marcos Boracchia⬤, and Patricia Pesado⬤

Computer Science Research Institute LIDI (III-LIDI), Facultad de Informática, Universidad
Nacional de La Plata, 50 y 120 La Plata, Buenos Aires, Argentina
{jspreisegger,apasini,marcosb,ppesado}@lidi.info.unlp.edu.ar

Abstract. Open data portals make a very important set of information available
to the community. Those interested in a particular topic, retrieve data on the topic
from different portals, but then, processing them together is difficult due to the
different publication criteria used by each portal. To assist in this process, a tool
called IndiMaker was developed, together with a framework that helps linking
these files to users with little technical experience in data analysis. Within the
framework, the tool allows applying different operations on the files, generating
graphics in a dashboard, which makes information analysis easier. The framework
was applied to the "environment" topic, in particular, to water and air quality and
energy generation.

Keywords: Open data · Data linking · Software engineering · Open
government · Environment

1 Introduction

A city thrives on the behavior of its citizens. Citizens, through different devices, are able
to register more and more information about the activities they carry out. Making intelligent use of the information registered by government authorities to improve the lives
of citizens is a great contribution to the community itself. But the contributions that can
be achieved from the recorded data may come not only from the government – different
agencies or individuals, who are capable of analyzing the information, processing it and
proposing improvements, are also important factors in this cycle of city improvement.
This difference is what makes a city a smart, sustainable and participatory [1].

To achieve citizen participation in this type of process, organizations make large
volumes of open data available to their community, so that those interested in the subject
can process them and generate contributions in the process of improving the city [2,
3]. But when accessing the data, technical differences appear such as file formats, file
structure, column names, data types, magnitudes, etc., which make it difficult, and in
some cases impossible, to analyze the information.

Computer Science Research Institute LIDI (III-LIDI) - Partner Center of the Scientific Research
Agency of the Province of Buenos Aires (CIC).

J. S. Preisegger, A. Greco, A. Pasini, M. Boracchia, P. Pesado—Fellow UNLP.

© Springer Nature Switzerland AG 2021
P. Pesado and J. Eterovic (Eds.): CACIC 2020, CCIS 1409, pp. 337–349, 2021.
https://doi.org/10.1007/978-3-030-75836-3_23

The proposed framework is aimed, on the one hand, at linking datasets obtained from open portals and about a specific subject, and, on the other, at allowing a joint analysis of these data in a simple way that does not require advanced technical expertise. This framework is based on five steps: *1) Search, 2) Preliminary analysis, 3) Direct loading, 4) Standardization, and 5) Linkage.* This process is supported by the use of the IndiMaker tool.

IndiMaker has the potential to process files in various formats, apply different operations to their contents, and link the files, creating a dashboard of indicators that helps the user visualize the operations performed on the files. This article incorporates a more detailed description of the tool presented in [4].

To validate the process, the framework was applied to open data related to the environment, in particular, to data sets obtained from different public portals on air quality, water quality and energy consumption.

The second section presents the concepts of sustainable smart cities and open data. Then, in the third section, the general concepts about the indicator dashboards and the IndiMaker tool are discussed. The fourth section introduces the open data linking framework. In the fifth section, the framework is applied to environment-related data, and finally, in the sixth section, our conclusions and future work are discussed.

2 Sustainable Smart Cities and Open Data

Cities thrive on the participation of their communities. Citizens constantly generate information that can later be used in making decisions about the development of that city and, after a while, will affect the lives of those citizens. Achieving that citizens have access to data and being allowed to participate in their analysis, thus contributing to the development of the city is an important contribution in order to turn a city into a smart city.

2.1 Smart Sustainable Cities

In general, the concept of smart cities is related to the use of technology to carry out city activities, but, in reality, it is much more than that. According to [1], Smart Sustainable Cities represent the last stages of progression through digital cities and smart cities, and are considered as a continuous transforming process, based on the collaboration and commitment of different actors, building different capacities (human, technical and institutional) in a way that improves quality of life, protects natural resources, and pursues socio-economic development. The International Telecommunications Union (ITU) of the United Nations established one of the pioneering definitions of a smart sustainable city: "A Smart Sustainable City is an innovative city that uses information and communication technologies (ICTs) and other means to improve quality of life, efficiency of urban operation and services, and competitiveness, while ensuring that it meets the needs of present and future generations with respect to economic, social, environmental as well as cultural aspects".

2.2 Open Data

Society expects increasingly more from its government and government officials. These demands include transparency and an efficient management of public goods, as well as collaboration with different sectors of society and participation in the decision-making process [5]. Based on these requirements, and assisted by new technologies, a new type of government with greater citizen inclusion came to be, allowing citizens to contribute to public policies and participate in the decision-making process [6, 7].

The implementation of an open government resulted in data opening, which consists in making available to society data about common citizen interests so that, in any way, they can develop new ideas or applications that will deliver new data, knowledge, or other services that the government is unable to deliver [3, 8, 9].

The data that made available to society are very diverse, and this sharing process is not only carried out by government agencies – international organizations, NGOs, and other organizations promote various measures to make gradually more data sources available to society, not only related to government management, but also to other areas, such as the rational use of resources and the protection of the environment.

3 Using Open Data to Create Dashboards

The data are used to generate indicators that are in turn used to build dashboards. For the generation of these dashboards, data sources and datasets must be analyzed, and tools that allow establishing relations among data must be available, which is used to build relevant information that becomes an indicator that allows improving the decision-making process.

3.1 Data Sources

The new paradigms, developed by the different organizations, coordinate actions to improve quality of life for society through data opening and the improvements proposed in city infrastructure. Various applications and tools were generated, from multiple sectors, to provide support and automate, or improve, the process of publishing, searching and, sometimes, processing information for the different sectors of society. Among these tools, catalogs and open data portals stand out. Organizations use these to publish data on different aspects of their activities and the environment in which they operate. For example, some countries, provinces, municipalities or organizations have portals where they unify data from the different regions or topics in which they specialize. Those that are most advanced in the area publish their data and describe them using data schemes, which helps make data more descriptive in terms of content.

A tool that uses this information to allow data to be searched more globally is Google Dataset Search, which is a search engine specialized in finding datasets stored on the web, through keywords, as long as they use schema.org dataset tags or equivalent structures represented in the Data Catalog Vocabulary (DCAT) format [10].

3.2 Datasets

A dataset is a collection of data that is usually tabulated, that is, it corresponds to the contents of a single database table or a single data matrix, where each column of the table represents a specific variable and each row represents a specific member of the data set.

Datasets are the backbone of data portals and catalogs. They group one or more data resources and, for their publication, they require prior preparation in order to be processed and reused by third parties. According to [11], this includes three activities: *1) Documentation*: this activity consists in defining the metadata that each of the datasets to be published will have. Metadata describe the basics of the dataset, and are used to organize, classify, relate, and find the necessary data (e.g., title, description, institution, license, category, publication date, etc.). *2) Structuring*: it consists in preparing the dataset to be published with a structured format, without inaccurate or empty fields, which allows reusing and processing in any software. *3) Data loading*: it consists of publishing the data on a platform that allows organization and easy access by those who are going to reuse the data.

3.3 Dashboards

An indicator can be defined as a piece of data, or a set of data, that helps to objectively measure the evolution of a process or an activity corresponding to any organization. Indicators can be organized and connected to form a dashboard. These dashboards allow a more exhaustive monitoring and evaluation of the process or activity. In addition, they generally allow visualizing their evolution graphically, which helps interpret the results.

3.4 Tool for Dashboard Generation - IndiMaker

IndiMaker is a system that can be accessed from any web browser and allows connecting datasets to build custom indicators in dashboards.

To start using the tool, a username and password are required. When you open the login screen, you will be asked for these credentials to begin.

Before building an indicator, it will be necessary to generate a dashboard, which will contain a set of indicators that will generally have common objectives to measure.

In addition to the set of indicators mentioned above, dashboards also have a name that identifies them, a description of their purpose, and a set of datasets that must be loaded by the user when building each dashboard. It should be noted that datasets can be removed if they are no longer necessary, and new ones can be added. This tool allows importing datasets in various formats (.xls, .xlsx, .xml, .ods and .csv).

An operation that is very interesting is the combination of datasets. This operation can be done using columns with common content between the datasets. The result of this operation will be a new dataset with richer information.

It can also be used to homogenize all this information and store it in the database; then, the user can perform operations on the data stored and build indicators. The indicators must be generated appropriately; otherwise, they can generate inaccurate, incorrect or subjective information, which would hinder data analysis. One of the great virtues of this tool is its simplicity when generating indicators, since it is designed to make use of the information in a way that makes it easy for the user to perform complex operations between the different data, avoiding *a priori* the generation of inaccurate indicators. Therefore, the indicators that are generated will allow developing a quantitative measure that will have meaning for those who analyze it.

At the same time, the tool can be adapted to different devices, like a desktop computer, a tablet or a smartphone, and it can also be used in both Spanish and English.

The tool has a role management system, which means that there will be different users in the system with different permissions and, thus, different operations available to them.

When accessing the tool, there is a menu on the left of the screen with all the options available to the user. These options include:

- General dashboard: This will be where, based on the different charts, the results of the indicators from the different dashboards can be viewed.
- Dashboards: Here, users can manage their dashboards, add new dashboards and remove or edit existing ones. This view will show a paginated list with all the dashboards for the logged-in user. The number of records to display per page can be configured, results can be sorted by name, and dashboard searches can be sorted by name, which improves access speed and favors simplicity if there are many results.

To build the indicators, their name, type of indicator, owner, measurement frequency, description, and reference levels must be indicated, in addition to the operation on which the corresponding indicator is based. The operations that can be performed on data include addition, subtraction, division, percentages, data grouping, and various logical comparisons, including the ability to use regular expressions for more advanced users. Users can build indicators by combining these operations.

The name field is used to identify the indicator.

The type field allows selecting a type from those already loaded in the system, and it will be used to classify the indicator.

The owner is the person responsible for defining the different roles associated with the indicator:

- Who is responsible for generating information
- Who gathers the information
- Who analyzes the information
- Who reports or presents the information obtained with the indicator

The frequency field allows selecting how often the indicator will be recalculated.

Calculation frequency should not be confused with information collection frequency. For example, to analyze the work of a supplier, it may be convenient to calculate the indicator every six months. However, is the information on the work of that provider going to be gathered after they have been working for six months? The answer is no. It will be more convenient to have a supplier control sheet where their weekly management is tracked.

The description field, optional but recommended, can be completed with free text by the user, and it is used to describe the objectives of the indicator.

Within a section called "Indicator formula" there are some fields that will allow carrying out operations on the data belonging to the sources in the dashboard. This is the process used to create the calculation for the indicator, known as its "formula".

An example of formula construction can be seen in Fig. 1. In this example, the "USA_Air" dataset was used, which contains information about the air in different cities of the United States for different years. This formula allows knowing the total number of days in 2020 for each of the cities in which air pollution is considered acceptable.

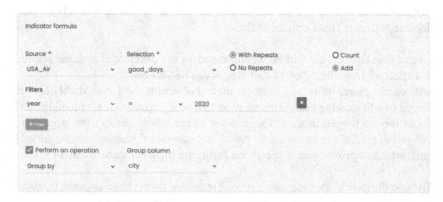

Fig. 1. Building the formula for an indicator

Finally, both the "Critical Level" and "Satisfactory Level" fields are optional.

These fields allow entering reference values for the user when calculating the indicator. These entered values will be represented when creating the chart for the indicator, and will allow alerting the user about possible deviations from the objectives established by the indicator.

It should be noted that, at all times, the user can search for a particular indicator. To do so, there is a search button located in a top menu bar that, when clicked on, will display a text field to be completed, where users can enter the name of the indicator (or part of it) that they want to search for.

The indicators in each dashboard can be represented in various ways, including different charts, which allows users to easily be alerted to potential deviations from previously established objectives. Figure 2 shows a sample representation for an indicator as a line graph.

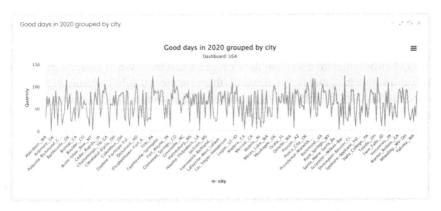

Fig. 2. Representation of an indicator as a line graph.

4 Open Data Linking Framework

When analyzing the data from the different catalogs or portals, there are incompatibility issues between the data formats used by the different providers. Given this situation, to achieve successful data linking, it is essential to analyze data sources and formats beforehand. Consequently, progress was made in generating a five-step data linking framework: *1) Search, 2) Preliminary analysis, 3) Direct loading, 4) Standardization, and 5) Linkage.*

1. *Search*: Searching for datasets related to the area of interest, through organizations' data portals or catalogs, or using the Google Dataset Search tool.
2. *Preliminary analysis:* Analyzing the datasets obtained, verifying that information is in a format supported by the tool and that all the columns have a header. Also, checking content format (completing rows and columns, transposing rows by columns in any of the datasets, etc.) for a successful linkage.
3. *File loading:* Loading the file into IndiMaker. When loading the file, the tool will perform a series of checks on the content. If validated, the comparison instance will begin. In the event that inconsistencies are detected, the content will be standardized.
4. *Standardization:* The standardization process can be done manually or automatically (using an external tool), depending on the size of the file. In this instance it is verified:

   a. The data in the columns of the datasets are of the same type.
   b. The data in the columns have some value.
   c. The max amount of data in each row is not exceeded.

5. *Linkage*: Consolidating the tables based on a common parameter, if necessary, to obtain more information and to be able to relate the data to analyze them in a simple and direct fashion.

5   Environment Open Data Linkage – Case Study

Governmental and non-governmental agencies make available to the community numerous sets of environmental data from their geographic region. When analyzing the information as a whole to obtain regional values, there are incompatibility issues between the data formats used by the different organizations. Data sources and their formats should be analyzed to make the process of information linkage possible.

Below, the five steps of the framework will be applied:

Search. The environment was selected as a case study. Among the different aspects that are relevant for this topic, it was decided to limit data to the aspects that affect society every day, such as water and air quality, which are essential for society and its future. Also, energy generation was included, which is often related to quality of life.

Data searches were carried out using the following terms: *Drinking water quality, Energy generation, Air quality*. In Table 1, below, shows the datasets selected among those obtained from the different countries.

Table 1. Datasets obtained per country.

Country	Water	Air	Energy
USA	✓	✓	✓
Chile	✓	✓	✓
Brazil	✓	✓	✓
Uruguay	✕	✓	✓
Paraguay	✕	✕	✓
Bolivia	✕	✕	✕
Peru	✕	✕	✕
Colombia	✓	✓	✕
Argentina	✓	✕	✓

Preliminary análisis. From the data obtained, data type, format and structure were analyzed in each case, so as to be able to link them using the proposed tool to carry out a more in-depth analysis of the environmental situation in the different regions.

Air and Water Data. In the case of air and water quality, it was possible to identify a certain standard to analyze existing magnitudes for different characteristics. It was observed that almost the same tests are carried out on different samples to analyze different characteristics and determine if they are within healthy margins for human consumption.

Energy Data. In the case of datasets regarding energy, the difference between the data published by the different organizations is greater. It was observed that some countries simply publish an annual percentage and the type of energy production on which the different published energy generation plants are based, while others simply publish the percentages of their energy generation sources without plant-level granularity, and yet others publish totals corresponding to each energy plant capacity, energy plant types, and even the companies that own them.

Direct Loading. After collecting the data, a direct loading process was carried out, as a starting point, to analyze whether the untreated data met tool requirements. It was found that not all files had the data in an orderly manner and without errors – only 35% of the datasets passed this minimum control, indicating that the data published by the organizations required further standardization before they could be processed. If the data are analyzed by area, it can be seen that, based on this standardization, progression is as follows: Water: 80% direct loading 20% indirect loading; Energy: 66% direct loading and 33% indirect loading; Air: 50% direct loading and 50% indirect loading.

Standardization. In all three areas, it was observed that, beyond the standardization of certain published data, data are in a very "raw" format that makes optimal processing impossible. In many cases, they have empty spaces, or even have more data in the rows than is declared. In each case we can see:

Air and Water Data. There are differences in the structure of the datasets, the units used for the different quantities that are analyzed, and how these are stored in the datasets. For example, variations in columns to rows or one field split into several ones. This makes datasets mapping difficult.

Energy Data. In this case, it was observed that the measurement units used in the different datasets vary greatly, which makes a linear comparison of the data impossible. At the same time, due to the great difference in terms of the data published by each organization, a selection of certain common fields to all datasets is required, based on their type, so as to be able to represent them in a typified way. This is difficult due to the existing dispersion.

Linkage. Once the data are standardized, it is possible to link different datasets that have data in common, allowing a regional analysis of the information. With these datasets, the tool allows selecting columns to perform operations and obtain values with which various charts can be generated for a linear analysis of magnitudes of interest. Then, the analysis carried out with each of the data sets can be made visualized.

Water Data. Among the information collected on water quality, data from Colombia and Brazil were selected, as an example. The number of measurements carried out in both countries were added up, and the vertical bar charts that can be seen in Figs. 3 and 4 were generated. As it can be seen, the information published by Colombia is split by state and, on the other hand, the information from Brazil is split based on the different natural effluents in the country. The tool allows, in any case, visualizing this information regardless of these differences.

In a further analysis, effluents could be mapped to their corresponding Brazilian states and data could be compared by geographic region.

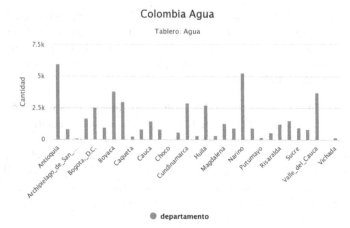

Fig. 3. Number of water quality measurements in Colombia

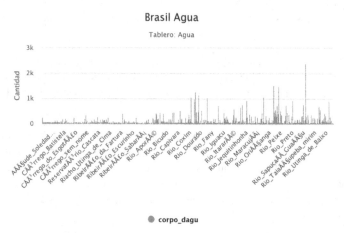

Fig. 4. Number of water quality measurements in Brazil

Air Data. As regards the information collected on air quality, suspended particulate values from the cities of Bogota in Colombia and Montevideo in Uruguay were selected to show how the tool can be used. Annual average values were calculated for Bogotá (this step was not necessary with Montevideo data because this city already records average values), and the horizontal bar charts shown in Figs. 5 and 6 were generated. In this case, the information published by Colombia was more detailed based on multiple measurements per year, so it had to be processed further to obtain a format similar to that published by Uruguay. The tool allows, in any case, visualizing this information regardless of these differences, for the same yearly periods.

Energy Data. Among the information collected on energy production, data from Paraguay and New York City were selected as an example. Beyond their differences in

Bogotá PM10

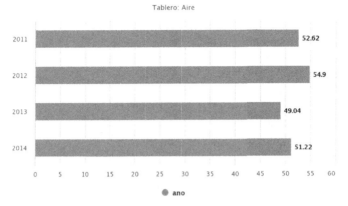

Fig. 5. PM10 measurements in Bogota.

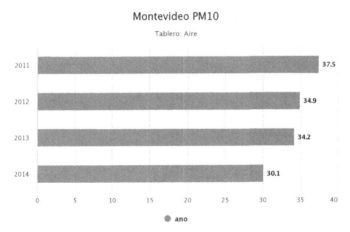

Fig. 6. PM10 measurements in Montevideo.

size and population, a comparison was made with these data to observe the differences in terms of energy production values, in GWh. In this case, the information published by both sources was very similar, although NYC also specified energy production plants. With this information, the line charts presented in Figs. 7 and 8 were generated, showing that NYC produced, in the period analyzed, more energy than all of Paraguay.

Fig. 7. Energy production per year in Paraguay

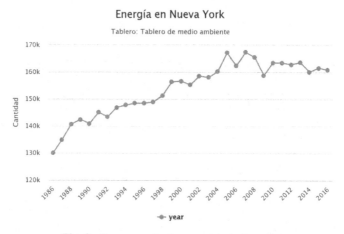

Fig. 8. Energy production per year in Paraguay

6   Conclusions and Future Work

Throughout the article, the basic concepts of Smart Sustainable Cities, Open Data, Data Sources, Datasets and Dashboards were introduced. Emphasis was placed on how these concepts can be combined to generate a higher level of information for society, which is achieved by linking already available data using the IndiMaker tool.

The tool was briefly described and a five-stage framework was generated to link the data made available by various organizations and compare them easily.

As a case study for the application of the framework, open data sources on water quality, air quality and energy production from 10 countries were downloaded, obtaining information in 8 of these data portals.

The information obtained was processed using the framework, standardizing the information where necessary, and then IndiMaker was used. The tool allowed performing operations on the data and easily generating indicators. The differences found in the information published on the same topic were notable; however, with the application of the proposed framework, the tool was able to process the information, generating indicators in a user-friendly way and various charts that facilitated data analysis. It should be noted that the model can be extended to any area of interest.

In the future, we expect to connect the tool with APIs from various data portals from several organizations and expand the range of operations offered by the tool, including the possibility of displaying various indicators on the same chart.

Acknowledgments. Project co-funded by the Erasmus+ Programme of the European Union. Grant no: 598273-EPP-1-2018-1-AT-EPPKA2-CBHE-JP.

References

1. Estevez, E., Lopes, N.V., Janowski, T.: Smart Sustainable Cities - Reconnaissance Study. Operating Unit ON Policy-Driven. Electronic Governance. United Nations University, Canada (2017)
2. Chun, S.A., Shulman, S., Sandoval, R., Hovy, E.: Government 2.0: making connections between citizens, data and government. Inf. Polity **15**(1–2), 1–9 (2010). https://doi.org/10.3233/IP-2010-0205
3. Concha, G., Naser, A.: Datos abiertos: Un nuevo desafío para los gobiernos de la region. Instituto Latinoamericano y del Caribe de Planificación Económica y Social (2012)
4. Preisegger, J.S., Greco, A., Pasini, A., Boracchia, M., Pesado, P.: Marco de vinculación de datos abiertos aplicado al contexto de datos medioambientales, pp. 684–694 (2020). https://sedici.unlp.edu.ar/handle/10915/113243
5. Calderón, C., Lorenzo, S.: Open Government. Gobierno Abierto (2010)
6. Naser, A., Ramírez-Alujas, Á., Rosales, D. (eds.): Desde el gobierno abierto al Estado abierto en America Latina y el Caribe: Planificación para el Desarrollo (2017)
7. Gil-García, J.R., Criado, J.I.: Las Tecnologías de Información y Comunicación en las Administraciones Públicas Contemporáneas (2017)
8. Pasini, A., Preisegger, J.S., Pesado, P.: Modelos de evaluación de gobiernos abiertos, aplicado a los municipios de la provincia de Buenos Aires. In: XXIV Congreso Argentino de Ciencias de la Computación, vol. XXIV, p. 10 (2018)
9. Pasini, A., Preisegger, J., Pesado, P.: Open Government assessment models applied to province's capital cities in Argentina and municipalities in the province of Buenos Aires. In: Pesado, P., Aciti, C. (eds.) CACIC 2018. CCIS, vol. 995, pp. 355–366. Springer, Cham (2019). https://doi.org/10.1007/978-3-030-20787-8_25
10. Noy, N., Burgess, M., Brickley, D.: Google dataset search: building a search engine for datasets in an open web ecosystem. In: The Web Conference 2019 - Proceedings of the World Wide Web Conference, WWW 2019, pp. 1365–1375 (2019). https://doi.org/10.1145/3308558.3313685
11. Naser, A., Ramirez, A.: Plan de gobierno abierto. Una hoja de ruta para los Gobiernos de la Región. CEPAL - Manuales **81**, 80 (2017)

Improving Usability and Intrusion Detection Alerts in a Home Video Surveillance System

María José Abásolo[1,2](✉) and Carlos Sebastián Castañeda[1,2]

[1] III-LIDI, Facultad de Informática, Universidad Nacional de La Plata, La Plata, Argentina
mjabasolo@lidi.info.unlp.edu.ar
[2] CICPBA, Buenos Aires, Argentina

Abstract. The purpose of this work is improving the functionality and usability of a low cost commercial surveillance system. The original system provides simple motion detection and sends alert messages by means of FTP or email. The modified system adds a software layer to the original system for implementing desirable image processing features. Particularly, people detection functionality was implemented by means of Oriented Gradient Histograms. The modified system also adds the use of Telegram messaging service for sending alerts. When the camera detects motion, the modified system improves the alert information with the results of the intruder detection algorithm. System Usability Scale (SUS) was used to compare the usability of both systems and the results showed that the modified system improved the original one in terms of usability.

Keywords: Computer vision · Motion detection · People detection · Video surveillance systems · Computer vision

1 Introduction

Monitoring and control in public places, banks, shops, airports has become a growing need in these times. There is a lot of work done in video surveillance systems in different environments and with different purposes. There are many tasks in surveillance monitoring such as object detection, person identification, activity and action recognition etc.

Recent proposals like Dong et al. [1] present methods for automatic object detection and tracking that can deal with object occlusion, with high real-time performance and robustness, suitable in long time video surveillance. Traffic surveillance helps detect incidents automatically. In the field of autonomous driving vehicles, the identification of vehicles and pedestrians minimize accidents. Many algorithms have been developed to improve efficient real-time detection of incidents. Sri Jamiya and Rani [2] present a survey on vehicle detection and tracking algorithms in real time video surveillance.

Face recognition is a challenging task for video surveillance, criminal investigations, and sports applications. Ennerhar Becheriet [3] presents a fast detection of multiple faces in complex backgrounds such as variation in illumination, human skin tone and facial expression, pose, and background. Alcanhal et al. [4] present person identification

© Springer Nature Switzerland AG 2021
P. Pesado and J. Eterovic (Eds.): CACIC 2020, CCIS 1409, pp. 350–364, 2021.
https://doi.org/10.1007/978-3-030-75836-3_24

based on a deep learning-based super resolution system that aims to enhance the faces images captured from surveillance video in order to support suspect identification. Also there are computer vision based approaches to age, gender and expressions prediction in surveillance video. In this way Ijjina et al. [5] approach leverages the effectiveness of wide residual networks and deep learning models to predict age and gender demographics of the consumers. The system can also detect customer facial expressions during purchase in addition to demographics, that can be utilized to devise effective marketing strategies. Recently many deep neural network based approaches have been proposed to automate Human Action Recognition in different domains Alturki and Ibrahim [6] perform real time action recognition in surveillance video using machine learning. Rashmi et al. [7] proposed a system for recognition and localization of student actions from still images extracted in a learning environment. Recently Zitouni and Śluzek [8] implemented social distancing monitoring related to the COVID-19 pandemic.

With technological advances in the area of security and the availability of low-cost hardware the use of security systems has become common in homes. Based on the development of embedded network technology and intelligent mobile phones used widely, the design for home security is put forward. Among the home systems that can be cited is the work of Zai-Ying and Liu [9] that use a microprocessor as the hardware core of embedded system whose function is coding and compressing the real-time image for transmitting data, and an intelligent mobile phone is used as the monitoring terminal, whose function is receiving and displaying data. Shete [10] proposes a monitoring system which includes a motion detection algorithm that is implemented along with some alarming features. The system proposed is an IOT based image processing unit with internet connectivity so that data can be transferred to any remote server. The main idea behind this system is to detect the presence of any moving object, especially a human, and then start recording a video from the motion being detected.

It is possible to acquire, at a low cost, fixed security cameras with embedded motion detection function, but a problem with these devices is that the algorithm used to be very sensitive to changes in the environment, such as changes in lighting conditions and shadows projections. In our previous related publication [11] we present the improvement of a low-cost camera-based surveillance system that implements motion detection based on background subtraction. We add a post processing of the image the camera sends when detecting motion. Particularly, we apply a people detector to determine based on the results of the algorithm, if it is a true alert in which a person is detected or if it is a warning when the algorithm does not detect people. In addition, since the original system uses a web application to activate and deactivate the alarm system, and on the other hand it uses the sending of alerts through email, it was proposed using Telegram both to activate and deactivate the alarm system, and to receive the alerts.

In this work we review the proposed system, as well as the usability tests to compare the proposed system with the original are detailed.

The rest of the article is organized as follows: in Sect. 2 we describe the algorithms used for motion and people detection. In Sect. 3 we describe the proposed system that improves a low cost commercial system. Section 4 shows the tests carried out to evaluate the usability of both original and modified surveillance systems. Finally, Sect. 5 presents the conclusions and future work.

2 Intruder Detection

It is possible to acquire fixed security cameras at low cost, but a problem that these devices can present is that the embedded motion detection algorithm is very sensitive to changes in the environment, such as changes in lighting conditions and shadows projections [12]. In general, cameras implement motion detection based on background subtraction techniques [13–18] and difference between frames [19–21].

2.1 Background Subtraction

In the background subtraction technique, the difference between the current frame and a frame representing the image background is used to detect moving objects. In this method, it is necessary to maintain a model that represents the background of the image. A background model could be obtained, for example, from the average image over a certain training period. Moving objects are easy to detect using this technique, but the background model must be updated regularly.

Wide variety of algorithms have been proposed to segment foreground objects from the background of a video sequence. Sobral et al. in [16] perform a review and evaluation of several of the algorithms, to detect movement by means of background subtraction, available in the bibliography. In general, all these algorithms share the same scheme, which consists of background initialization, foreground object detection, and background model maintenance. The authors classify the different algorithms, according to the technique used to initialize and update the background model, into basic models, statistical models, blurred models, neural and neuro-blurred methods.

Background subtraction is the most commonly used technique in fixed security cameras. The statistical model based on background subtraction is flexible and fast but the camera must be stationary. Figure 1 shows background subtraction used to motion detection of a person. This technique is simple to implement but has the disadvantage of being very sensitive to changes in the environment, making it difficult to isolate the interference of the real movement of objects in the image. In Fig. 2 it can see examples of false positives of the background subtraction based motion detector of the camera.

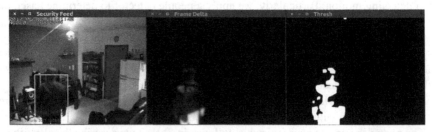

Fig. 1. Background subtraction OpenCV algorithm applied to a video stream for motion detection of a person (own source)

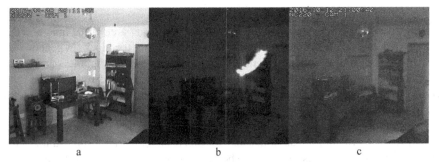

a   b   c

Fig. 2. Examples of false positives informed by the background subtraction based motion detector of the camera: a) during daylight; b) at night, generated by brightness reflected on any of the objects in the image; c) at night (Source: own)

2.2 People Detection

Molchanov et al. [22] point out that more than 80% of video surveillance systems are used for monitoring people.

On the other hand, there are different techniques or algorithms in the bibliography to detect people in images or video streams. Viola et al. in [23] proposes to use cascade classifiers, a method widely used in real-time applications. This method has been extended to employ different types of characteristics and techniques, but fundamentally the cascade concept has been used to achieve real-time detection. Hamdoun in [24] proposes Keypoints-based, such as SIFT and SURF, combined with background subtraction to detect pedestrians. Molchanov et al. [22] remarks that human detection algorithms based on background and foreground modelling could not even deal with a group of people or a crowd. Based on modern approaches in deep learning robust and highly effective pedestrian detection algorithms are a recent milestone of video surveillance systems. These algorithms produce very discriminative features that can be used for getting robust inference in real visual scenes. They deal with such tasks as distinguishing different persons in a group, overcome sufficient enclosures of human bodies by the foreground, and detect various poses of people. In their work they combine detection and classification tasks into one challenge using convolution neural networks. While Angelova et al. in [25] combines the efficiency of cascade classifiers with the accuracy of neural networks.

2.3 Oriented Gradient Histogram

In our work we choose to work with one of the most popular features used for human detection, the Oriented Gradient Histograms (OGH) developed by Dalal and Triggs, for people detection [26].

The HOG technique counts the occurrences of the orientation of the gradients located in an area of an image. The essential rationale behind HOG descriptors is that the appearance and shape of objects within an image can be described by the distribution of intensity gradients or edge directions. The image is divided into small regions called cells, and for the pixels within each cell, a histogram of gradient directions is compiled. Descriptors are the concatenation of these histograms. To improve precision, local histograms can be normalized in contrast, by calculating the intensity in a larger area of the image, called a block; and then use this value to normalize the cells within the block. In general, this normalization results in obtaining better invariants to changes in brightness and reflections that may appear in the images. HOG descriptors have some advantages over other types of descriptors, since they operate on local cells, they are invariant to geometric (for example: mirror the image) or photometric (example: increase contrast or convert to grayscale) transformations. Furthermore, as Dalal and Triggs describe, wide spatial sampling, finer orientation sampling, and localized photometric normalization allow individual body movements of people to be ignored as long as they maintain a position closest to being upright. For this reason, this technique is very effective for detecting people in images. Figure 3 shows a visual representation of the HOG descriptors of an image and can be noticed that, in the image area where a person is, the orientation of the gradients is different from the rest of the image.

Fig. 3. Visualization of the descriptors of histograms of oriented gradients in images with people a) Original image b) Oriented gradients of the original image c) Superposition of the gradients on the original image d) Detail of the orientation of the gradients in the area where a person is viewed (Source: own)

HOG descriptors are used in conjunction with a classifier trained to determine if an image contains people, such as Least Square Vector Machine (LSVM). When working with object detection in images, it is very likely to run into the problem of getting multiple frames on the object to be detected. Basically, a procedure is needed to remove these redundant boxes and get the box that best represents the area of the detected object. There are different techniques to accomplish this task. Rosebrock A in [27], proposes to use the non-maximum suppression method that aims to eliminate the multiple detected boxes and merge them into one. Figure 4 shows the results of people detection on an arbitrary video stream obtained from YouTube.

Fig. 4. Detection test of people with HOG + LSVM in OpenCV, on a video stream obtained from YouTube (Walking tour around Times Square in Midtown Manhattan, New York City https://www.youtube.com/watch?v=u68EWmtKZw0&t=108s)

3 Proposed Home Video Surveillance System

3.1 Original System

We analyze a TP-LINK model NC220 camera[1] which has the following features: low cost; wireless connectivity and Wi-Fi signal amplifier; night vision; motion and sound detection that can be enabled and disabled; sending alert notifications by email or FTP; application for live video streaming for Android, IOS, Windows platforms or through the TP-LINK cloud platform[2]. The camera is connected to a Wi-Fi internal network through which an integrated web application is accessed that allows enabling/disabling alerts. Motion detection alerts are sent to an email or to an FTP server which can be accessed directly to inspect the attached images.

In our previous related publication [11] we show the tests carried out with this camera where the results of the evaluation show 35.60% false positives from the total of alerts that were sent during the experiment.

3.2 Modified System

With the objective of improving the original commercial system we proposed:

– Processing the images resulting from the motion detection provided by the camera to detect the presence of intruders, and then to emphasize the alerts;

---

[1] https://www.tp-link.es/products/details/cat-19_NC220.html.

[2] https://www.tplinkcloud.com/.

– Use Telegram notification system as the interface to activate and deactivate the alarm system, and the notification of alerts every time the camera detects motion.

The new proposed architecture can be seen in Fig. 5.

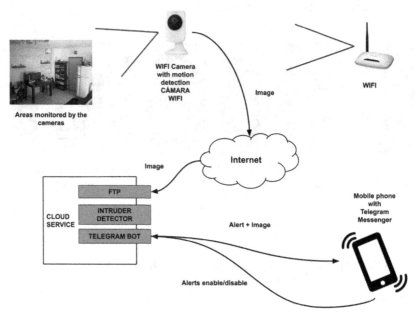

Fig. 5. Proposed architecture system that interacts with the TP-LINK nc220 security camera [11]

The original system sends to an FTP server the corresponding image when a sound or motion detection event occurs. The sent images are processed with an added image processing module. The code was structured in such a way that it is possible to add new detection algorithms. Particularly, our objective was to implement an intruder detector and we use the HOG-SVM implementation in Opencv by Rosebrock [28].

The alert is then classified according to the results of the processing as a true or a false positive, depending on whether or not the algorithm detected people respectively. The image is sent jointly with a text notification indicating if it is a true alert where the intruder was detected, if it is only a warning since no intruder was detected. In true positives images the detected people are highlighted.

Telegram is used as the notification application, and the alerts can be read from almost any current mobile device. From the instant messaging program it is also possible to send a command to enable/disable the reception of notifications.

The system was implemented with DJANGO[3] framework. The project consists of four modules: Django Admin, FTPserver, Image processing, and Notifications (see

---

[3] https://www.djangoproject.com.

Fig. 6). More details of the implementation were included in [11] and the code can be downloaded from GitHub[4].

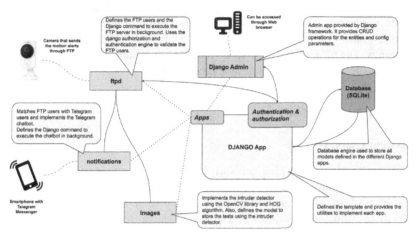

Fig. 6. Organization of the django project (own source)

Figure 7 shows four types of images that were found in this test: true positive is an alert; false negative is a missing alarm that was sent just as a warning; false positive is a false alarm; and true negative is a true warning.

Fig. 7. a) True positive is a true alarm; b) False negative is a missing alarm; c) False positive is a false alarm; d) True negative is a warning.

---

[4] https://github.com/seba3c/scamera.

In [11] we detailed the test carried out of the intruder detector algorithm. We classified the received images into true or false positives with an accuracy of 76%. There were 6% of false alarms where a false positive is treated as true alert. There were also 18% of missed alarms where a true positive was treated just as a warning. The 87% of the alerts corresponds to true alerts and the remaining 13% are false alerts that should be just warnings. The 65% of the warning notifications corresponds to true warnings, and the remaining 35% are warnings that should be alerts.

4 Usability Evaluation

4.1 System Usability Scale

Usability is the degree to which software can be used by a set of specific users to achieve specific objectives with effectiveness, efficiency and satisfaction within a context of specific use [29]. There are a wide variety of methods and techniques of varying complexity to evaluate the usability of a software system, among them it is the System Usability Scale (SUS) usability test [30]. SUS is a simple and fast usability test consisting of ten questions, which accept as a response a value within a scale that can range from 1 to 5. Odd questions correspond to positive questions in which a high score means high satisfaction. For calculating SUS final score the value of odd questions is the score minus one. On the other hand, even questions correspond to negative questions in which a high score means high dissatisfaction. The value of even questions is the absolute value of the score minus five. To calculate the final score the values of each question are added, and a factor of 2.5 is applied. SUS final score varies between 0 and 100. This score allows obtaining a global vision of the subjective usability ratings of a system and it is used to compare two or more systems.

4.2 Evaluation Description

The usability of both the web application of the original commercial system and the proposed Telegram based application were evaluated. The tests were performed with six users between 20 and 30 years old, with familiarity in the use of mobile devices and computers, and instant messaging and email applications both desktop and mobile. In the evaluation, each user is asked to carry out two tasks with each of the two systems:

T1. Activate and deactivate the alert system.
T2. Visualize an alert notification.

In the original system T1 has to be done by means of the web application that is embedded in the camera, meanwhile in the proposed system the Telegram application is used. Table 1 shows the actions that a user must carry out to activate and deactivate the alarm system (T1), using each of the compared systems. Figure 8 shows the interface of each system to complete T1.

Table 1. Actions that a user must carry out to activate and deactivate the alarm system

		Original system (web application)	Proposed system (telegram bot)
Preconditions		Be connected with a computer or mobile device to the same WIFI where the camera is installed and be within the range of the WIFI network signal	Have a mobile device with an internet connection and telegram application installed and registered to operate with the chatbot@*scamerabot*
Actions	1	Open a WEB browser	Open telegram
	2	Type the IP address of the camera	Search and select the chatbot @scamerabot within the contacts
	3	Enter username and password to access the web application embedded in the camera	Click on the command list [/]
	4	Click in login	Click "/activate" to activate and "/deactivate" to deactivate alerts
	5	Go to the advanced section	
	6	Go to motion detection section	
	7	Select between the enabled and disabled options to activate or deactivate the alerts respectively	
	8	Click save option	

a)   b)

Fig. 8. Activating and deactivating alarms a) original system (Source: P-LINK User Guide - NC220 Day/Night Cloud Camera, 300 Mbps Wi-Fi) b) Telegram based proposal

In the original system T2 has to be done by means of e-mail application, meanwhile in the proposed system the Telegram application is used again. Table 2 shows the actions that a user must carry out to visualize a received alert (T2), using each of the compared systems. Figure 9 shows the interface to complete T2 in the original system, both desktop and mobile version of email. Figure 10 shows the alerts received in the proposed system, and can be seen that a message is received categorizing the alert in warning or a true alert, according to the results of the intruder detector algorithm.

Table 2. Actions that a user must carry out to visualize an alert notification

		Original system (email)	Proposed system (telegram bot)
Preconditions		Have a device with an internet connection with access to the email box configured to receive alerts from the camera	Have a mobile device with an internet connection and telegram application installed and registered to operate with the chatbot@*scamerabot*
Actions	1	Open email application	Open telegram
	2	Find the alert email in the inbox	Search and select the chatbot @scamerabot within the contacts
	3	Open the email	View the last messages received in the chatbot in which the images sent by the camera will be seen
	4	Open the attachments in the email to see the images sent by the camera	

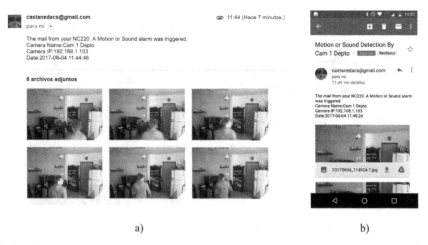

a)   b)

Fig. 9. Visualizing alert notifications sent by email in the original system: a) desktop; b) mobile

4.3 Results of the Usability Evaluation

After completing the tasks with each system, each user was asked to complete the SUS usability questionnaire with values on the scale from 1 to 5. Table 3 shows the average value assigned for each question in the questionnaire and the average SUS score for each system. The scores assigned to the proposed system in each question are significantly better than those of the original system. It should be noted that in the even questions a lower score is a better result.

Regarding ease of use (question 2), the proposed system has a perfect score, and the original system was found unnecessary complex (question 3). On the learning time to learn to use the system by anyone, users assigned a score twice better for the proposed system than for the original (question 7). Also the users found that the functions in the proposed system are much better integrated than in the original (questions 5 and 6). In both systems the users indicated that they would not need the support of a technical person to be able to use this (question 4). In relation to confidence when using both systems the users assigned similar scores, being the score of the proposed system slightly higher. A SUS final score of 95 was obtained for the proposed system against 57.08 for the original system. According to these results, the users that test the system think that the proposed system noticeably improves usability of the original commercial system.

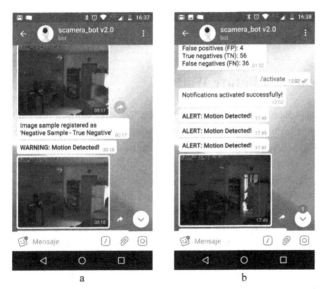

Fig. 10. Interface to visualize alert notifications in the Telegram based proposed a) Warning when an intruder is not detected and b) True alert when intruder is detected and highlighted

Table 3. Final average score of SUS usability test

SUS questionnaire		Original system scores	Proposed system scores
1	I think that i would like to use this system frequently	3.5	4.83
2	I found the system unnecessarily complex	4.0	1.5
3	I thought the system was easy to use	3.0	5.0
4	I think that i would need the support of a technical person to be able to use this system	1.33	1.0
5	I found the various functions in this system were well integrated	3.33	4.83
6	I thought there was too much inconsistency in this system	3.0	1.33
7	I would imagine that most people would learn to use this system very quickly	2.16	4.33
8	I found the system very cumbersome to use	3.66	1.0
9	I felt very confident using the system	4.0	4.83
10	I needed to learn a lot of things before i could get going with this system	1.16	1.0
SUS final score		57.08	95

5 Conclusions and Future Work

In this work, we presented the improvement of a low-cost commercial security camera system which can be useful for monitoring homes. We attended some problems such as the mechanism to activate and deactivate alerts, and the reception of many false alarms by email. We implemented a software level that interacts with the commercial system, adding an image processing module. We particularly implemented the detection of intruders using a people recognition algorithm based on OGH. This allows to enhance the notifications sent separating them into alerts and warnings. Also we add a Telegram based communication between the user and the system, both to activate and deactivate alerts, and to receive the notifications every time the system detects motion.

The results showed that the proposed system improved the notifications, and the usability tests showed that the proposed system improves the usability and interactions of users with the system.

As potential future work, it is proposed to add other different functionality by other image processing algorithms. Particularly, methods of detecting people based on neural networks or on machine learning are being incorporated. Also it is intended to incorporate detection of other particular objects, such as vehicles and people identification.

References

1. Dong, E., Zhang, Y., Du, S.: An automatic object detection and tracking method based on video surveillance. In: 2020 IEEE International Conference on Mechatronics and Automation (ICMA), pp. 1140–1144. IEEE (2020)

2. Jamiya, S.S., Rani, E.: A survey on vehicle detection and tracking algorithms in real time video surveillance. Int. J. Sci. Technol. Res. **8**(10) (2019). ISSN 2277-8616

3. Ennehar, B.C.: New face features to detect multiple faces in complex background. Evol. Syst. **10**(2), 79–95 (2019). https://doi.org/10.1007/s12530-017-9211-y

4. Alkanhal, L., et al.: Super-resolution using deep learning to support person identification in surveillance video (IJACSA). Int. J. Adv. Comput. Sci. Appl. **11**(7) (2020)

5. Ijjina, E.P., Kanahasabai, G., Joshi, A.S.: Deep learning based approach to detect customer age, gender and expression in surveillance video. In: 2020 11th International Conference on Computing, Communication and Networking Technologies (ICCCNT), pp. 1–6. IEEE (2020)

6. Alturki, A.S., Ibrahim, A.H.: Real time action recognition in surveillance video using machine learning. Int. J. Eng. Res. Technol. **13**(8), 1874–1879 (2020). ISSN 0974-3154

7. Rashmi, M., Ashwin, T.S., Guddeti, R.M.R.: Surveillance video analysis for student action recognition and localization inside computer laboratories of a smart campus. Multimed. Tools Appl. **80**(2), 2907–2929 (2021). https://doi.org/10.1007/s11042-020-09741-5

8. Zitouni, M., Śluzek, A.: Video-surveillance tools for monitoring social responsibility under covid-19 restrictions. In: Chmielewski, L.J., Kozera, R., Orłowski, A. (eds.) ICCVG 2020. LNCS, vol. 12334, pp. 227–239. Springer, Cham (2020). https://doi.org/10.1007/978-3-030-59006-2_20

9. Zai-Ying, W., Liu, C.: Design of mobile phone video surveillance system for home security based on embedded system. In: The 27th Chinese Control and Decision Conference (2015 CCDC), pp. 5856–5859. IEEE (2015)

10. Shete, V., et al.: Intelligent embedded video monitoring system for home surveillance. In: 2016 International Conference on Inventive Computation Technologies (ICICT), pp. 1–4 IEEE (2016)

11. Castañeda, C.S., Abásolo, G.M.J.: Improving a low cost surveillance system. In: XXVI Congreso Argentino de Ciencias de la Computación. Red UNCI, pp. 777–786 (2020). ISBN 978-987-4417-90-9

12. Shirbhate, R.S., Mishra, N.D., Pande, R.: Video surveillance system using motion detection: a survey. Adv. Network. Appl. **3**(5), 19 (2012)

13. Zivkovic, Z.: Improved adaptive Gaussian mixture model for background subtraction. In: Proceedings of the 17th International Conference on Pattern Recognition, Cambridge, UK, 26 de agosto (2004)

14. Zivkovic, Z., van der Heijden, F.: Efficient adaptive density estimation per image pixel for the task of background subtraction. Pattern Recogn. Lett. **27**(7), 773–780 (2006)

15. Kaewtrakulpong, P., Bowden, R.: An improved adaptive background mixture model for real time tracking with shadow detection. In: Remagnino, P., Jones, G.A., Paragios, N., Regazzoni, C.S. (eds.) Video Based Surveillance Systems, pp. 135–144. Springer, Boston (2001). https://doi.org/10.1007/978-1-4615-0913-4_11

16. Sobral, A., Vacavant, A.: A comprehensive review of background subtraction algorithms evaluated with synthetic and real videos. Comput. Vis. Image Underst. **122**, 4–21 (2014)

17. Dou, J., Qin, Q., Tu, Z.: Background subtraction based on circulant matrix. SIViP **11**(3), 407–414 (2016). https://doi.org/10.1007/s11760-016-0975-5

18. Brutzer, S., Hoferlin, B., Heidemann, G.: Evaluation of background subtraction techniques for video surveillance. In: IEEE Conference on Computer Vision and Pattern Recognition, pp. 1937–1944 (2011)

19. Singla, N.: Motion detection based on frame difference method. Int. J. Inf. Comput. Technol. **4**(15), 1559–1565 (2014)

20. Sengar, S.S., Mukhopadhyay, S.: A novel method for moving object detection based on block based frame differencing. In: 3rd International Conference on Recent Advances in Information Technology, pp. 462–472 (2016)

21. Fei, M., Li, J., Liu, H.: Visual tracking based on improved foreground detection and perceptual hashing. Neurocomputing. **152**(C), 413–428 (2015)
22. Molchanov, V.V., Vishnyakov, B.V., Vizilter, Y.V., Vishnyakova, O.V., Knyaz, V.A.: Pedestrian detection in video surveillance using fully convolutional YOLO neural network. In: Proceedings. SPIE 10334, Automated Visual Inspection and Machine Vision II, p. 103340Q (2017)
23. Viola, P., Jones, M.J., Snow, D.: Detecting pedestrians using patterns of motion and appearance, In: Proceedings Ninth IEEE International Conference on Computer Vision, Nice, France (2005)
24. Hamdoun, O., Moutarde, F.: Keypoints-based background model and foreground pedestrian extraction for future smart cameras. In: 3rd ACM/IEEE International Conference on Distributed Smart Cameras, Como, Italy (2009)
25. Angelova, A., Krizhevsky, A., Vanhoucke, V., Ogale, A., Ferguson, D.: Real-time pedestrian detection with deep network cascades. In: Proceedings of BMVC (2015)
26. Dalal, N., Triggs, B.: Histograms of oriented gradients for human detection. In: IEEE Computer Society Conference on Computer Vision and Pattern Recognition, San Diego, CA, USA (2005)
27. Rosebrock: Histogram of oriented gradients and object detection. https://www.pyimagese arch.com/2014/11/10/histogram-oriented-gradients-object-detection. Accessed 12 Mar 2021
28. Rosebrock: Pedestrian Detection OpenCV. https://www.pyimagesearch.com/2015/11/09/ped estrian-detection-opencv. Accessed 12 Mar 2021
29. ISO: Ergonomic requirements for office work with visual display terminals, 9241-11. ISO, Marzo (1998)
30. Bangor, A., Kortum, P.T., Miller, J.T.: An empirical evaluation of the system usability scale. Int. J. Hum Comput Interact. **24**(6), 574–594 (2008)

Author Index

Printed in the United States
by Baker & Taylor Publisher Services